MULTIPLE TEACHERS IN BIBLICAL TEXTS

CONTRIBUTIONS TO BIBLICAL EXEGESIS AND THEOLOGY

SERIES EDITORS

K. De Troyer (St Andrews)
G. van Oyen (Louvain-la-Neuve)

ADVISORY BOARD

Lutz Doering (Münster)
Beverly Gaventa (Baylor)
Annette Merz (Groningen)
Jack Sasson (Nashville)
Bas ter Haar Romeny (Amsterdam)
Jacob Wright (Atlanta)

B.J. KOET and A.L.H.M. VAN WIERINGEN

MULTIPLE TEACHERS
IN BIBLICAL TEXTS

PEETERS
LEUVEN – PARIS – BRISTOL, CT
2017

A catalogue record for this book is available from the Library of Congress.

© 2017 — Peeters, Bondgenotenlaan 153, B-3000 Leuven
ISBN 978-90-429-3542-6
D/2017/0602/131
All rights reserved. No part of this publication may be reproduced, stored in a retrieval system, or transmitted, in any form or by any means, electronic, mechanical, photocopying, recording or otherwise, without the prior permission of the publisher.

TABLE OF CONTENTS

Bart J. Koet – Archibald L.H.M. van Wieringen
In Search of Teachers and Disciples   1

Piet J. van Midden – Archibald L.H.M. van Wieringen
Moses as a Teacher in the Narration about the Gold Bullock:
A Communication-Oriented Exegesis of Exodus 32   9

Christiaan Erwich – Eep Talstra
The Text as our Teacher: Participant tracking in Psalm 64. 29

Harm W.M. van Grol
Coping with Hellenistic Neighbours: Psalms 137–145: An initiation
into royal warriorship 49

Sehoon Jang
God as the Wise Teacher in Job. 73

Archibald L.H.M. van Wieringen
The Triple-Layered Communication in the Book of Amos and its
Message of Non-appropriation Theology 89

Solomon Pasala
Multiple Teachers and Disciples in Mt 8-9 107

Lauri Thurén
Multiple Communication Layers and the Enigma of the Last
Judgment (Matt 25,31-46). 125

Bart J. Koet
A Tale of Two Teachers: Jesus about Jesus and John the Baptist
(Luke 7,18-35). 147

Jan van der Watt
Education and Teaching in John's Gospel 169

Peter J. TOMSON
Paul as a Recipient and Teacher of Tradition 185

Eric OTTENHEIJM
Hillel as a Teacher: Sayings and Narratives 207

Toke ELSHOF
Religious Teachers and Students on Biblical Teaching and Discipleship: An Account of a Recent Exploration 225

INDEX OF REFERENCES 239

ABBREVIATIONS

AB	Anchor Bible
ACEBT (Suppl. Series)	Amsterdamse Cahiers (Supplement Series)
AJEC	Ancient Judaism and Early Christianity
ASNU	Acta Seminarii Neotestamentici Uppsaliensis
ATANT	Abhandlungen zur Theologie des Alten und Neuen Testaments
BBB	Bonner Biblische Beiträge
BBR	Bulletin for Biblical Research
BDAG	Bauer – Danker – Arndt – Gingrich (eds. Greek-English Lexicon)
BEAT	Beiträge zur forschung des Alten Testaments und des antiken Judentums
BETL	Bibliotheca Ephemeridum Lovaniensa Theologica
BHS	Biblia Hebraica Stuttgartensia
BI	Biblical Interpretation
Bib	Biblica
BIS	Biblical Interpretation Series
BiSe	Biblical Seminar
BJRE	British Journal of Religious Education
BJS	Brown Judaic Studies
BN	Biblische Notizen
BNTC	Black's New Testament Commentaries
BOT	de boeken van het Oude Testament
BSac	Bulletin de la Société de l'Archéologie Copte
BTB	Biblical Theology Bulletin
BZAW	Beihefte zur Zeitschrift für die alttestamentliche Wissenschaft
BZNW	Beihefte zur Zeitschrift für die neutestamentliche Wissenschaft
CBAA	Catholic Biblical Association of America
CBC NEB	The Cambridge Bible Commentary on the New English Bible
CBET	Contributions to Biblical Exegesis and Theology
CBQ	Catholic Biblical Quarterly
COT	Commentaar Op Het Oude Testament
CRINT	Compendia Rerum Iudaicarum Novum Testamentum
DC	Documentation Catholique
DCLS	Deuterocanonical and Cognate Literature Studies
DCLY	Deuterocanonical and Cognate Literature Yearbook
EKKNT	Evangelisch-Katholischer Kommentar zum Neuen Testament

ETCBC	Eep Talstra Centre for Bible and Computer
EstB	Estudios Biblicos
FARMS Review	Foundation for Ancient Research and Mormon Studies
FOTL	The Forms of the Old Testament Literature
FS	Festschrift
HNT	Handbuch zum Neuen Testament
HTKAT	Herders theologische Kommentar zum Alten Testament
HUT	Hermeneutische Untersuchungen zur Theologie
ICC	International Critical Commentary
ISHR	International Studies in the History of Rhetoric
JBL	Journal of Biblical Literature
JBV	Journal of Beliefs and Values
JCP(S)	Jewish and Christian Perspectives (Series)
JNSL	Journal of Northwest Semitic Languages
JPS	Jewish Publication Society
JSJ (Suppl.)	Journal for the Study of Judaism (Supplement)
JSNT.S	Journal for the Studies of the New Testament, Supplement Series
JSOT.S	Journal for the Study of the Old Testament; Supplement Series
JTS	Journal of Theological Studies
JTSA	Jewish Theological Seminary of America
KBS	Katholieke Bijbelstichting
KBW	Katholisches Bildungswerk
KJV	King James Version (Bible)
LAHR	Late Antique History and Religion
LHBTS	Library of Hebrew Bible/Old Testament Studies
LNTS	Library of New Testament Studies
LQHR	London Quarterly and Holborn Review
LSJ	Liddell – Scott – Jones, Greek-English Lexicon
NBG	Nederlands Bijbelgenootschap
NCBC	New Cambridge Bible Commentary
Neot.	Neotestamentica
NIB	New Interpreter's Study Bible
NICNT	The New International Commentary on the New Testament
NIV	New International Version (Bible)
NKJV	New King James Version (Bible)
NRSV	New Revised Standard Version (Bible)
NT	Novum Testamentum
NTD	Das Neue Testament Deutsch
NTS	New Testament Studies
NTT	Nederlands Theologisch Tijdschrift
ÖBS	Österreichische Biblische Studien
OOM	Oxford Oriental Monographs
OTS	Old Testament Studies
POT	De Prediking van het Oude Testament
RB	Rhétorique Biblique

ReBib	Retorica Biblica
RNT	Regensburger Neues Testament
RTP	Revue de théologie et de philosophie
SBL	Society of Biblical Literature
SBLDS	Society of Biblical Literature Dissertation Series
SBS	Stuttgarter Bibelstudien
SC	Sources Chrétiennes
SHBC	Smyth & Helwys Bible Commentary
SNTA	Studiorum Novi Testamenti Auxilia
SPCK	Society fot Promoting Christian Knowledge
SSN	Studia Semitica Neerlandica
STJ	Stellenbosch Theological Journal/Theologiese Joernaal
STKSJ	Suomalaisen teologisen kirjallisuusseuran julkaisuja
STPS	Studien zur Theologie und Praxis der Seelsorge,
StRBS	Studia Rhetorica Biblica et Semitica
SubBi	Subsidia Biblica
Supp. VC	Supplements to Vigilae Christianae
Theol. Persp. (Suppl.)	Theologische Perspectieven (Supplement)
TGl	Theologie und Glaube
THOC	Two Horizons Old Testament Commentary
TSAJ	Texts and Studies in Ancient Judaism
TTS	Tilburg Theological Studies
TWNT	Theologisches Wörterbuch zum Neuen Testament
TynBul	Tyndale Bulletin
UTB	Uni-Taschenbücher
UTR	Utrechtse Theologische Reeks
VC (Suppl.)	Vigilae Christianae (Supplement)
VT	Vetus Testamentum
VT.S	Vetus Testamentum, Supplements
WA	Weimarer Ausgabe (Luthers Werke)
WBC	Word Biblical Commentary
WBG	Wissenschaftliche Buchgesellschaft
WdF	Wege der Forschung
WTJ	Westminster Theological Journal
WUNT	Wissenschaftliche Untersuchungen zum Neuen Testament
ZNW	Zeitschrift für Neutestamentliche Wissenschaft

IN SEARCH OF TEACHERS AND DISCIPLES

Bart J. KOET – Archibald L.H.M. VAN WIERINGEN
Tilburg, the Netherlands

In several countries there is hot debate on learning. Adherents of the so-called "New Learning" claim that it is time for new educational concepts.[1] They argue that classical learning was teacher- and content-centred, while for the future it is necessary to be pupil-centred. The discussions initiated by the so-called New Learning call for attention to be given to communication and relations in learning processes. New Learning is not simply about the fact that in recent decades mankind has had to deal with new ways of communication and learning due to the digitalisation of our world. The change in the classroom to new forms, including computers on the desks and the so-called interactive whiteboard instead of the old-fashioned blackboard, is only a stepping stone to argue that education should not be content-centred, but pupil-centred, i.e. student-centred. This implies that the communicative process from teacher to student is in the spotlight.[2]

Of course, one can wonder whether being pupil-centred is really new. Could there also be some continuity between learning nowadays and learning in the past?[3] For example, in the past memorizing was an important element of teaching,[4] but this competency is nowadays neglected and quite often even reviled. However, it is remarkable that quite a lot of young people dealing with computers especially use their memory when dealing with all the commands in navigating through the digital world of the computer and all its kinds of games. They do not need a manual.

---

[1] See for example M. KALANTZIS – B. COPE, *New Learning: Elements of a Science of Education*, Cambridge, Cambridge University Press, 2nd ed., 2012.
[2] See for biblical studies e.g. K.A. REYNOLDS, *Torah as Teacher: The exemplary Torah Student in psalm 119* (VT.S, 137), Leiden, Brill, 2010; R.T. FRANCE, *Matthew: Evangelist and Teacher* (New Testament Profiles), Westmont, InterVarsity Press, 1998.
[3] For an interesting case study, see I. ABRAM, *Jewish Tradition as Permanent Education*, 's-Gravenhage, 1986.
[4] For the importance of memory regarding biblical texts see especially: T.E. VAN LEVY – T. SCHEIDER – W.H. PROPP (eds.), *Israel's Exodus in Transdisciplinary Perspective: Text, Archaeology, Culture, and Geoscience*, Cham, Springer, 2015; B. GERHARDSSON, *Memory and Manuscript: Oral Tradition and Written Transmission in Rabbinic Judaism and Early Christianity*, Uppsala, Gleerup, 1961 (2nd ed.).

In theological research, the interest in initiation and mystagogy as an ongoing process in which people in various roles are involved, has been studied for the past decades.[5] In this way, initiation and mystagogy can be considered not primarily being content-centred, but rather focussing on the person who is admitted by initiation and who is developing through mystagogy. The initiated one is taught and he/she is therefore part of a teacher-disciple-process. In other words: initiation and mystagogy are also student-centred.[6]

For example, poetry that plays a role in religious growth, does not appear to reflect only the religious mind of the poet, but wishes to transform the addressee of the poem. Transformative poetry is therefore reader-centred. In the well-known poem *Adoro Te Devote* by Thomas Aquinas, the 'I'-figure is not simply a textual reflection of the historical Thomas Aquinas, but rather an open invitation to the addressee of the poem for religious growth while attending Mass. The poem is not teacher-centred, i.e. a poem about Thomas Aquinas, but student-centred, i.e. a poem that enables the reader to grow in his/her faith.[7]

These examples of the current interest in relations and communication evoke the question whether relations and communication, especially between teacher and pupil, can be found in the Bible as well. Thorough research makes clear that teachers and pupils are present in biblical texts in abundance. Just two short examples.

The book of Deuteronomy consists of a couple of speeches (or maybe better, sermons) by Moses to the people just before crossing the river Jordan into the promised land. In these speeches, Moses retells the journey through the desert, how the Lord revealed himself and how he gave the Torah as a teaching about the good life in the new land. Deut 18,15-18 is of special interest.[8] In this text Moses is initiated as the beginning of a continuous line of prophets, who teach the people the Torah of the

---

[5] P.J.J. VAN GEEST (ed.), *Seeing Through the Eyes of Faith: New Approaches to the Mystagogy of the Church Fathers* (LAHR, 11), Leuven, Peeters, 2016.

[6] See for instance G. BUNGE, *Spiritual Fatherhood: Evagrius Ponticus on the role of the spiritual father*, Yonkers NY, St Vladimir's Seminary Press, 2016; G. BOSELLI, *The spiritual meaning of the liturgy: school of prayer, source of life*, Collegeville MN, Liturgical Press, 2014.

[7] H.J.M. SCHOOT, *Eucharistic Transformation: Thomas Aquinas' Adoro Te Devote*, in *Perichoresis* 14 (2016), 67-79. See further: A.L.H.M. VAN WIERINGEN, *Transformative Poetry: A General Introduction and a Case Study of Psalm 2*, in *Perichoresis* 14 (2016), 3-20.

[8] *Cf.* also J.D. ATKINS, *Reassessing the Origins of Deuteronomic Prophecy: Early Moses Traditions in Deuteronomy 18:15-22*, in *BBR* 23 (2013), 323-341.

Lord in every new age. Actually, this idea of a continuous line of prophets originates from the people themselves. They were so much impressed by the appearance of the Lord, that their reaction is interpreted by the Lord as a request for an indirect way of being taught, namely by prophets. This line of prophets goes on even beyond the book of Deuteronomy, and can therefore reach the reader as well.[9]

This aspect is supported by the location of Moses' speeches: the banks of the river Jordan. This implies that the continuous line of prophets is meant for the promised land, in order to live the good life there. That the reader of the text is also connected to this land, is made clear at the very beginning of the book. In Deut 1,1, Moses is situated at בְּעֵבֶר הַיַּרְדֵּן *the other side of the river Jordan*. From Moses' perspective, the other side is the promised land. Calling the riverbank Moses is standing on, 'the other side' means that the author's perspective is from the promised land. The author's concern is the promised land. By creating a continuous line from the desert, across the river Jordan, into the land, the author connects the reader of his book to that line as well. In this way, Moses can be the teacher of the reader and via the continuation of his teaching, the reader can continuously be a pupil in the land given by the Lord.[10]

In the formulation of the future task of John the Baptist, Gabriel announces that John will go before the Lord in the spirit and power of Elijah (Lk 1,17). By referring explicitly to Elijah as a kind of spiritual father of John the Baptist, Luke makes clear to his readers that the phrase *to turn the hearts of the fathers to their children* recalls the Elijah-tradition of inspiring father(s) to turn their hearts to their children (sons), a tradition found in both Malachi (3,23) and Ben Sira (48,10).[11] In 1 Kings 17,1, Elijah came to the fore after Hiel's sacrifice of his sons, which is a flagrant violation of the biblical law that a father may not sacrifice his son. Such a sacrifice cries out for a prophetic answer and Elijah is this answer. In biblical traditions, one of the aspects of Elijah was his aim to atone the different generations, especially between fathers and their sons or children. In a world where the father, who even punishes using the rod, is the most

---

[9] *Cf.* also J.P. SONNET, *La construction narrative de la figure de Moïse comme prophète dans le Deutéronome*, in *RTP* 142 (2010), 1-20. *Cf.* further E. OTTO, *Deuteronomium 12,1-23,15* (HTKAT), Freiburg, Herder, 2016, 1500.1502.
[10] *Cf.* E. OTTO, *Deuteronomium 1-11* (HTKAT), Freiburg, Herder, 2012, p. 306.
[11] See B.J. KOET, *Elijah as Reconciler of Father and Son: From 1 Kings 16:34 and Malachi 3:22-24 to Ben Sira 48:1-11 and Luke 1:13-17*, in J. CORLEY – H. VAN GROL (eds.), *Rewriting Biblical History: Essays on Chronicles and Ben Sira in Honor of Pancratius Beentjes* (DCLS, 7), Berlin, De Gruyter, 2011, 173-190.

important authority in a family, the task of John the Baptist, acting in the spirit of Elijah, is quite an unexpected directive. It means that the father will start to listen to his son, and will maybe even have to wait before speaking! When fathers direct themselves to their children, the gap between the generations will be less great. This suggests a special form of teaching.

It is clear that, either implicitly or explicitly, the roles of teacher and disciple are a part of biblical[12] traditions, although often neglected in biblical exegesis.[13] In this volume we would like to explore the roles of teacher and disciple from a textual perspective. This perspective contains two aspects. Firstly, the relation teacher-disciple is present in the text itself. It indicates the relation between characters acting in the text. Secondly, through the relation teacher-disciple at the textual level of the characters, the author and reader create a similar relationship of teacher and disciple at the level of their communication. Texts, therefore, have a double communication, which is disciple-centred: from the character of the teacher towards the character of the disciple, as well as from the textual author as a teacher towards the textual reader as a disciple.[14]

The authors of the contributions of this volume will emphasise both aspects in their own way, but always focussing on the communicative relation of teacher and disciple. *Piet van Midden* and *Archibald van Wieringen* explore Ex 32. The story of the gold bullock appears to be a communicatively multi-layered narrative in which Moses turns out to be a teacher not only for his fellow-characters, including the Lord God, but also for the

---

[12] Jewish traditions, however, often refer to Moses, with a clear undertone of love and esteem, as משה רבנו *Moshe rabbenu*, *Moses, our teacher*. Cf. E.E. URBACH, *The Sages*, Cambridge MA, Harvard University Press, 1979, p. 646.

[13] For the neglect of Moses as teacher, see for example K. FINSTERBUSCH, *"Du sollst sie lehren, auf dass sie tun": Mose als Lehrer der Tora in Buch Deuteronomium*, in B. EGO – H. MERKEL (eds.), *Religiöses Lernen in der biblischen frühjüdischen und frühchristlichen Überlieferung* (WUNT, 180), Tübingen, Mohr-Siebeck, 2005, 27-45, p. 27. Of course, it is understandable that there are also some specific studies about Jesus as teacher: R. RIESNER, *Jesus als Lehrer: Eine Untersuchung zum Ursprung der Evangelien-Überlieferung* (WUNT, 2.7), Tübingen, Mohr-Siebeck, 1981; repr. 1984; repr. 1988); V. Tropper, *Jesus Didáskalos: Studien zu Jesus als Lehrer bei den Synoptikern und im Rahmen der antiken Kultur- und Sozialgeschichte* (ÖBS, 42), Frankfurt am Main, Peter Lang, 2012. For the first centuries CE, see K.O. SANDNES, *The Challenge of Homer: School, Pagan Poets and Early Christianity* (LNTS, 400), London, T&T Clark International, 2009.

[14] For a short description of various textual readers see: A.L.H.M. VAN WIERINGEN, *Two Reading Options in Psalm 114: A Communication-Oriented Analysis*, in *Revue Biblique* 122 (2015), 46-58, pp. 46-47. See further: A.L.H.M. VAN WIERINGEN, *Communicatiegeoriënteerde exegese en tekstuele identiteit: geïllustreerd aan het boek Amos*, in A.L.H.M. VAN WIERINGEN (ed.), *Theologie & Methode* (Theol. Persp. Suppl., 4), Bergambacht, 2VM, 2012, 3-46.

text-immanent reader. Moses' teaching is related to the gold bullock and the ambiguous question as to who made it. The Lord is taught to keep loyal to himself, and the characters and text-immanent reader are incited to be loyal to the Lord.

Christiaan Erwich and *Eep Talstra* wonder why exegetical tradition chooses to see the 'I' who is praying in Psalm 64 as the sole text-immanent reader's teacher. In many translations this voice is not only first complaining (verse 2f.), but after that the very same voice is also seen to express confidence in God and even to summon us to enjoy. This implies first, that the translator has to violate patterns of Hebrew verbal syntax, in reading a narrative past (verse 8f.) as if it were a future tense. Secondly, one easily promotes the frightened praying voice into a hero of faith who claims to be sure of being rescued. This disregards the variation of participants communicating in the text and it dissolves the tension between personal prayer and the narrative of religious tradition as the text presents it. The text, i.e. its text-immanent author, allows various competing voices to take the floor, be it in a particular and inspiring order. Erwich and Talstra experiment with linguistic, computer-assisted, techniques of participant tracking to propose their reading of the text as text.

Harm van Grol reads Psalm 137 as the intro to the Davidic Psalms 138-145. The resulting editorial collection facilitates the initiation of individuals into a community of anti-assimilationists (Hasidic anti-Hellenists at the end of the third century BCE) by offering three role models and role-'situations': a Judean in exile (Ps 137), David and his inner struggle (Pss 138-143), David as royal warrior (Ps 144,1-8). The collection is a textbook that stresses the importance of a personal choice against assimilation, that guides the potential member through an inner struggle, and that teaches him a militant spirituality. The major instrument in this initiation/teaching is the role model/situation that confronts the reader with exemplary individuals in crisis.

Sehoon Jang discusses the role of the character God in the book of Job. He demonstrates that God acts as a wise teacher, using creation as his educatory material. God teaches Job at the level of the characters,. However, through this level, the text-immanent author wishes to present God as a wise teacher for his text-immanent readers as well.

Archibald van Wieringen points out that in the book of Amos the relation teacher-disciple is present at three communicative levels: at the level of communication with the Northern Kingdom, at the level of the communication with the Southern Kingdom and, finally, at the level of communication with the text-immanent reader. All three of them can be characterised as communication by a teacher to a pupil. The teaching remains the same, but is each time realised at a higher textual level.

How do we explain the response of Matthew, the tax collector, who went up and followed Jesus immediately without knowing him? *Solomon Pasala* tries to find out how the Evangelist Matthew has constructed the text-immanent author and the text-immanent reader in Matt 8-9. There appears to be a certain pattern in the usage of the imperative and the indicative tense. While the imperative is reserved to the Teacher, the indicative tense is reserved for the disciple. When this combination does not work, there is something wrong in their dialogues and relationships. He is able to strengthen his argument and to get some clarity, when he applies the rules of "Drama", as defined by Aristotle and others, to the text. In the call of the tax collector, we have a fine example of a text-immanent disciple, who responds to the text-immanent Teacher.

Jesus' teaching about the Last Judgment reports 14 individuals or groups interacting on at least six different levels. Moreover, it combines aspects of parable and prophecy. The interpreters' careless mixing of these levels, combined with a preoccupation for conditions of salvation or guidelines for decent living, have resulted in losing the story's own message in its context. The contribution of *Laurí Thurén* seeks to discover the text's message by focusing on the narrative, by using tools from modern narrative and argumentation analysis. He argues that the narrative itself plays a key role in Matthew's literary strategy, as he prepares his readers for the forthcoming passion narrative.

Bart Koet poses the question as to where we can find a great wisdom teacher who uses children's rhymes to depict his teachings. Such a teacher can be found in Lk 7,31-35, where Jesus explains both his own teaching and John the Baptist's and defends their teachings, which are so different from each other, by referring to a children's song. An analysis of the communication shows that in 7,35 there is a reference to the fact that all the people and even all the tax collectors choose the baptism of John and that therefore there is a possibility for the audience to become children of Wisdom by joining one of the teachers.

In his article *Jan van der Watt* tries to determine the dynamics of education or educational processes in John by investigating the use of relevant educational terminology, and thereafter by analysing the conceptual references to education. He investigates the semantic field of education in that Gospel. The theme of teaching in John proves to be a central concept in its theological structure. Without this information it would not be clear where Jesus got his teachings from or how, which would be problematic in a document that deals with significant dogmatic issues related to the presence of God. Jesus is described as ῥαββί, which colours the narrative significantly. His movement with disciples frames him as an authoritative figure on a mission and also ensures the continuation of the message through the mission of the disciples.

Under the influence of especially Protestant exegesis and with an appeal to Gal 1,12, scholars have often supposed that Paul's teaching was based on revelation rather than tradition. Other scholars, however, have studied the importance of 'schools of life', both in the Hellenistic and the Jewish world, concluding that a 'school of Paul' was not at all out of line with that situation. With this in mind, *Peter Tomson* analyses the halakhic Jesus-traditions and the mystical Jesus-traditions that Paul refers to in a number of passages, as well as the specific terminology he uses in doing so.

As an example of Rabbinic traditions about teacher and disciple, *Eric Ottenheijm* discusses Hillel tutoring new disciples. Although the parallel between Hillel as a teacher and Jesus as a teacher has been viewed as remarkable, there are differences as well, which demonstrates that various teaching models existed in early Judaism.

Toke Elshof, specialised in catechesis and religious education, concludes this volume with a reflection on religious teachers from the perspective of biblical teaching and discipleship. Her contribution consists of a case study, based upon the written material in which future teachers of Religious Education go into the meaning of biblical narratives about Jesus for their work. Being familiar with biblical texts is important for their three professional roles: the role of the Witness, of the religious Specialist and of the Moderator. A limited familiarity with biblical models of teaching appears always to be coupled with a biased and optimistic approach to their future teaching profession. A broader knowledge of biblical texts would prove very helpful to the schooling of future teachers of Religious Education, especially because of the fact that these texts offer models of teaching and learning for more obstinate and complex situations in the actual practice of teachers of Religious Education.

As in biblical traditions, being a disciple is of upmost importance. Therefore, we are very honoured to dedicated this volume to Wim Beuken, who, according to 2 Tim 2,24, is a gentle and patient διδακτικός, for some of us even as *Doktorvater*, and to whom we are grateful to be one of his disciples.[15]

---

[15] We would like to thank Drs. Maurits J. Sinninghe Damsté for correcting the English text of the manuscript and Alette H.C. Warringa MA for editing the footnotes.

MOSES AS A TEACHER IN THE NARRATION ABOUT THE GOLD BULLOCK
A Communication-Oriented Exegesis of Exodus 32

Piet J. van Midden – Archibald L.H.M. van Wieringen
Tilburg, the Netherlands

Exodus 32, the narration about the gold bullock,[1] is a communicatively layered text.[2] In this contribution we will examine the role of the character Moses: which role does he play amid the various roles in the narration about the gold bullock?

We have primarily based ourselves on the syntactic computer-assisted analysis provided by the Eep Talstra Centre for Bible and Computer, situated at the VU-University in Amsterdam. We must acknowledge that the computer script used, is based on certain syntactic decisions having already been made.

On the basis of this syntactic analysis, the successive narrative units, which can be distinguished from each other by the various characters acting in the narration, become clear. We will focus on the role of Moses, who not only appears to fulfil the role of teacher in relation to all the other characters in the text, but also in relation to the text-immanent reader.

---

[1] Although this narration is widely known as the narration about the 'golden calf', we use the expression 'gold bullock' to emphasize that the statue is fashioned from molten gold and that the animal reproduced is a young, male (i.e. masculine and fertile), uncastrated bull.

[2] Cf. also C. MEYERS, *Exodus* (NCBC), Cambridge, Cambridge University Press, 2005, p. 259.

A CONCISE SYNTACTIC HIERARCHY OF EXODUS 32[3]

```
                              [<Su> העם] [<Pr> ירא] [<Cj> ו]    | EXO 32,01
                    [<Su> משה] [<Pr> בשש] [<Cj> כי]    |    |    | EXO 32,01
                              [<Co> מן ההר] [<Pr> לרדת]    |    | EXO 32,01
                 [<Co> על אהרן] [<Su> העם] [<Pr> יקהל] [<Cj> ו]  | EXO 32,01
                             [<Co> אליו] [<Pr> יאמרו] [<Cj> ו]  | EXO 32,01
==============================================================+ | |
                                           [<Pr> קום]    ||    | EXO 32,01
                   [<Ob> אלהים] [<Co> לנו] [<Pr> עשה]    ||    | EXO 32,01
       [<Co> לפנינו] [<Pr> ילכו] [<Re> אשר]    |         ||    | EXO 32,01
            [<Fr><ap> האיש / משה / זה] [<Cj> כי]         ||    | EXO 32,01
[<Co> מארץ מצרים] [<PO> העלנו] [<Re> אשר]    |           ||    | EXO 32,01
                             [<Pr> ידענו] [<Ng> לא]      ||    | EXO 32,01
                   [<Co> לו] [<Pr> היה] [<Su> מה]        ||    | EXO 32,01
==============================================================+ |
                    [<Su> אהרן] [<Co> אלהם] [<Pr> יאמר] [<Cj> ו] | EXO 32,02
==============================================================+|
                             [<Ob> נזמי הזהב] [<Pr> פרקו]    |   | EXO 32,02
[<PC> באזני נשיכם בניכם ובנתיכם] [<Re> אשר]    |                 | EXO 32,02
                             [<Co> אלי] [<Pr> הביאו] [<Cj> ו]    | EXO 32,02
/=============================================================+|
[<Ob> את נזמי הזהב] [<Su> כל העם] [<Pr> יתפרקו] [<Cj> ו]         | EXO 32,03
                             [<PC> באזניהם] [<Re> אשר]    |      | EXO 32,03
                   [<Co> אל אהרן] [<Pr> יביאו] [<Cj> ו]          | EXO 32,03
                             [<Co> מידם] [<Pr> יקח] [<Cj> ו]     | EXO 32,04
         [<Aj> בחרט] [<Ob> אתו] [<Pr> יצר] [<Cj> ו]              | EXO 32,04
         [<Ob><ap> עגל / מסכה] [<PO> יעשהו] [<Cj> ו]             | EXO 32,04
                             [<Pr> יאמרו] [<Cj> ו]               | EXO 32,04
==============================================================+
                             [<PC> אלהיך] [<Su> אלה]    |        | EXO 32,04
                             [<Vo> ישראל]    |                   | EXO 32,04
         [<Co> מארץ מצרים] [<PO> העלוך] [<Re> אשר]    |          | EXO 32,04
/=============================================================+|
                    [<Su> אהרן] [<Pr> ירא] [<Cj> ו]              | EXO 32,05
         [<Aj> לפניו] [<Ob> מזבח] [<Pr> יבן] [<Cj> ו]            | EXO 32,05
                    [<Su> אהרן] [<Pr> יקרא] [<Cj> ו]             | EXO 32,05
                             [<Pr> יאמר] [<Cj> ו]                | EXO 32,05
==============================================================+
                    [<Ti> מחר] [<Co> ליהוה] [<PC> חג]    |       | EXO 32,05
==============================================================+
                    [<Ti> ממחרת] [<Pr> ישכימו] [<Cj> ו]          | EXO 32,06
                             [<Ob> עלת] [<Pr> יעלו] [<Cj> ו]     | EXO 32,06
                    [<Ob> שלמים] [<Pr> יגשו] [<Cj> ו]            | EXO 32,06
                    [<Su> העם] [<Pr> ישב] [<Cj> ו]               | EXO 32,06
```

[3] By kind permission of the Eep Talstra Centre for Bible and Computer (ETCBC), VU-University Amsterdam. See for the account of the method E. TALSTRA, *A Hierarchy of Clauses in Biblical Hebrew Narrative*, in E. VAN WOLDE (ed.), *Narrative Syntax and the Hebrew Bible* (BIS, 29), Leiden, Brill, 1997; E. TALSTRA, *Tense, Mood, Aspect and Clause Connections in Biblical Hebrew: A Textual Approach*, in *JNSL* 23 (1997), 81-103; E. TALSTRA, *Deuteronomy: Confusion or Conclusion? The Story of Moses' Threefold Succession*, in M. VERVENNE – J. LUST (eds.), *Deuteronomy and Deuteronomic Literature* (BETL, 133), Leuven, Peeters, 1997, pp. 87-110. In this volume, see the contribution by ERWICH – TALSTRA. See f[urther]: P. VAN MIDDEN, *Broederschap en Koningschap: Een onderzoek naar de betekenis van Gideon en Abimelek in het boek Richteren*, Maastricht, Shaker Publishing, 1998, pp. 19-20; A.L.H.M. VAN WIERINGEN, *The Reader-Oriented Unity Of The Book Isaiah* (ACEBT Suppl. Series, 6), Vught, Skandalon, 2006, pp. 7-8.

MOSES AS A TEACHER 11

```
                                    [<Pr> לאכל]   |        |   EXO 32,06
                         [<Pr> שתו]  [<Cj> ו]     |        |   EXO 32,06
                         [<Pr> יקמו] [<Cj> ו]     |        |   EXO 32,06
                                    [<Pr> לצחק]   |        |   EXO 32,06
                [<Co> אל משה] [<Su> יהוה] [<Pr> וידבר] [<Cj> ו] |   EXO 32,07
|============================================================+|
                                       [<Pr> לך] ||           EXO 32,07
                                       [<Pr> רד] |            EXO 32,07
                    [<Su> עמך] [<Pr> שחת] [<Cj> כי]  |        EXO 32,07
    [<Co> מארץ מצרים] [<Pr> העלית] [<Re> אשר]      |          EXO 32,07
          [<Co> מן הדרך] [<Pr> מהר] [<Mo> סרו]     |          EXO 32,08
              [<PO> צויתם] [<Re> אשר]              |          EXO 32,08
   [<Ob><ap> עגל / מסכה] [<Co> להם] [<Pr> עשו]     |          EXO 32,08
---------------------------------------------+      |          ||
              [<Co> לו] [<Pr> ישתחוו] [<Cj> ו]    |           EXO 32,08
              [<Co> לו] [<Pr> יזבחו] [<Cj> ו]     |           EXO 32,08
                        [<Pr> יאמרו] [<Cj> ו]     |           EXO 32,08
|============================================+      |          ||
                 [<PC> אלהיך] [<Su> אלה]          |  |        EXO 32,08
                         [<Vo> ישראל]             |  |        EXO 32,08
   [<Co> מארץ מצרים] [<PO> העלוך] [<Re> אשר]      |  |        EXO 32,08
|===========================================================+
                [<Co> אל משה] [<Su> יהוה] [<Pr> ויאמר] [<Cj> ו]  EXO 32,09
|============================================================+|
              [<Ob> את העם הזה] [<Pr> ראיתי]     |            EXO 32,09
                        [<Ij> הנה] [<Cj> ו]      |            EXO 32,09
           [<Su> הוא] [<PC> עם קשה ערף]          |            EXO 32,09
                        [<Mo> עתה] [<Cj> ו]      |            EXO 32,10
                    [<Co> לי] [<Pr> הניחה]       |            EXO 32,10
   [<Co> בהם] [<Su> אפי] [<Pr> ויחר] [<Cj> ו]    |            EXO 32,10
                    [<PO> ואכלם] [<Cj> ו]        |            EXO 32,10
   [<Co> לגוי גדול] [<Ob> אותך] [<Pr> אעשה] [<Cj> ו] |        EXO 32,10
|===========================================================+
         [<Ob><ap> את פני יהוה / אלהיו] [<Su> משה] [<Pr> ויחל] [<Cj> ו]  EXO 32,11
                              [<Pr> יאמר] [<Cj> ו] |          EXO 32,11
|===========================================================+
                                 [<Qu> למה]     |    |        EXO 32,11
                         [<Vo> יהוה]            |    |        EXO 32,11
            [<Co> בעמך] [<Su> אפך] [<Pr> יחרה]  |    |        EXO 32,11
[<Aj> [<Co> בכח גדול וביד חזקה] [<Co> מארץ מצרים] [<Pr> הוצאת] [<Re> אשר] |  | EXO 32,11
                                                                           
              [<Su> מצרים] [<Pr> יאמרו] [<Qu> למה]  |         EXO 32,12
                               [<Pr> לאמר]     |    |         EXO 32,12
|============================================+      |         |
                 [<PO> הוציאם] [<Aj> ברעה]     |    |         EXO 32,12
          [<Lo> בהרים] [<Ob> אתם] [<Pr> להרג]  |    |         EXO 32,12
     [<Lo> מעל פני האדמה] [<PO> לכלתם] [<Cj> ו] |   |         EXO 32,12
|============================================+      |         |
                    [<Co> מחרון אפך] [<Pr> שוב]   |           EXO 32,12
          [<Aj> לעמך] [<Co> על הרעה] [<Pr> הנחם] [<Cj> ו] |   EXO 32,12
   [<Co><ap> לאברהם ליצחק / ולישראל / עבדיך] [<Pr> זכר]  |    EXO 32,13
              [<Aj> בך] [<Co> להם] [<Pr> נשבעת] [<Re> אשר] |  EXO 32,13
---------------------------------------------+      |         |
              [<Co> אלהם] [<Pr> תדבר] [<Cj> ו]    |           EXO 32,13
|============================================+      |         |
[<Aj> ככוכבי השמים] [<Ob> את זרעכם] [<Pr> ארבה]  |  |         EXO 32,13
              [<Ob> כל הארץ הזאת] [<Cj> ו]       |  |         EXO 32,13
             [<Pr> אמרתי] [<Re> אשר]             |  |         EXO 32,13
             [<Co> לזרעכם] [<Pr> אתן]            |  |         EXO 32,13
   [<Ti> לעלם] [<Pr> ונחלו] [<Cj> ו]             |  |         EXO 32,13
|===========================================================+
            [<Co> על הרעה] [<Su> יהוה] [<Pr> וינחם] [<Cj> ו]  EXO 32,14
                         [<Pr> דבר] [<Re> אשר]  |             EXO 32,14
              [<Co> לעמו] [<Pr> לעשות]          |             EXO 32,14
```

```
                                       [<Pr> ויפן] [<Cj>ו]   |   |  EXO 32,15
                     [<Co> מן ההר]  [<Su>משה] [<Pr>וירד] [<Cj>ו] |   |  EXO 32,15
           [<PC><sp>בידו / לחת] [<Su>שני לחת העדת] [<Cj>ו]   |   |  EXO 32,15
          [<Aj>משני עבריהם] [<PC>כתבים]  |  |                |   |  EXO 32,15
     [<PC>כתבים] [<Su>הם] [<Aj>מזה ומזה]  |                  |   |  EXO 32,15
                         [<Fr>הלחת] [<Cj>ו]                  |   |  EXO 32,16
            [<Su>המה]  | [<PC>מעשה אלהים]                    |   |  EXO 32,16
                  [<Fr>המכתב] [<Cj>ו]                        |   |  EXO 32,16
            [<Su>הוא] [<PC>מכתב אלהים]                       |   |  EXO 32,16
                  [<Lo>על הלחת] [<PC>חרות]                   |   |  EXO 32,16
  [<Aj>ברעה] [<Ob>את קול העם] [<Su>יהושע] [<Pr>ישמע] [<Cj>ו] |   |  EXO 32,17
                  [<Co>אל משה] [<Pr>יאמר] [<Cj>ו]   |  |     |   |  EXO 32,17
=================================================================+|   |   |
                  [<PC>במחנה] [<Su>קול מלחמה]  ||            |   |  EXO 32,17
=================================================================+|   |   |
                              [<Pr>יאמר] [<Cj>ו]   |  |      |   |  EXO 32,18
=================================================================+|   |   |
              [<PC>קול ענות גבורה] [<NC>אין]   ||            |   |  EXO 32,18
    [<PC>קול ענות חלושה] [<NC>אין] [<Cj>ו]   ||              |   |  EXO 32,18
             [<PC>שמע] [<Su>אנכי] [<Ob>קול ענות]    ||       |   |  EXO 32,18
=================================================================+|   |
                              [<Pr>יהי] [<Cj>ו]   |          |   |  EXO 32,19
            [<Co>אל המחנה] [<Pr>קרב] [<Cj>כאשר]   |          |   |  EXO 32,19
      [<Ob>את העגל ומחלת] [<Pr>ירא] [<Cj>ו]       |          |   |  EXO 32,19
            [<Su>אף משה] [<Pr>יחר] [<Cj>ו]        |          |   |  EXO 32,19
    [<Ob>את הלחת] [<Aj>מידו] [<Pr>ישלך] [<Cj>ו]              |   |  EXO 32,19
    [<Lo>תחת ההר] [<Ob>אתם] [<Pr>ישבר] [<Cj>ו]               |   |  EXO 32,19
            [<Ob>את העגל] [<Pr>יקח] [<Cj>ו]                  |   |  EXO 32,20
                  [<Re>אשר] [<Pr>עשו]   |                    |   |  EXO 32,20
            [<Co>באש] [<Pr>ישרף] [<Cj>ו]                     |   |  EXO 32,20
                         [<Pr>יטחן] [<Cj>ו]                  |   |  EXO 32,20
                  [<Pr>דק] [<Cj>עד אשר]    |                 |   |  EXO 32,20
       [<Lo>על פני המים] [<Pr>יזר] [<Cj>ו]                   |   |  EXO 32,20
       [<Ob>את בני ישראל] [<Pr>ישק] [<Cj>ו]                  |   |  EXO 32,20
    [<Co>אל אהרן] [<Su>משה] [<Pr>יאמר] [<Cj>ו]               |   |  EXO 32,21
=================================================================+|   |
    [<Su>העם הזה] [<Co>לך] [<Pr>עשה] [<Ob>מה]    |  |        |   |  EXO 32,21
  [<Ob>חטאה גדלה] [<Co>עליו] [<Pr>הבאת] [<Cj>כי]    |        |   |  EXO 32,21
=================================================================+|   |
                  [<Su>אהרן] [<Pr>יאמר] [<Cj>ו]   |          |   |  EXO 32,22
=================================================================+|   |
            [<Su>אדני] [<Pr>יחר] [<Ng>אל]   |                |   |  EXO 32,22
            [<Pr>ידעת] [<Su>אתה]  |                          |   |  EXO 32,22
       [<Ob>את העם] [<PC>ברע] [<Cj>כי]   |                   |   |  EXO 32,22
       [<Su>הוא]    |                                        |   |  EXO 32,22
-----------------------------------------------------------------|   |
            [<Co>לי] [<Pr>יאמרו] [<Cj>ו]   ||                |   |  EXO 32,23
=================================================================+|   |
  [<Ob>אלהים] [<Co>לנו] [<Pr>עשה]   |    ||                  |   |  EXO 32,23
[<Co>לפנינו] [<Pr>ילכו] [<Re>אשר]   |    ||                  |   |  EXO 32,23
[<Fr><ap>האיש / משה / זה] [<Cj>כי]   |   ||                  |   |  EXO 32,23
[<Co>מארץ מצרים] [<PO>העלנו] [<Re>אשר]  |   ||               |       EXO 32,23
       [<Ng>לא] [<Pr>ידענו]   |   ||                         |   |  EXO 32,23
  [<Co>לו] [<Pr>היה] [<Su>מה]   |   ||                       |   |  EXO 32,23
=================================================================+   |   |
       [<Co>להם] [<Pr>אמר] [<Cj>ו]   ||                      |   |  EXO 32,24
=================================================================+   |
            [<Su>זהב] [<PC>למי]   |   ||                     |   |  EXO 32,24
                         [<Pr>התפרקו]   |   ||               |   |  EXO 32,24
=================================================================+   |
            [<Co>לי] [<Pr>יתנו] [<Cj>ו]   ||                 |   |  EXO 32,24
       [<Co>באש] [<PO>אשלכהו] [<Cj>ו]   ||                   |   |  EXO 32,24
  [<Su>העגל הזה] [<Pr>יצא] [<Cj>ו]   ||                      |   |  EXO 32,24
=================================================================+   |   |
```

MOSES AS A TEACHER   13

		[<Cj>ו] [<Pr>וירא] [<Su>משה] [<Ob>את העם]		EXO 32,25
		[<Cj>כי] [<PC>פרע] [<Su>הוא]		EXO 32,25
[<Aj>בקמיהם] [<Aj>לשמצה] [<Su>אהרן] [<PO>פרעה] [<Cj>כי]				EXO 32,25
	[<Co>בשער המחנה] [<Su>משה] [<Pr>ויעמד] [<Cj>ו]			EXO 32,26
		[<Pr>ויאמר] [<Cj>ו]		EXO 32,26
	[<PC>ליהוה] [<Su>מי]			EXO 32,26
	[<Co>אלי]			EXO 32,26
	[<Su>כל בני לוי] [<Co>אליו] [<Pr>ויאספו] [<Cj>ו]			EXO 32,26
	[<Co>להם] [<Pr>ויאמר] [<Cj>ו]			EXO 32,27
[<Su><ap>אלהי ישראל / יהוה] [<Pr>אמר] [<Mo>כה]				EXO 32,27
		[<Pr>שימו]		EXO 32,27
[<Co>על ירכו] [<Ob>חרבו] [<Su>איש]				EXO 32,27
		[<Pr>עברו]		EXO 32,27
[<Co>במחנה] [<Lo>לשער] [<Lo>משער] [<Pr>ושובו] [<Cj>ו]				EXO 32,27
		[<Pr>והרגו] [<Cj>ו]		EXO 32,27
	[<Ob>את אחיו] [<Su>איש]			EXO 32,27
	[<Ob>את רעהו] [<Su>איש] [<Cj>ו]			EXO 32,27
	[<Ob>את קרבו] [<Su>איש] [<Cj>ו]			EXO 32,27
	[<Co>כדבר משה] [<Su>בני לוי] [<Pr>ויעשו] [<Cj>ו]			EXO 32,28
<Aj>כשלשת אלפי איש] [<Ti>ביום ההוא] [<Aj>מן העם] [<Pr>ויפל] [<Cj>ו]			EXO 32,28
	[<Su>משה] [<Pr>ויאמר] [<Cj>ו]		EXO 32,29
[<Aj>ליהוה] [<Ob>היום] [<Ti>ידכם] [<Pr>מלאו]			EXO 32,29
[<PC>בבנו ובאחיו] [<Su>איש] [<Cj>כי]			EXO 32,29
[<Ob>ברכה] [<Ti>היום] [<Co>עליכם] [<Pr>לתת] [<Cj>ו]			EXO 32,29
	[<Ti>ממחרת] [<Pr>ויהי] [<Cj>ו]		EXO 32,30
	[<Co>אל העם] [<Su>משה] [<Pr>ויאמר] [<Cj>ו]		EXO 32,30
[<Ob>חטאה גדלה] [<Pr>חטאתם] [<Su>אתם]			EXO 32,30
	[<Mo>עתה] [<Cj>ו]		EXO 32,30
	[<Co>אל יהוה] [<Pr>אעלה]		EXO 32,30
[<Co>בעד חטאתכם] [<Pr>אכפרה] [<Mo>אולי]			EXO 32,30
	[<Co>אל יהוה] [<Su>משה] [<Pr>וישב] [<Cj>ו]		EXO 32,31
	[<Pr>ויאמר] [<Cj>ו]		EXO 32,31
[<Ob>חטאה גדלה] [<Su>העם הזה] [<Pr>חטא] [<Ij>אנא]			EXO 32,31
[<Ob>אלהי זהב] [<Co>להם] [<Pr>ויעשו] [<Cj>ו]			EXO 32,31
	[<Mo>עתה] [<Cj>ו]		EXO 32,32
[<Ob>חטאתם] [<Pr>תשא] [<Cj>אם]			EXO 32,32
	[<Ng>אין] [<Cj>אם] [<Cj>ו]		EXO 32,32
[<Co>מספרך] [<Ij>נא] [<PO>מחני]			EXO 32,32
	[<Pr>כתבת] [<Re>אשר]		EXO 32,32
	[<Co>אל משה] [<Su>יהוה] [<Pr>ויאמר] [<Cj>ו]		EXO 32,33
		[<Fr>מי]		EXO 32,33
[<Co>לי] [<Pr>חטא] [<Re>אשר]			EXO 32,33
[<Co>מספרי] [<PO>אמחנו]			EXO 32,33
	[<Mo>עתה] [<Cj>ו]		EXO 32,34
	[<Pr>לך]		EXO 32,34
	[<Ob>את העם] [<Pr>נחה]		EXO 32,34
[<Co>לך] [<Pr>דברתי] [<Re>אל אשר]			EXO 32,34

```
                                              [<Ij> הנה]                |  |  EXO 32,34
                        [<Co> לפניך] [<Pr> ילך] [<Su> מלאכי]             |  |  EXO 32,34
                                 [<Fr> וביום פקדי] [<Cj> ו]              |  |  EXO 32,34
[<Ob> חטאתם] [<Co> עליהם] [<Pr> ופקדתי] [<Cj> ו]                         |  |  EXO 32,34
=================================================================================+
                   [<Ob> את העם] [<Su> יהוה] [<Pr> ויגף] [<Cj> ו]        EXO 32,35
                        [<Ob> את העגל] [<Pr> עשו] [<Cj> אשר]             EXO 32,35
                                 [<Su> אהרן] [<Pr> עשה] [<Re> אשר]       EXO 32,35
```

WORKING TRANSLATION

For the sake of convenience we would like to first give a working translation. In this translation, every single clause(-atom) is written on a new line, as in the syntactical scheme. All new direct speeches are marked by a tab from the left margin. A blank line is added to separate the narrative units we will discuss in the next paragraph.

1 a The people saw
    b that Moses delayed
    c to come down from the mountain;
    d whereupon the people congregated before Aaron
    e and said to him:
    f   'Up,
    g   make us a god
    h   who shall go before us.
    i   For this Moses, the man
    j   who brought us up out of the land of Egypt,
    k   we do not know
    l   what has become of him.'
2 a Thereupon Aaron said to them:
    b   'Take off the gold rings
    c   that are in the ears of your wives, your sons, and your daughters,
    d   and bring them to me.'
3 a So all the people took off the gold rings
    b that were in their ears
    c and brought them to Aaron.
4 a And he took the gold from their hand
    b and fashioned it with a graving tool
    c and made a moulded bullock.
    d And they said:
    e   'This is your god,
    f   oh Israel,
    g   that brought you up out of the land of Egypt!'

5 a Aaron saw [this].
  b He built an altar before it.
  c And Aaron proclaimed
  d and said:
  e   'Tomorrow shall be a feast to YHWH.'
6 a And they rose up early the next day
  b and offered burnt offerings
  c and brought peace offerings.
  d And the people sat down to eat
  e and drink
  f and rose up
  g to play.

7 a YHWH said to Moses
  b   'Go
  c   get down
  d   for your people has corrupted itself
  e   whom you brought up out of the land of Egypt
8 a   They have turned aside quickly out of the way
  b   that I commanded them.
  c   They have made for themselves a moulded bullock;
  d   they have worshipped it
  e   sacrificed to it
  f   and said:
  g   "This is your god,
  h   oh Israel,
  i   who brought you up out of the land of Egypt!"
9 a And YHWH said to Moses:
  b   'I have seen this people
  c   and indeed, it is a stiff-necked people.
10 a   Now therefore,
   b   let me alone
   c   that my anger may burn hot against them
   d   and I may consume them;
   e   but I will make a great nation of you.
11 a But Moses sought the favour of YHWH his God;
   b he said:
   c   'Why
   d   oh YHWH,
   e   does your anger burn hot against your people

	f	whom you have brought out of the land of Egypt with great power and with a mighty hand?
12	a	Why should the Egyptians say:
	b	"With evil intent did he bring them out
	c	to kill them in the mountains
	d	and to consume them from the face of the earth"!
	e	Turn from your burning anger
	f	and relent from this disaster against your people.
13	a	Remember Abraham, Isaac, and Israel, your servants,
	b	to whom you swore by your own self,
	c	and said to them:
	d	"I will multiply your offspring as the stars of heaven,
	e	and all this land
	f	that I have promised
	g	I will give to your offspring,
	h	and they shall inherit it forever."'
14	a	Thereupon YHWH relented from the disaster
	b	that he had spoken
	c	of making for his people.

15	a	Then Moses turned
	b	and went down from the mountain
	c	with the two tablets of the testimony in his hand, tablets
	d	that were written on both sides; on the front and on the back they were written,
16	a	the tablets were the work of God,
	b	and the writing was the writing of God,
	c	engraved on the tablets.

17	a	When Joshua heard the noise of the people as they shouted,
	b	he said to Moses:
	c	'There is a noise of war in the camp.'
18	a	But he said:
	b	'It is not the sound of shouting for victory,
	c	or the sound of the cry of defeat,
	d	but the sound of singing that I hear.'

19	a	And as soon as he came near the camp
	b	and saw the bullock and the dancing,
	c	Moses' anger burned hot,

	d	and he threw the tablets out of his hand
	e	and broke them at the foot of the mountain.
20	a	He took the bullock
	b	that they had made
	c	and burned it with fire
	d	and ground it to powder
	e	and scattered it on the water
	f	and made the sons of Israel drink it.

21	a	Moses said to Aaron:
	b	'What did this people do to you
	c	that you have brought such a great sin upon them?'
22	a	And Aaron said:
	b	'Let not the anger of my lord burn hot.
	c	You know the people,
	d	that it is set on evil.
23	a	For they said to me:
	b	"Make us a god
	c	who shall go before us.
	d	As for this Moses, the man
	e	who brought us up out of the land of Egypt,
	f	we do not know
	g	what has become of him."
24	a	So I said to them:
	b	"Let any
	c	who have gold
	d	take it off."
	e	So they gave it to me,
	f	and I threw it into the fire,
	g	and out came this bullock.'
25	a	And when Moses saw
	b	that the people had broken loose
	c	–for Aaron had let them break loose, to the derision of their enemies–,
26	a	then Moses stood in the gate of the camp and said:
	b	'Who is on YHWH's side?
	c	Come to me.'
	d	And all the sons of Levi gathered around him.
27	a	And he said to them:
	b	'Thus said YHWH, God of Israel:

	c	"Put your sword on your side each of you,
	d	and go to and fro from gate to gate throughout the camp,
	e	and each of you kill his brother and his companion and his neighbour." '
28	a	And the sons of Levi did according to the word of Moses.
	b	That day about three thousand men of the people fell.
29	a	Moses said:
	b	'Today you have been ordained for the service of Y<small>HWH</small>,
	c	each one at the cost of his son and of his brother,
	d	so that he might bestow a blessing upon you this day.'
30	a	The next day Moses said to the people:
	b	'You have sinned a great sin.
	c	And now,
	d	I will go up to Y<small>HWH</small>;
	e	perhaps I can make atonement for your sin.'
31	a	So Moses returned to Y<small>HWH</small>
	b	and said:
	c	'Alas, this people has sinned a great sin.
	d	It has made for itself a god of gold.
32	a	But now,
	b	if you will forgive their sin
	c	– but if not,
	d	please blot me out of your book
	e	that you have written.'
33	a	But Y<small>HWH</small> said to Moses:
	b	'Whoever has sinned against me,
	c	I will blot out of my book.
34	a	But now,
	b	go,
	c	lead the people to the place
	d	about which I have spoken to you;
	e	behold, my angel shall go before you.
	f	Nevertheless, in the day when I visit,
	g	I will visit their sin upon them.'
35	a	Then Y<small>HWH</small> sent a plague on the people,
	b	because they made the bullock,
	c	the one that Aaron made.

Narrative units

Based on the syntactic analysis we mark the following narrative units and protagonists:[4]

32,1-6	the people, tired of waiting for Moses
32,7-13	Yhwh and Moses, in response to the people's action
32,14	Yhwh's repentance
32,15-16	narrative continuation, with text-immanent author's information
32,17-18	Joshua and Moses in response to the people's action
32,19-20	narrative continuation
32,21-29	Moses and Aaron in response to the people's action
32,30-34	Moses and Yhwh, in return
32,35	narrative closure, with text-immanent author's new information

The first narrative unit (the verses 1-6) contains the actions between the characters 'people' and 'Aaron'.

Moses is out of view. He is introduced only indirectly, sideways, by means of a כִּי-clause in the text-immanent author's text in verse 1b as well as in the direct speech of the people itself in verse 1i: he delayed in coming down from the mountain.[5] He does not play a role on this stage.

Yhwh seems to be out of view as well. He is only mentioned in verse 5e. His appearance in the first narrative unit is more or less unexpected, because it is not made clear in the text what Yhwh has to do with the bullock which was made out of the gold jewellery.

The action of making the gold bullock is both the introduction to and the cause of the rest of the chapter. The rest of the chapter is almost completely dedicated to the conversations between Yhwh and Moses, between Joshua and Moses, between Moses and Aaron, between Moses and the people, and once again between Moses and Yhwh, after which new information is given at the end of the story.

The second narrative unit (the verses 7-13) contains the communication between Yhwh and Moses. After the verses 1-6, a change of scene occurs.

---

[4] For narrative units in Ex 32 see also: Y.H Chung, *The Sin of the Calf: The Rise of the Bible's Negative Attitude Toward the Golden Calf* (Library of Hebrew Bible/OTS, 523), New York NY, T&T Clark Int., 2010, p. 30; R.E. Hendrix, *A Literary Structural Analysis of the Golden-Calf Episode in Exodus 32:1-33:6*, in *Andrews University Seminary Studies* 28 (1990), 211-217.

[5] See also: U. Cassuto, *A Commentary on the Book of Exodus*, Jerusalem, Magnes Press, 1967, repr.1997, p. 411.

Moses, at first having delayed in coming, is now the eye-catcher in the narration. Although YHWH starts the communication, it is Moses who plays the active role by searching after the favour of YHWH, who is his God.

The third narrative unit is formed by verse 14 only. This verse is syntactically not part of the composition. In the text hierarchy, no other sentences depend on it. Verse 14 is grammatically not dependent on the previous verses. This syntactical position of verse 14 makes this verse of high importance within the narration. Only the character YHWH is present in it, and no other characters are mentioned.

The fourth narrative unit contains the verses 15-16.[6] Only the first two clauses of the seven clauses of which this unit is constructed, describe narrative actions, indicated by the *wayyiqtol*-forms וַיִּפֶן and וַיֵּרֶד. Therefore, this unit is mainly a retarding element in the narrative, in which the text-immanent author focusses on the tablets themselves.

The verses 17-18, forming the fifth narrative unit, continue the narrative line by introducing a new character, Joshua. This unit contains the communication between Joshua and Moses.

From a semantic point of view, this unit is held together by the word קוֹל *noise / sound*, which occurs five times in these verses (17a.d; 18b.c.d).[7]

The next narrative unit is formed by the verses 19-20. The unit is introduced by the macro-syntactical sign וַיְהִי in verse 19a and Moses is renominalised in verse 19c. Whereas the fourth unit is characterised by only a few narrative actions, this unit contains a rapid enumeration of successive narrative actions in the verses 19d-20f.

The verses 21-29 form the sixth narrative unit. The character Moses is renominalised again in verse 21a, and the character Aaron is reintroduced in the same verse, having last been mentioned in the first narrative unit. This sixth narrative unit contains the communication between Moses and Aaron, which, from verse 25a onwards, develops into the communication between Moses and the sons of Levi.

The seventh narrative unit consists of the verses 30-34. This unit narrates the communication between Moses and YHWH, after the introductory verse 30, in which Moses communicates with the people. This seventh

---

[6] *Pace*: CASSUTO, *Commentary* (n. 5), p. 417; M. O'BRIEN, *The dynamics of the golden calf story (Exodus 32-34)*, in *Australian Biblical Review* 60 (2012), 18-31, p. 20, who consider the verses 15-16 as being part of Moses' actions.

[7] *Cf.* for Moses' direct speech in the verses 18b-d the translation of M. BUBER – F. ROSENZWEIG, *Die fünf Bücher der Weisung*, Berlin, L. Schneider, 1930: *Kein Schall, der sänge Überwiegen, / Kein Schall, der sänge Unterliegen – / Schall von Wächselgesängen höre ich*.

unit is the continuation of the communication in the second unit; however, whereas YHWH initiates the communication in the second unit, Moses does so in the seventh.

This unit is constructed by using the particle וְעַתָּה three times, in each direct speech once: Moses uses this emphatic particle in verse 30c in his communication with the people and in verse 32a in his communication with YHWH, while YHWH uses it in verse 34a in his reply to Moses.

The eighth and concluding narrative unit is formed by verse 35. The narrative sequel is clearly marked by the use of the *wayyiqtol*-form וַיִּגֹּף in verse 35a. The information given, however, is new in the narrative and has not been told before by the text-immanent author.

WHO HAS BROUGHT UP ISRAEL OUT OF EGYPT?

Within these narrative units, several semantic lines occur. We will focus on two of them, because of their role in the content of the various communications taking place in the narrative.

The first semantic item concerns the one who is responsible for the exodus. The communication about the question of who has brought Israel up out of Egypt is not fluent at all levels. The responsibility for the exodus from Egypt is a crucial question. The people says in verse 1: 'Up, make us a god who shall go before us. For this *Moses, the man who brought us up out of the land of Egypt*, we do not know what has become of him.'

Aaron executes the people's demand apparently without protest. That protest should be expected, in view of the Ten Commandments, which are given in Exodus 20 and start with *I am YHWH your God, who brought you out of the land of Egypt*, to the exclusion of all other deities.

In verse 4, however, the Israelites respond with regard to the moulded bullock: 'This is *your god*, O Israel, *that brought you up out of the land of Egypt!*'

This 'confession' serves as a prelude to the statement of Jeroboam at the occasion of the unveiling of the two gold bull-calfs he has made for the sanctuaries in Dan and Bethel: *Here is your god, oh Israel, who brought you up out of Egypt* (1 Ki 12,28).[8]

---

[8] See e.g. H. SCHÜNGEL-STRAUMANN, *Der Dekalog – Gottes Gebote?* (SBS, 67), Stuttgart, KBW, 1973, p. 90.

In the second narrative unit the exodus from Egypt is again a topic. In verse 7, YHWH reproaches Moses with: '...for your people has corrupted itself *who you brought up out of the land of Egypt*'. YHWH seems to consent to the people's view that appoints Moses as the leading man.

However, Moses draws YHWH's attention to his responsibility in verse 11 by stating that it is YHWH who actually has brought up Israel out of the land of Egypt: '...against your people *whom you have brought out of the land of Egypt* with great power and with a mighty hand...'. By adding the prepositional phrase בְּכֹחַ גָּדוֹל וּבְיָד חֲזָקָה *with great power and with a mighty hand* he strengthens his claim. Neither another god nor Moses could have led the people out of Egypt: neither have such capabilities.

In verse 23 Aaron literally repeats what the people, in verse 1, said as an excuse for making the statue: 'As for this *Moses, the man who brought us up out of the land of Egypt*, we do not know what has become of him.' However, this excuse is not adequate. The theme continues in chapter 33, starting with: 'Depart, go up hence, you and the people *who you have brought up out of the land of Egypt*.' YHWH distances himself from one of his most important acts, while Israel's birth coincides with the exodus from Egypt.

It is important to notice that it is only in Exodus, that the people of Israel is indicated by using the word הָעָם. In the promise in Gen 12,2; 17,20; 46,3 – see also Ex 32,10 – to make Israel a great nation, the word גּוֹי is used. The relation between Israel and YHWH is expressed by the word עַמִּי, *my people*. The expression is not free of emotion.[9] Moses appeals to YHWH's promise in Ex 32,13.

THE GOLD BULLOCK: WHO MADE IT?

The second theme that is communicatively important, is the question of who made the gold bullock.

According to verse 4, Aaron fabricates a bullock out of molten gold, and it is meant to be a god that should be considered to have brought the people up out of Egypt.[10] However, verse 5b is ambiguous: Aaron builds an altar לְפָנָיו, *before it / him*. In this sentence it is not immediately clear what the antecedent of the suffix is: the bullock, the people or Aaron himself. It is even possible to consider YHWH as the antecedent, because

---

[9] See, regarding to emotions in עמי: Hos 1,9.12; 2:22. *Cf.* also בת־עמי in Jer. 14,17.
[10] *Cf.* CASSUTO, *Commentary* (n. 5), p. 413.

Aaron proclaims: 'Tomorrow is a feast to YHWH'. The text therefore could suggest that Aaron does not intend to replace YHWH with a gold bullock.[11]

In verse 8 YHWH holds the Israelites responsible for making the gold bullock. The name of the fabricator is not mentioned. Moreover YHWH accuses the Israelites of bowing down before the bullock and offering to it. Although burnt offerings and peace offerings are made in verse 6, the text does not mentioned whether these are offered to the moulded bullock.

The perspective of YHWH is adopted by the text-immanent author in verse 20b: Moses destroys the gold bullock that the people made, with fire. This position of the text-immanent author confirms the ambiguity about Aaron's role in the first narrative unit and seems to solve it in favour of Aaron.

When in verse 21 the communication between Moses and Aaron starts, Moses does not reproach Aaron for fabricating the gold bullock. In reaction, Aaron tells in his own words what happened. He mentions the people's unrest and his attempts to deal with it, but he does not say that he himself made the gold bullock. Not before the last line of his direct speech, does Aaron mention the origin of the gold bullock: it simply came out of the fire (verse 24f).

This view that the people fabricated the gold bullock, is continued in verse 31d. In the communication between Moses and YHWH, YHWH's evaluation of the situation is not changed. In the eyes of both YHWH and Moses, the people fabricated it.

However, in the concluding narrative unit, on the one hand, the text-immanent author confirms the view that the people made the gold bullock (verse 35b), but on the other hand, he also mentions Aaron as the fabricator, and for the first time explicitly.

Moses as a multiple teacher:
Teaching the two minor helpers' roles

Against the background of these two main semantic ambiguities found in the narrative, Moses plays the role of teacher to explain what is going on. Moses does so in relation to the various characters in the text as well as in relation to the text-immanent reader. Examining this role of Moses, we would like to start with the two minor roles of Moses' helpers: Joshua and the sons of Levi.

---

[11] *Cf.* P.Y. HOSKISSON, *Aaron's Golden Calf*, in *FARMS Review* 18 (2006), 375-387, p. 381.

After YHWH has informed Moses about what is happening at the foot of the mountain, the noise of the people reaches the mountain. As can be deduced from Joshua's remark in verse 17d, he appears not to know about what is happening at the foot of the mountain, whereas Moses is.

Until this moment Joshua has been invisible. As from Ex 24,13 the text-immanent reader knows that he is accompanying Moses on his journey on the mountain. After the verses 17-18, Joshua again becomes invisible in the narrative.[12] His function, however, is related only to the verses 15-16. The text-immanent author describes the specific value of the tablets to the text-immanent reader in the verses 15c-16c. In view of these tablets, the text-immanent reader knows that idolatry cannot be an option for the people of God. In verse 17 Joshua explains the noise from the perspective of the tablets. Joshua, therefore, is the character in the text that gives utterance to the idea that the text-immanent reader would wish were to be the case. Unfortunately, this is not the case.

That Joshua thinks of warring, is not strange: from his first appearance in Ex 17,9 he is marked as a general. Moses, informed by YHWH, can explain it better: the journey in the desert is in danger of stranding and devolving into dancing and singing. YHWH's outburst however, escaped Joshua's observation and neither is he informed about it. Joshua is situated outside the people's misbehaviour. In a way, therefore, Joshua is the text-immanent reader in the form of a character. Unfortunately, this option of being in an outside position is not possible for the text-immanent reader, who is present in the entire narrative, though he would wish he could join with Joshua in his position.

The second helpers' role is formed by the sons of Levi. From Ex 24 on, the text focuses on the cult and the tasks of Aaron and his sons. Aaron and his sons accompany Moses going up on the mountain. The first thing they hear is that the tabernacle should be set up and how its interior should be arranged. The sons of Levi are therefore well-informed. In verse 25 Moses asks for help by choosing YHWH's side. It is not a surprise that all the Levites respond to this request positively. Moses explains to them how they should act in the actual crisis.

---

[12] *Pace*: CASSUTO, *Commentary* (n. 5), p. 419, who adds *accompanied by Joshua* to the description of Moses' coming down to the camp.

The positive role of the Levites also creates an ambiguity.[13] For the most important Levite, Aaron, was the instigator of the chaos and his tribe Levi can now clean up the mess he made. This means a purge, which is similar to the purge in Sittim, where the priest Phinehas plays an important role (Num 25).

The text-immanent reader is also confronted with this ambiguity. He is challenged to make the right choice, i.e. to sympathize with the sons of Levi, and not with Aaron. On the other hand, the punishment meted out by the sons of Levi at the order of Moses, makes the choice in favour of Levi's sons a difficult one to make.

The two minor roles of Moses' helpers confront the text-immanent reader with an ambiguous situation: on the one hand he would like to join the safe and unknowing position of Joshua, which is impossible, and, on the other hand, he would like to choose in favour of YHWH, like the sons of Levi, but which has it dark sides as well.

MOSES AS A MULTIPLE TEACHER: TEACHING THE PEOPLE

The communication between Moses and the people is only mentioned twice in the narrative. In the sixth narrative unit, the verses 19-20, this relation is described from the text-immanent author's perspective. Only Moses' actions are mentioned, without any direct speech. Moses acts drastically: he destroys the gold bullock and makes the people drink it. The action performed by Moses in relation to the people, is stressed by using the expression בני ישראל *the sons of Israel* (verse 20f), which is used only once in the narrative.

In verse 30, the opening scene of the eighth narrative unit, the relation between Moses and the people is expressed by using a direct speech. The content of this direct speech is mild: Moses does not focus on the great sin, but explains to the people the possibility of atonement for which he himself will do his best on their behalf.[14]

---

[13] *Cf.* J.W. WATTS, *Aaron and the Golden Calf in the Rhetoric of the Pentateuch*, in *JBL* 130 (2011), 417-430, pp. 428-429.

[14] *Cf.* B.S. CHILDS, *Biblical Theology of the Old and New Testament: Theological Reflections on the Christian Bible*, Minneapolis MN, Fortress, 1993, pp. 505-506. *Cf.* further: D. TIMMER, *Small Lexemes, Large Semantics: Prepositions and Theology in the Golden Calf Episode (Exodus 32–34)*, in *Bib* 88 (2007), 92-99, p. 99.

Moses as a multiple teacher: teaching YHWH

In the second narrative unit, Moses starts off with being a pupil. He forms YHWH's sounding board. YHWH bursts out in anger. Moses does not know why. He is positioned as someone who is not to blame in this situation. He is a *tabula rasa* who has to be informed by YHWH.[15]

However, as the second narrative units develop, pupil Moses becomes a teacher to YHWH.[16] Whereas YHWH's first direct speech in the verses 7-8 is meant to inform Moses, his second direct speech in the verses 9-10 makes clear that Moses functions as more than a pupil and becomes a teacher as well. In his role as representative of the people, Moses stands in YHWH's way, as the imperative הַנִּיחָה לִי *let me alone* in verse 10b makes clear. The narrative is very anthropomorphous: YHWH cannot bypass Moses.

YHWH has in mind to destroy the entire people, not indicated as עַמִּי, but as הָעָם הַזֶּה *this people* (verse 9b),[17] but wishes to make an exception for Moses: he will make of Moses a great nation, גּוֹי גָּדוֹל (verse 10e). Here, the promise to Abraham, Isaac and Jacob is given regarding Moses. The promise to the patriarchs is not cancelled: Moses is a son of Abraham. It is a new beginning for the Israel, realised in Moses.

Moses' reaction is striking. He not only acts on behalf of the people, to preserve the people from doom, but also tries to keep YHWH from doing wrong, using the exact same appeal. Moses teaches YHWH that, if he sticks to his decision, it will result in only losers. And the greatest loser will be YHWH himself!

Moses explains this by giving two arguments.[18] Firstly, if YHWH cancels his plan of liberation, his image and reputation in Egypt will be shattered (the verses 11f-12d). Secondly, if YHWH cancels his plan of liberation, he violates his promises to Abraham (verse 13). With these two arguments, Moses instructs YHWH what he should do: turn away from his anger (the verses 12e-f).

---

[15] For the contrast between Moses and the people *cf.* J.N. OSWALT, *The Golden Calves and the Egyptian Concept of Deity*, in *Evangelical Quarterly* 45 (1973), 13-20, p. 19.

[16] *Pace* among others: F. DELITZSCH, *The Pentateuch; Commentary on the Old Testament*, Vol. 1, Edinburgh, T.&T. Clark, 1864; repr. Grand Rapids MI, Eerdmans, 1981, p. 224, who considers the situation as a test of Moses by YHWH.

[17] See also O'BRIEN, *The Dynamics* (n. 6), p. 21.

[18] See also J. ASSMANN, *Exodus: Die Revolution der Alten Welt*, Darmstadt, WBG Verlag, 2015³, p. 364.

The climax of Moses' teaching is found in the fourth narrative unit: does the narrative of Abraham and his kinship with YHWH end here, or is the people offered another chance? The text continues: וַיִּנָּחֶם יְהוָה *and YHWH relented...*, and changes his mind (verse 14).[19]

In the sixth narrative unit, the verses 19-20, the text-immanent author gives Moses a new role. At the top of the mountain Moses was the representative of the people and the teacher of YHWH, who convinced him not to quit his relation with Israel. But now he represents YHWH in his anger. The parallel emotion is striking: Moses bursts with anger in seeing the bullock and the dancing (verse 19), just as YHWH exploded with anger in verse 10.

First of all, Moses destroys the two tablets (verse 19). This seems to be as radical as the destruction YHWH had in mind, because destroying the two tablets is destroying YHWH's words of relation with his people. Next, Moses destroys the gold bullock (verse 20) – whereas, strikingly, YHWH in his own rage did not mention destroying it. Furthermore, Moses destroys the perpetrators (the verses 25-29).

This last element of the destruction performed by Moses is based on a direct speech of YHWH. In verse 27, Moses tells what YHWH, indicated as אֱלֹהֵי יִשְׂרָאֵל *the God of Israel*, an expression only used here in the narrative, has said. However, this direct speech is not mentioned in the text as being spoken by YHWH himself: the text-immanent reader has not been informed about these words of YHWH before. Here, Moses' role of being a teacher also develops into being a teacher for the text-immanent reader.

MOSES AS A MULTIPLE TEACHER: TEACHING THE TEXT-IMMANENT READER

Moses does not only teach his fellow-characters, but also the text-immanent reader. The embedded direct speech of YHWH in Moses' direct speech in verse 27 is of importance here. This embedded direct speech can only be understood if the text-immanent reader is aware of the ellipsis, which implies that he does not have access to the words of YHWH unless through Moses. In other words, the choice in favour of Moses implies a choice in favour of YHWH and the other way round, a choice in favour of YHWH implies a choice in favour of Moses.

---

[19] For later theological readings of the text, a change in the mind of YHWH is impossible; see e.g. D.U. ROTTZOLL, *Abraham Ibn Esras langer Kommentar zum Buch Exodus* (Studia Judaica, 17), Berlin, De Gruyter, 2000, p. 985.

The new information at the end of the narrative in the ninth narrative unit confirms Moses' teaching to the text-immanent reader. In verse 35 the loss of people is attributed to a plague sent by YHWH. This implies that not Moses is responsible for the destruction of the perpetrators among the people, but that YHWH himself is the acting character in the perpetrators' destruction, in accordance with his embedded direct speech in Moses' direct speech.[20]

Even the closing words אֲשֶׁר עָשָׂה אַהֲרֹן *the one that Aaron made*, which seems to continue the ambiguity at the text-immanent reader's level, confirms the importance of Moses' teaching: the choice to be made in favour of YHWH (and of Moses and of the sons of Levi) is independent of the final answer to the question of who made the gold bullock.

In sum, we can conclude that Ex 32 is an interesting narrative with a complex communicative structure, incorporating semantic ambiguities. Within the various communications, Moses appears to be a teacher, primarily for the other characters in the narrative, including YHWH, but also for the text-immanent reader.

---

[20] Besides Ex 32:27, in the five books of the Torah, the introductory formula כי כה אמר יהוה functions only in Exodus in the narratives of the plagues upon Egypt; see: S.A. MAIER, *Speaking of speaking: Marking Direct Discourse in the Hebrew Bible* (VT.S, 46), Leiden, Brill, 1992, p. 274.

THE TEXT AS OUR TEACHER
Participant tracking in Psalm 64

Christiaan ERWICH – Eep TALSTRA
Amsterdam, the Netherlands

READING THE TEXT

Hear, God, my voice in my complaint.
Hide me from those doing evil.

God shot at them an arrow.

How should one read a Psalm where someone ('I') begins with praying to God (vocative and imperative) requesting him to listen, and next, after a number of lines, suddenly presents a short narrative about what God ('he') *did* to 'them'? Where does this text locate its reader? Are we invited to join the prayer of the first speaker? Or to listen to someone else's story about God? Who wants to teach us what?

When analysing Biblical Hebrew texts one quickly finds oneself entering a field of research that requires giving simultaneous attention to a variety of data and data types. We have to understand the language being used, and then interpret what is actually being said about God and humans. In addition we also have to keep track of the repeated change of dialogues in the text and try to understand the discourse of the text as composition. As the lines quoted above demonstrate: God is the addressee in verse 2, but from verse 8 on he is being narrated about. So who speaks to whom in the various parts of the Psalm? How do the various dialogues in this Psalm contribute to the Psalm as a whole? A small map of Psalm 64 may suffice here as a first introduction to our search to understand its discourse:

Verses 2-3 form a dialogue between *I* and *you* = *God*, using verbal forms of request, *imperative* and 2nd person *yiqtol*:
God, listen to me and hide me from those doing evil.

Verses 4-5a elaborate upon the actions of these evildoers, expressed by *qatal* verbal forms and beginning with a relative clause. So the speaker seems to continue, however, the 'I' and 'you' are no longer present. The one being attacked no longer is the 'I', but *a blameless one*. Is the 'I' here still speaking to 'you, God'?
they are the ones that have sharpened like a sword their tongue...
to shoot from an ambush a blameless one.

Verses 5b-7 describe what the evildoers do or will do. This section uses mainly *yiqtol* verbal forms. The victim, *the blameless one* is mentioned again, but no 'I' or 'you'. Is God still the addressee?
Suddenly they will shoot him ...

Verses 8-10 again change the main verbal tense used. Four times we find *wayyiqtol*, the tense form of narrated action, the first action here coming from God. So it cannot be God who is being addressed here as in verses 2 and 3 of the Psalm. Who is narrating here, and to whom? Can it still be the 'I' who began with a prayer?
God shot at them an arrow.

Verse 11 concludes the discourse with a change of subject and again with a change of verbal tenses. We now find *yiqtol* with modality, elaborated by *wᵉqatal* and *wᵉyiqtol*.
Let a righteous one rejoice in YHWH.

1. The text: what are our data?

Before asking the question as to what this volatile text might mean, one has to ask the linguistic question: what kind of data do we have here on our desk or screen and in what way do the different types of data interact?

First, the text reflects classical Hebrew as a linguistic system. Questions of grammar and syntax arise, especially when one wants to propose a translation of the Psalm. How to understand the variety of verbal forms used here? Can one really render all of the *yiqtol*s, the *qatal*s and *wayyiqtol*s simply by using present or future tenses as modern translations often do?[1] What kind of discourse results from this translation strategy?[2] Is it always

---

[1] See for example the *New Revised Standard Version*, Cambridge, Cambridge University Press, 1989, and in Dutch the *Nieuwe Bijbelvertaling* (NBV), Haarlem, NBG, 2004; *Bijbel in Gewone Taal* (BGT), Haarlem, NBG, 2014; *Willlibrordvertaling* (W95), Boxtel, KBS, 1995.

[2] See the discussion in F-L. HOSSFELD – E. ZENGER, *Psalmen 51-100* (HTKAT), Freiburg, Herder, 2000, pp. 202-203.

the same speaker who is addressing either God or the reader in the various sections of the text?

Secondly, the text reflects its history of textual transmission. One encounters a number of complexities or textual errors in the traditional text which must be explained or corrected. For example:

verse 4 דָּרְכוּ חִצָּם *those who have aimed their arrow, a bitter word*. Should one not read *bow* instead of *arrow*?

verse 7 תַּמְנוּ חֵפֶשׂ מְחֻפָּשׂ *We have completed a well-designed plan*, translating *complete* תמם instead of *hide* טמן as found in some manuscripts (BHS-crit.app);

verse 9 וַיַּכְשִׁילוּהוּ עָלֵימוֹ לְשׁוֹנָם. What is the meaning of the text line as it stands: *they made him stumble against them their tongue*? Can the 'they', the evildoers, really function as subject here? Should we 'repair' the text, by reading, for example, the first word as two: וַיַּכְשִׁיל יהוה (Y*HWH made stumble* ...)?[3]

Thirdly, a biblical text such as Psalm 64 also reflects some episode from the history of Israelite religion, even when, as the history of its interpretation demonstrates, we hardly know in what historical context to locate this Psalm. For example, is the text referring to episodes from David's life (*e.g.* NIV[4]), or is that only a literary construct? Does the Psalm have an origin in the temple liturgy? Does it reflect exilic times of oppression? Or rather postexilic experiences? So the question is: is it always necessary for exegesis to make suggestions about the text's original genre and usage and how that would influence its interpretation?

From such observations various questions arise about the instruments and the goal of our exegetical task: what is it one wants to know about this text? Are we in search of knowledge about history of religion? Are we trying to identify the message expressed by some author in a particular situation he shares with his audience? Or is our research more of a synchronic type and are we interested in particular religious positions represented by those who enter into dialogue in this text? What kind of communication is expressed by the text's discourse: who speaks to whom?

---

[3] See the text alteration suggested by M.L. BARRÉ, *A proposal on the crux of Psalm lxiv 9a*, VT 46 (1996), 115-118. A problem, however, is that Barré also easily changes the *wayyiqtols* into *weyiqtols*.

[4] *New International Version*, Grand Rapids MI, Zondervan, 2002.

In this article we will concentrate mainly on the domain of research mentioned first: language and linguistic system. This is important, since exegetical tradition shows a tendency to begin elsewhere, i.e. with an identification of genre or text type. Consequently, we also found that there is a tendency to adjust the text's linguistic phenomena into the genre suggested. For example, the heading of Psalm 64 in NRSV is: *Prayer for Protection from Enemies*. Actually, this would only apply to verses 2 and 3. For can someone also pray while narrating about YHWH's actions, as the *wayyiqtol*s in verse 8 do? Apparently not, for instead of *God shot them...* NRSV has to make a move and translates: *But God will shoot...* NIV characterizes Psalm 64 as a *Confident prayer to God for protection* and accordingly analyses the *wayyiqtol*s of verse 9 as expressing confidence in God's righteous judgment, also translating *But God will shoot...* In this way one forces the attitude of praying to continue in verse 8. Thus, in our view, linguistic data are too easily overruled in the tradition of textual interpretation and translation. As a result, it is the proposed genre of the Psalm, indicated by the added superscriptions, that acts as the teacher of its reader rather than the text itself. 'Praying for help' however, is not expressed by the narrative of verses 8-10, which states that God reacted appropriately to the threat. And what about the final call for joy of verse 11?

So the goal of our research presented in this paper, is to address a basic question of exegetical method: if we make a choice to postpone proposals of genre or rhetorical structure until we have found out more about the text's syntactic structure and the interaction of the various participants active in it, how would that contribute to its interpretation?

2. Analysis of text syntactic hierarchy

We begin our research by bringing our experiences with text grammatical analysis and the construction of a Biblical Hebrew database into the debate on biblical interpretation. First, we offer some explanation of the text syntactic analysis used to construct the database. Next, we give an overview of the resulting syntactic text structure that will become the starting point of our discussion about discourse and interpretation.

Text syntactic analysis starts from the point where the text has already been analysed in terms of text lines, clauses and clause types, clause constituents (*e.g.* verbal predicate <Pr>, verbal predicate with pronominal object <PO>, object <Ob>, complement <Co>). From here, guided by a computer program calculating and presenting proposals for clause connections,[5] we try to establish a hierarchy of clauses. An example of this process is presented below. Assuming we have already found out where to locate lines 3-11 in the textual hierarchy, then the question is: where to locate line 12 (verse 5b)?

Verb ClType		Line	Clause with parsing of constituents
Ps64,2 2sgM ZIm0		3	[שְׁמַע <Pr>]
Ps64,2 ---- Voct		4	| | | [אֱלֹהִים <Vo>]
Ps64,2 ---- Defc		5	| | [בְּשִׂיחִי <Aj>] [קוֹלִי <Ob>] | | Hear, God, my voice in my complaint,
Ps64,2 2sgM xYq0		6	| [חַיָּי <Ob>] [תִּצֹּר <Pr>] [מִפַּחַד אוֹיֵב <Co>] | from a frightening enemy protect my live.
Ps64,3 2sgM ZYq0		7	| [מִסּוֹד מְרֵעִים <Co>] [תַּסְתִּירֵנִי <PO>] | | Hide me from the planning of bad people,
Ps64,3 ---- Ellp		8	| | [מֵרִגְשַׁת פֹּעֲלֵי אָוֶן <Co>] | | from the action of those doing evil,
Ps64,4 3pl- xQt0[attr]		9	| [לְשׁוֹנָם <Ob>] [כַחֶרֶב <Aj>] [שָׁנְנוּ <Pr>] [אֲשֶׁר <Re>] | | who have sharpened like a sword their tongue
Ps64,4 3pl- ZQt0[coor]		10	| [דָּבָר מָר / חִצָּם <sp><Ob>] [דָּרְכוּ <Pr>] | | who have aimed their arrow, a bitter word
Ps64,5 ---- InfC[adju]		11	| [תָּם <Ob>] [בַּמִּסְתָּרִים <Aj>] [לִירֹת <Pr>] | | to shoot from an ambush a blameless one
Ps64,5 3plM xYq0		12	| [יֹרֻהוּ <PO>] [פִּתְאֹם <Mo>] | Suddenly they shoot him.

---

[5] The program *syn04types* has been developed in our research group since we started creating a text syntactic database of the Hebrew Bible. It is a program used both in syntactic research and in data production, cf. E. TALSTRA, *A Hierarchy of Clauses in Biblical Hebrew Narrative*, in E.J. VAN WOLDE (ed.), *Narrative Syntax and the Hebrew Bible: Papers of the Tilburg Conference 1996* (BIS, 29), Leiden, Brill, 1997, 85-118.

Results for lines 3-11, already produced:

Lines 3-5 (*imperative*) constitute one clause, interrupted by a vocative. In our database we take the vocative not as a constituent, but as a separate linguistic utterance.

Line 6 (*yiqtol*, 2nd person singular) connects back to the *imperative* of line 3.

Line 9 (*qatal*, 3rd person plural) elaborates on the evildoers from line 8 by characterizing their actions in an אֲשֶׁר clause that is continued in lines 10 and 11.

Now where can line 12 be located in this syntactic hierarchy? It is a *yiqtol* clause, without an upwards connecting conjunction. The suffix הוּ refers to the תָּם (*blameless one*) who was introduced in line 11, but it is attached to the *yiqtol* plural יִרְהוּ that connects back to the evildoers who are active in lines 7-11. This is a block of text which also starts with a *yiqtol* clause without a conjunction. The combination of these observations (tenses and participants) suggests that line 12 continues the presence of two participants of the text block of lines 7 – 11 (*the evildoers* and *the blameless one*), and therefore, line 12 can be connected upwards to the starting clause of that section, i.e. to line 7.

This is just to give some idea of the analytical procedure. Similar questions about the position of particular clauses in the textual hierarchy come up with the *wayyiqtol* clause with explicit subject אֱלֹהִים of verse 8, line 22 and also with the *yiqtol* clause of verse 11, line 31. At this level of the analysis it appears that syntactic arguments for inserting these clauses somewhere into the larger textual hierarchy fail, so that one has to conclude that with verse 9 (*God shot at them*) and with verse 11 (*Let rejoice*) we find separate syntactic sections of the text. This is not uncommon: see the *wayyiqtol* of Psalm 94:22f. Also, based on such experiences, we think that an analysis of participants is needed before we make further proposals on the structure of the Psalm as a whole.

This procedure results in a proposal of textual segmentation and structure. This allows for a next step in syntactic analysis, *i.e.* to establish the various paragraphs of the text and the participants active in them. It will provide us with the linguistic data needed to enter into discussion with existing exegetical proposals of textual division and interpretation.

Textual structure: paragraphs and participants

[1]
    To the music leader   1 לַמְנַצֵּחַ
      A psalm by David   מִזְמוֹר לְדָוִד

[2]
You (אֱלֹהִים) + I + they (3rd plur פֹּעֲלֵי אָוֶן); *imperative* + *yiqtol*

Hear, God, my voice in my complaint,	שְׁמַע אֱלֹהִים קוֹלִי בְשִׂיחִי 2
from a frightening enemy protect my life.	מִפַּחַד אוֹיֵב תִּצֹּר חַיָּי
Hide me from the planning of bad people,	תַּסְתִּירֵנִי מִסּוֹד מְרֵעִים 3
from the alarming action of those doing evil.	מֵרִגְשַׁת פֹּעֲלֵי אָוֶן

[3]
They (3rd plur פֹּעֲלֵי אָוֶן) + someone blameless (3rd sg תָּם); אֲשֶׁר + *qatal*

They who have sharpened like a sword their tongue,	אֲשֶׁר שָׁנְנוּ כַחֶרֶב לְשׁוֹנָם 4
who have aimed their arrow, a bitter word	דָּרְכוּ חִצָּם דָּבָר מָר
to shoot from an ambush a blameless one.	לִירֹת בַּמִּסְתָּרִים תָּם 5

[4]
They (3rd plur פֹּעֲלֵי אָוֶן) + someone blameless (3rd sg תָּם); mainly *yiqtol* (and speeches)

Suddenly they shoot him	פִּתְאֹם יֹרֻהוּ
and have no fear.	וְלֹא יִירָאוּ
They encourage themselves to something evil,	יְחַזְּקוּ לָמוֹ דָּבָר רָע 6
calculate to hide snares	יְסַפְּרוּ לִטְמוֹן מוֹקְשִׁים
having said:	אָמְרוּ
'Who will notice them?'	מִי יִרְאֶה לָּמוֹ
They design criminal deeds:	יַחְפְּשׂוּ עוֹלֹת 7
'We have completed a well-designed plan.'	תַּמְנוּ חֵפֶשׂ מְחֻפָּשׂ
So the human mind and heart is deep.	וְקֶרֶב אִישׁ וְלֵב עָמֹק

[5]
He (3rd sg אֱלֹהִים) + 3rd plur: them (פֹּעֲלֵי אָוֶן) + mankind; *wayyiqtol*: narrated action;

God shot at them an arrow,	וַיֹּרֵם אֱלֹהִים חֵץ 8
suddenly they have got wounds.	פִּתְאוֹם הָיוּ מַכּוֹתָם
They made him stumble,	וַיַּכְשִׁילוּהוּ 9
their tongue being against themselves.	עָלֵימוֹ לְשׁוֹנָם
They shake the head, anyone seeing them	יִתְנֹדֲדוּ כָּל רֹאֵה בָם
All mankind feared,	וַיִּירְאוּ כָּל-אָדָם 10
they made known the work of God	וַיַּגִּידוּ פֹּעַל אֱלֹהִים
and his work they have understood.	וּמַעֲשֵׂהוּ הִשְׂכִּילוּ

[6]
He (3rd sg צַדִּיק) + 3rd sg יהוה + 3rd plur: they (לֵב יִשְׁרֵי כָל); *yiqtol:* fronting position:

Let a righteous one rejoice in Yhwh	יִשְׂמַח צַדִּיק בַּיהוָה 11
And take refuge in him.	וְחָסָה בוֹ
And let rejoice all upright of heart!	וְיִתְהַלְלוּ כָּל יִשְׁרֵי לֵב

The calculation and the presentation of the text's structure visualize its text syntactic features: (1) the segmentation of the text, and (2) for each segment the (verbal) clauses, main tenses and type of communication, and (3) the participants and participant shifts.⁶ These are the elements of syntactic analysis to be considered when we enter into dialogue with the literary approach found in most commentaries and translations.

COMMENTARIES AND TRANSLATIONS

In our research, the next step is to see whether and how commentaries analyse and apply the text syntactic features listed above. Below we have listed the proposals for text segmentation found in ten commentaries.⁷ In addition we consulted a set of fifteen Bible translations, in four languages.⁸ When relevant, some of the translation strategies of the translations will be presented.

1. Text segmentation and textual structure

The way the commentaries structure Psalm 64 varies greatly, as can be observed from the presentation below. In most cases the authors describe each segment of text they propose, together with some of the theological characteristics of its content. We have tried to summarize them below (italics added are ours). At the same time, this semantic labelling seems

---

⁶ Participant shifts are recognizable by syntactical shifts in subject, predicate and first, second or third person addressee. They are also called: PNG shifts: shifts in Person, Number, or Gender.

⁷ C.A. BRIGGS – E.G. BRIGGS, *A Critical and Exegetical Commentary on the Book of Psalms* (ICC), Edinburgh, T&T Clark, 1916; J. RIDDERBOS, *De Psalmen II* (COT), Kampen, Kok, 1958); M. DAHOOD, *Psalms II 51-100* (AB), Garden City NY, Doubleday, 1968; J.W. ROGERSON – J.W. MCKAY, *Psalms* (CBC NEB), Cambridge, Cambridge University Press, 1977; N.A. VAN UCHELEN, *Psalmen deel II (41-80)* (POT), Nijkerk, Callenbach, 1977; M.E. TATE, *Psalms 51-100* (WBC), Waco, TX, Word Books, 1990, p. XX; J.C. MCCANN JR., *The Book of Psalms* (NIB), Nashville TN, Abingdon Press, 1994, p. IV; F-L. HOSSFELD – E. ZENGER, *Psalmen 51-100* (HTKAT), Freiburg, Herder, 2000; E.S. GERSTENBERGER, *Psalms, part 2, and Lamentations* (FOTL, 15), Grand Rapids MI, Eerdmans, 2001; S.L. TERRIEN, *The Psalms: Strophic Structure and Theological Commentary*, Grand Rapids MI, Eerdmans, 2003).

⁸ The translations ordered per language, as consulted in BibleWorks 9: *Afrikaans*: Zuid-Afrikaanse Bijbel 1983: A83; *Dutch:* Revised Leidse Vertaling 1912/1994: LEI; Nieuwe Vertaling, 1951: NBG; Statenvertaling 1637/1995: SV; Willibrordvertaling 1978: W78; Willibrordvertaling 1995: W95; *English*: American Standard Version 1901: ASV; English Standard Version 2011: ESV; 1769 Blayney Edition of the 1611 King James Version: KJV; The New American Standard Bible 1995: NAU; New International Reader's Version 1998: NIRV; The New International Version 2011: NIV, New Jerusalem Bible 1985: NJB; *German*: the German translation from the Herders Bibelkommentar 2005: HRD; The German Lutherbibel 1912/1995: LUO.

to be the rationale behind the text segmentation. Syntactic observations or the question of sender and addressee can hardly be found to have served as arguments.

Commentary	(strophic) Structure with content
Briggs[9]	S1: vv. 2-4 (*Plaintive cry of Israel* to YHWH for preservation against enemies S2: vv. 5-7a who slander and plot against him) S3: vv. 7b-11 (*Assurance* that the enemy's plot will fail, because YHWH will overcome them; assurance of eventual joy and glory for the righteous.)
Ridderbos[10]	S1: vv. 2-3 (Complaint about the threat of the enemy; request for Gods protection) S2: vv. 4-5 (Description of the enemy's plans against the innocent) S3: vv. 6-7 (Description of the enemy's plans against the innocent) 4S: vv. 8-9 (Poets expression of *confidence* that God will punish the wicked) 5S: vv. 10-11 (*Description* of the praise of God and the joy of the righteous)
Dahood	–
Rogerson-McKay[11]	S1: vv.1-4 (Appeal for protection from enemies who expertly camouflage their treachery) S2: vv. 5-7 (Though they feel safe in their secrecy, God knows their deeds and will reward them accordingly) S3: vv. 8-10 (The *consequence* of God's judgment is that the faithful will rejoice; all who see it will learn to fear God)
van Uchelen[12]	S1: vv. 2-7 (Request and complaint) S1.1: vv. 2-3 (Urgent request to God) S1.2: vv. 4-7 (*Complaint* to God about the enemies) S2: vv. 8-11 (*Description* of God's answer in the form of the punishment of the enemies)
Tate[13]	S1: vv. 2-3 (Opening call for help with a familiar vocative address to God) S2: vv. 4-7 (Description of the enemy) S3: vv. 8-10 (*Expected* judgment of God) S4: v. 11 (*Happy conclusion* about the joy and security of the righteous)

[9] BRIGGS, *Book of Psalms* (n. 7), pp. 76-78.
[10] RIDDERBOS, *Psalmen* (n. 7), pp. 159-162.
[11] ROGERSON-MCKAY, *Psalms* (n. 7), pp. 68-71.
[12] VAN UCHELEN, *Psalmen* (n. 7), pp. 164-166.
[13] TATE, *Psalms 51-100* (n. 7), pp. 132-133.

Commentary	(strophic) Structure with content
McCann[14]	S1: vv. 1-2 (Petition) S2: vv. 3-6 (Complaint in the form of a description of the enemy) S3: vv. 7-9 (*Affirmation of faith* in God's activity) S4: v. 10 (Calls for *joyful trust* and praise)
Hossfeld-Zenger[15]	S1: vv. 2-3 (Invocation of God with a summarizing question for protection and rescue from threats of the enemy) S2: vv. 4-7 (Complaining description of the plans of the enemy) S3: vv. 8-9 (*Description* of God's intervention) S4: vv. 10-11 (Reaction to God's actions)

Gerstenberger[16]	S1: v. 1 (Superscription)
	S2: vv. 2-3 (Invocation and plea)
	S3: vv. 4-7 (Complaint)
	S4: vv. 8-9 (*Announcement* of destruction: imprecation)
	S5: vv. 10-11 (*Announcement* of salvation; beatitude)
	  A. v. 10 (*Announcement* of salvation)
	  B. v. 11 (*Announcement* of bliss; beatitude)

Terrien	S1: vv. 2-7a (The scheming of magicians) S2: vv. 7a [*sic*]-11 (God's own arrow)

In this context, a statement made by Tate is revealing. Although he admits that the transmitted text of verses 7 and 8 is very troublesome, he remarks: ...*the literary structure seems simple enough.*[17] Apparently literary analysis is considered possible in a direct way, independent of syntactic and linguistic analysis. Nevertheless, the various structures presented in the scheme above expose how interpretations of the text as discourse are related to different views on its literary or exegetical analysis. The way the commentaries structure this Psalm is apparently based mainly on a thematic division of the verses. As a next step, one matches that division to a particular genre of psalms. A typical example of this way of working is presented by Gerstenberger who, in his *The Forms of the Old Testament Literature*, attempts to apply with consistency the terminology used for the genres and formulas of biblical literature. According to Gerstenberger Psalm 64 is a *complaint of the individual*, which is characterized by elements occurring in verses 2-7: the invocation, petition and complaint.

[14] McCann, *Book of Psalms* (n. 7), pp. 930-931.
[15] Hossfeld – Zenger, *Psalmen 51-100* (n. 7), pp. 202-204.
[16] Gerstenberger, *Psalms 2 and Lamentations* (n. 7), pp. 17-19.
[17] Tate, *Psalms 51-100* (n. 7), p.132.

The words or thoughts of the foes are 'quoted verbatim' in verses 4-7. However, he faces trouble when trying to fit the elements of the last verses into the genre he has just construed for the Psalm. The peculiar verbal forms in verses 8-9 (mainly *wayyiqtol*) he interprets as an *announcement of destruction* with an affinity to a spoken curse. Next, he considers also verses 10-11 to be an announcement, expressing salvation and beatitude, since this last element of Ps. 64 mirrors the announcement of destruction of the preceding verses.[18] Gerstenberger finds these last verses to be more generalizing: ridiculing not personal, but rather communal enemies, while addressing a larger audience (he cites *all men* in verse 10a and *the upright of heart* in verse 11b). These lines use language and concepts from wisdom literature, but lack the individual suppliant's voice. In order to fit the formal elements of Ps. 64 into the genre, he remarks: *According to the basic liturgical pattern of individual complaints, we would expect deft, extensive imprecations of foes and warm, personal vows of thanksgiving. But the elements at hand (a) echo faintly the vigorous denunciations, and (b) dissipate into a vague benediction for all humankind.*[19] He therefore adjusts his genre and concludes: *the older genre 'complaint of the individual' has been adapted somewhat to the needs of later community life and worship.*[20] It is not clear how Gerstenberger processes these insights into a translation, since he does not present one in his commentary.[21]

The majority of the commentators (Ridderbos, Rogerson-McKay, van Uchelen, Tate and McCann) combine the thematic structuring of Psalm 64 with a rhetorical segmentation of the text into strophes. Terrien considers the two strophes he finds in the text to be regular, each strophe constituted of three bicola and two tricola. The meter may reflect the chaotic emotions of the psalm (4+3; 3+3; 3+3+3; 2+2+2).[22] Briggs perceives some kind of stairlike advance in the argument of the psalm, and structures Ps. 64 in three strophes, with a division, like Terrien does, of verse 7 into two parts.

This overview suggests even more strongly that in literary research one could have direct access to a literary analysis without initially having to pay attention to markers of syntactic structure, or to ask how syntactic and literary divisions might interact.

---

[18] GERSTENBERGER, *Psalms 2 and Lamentations* (n. 7), pp. 18-19.
[19] *Ibid.*, p. 19.
[20] *Ibid.*, p. 19.
[21] *Ibid.*, p. 19.
[22] TERRIEN, *The Psalms* (n. 7), pp. 466-467. It is unclear whether the poet really used this meter as a way to reflect chaotic emotions.

2. Verbal tenses and type of communication

A number of commentaries hardly address the verbal tenses used in the Psalm, let alone the four *wayyiqtols* in verses 8-10, *e.g.*: Dahood, Rogerson-McKay, van Uchelen, McCann, Terrien. Briggs, however, gives for each verse very detailed notes on his translation and exegesis. For וַיֹּרֵם in verse 8 he remarks that with the *wayyiqtol* a new clause could start, since it is a different tense than the ones in preceding verses. Nevertheless he translates the form as dependent on the previous *qatals* (such as the one in verse 6) and renders the *wayyiqtol* as its continuation, by using 'then' + present tense: *Then Yahweh, doth shoot at them: sudden is their wound.*[23] Commentaries that in some way do notice and analyse the interesting sequence of the *wayyiqtols* are Ridderbos, Tate, Hossfeld-Zenger and Gerstenberger. Tate, in his *Word Biblical Commentary*, describes in his translation notes on verses 8-10, the way these exegetes handle verbal tense analysis strikingly well: *The normal usage of the waw-consecutive with imperfect produces past tense. However, this seems unlikely in this context. One option is to read the verbs as equivalent to the so-called prophetic perfects or perfects of certainty, which have future reference ... The translation takes the verbs as future (...) with a model force appropriate for the supplicatory context of the psalm.*[24] Tate thus translates accordingly:

> 8. Surely – God *will* shoot an arrow without warning,
>   (and) suddenly they *will* have wounds!
> 9. Surely they *will* ruin themselves with their tongues
>   (and) everyone who sees them *will* be shocked.
> 10. And then all mankind *will* fear,
>   and declare the works of God,
>   and his doings which they (then) *will* comprehend.[25]

Ridderbos, Gerstenberger and Tate take note of the narrative verbal tenses, but these authors all prefer the future tense to the past tense, since the content of the Psalm anticipates the full result of the activity of the evildoers in contrast to God's future actions, that have not yet taken place.[26] The same theological position seems to have guided the majority of the

---

[23] BRIGGS, *Book of Psalms* (n. 7), pp. 77, 80. Bible translations A83, LEI, NBG, ESV and HRD do the same for verse 8, *e.g.* NBG: *Maar plotseling treft God hen met een pijl; daar zijn nu hun wonden.*
[24] TATE, *Psalms 51-100* (n. 7), p. 131. The italics are ours.
[25] TATE, *Psalms 51-100* (n. 7), p. 130.
[26] RIDDERBOS, *Psalmen* (n. 7), p. 161; GERSTENBERGER, *Psalms 2 and Lamentations*, pp.18-19; TATE, *Psalms 51-100* (n. 7), pp. 132-133.

Bible translations we studied: SV, ASV, KJV, NAU, NIRV, NIV and LUO. Like Tate, they all translate the verbs in verses 8-10 with *futurum*.[27] By exception W78 stays more close to the Hebrew verbal tenses, in translating verse 9: *Zo heeft hun schandelijk woord hun val teweeg gebracht. Het hoofd schudt wie hen aanziet.*[28]

Hossfeld-Zenger do pay attention to the translation problem of the verbal tenses and remark that it pertains to the understanding of whole text. They decide to stay close to the text (*Textnähe*), and add a disclaimer to their translation by stating that the syntax of Hebrew poetry is a scarcely researched field.[29] Like Tate, Hossfeld-Zenger interpret the *wayyiqtol* forms theologically, not linguistically. They read the Psalm as an individual psalm of lament and counter interpretations that understand Ps. 64 as a psalm of gratitude for the rescue from oppression. This genre interpretation depends, in their view, on the way the *wayyiqtol* forms in verses 8-10 are understood: as narrative past tense (also in the sense of prophetic perfect), as present tense, or as future tense. Hossfeld-Zenger choose to translate the *wayyiqtol* forms as past tense, but interpret them as prophetic perfect. According to them, verses 8-9 proclaim YHWH's battle against the wicked and evil.[30] Their translation (taking verses 8-9 and verses 10-11 as separate paragraphs):

> 8. Da schoß Gott auf sie mit dem Pfeil,
>   plötzlich waren sie verwundet.
> 9. Man/er ließ jeden einzelnen stürzen, indem ihre eigene Zunge über sie kam,
>   es schüttelten sich (vor Hohn) alle, die auf sie sahen.
> 10. Da fürchteten sich (vor Gott) alle Menschen
>   und verkündeten das Tun Gottes
>   und verstanden sein Werk.[31]

---

[27] An exception is NJB for verse 8: *God has shot them with his arrow, sudden were their wounds.* For verse 9 A83, LEI, NBG, NJB and HRD translate in the present tense, e.g. HRD: *Untergang bereitet ihnen die eigene Zunge. / Alle, die sie sehen, schütteln das Haupt über sie.* Verse 10 is translated in the present tense by A83, LEI, NBG and W78. NJB and ESV combine present and past tense, e.g. ESV: *Then all mankind fears; they tell what God has brought about and ponder what he has done.* ESV applies the same strategy in verse 9 by combining a present and future tense: *They are brought to ruin and all who see them will wag their heads.*

[28] The later edition, W95, has changed that again into present tense.

[29] HOSSFELD – ZENGER, *Psalmen 51-100* (n. 7), pp. 202-203. See however the dissertation of G.J. KALKMAN, *Verbal Forms in Biblical Hebrew Poetry: Poetic Freedom or Linguistic System?*, 's-Hertogenbosch, Box Press, 2015. Kalkman proposes a new methodological paradigm for the analysis of verbal forms in which the highest priority is assigned to a search for syntactic patterns attested within clauses and in sequences of clauses.

[30] HOSSFELD – ZENGER, *Psalmen 51-100* (n. 7), pp. 203, 205-206, 209.

[31] *Ibid.*, p. 202.

Hossfeld-Zenger is the only commentary that explicitly uses syntactic signals in the text to make remarks about the overall structure. According to them, the description of distress in verses 4-7 is connected by means of the conjunction 'אֲשֶׁר' to verses 2-3. The description itself, however, speaks about the threat of the innocent (verse 5) in the third person and concentrates solely on the secret plans of the enemies. For them this implies that the paragraph about God's intervention (verses 8-9) only describes the failure of the evil and that in the reaction in verses 10-11, the 'I' of the supplicant (*all of the right of heart*) occurs only implicitly, or in the third person (*righteous one*).[32] Even when Hossfeld-Zenger more or less directly connect these linguistic remarks with theological reflections on the text, in our view the focus on linguistic markers supports our own approach. Their analysis of the text not only includes emphasis on its syntactic structure, but it also demonstrates that to analyse the overall textual structure and discourse, it is imperative to study which participants are active in a text. In the next section we will take a look at what the commentators do with the participants in Psalm 64.

3. Participants and participant shifts

Ridderbos, Dahood, Rogerson-McKay and Terrien do not make any remarks about the interaction of participants that play a role in Psalm 64. Briggs does notice (sudden changes of) participants, but in the case of incongruence he utilizes them to emend the text. Thus, the sudden change of person in verse 7 (that seems to be part of an inserted direct speech section), he finds improbable and emends the 1 plur of (תַּמְנוּ *we have completed*) into a 3 (m.) plur *They search out injustice; they have hidden a plot*.[33] Briggs also thinks it is improbable that the 3 plur and 3 sg of (וַיַּכְשִׁילוּהוּ *they made him stumble*) refer to the enemies, so he emends the text: *And He causeth them to stumble by their own tongue*, with 'He' being God.[34] McCann interprets the shift from 3 plur to 1 sg in verse 7 theologically as a marked reference to God in the third person. It gives the affirmation of faith in verses 7-9 a sort of instructional tone. Other commentaries, *e.g.* Tate and Gerstenberger, try to identify the general speakers of the Psalm immediately, without taking a closer look at the various sets of participants in the Psalm itself. Tate takes cue from the use of *blameless*

---

[32] *Ibid.*, p. 204.
[33] BRIGGS, *Book of Psalms* (n. 7), p. 79.
[34] *Ibid.*, p. 80.

in verse 5 and *righteous* and *upright* in verse 11 and identifies them as faithful members of a Yahwistic community, without attempting to relate Ps. 64 directly to a specific context of worship. Seeing a 'cult prophetic lament-liturgy' in the same category as Ps. 12, 14 and 52 being reflected in the Psalm, Tate is of the opinion that the speaker could be a leader of the community, a prophet, or a prophet-like person.[35] Next, he hastens to say: *In any case, the psalm is a literary entity, apparently without any strong ties to a specific ancient context. The text generates its own context in interaction with the reader.*[36] By placing the participant analysis and the text outside its context, this reading has to face the question of what could then be the discourse of the Psalm itself. An almost opposite approach can be found with van Uchelen. Though he analyses stylistic repetition and does not analyse any concrete participants in Psalm 64, he comments more generally that an effective repetition of words and word stems cause the prayer, the answer to the prayer, the accusation and punishment to be intertwined. Van Uchelen thus seems to detect some dialogue between the participants, albeit only at the level of semantics and presented only through the view of the poet.[37]

4. Conclusion

From our observations on how interpreters of the Psalm deal with the obvious linguistic features of the text: (1) syntax and text segmentation, (2) function of verbal clauses and (3) the sets of participants, it can be concluded that most of them prefer a literary analysis. What is more, they present the Psalm as a kind of theological process that guides the reader from an initial complaint into confidence in God's reaction to the persecution of the 'I' and a final invitation to joy. Having taken this as the design of the poem, they frequently also take the liberty to overrule the grammatical function of verbal forms and to neglect the repeated shift of participants. As a result, this literary approach suggests that it is the reconstructed literary design, or in fact the theology ascribed to the author, that has to be regarded as our teacher, the lesson being for the reader: after complaining, be reassured, God will save you.

Our approach is: if one takes a closer look at the linguistic markers used in the text, one should first try to proceed further along the lines of

---

[35] TATE, *Psalms 51-100* (n. 7), p. 133.
[36] *Ibid.*
[37] VAN UCHELEN *Psalmen* (n. 7), pp. 164-165.

what Hossfeld-Zenger and van Uchelen suggest and explore syntax to find more of the interaction and the dialogues between textual participants. In the final paragraph we will continue our research into that direction.

PARTICIPANTS, DISCOURSE AND INTERPRETATION

In the biblical exegesis of the psalms it is quite a common practice to identify the speaker of a text with its author, the poet. Even if one accepts the fact that the poem actually might represent the voice of the religious community, it is poet's voice that is responsible for the design of the psalm and the message it is thought to express. Following this type of analysis, one may conclude that the poet, in the way he expresses experiences and religious viewpoints, is our, *i.e.* the reader's teacher. Regarding the design of the complete text, one may choose to read the text in this way. However, before doing so, one has to study what the great variety of voices in the text express. Are they all merely the changing feelings of the same author? This is actually the implication of most of the interpretations we have encountered. The psalm is read as one speech, a discourse with a religious plot that mirrors the development of its author's piety. Consequently this view also determines the action of the verbs, whether in agreement with syntax or not.

So, apart from the problems with the interpretation of verbal syntax we have detected, we also found problems in the way interpreters deal with the shifts of participants in the text – if any attention is paid to that phenomenon at all. The most challenging case is the first line of verse 8: *God shot at them an arrow*, where we not only encounter the first *wayyiqtol* of the Psalm, but also see a shift from אֱלֹהִים being addressed in 2nd person (verse 2) to אֱלֹהִים as a 3rd person subject. This combined shift does not appear to be elaborated upon by most exegetes. The usual assumption seems to be that the 'I', the first speaker, actually continues to speak and now turns to the reader with a confident statement about Gods reaction, to be translated with a future tense: *he will shoot*. This translation is proposed by only discussing options for the *wayyiqtol*, not by also discussing the participant shift.

This is even the case in Hossfeld-Zenger's commentary. Though these authors pay much attention to the possible function of the *wayyiqtol*, they are in no doubt about who might be the speaker here in verse 8. *Da redet der Beter nicht mehr (vgl. V.2) von einer Rettung seiner Person. Er schildert (...) wie Jahwe (...) plötzlich energisch eingreift.*[38] The participant

---

[38] HOSSFELD – ZENGER, *Psalmen 51-100* (n. 7), p. 206.

shift is reduced to merely a shift in attitude within the poet: from praying to painting. However, what about the shift of addressee here?

This article is not meant to be an introduction into the more technical details of our actual research of the interaction of verbal tenses and participant shifts in the Psalms. However, it may be clear that text databases provide us with an effective instrument to search and sort the linguistic data that we need for both syntactic and for exegetical research.[39] The main point is a methodological one: before one decides to propose a translation that seems to best fit a particular Psalm, one can experiment with collecting syntactic parallel material, such as: (1) all cases of 3rd person *wayyiqtol* clauses in the Psalms, with אֱלֹהִים, יהוה or another name for God as its subject;[40] (2) all cases of 3rd person *wayyiqtol* clauses in the Psalms, with any noun phrase as its subject;[41] or (3) all 3rd person *wayyiqtol* clauses in the Psalms.[42] The actual PhD research project by Christiaan Erwich has as one of its goals the establishment of the interaction of tense shifts and participant shifts in the Psalms. The Psalm discussed here presents a clear case of this work.

In our view, the observation of participant shifts in the text will lead the reader to a different interpretation of Psalm 64. We need not assume a unified plot, expressing only the speaker's progress in personal piety, which is trying to convince us to follow him in this. Our proposal is to refrain from overruling the various linguistic types of communication found in the text. They each in their own way contribute to the text as discourse. Of course, the complete discourse has an implied speaker, our teacher, so to speak, but he is not *der Beter*. We first need an inventory of the 'senders', whether explicitly marked or implied as 'speaker' in each separate paragraph. Below, we present each individual paragraph, indicating who, in terms of linguistics, might be its sender and its addressee communicating there. (We skip [1], the meta text in verse 1.)

[2] Verses 2-3

Dialogue: Sender = 'I' Addressee = You (אֱלֹהִים), marked linguistically.
Participants: You (אֱלֹהִים) – 'I' – They (3rd plur פֹּעֲלֵי אָוֶן)
Verbs: imperative + *yiqtol* (complaint and request)

Hear, God, my voice in my complaint,…
Hide me from those doing evil.

---

[39] https://shebanq.ancient-data.org/.
[40] https://shebanq.ancient-data.org/hebrew/query?version=4b&id=1394.
[41] https://shebanq.ancient-data.org/hebrew/query?version=4b&id=1396.
[42] https://shebanq.ancient-data.org/hebrew/query?version=4b&id=1395.

[3] Verses 4-5

Dialogue: 'I' and 'you' are no longer marked; as Sender and Addressee still active.
Participants: They (3rd plur פֹּעֲלֵי אָוֶן) + 3rd sg: someone being תָּם
Verbs: אֲשֶׁר + *qatal* = actions known of those doing evil. (attrib. to previous section)

They who have sharpened like a sword their tongue, ...
to shoot from an ambush a blameless one.

[4] Verses 5-7

Dialogue: new paragraph, independent from the previous section with אֲשֶׁר Sender = writer, Addressee = reader, about common knowledge.
Participants: They (3rd plur פֹּעֲלֵי אָוֶן) + 3rd sg: someone being תָּם
Verbs: *yiqtol*: action; actual, generally known.

Suddenly they shoot him,...
having said: 'Who will notice them?'...

[5] Verses 8-10

Dialogue: Narrator = presenting knowledge from tradition. Addressee = reader.
Participants: He (3rd sg אֱלֹהִים) + 3rd plur: them (as in verse 4 – 5: פֹּעֲלֵי אָוֶן) + mankind
Verbs: *wayyiqtol* + *qatal*: אֱלֹהִים is now being narrated about; to the reader.

God shot at them an arrow, suddenly they have got wounds. ...
They wag the head, anyone seeing them. (*yiqtol*, general effect) ...
All mankind feared, and his work they have understood.

[6] Verse 11

Dialogue: Sender = writer, Addressee = reader.
Participants: He (3rd sg צַדִּיק) + 3rd sg יהוה + 3rd plur: they + (כָּל יִשְׁרֵי לֵב)
Verbs: *yiqtol* in fronting position: modality; *w^eqatal, w^eyiqtol*: modality]

LET A RIGHTEOUS ONE REJOICE IN YHWH

The shifts of participants and of the tenses imply that the text makes us read contrasting experiences: first [2], [3] those from personal life in particular situations, leading to prayer; next [4] common knowledge shared by writer and reader about the aggression of those doing evil; after that [5] competing experiences known from tradition, understood by all and finally [6] a summon to the צַדִּיק to be joyful. The repeated shifts of participants should prevent us from interpreting the various voices as only steps in the expression of the author's individual insights or progress of personal faith. Rather they express the experience of conflict between real life ('I') and tradition (*all humans* and *all the upright of heart*).

As a final step, and only after these observations, can one ask what the complete text as a particular composition expresses. How does the discourse of the complete composition unfold itself between the (implied) writer and the reader? The composition as a whole leads its reader through these contrasting experiences. It does so through confronting the reader with the communication by the changing sets of participants in the individual paragraphs. The text presents them in a particular order. Personal experiences may lead to praying to אֱלֹהִים for help. Writer and reader share the experience of having encountered this type of aggression. At the same time this praying is done within a tradition that narrates about אֱלֹהִים who has countered the attacks in the past. Humans have witnessed this before and have understood it. Therefore, if one has a good reason to pray, one enters onto a scene where others share one's experiences with this type of aggression. In addition, one also enters into a narrative tradition about אֱלֹהִים who has taken action before. So, righteous ones, enjoy!

Psalm 64 is not about a poet, the writer, who at the same time is the one who prays and teaches us to join him in his own strong faith. Rather, the Psalm places the reader on a stage where individual prayer is seen to be embedded in both common experience and in a much broader and much older narrative tradition of אֱלֹהִים and 'his work'. It is therefore the text itself that teaches us about real life. The tradition is out there and one can rely on it. The reader does not have to become a hero of faith, expecting immediate salvation. Within the narrative tradition of God's work, pray, be a צַדִּיק and enjoy!

COPING WITH HELLENISTIC NEIGHBOURS
Psalms 137–145: An initiation into royal warriorship

Harm W.M. VAN GROL
Tilburg, the Netherlands

Psalms 137–145 do not contain any teaching. Psalms are prayers and hymns, and sometimes reflections, but certainly not lessons. This may be true for individual psalms, but collections of psalms could be more interesting to our theme. Editorial work could create educational significance through the combination of texts. There are no teachers and disciples in Psalm 137–145, but transformation and initiation are the point of this collection, with role model and 'role situation' being its central instruments.

Psalms 137–145 are an editorial collection.[1] We will take the different first-person personages in this collection as a key to its meaning (§ Personages), basing our hypothesis on their distribution and relations (§ Initiation / learning process). We will describe the collection as a textbook for initiation into a community of anti-assimilationists. It stresses the importance of a personal choice against assimilation (§ 1 of Phases of an initiation: Ps 137), it guides the potential member through an inner struggle (§ 2 of Phases an initiation: Pss 138–143), and it teaches him a militant spirituality (§ 3 of Phases of an initiation: Ps 144,1-8). At the end, the one initiated

---

[1] In this study, we will not go into the composition-critical details. We have published such an analysis elsewhere: H. VAN GROL, *David and his Chasidim: Place and Function of Psalms 138-145*, in E. ZENGER (ed.), *The Composition of the Book of Psalms* (BETL, 238), Leuven, Peeters, 2010, 309-337. In that study we discussed the evidence for the existence of Pss 137–145 as an editorial collection and commented upon other studies of these psalms, especially E. BALLHORN, *Zum Telos des Psalters: Der Textzusammenhang des Vierten und Fünften Psalmenbuches (Ps 90-150)* (BBB, 138), Berlin, Philo, 2004, and M. LEUENBERGER, *Konzeptionen des Königtums Gottes im Psalter: Untersuchungen zu Komposition und Redaktion der theokratischen Bücher IV-V im Psalter* (ATANT, 83), Zürich, Theologischer Verlag, 2004. Of course, some observations are new, especially of the parallels between Pss 137 and 144, and I have changed my opinion about עמי in Ps 144,2. We will discuss some views of D. TUCKER in his recent *Constructing and Deconstructing Power in Psalms 107-150* (Ancient Israel and its Literature, 19), Atlanta GA, SBL, 2014.

comes into his textual existence, and the post-war future of the community is sketched (§ The initiated: Ps 144,9-15). We will conclude with some words about the historical writer-reader community that valued this anti-assimilationist spirituality (§ The external writer-reader community).

A special characteristic of the collection is its inclusive language. The person to be transformed and to be initiated is not addressed. From the start, the text-immanent reader is invited to identify with the community (WE) and its members (I). At the end, he himself may be the freshly initiated (I) and a new member of a great community (WE).

Personages

All parts of the collection have a first-person personage plural and/or single, but they belong to different worlds. There is a (post)exilic individual and community in Psalm 137, David in Psalms 138–145, and a (textual!) present-day individual and community in Psalm 144,9-15. We will give a preliminary description of these different worlds and we will claim that they are parallel worlds.

The collection hits ground only in the penultimate psalm. There we find a present-day personage I and a community WE. They are what the collection is about, the heroes, the protagonists. The text-internal reader will identify with them and they can be linked to the external writer and reader community. Both personages are talking, the individual prays to God and the community declares itself blessed (Ps 144,9-11.12-15). The next and last psalm of the collection will speak about them as Gods favourites: 'your favourites, let them bless you!' (Ps 145,10).

144,9-15		
personage		
I & WE textual present	→ internal reader	→ external writer-reader community

The present-day individual is not the only first-person personage in Psalm 144. In the first part of the psalm another I is present, who is David, according to the heading, לדוד. This David is a warrior and is later on called king and servant of God (Ps 144,1-2.10). The internal reader will identify (also) with him.

144,1-8
personage
I → internal David reader the royal warrior

The presence of two different first-person personages in one psalm is strange and demands explanation. Both characters are explicitly characterized as parallel. David the royal warrior prays to God, blessing and supplicating him. The unnamed individual does the same, supplicating and praising him. Moreover, he states that he will sing *a new song*, obviously over and against the old one of King David (Ps 144,9).[2] His plea is an application of David's one. He just quotes him: '... rescue me, / save me from the hand of foreigners ...' (Ps 144,7-8//11), and he suggests that he stands in the line of David and the kings of Judah, who were rescued by God before (Ps 144,10).[3]

The worlds of David and of his present-day follower are parallel worlds. In a very explicit way the follower is the first internal reader of the old song of David and stands, in a sense, between the song of David and the internal reader of the collection. The follower may be seen as the exemplary internal reader.

144,1-8	144,9-15	
parallel personage	embedded internal reader	
I → David the royal warrior	I & WE → textual present	internal reader
	personage	
	I & WE → textual present	internal reader

---

[2] The song of David is 'really' old, in being an adapted quote from psalms of David in the first two books of the Psalter, especially Ps 18.
[3] Verse 10 has hymnic participia, verb forms that are used to describe God's characteristic behaviour, instead of *qatal*-forms, that point to the past. The verse describes God's potential: 'the one who gives (הנותן) victory to kings, / who rescues (הפוצה) his servant David.'

Psalm 144 is not the first psalm of David in our collection, but it is the first one in which David has the role of royal warrior. Elsewhere in the collection (Pss 138-143) he is the exemplary supplicant as known from the first two books of the Psalter. There is a community around this first-person personage, but it is mentioned only in the third person, for example: 'around me the righteous will crowd' (Ps 142,8). Of course, the internal reader will identify with David.

The textual worlds of David, the supplicant, and of the present-day first-person personage are parallel worlds. By extension we may suppose that our present day personage is the embedded internal reader of this part of the collection too. Why should he identify with David the royal warrior and not with this other role of David? We may note that the phrase 'his servant David' in Psalm 144,10 goes back to the clause 'for I am your servant' in the previous psalm (Ps 143,12).

138-143			144:9-15		
parallel personage			embedded internal reader		
I David the supplicant	→	→	I & WE textual present	→	internal reader

The first textual world of the collection is that of Psalm 137. The psalm depicts an exilic situation and a post-exilic reflection. A first-person plural personage tells about the exile and first-person plural and single personages reflect upon that situation (Ps 137,1-3.4-5).

This exilic world has a lot in common with the present-day world, in a formal way. First of all, there is the presence of a first-person individual and community, which mirror, moreover, those of Psalm 144. Here, in the textual past, the community goes in front and the individual follows, and later on, in the textual present, the individual paves the way and the community follows (WE & I <> I & WE). Secondly, both psalms characterize the enemy with the adjective נכר, *foreign*, the land of Babylon being *foreign soil*, אדמת נכר, and the enemies in Psalm 144 being *foreigners*, בני נכר. Thirdly, both psalms close with two parallel beatitude formulas (Pss 137,8//9 and 144,15a//b). Finally, the Edomites and Babylon are characterized as *the sons of Edom*, בני אדום, and *daughter Babel*, בת־בבל, whereas the present-day community proudly speaks about *our sons* and *our daughters*, בנינו and בנותינו, which are 'full-grown in their youth', whereas the 'babies' of Babylon should be 'dashed against the rocks' (Pss 137,7-9 and 144,12).

Because of these explicit parallels, we may suppose that our present-day personage is the embedded internal reader of this part of the collection too. The present-day individual parallels David, the royal warrior, David, the supplicant, and the exilic/post-exilic individual of Psalm 137.

We combine the four textual worlds in one scheme. They stand next to each other, unconnected in a narrative or dramatic sense. The explicit parallels, between the first world and the fourth and between the third and the fourth, make clear that they belong together. The first-person individual of the textual present is the embedded internal reader of the three worlds we meet in Psalms 137, 138–143 and 144,1-8.

Ps 137	138–143	144,1-8		144,9-15		
parallel personage				embedded internal reader		
WE & I exile	→	→	→	I & WE textual present	→	internal reader
	parallel personage			embedded internal reader		
	I David the supplicant	→	→	I & WE textual present	→	internal reader
		parallel personage		embedded internal reader		
		I David the royal warrior	→	I & WE textual present	→	internal reader
				personage		
				I & WE textual present	→	internal reader

INITIATION / LEARNING PROCESS

We have given a preliminary description of the four different textual worlds in the collection and have noted their parallels. Now the question will be posed as to what the relation is between the different first-person personages. Why are they paralleled?

The four different textual worlds are not connected by narrative or dialogical sequence. The collection is not a narrative or a drama. The four parts are sequentially unconnected but paralleled. If we focus on the first-person personages, especially David the royal warrior and his follower, we may interpret their relations as that of an individual and his role models. A person will imitate his role model(s), until he has grown up and can live his own life. Role models are important within a learning process or initiation.

The first three textual worlds each contain a role model: an exilic/post-exilic person, David the supplicant and David the royal warrior, whereas the last textual world is that of the person who learns from these role models. Nothing is said about the initiation or the learning process as such. On the contrary, the present-day first-person personages become a textual reality only at the moment that their learning process has been completed, when their initiation is finished. At that moment they are the new generation, the initiated. They are ready to stand up against the foreigners and after the war they may enjoy a life of progeny, prosperity, and peace. Seen in this way, the collection is a spiritual text book for new members of the community. The internal reader is supposed to identify with all the first-person personages and to learn from each of them.

The collection is neither narrative nor drama. Even so, the parallel worlds are as sequential as the phases of a learning process. The first phase teaches the importance of making a radical choice against assimilation (Ps 137), the second teaches to integrate this insight into one's personal life (Pss 138–143), and the third teaches to stand up against the enemy as a warrior (Ps 144,1-8). Once the initiation has been completed, the natural effects of the spiritual life of this community are depicted (Ps 144,12-15). The collection closes with a hymn (Ps 145).

Phases of an Initiation

In this section we will describe the three phases of the initiation, corresponding to the first three textual worlds. By doing so, we will clarify what the challenge for the one to be initiated is, what he has to learn, and how he may prepare himself for his life in the community.

1. The importance of a personal choice against assimilation

Psalm 137 is about the exile. It sees in it a fundamental problem, that of assimilation, and gives as an answer the refusal to assimilate. It proudly promotes the importance of a personal choice against assimilation.

The following exposition will consist of a translation, a comment about the strophic structure, and a thematic analysis.

> 1 By the rivers of Babylon[4],
> there we sat and even wept,
> as we thought of Zion;
> 2 on the willows in her midst
> we hung up our lyres,
>
> 3 for there they asked us,
> our captors, for songs,
> our tormentors, for joy:
> 'Sing us
> one of the songs of Zion!'

> 4 How can we sing a song of Y<small>HWH</small>
> on foreign soil?!
> 5 If I forget you, Jerusalem,
> may my right hand forget!
>
> 6 May my tongue stick to my palate,
> if I cease to think of you,
> if I do not set Jerusalem
> above my highest joy!

> 7 Remember, Y<small>HWH</small>,
> against the sons of Edom
> the day of Jerusalem's fall –
> who said: 'Strip, strip
> down to her foundation!'
>
> 8 Daughter Babylon, you are dead,
> happy who repays you in kind
> the infliction you inflicted on us;
> 9 happy who seizes and dashes
> your babies against the rocks!

In many ways, interpretation depends on structure; in the case of poetry, strophic structure. We will confine ourselves to a sketch of the strophic structure and discuss one major question.[5]

---

[4] The translations are 'home-made'. They will clarify our reading of difficult passages and they present the strophic structure. The strophes are divided by a vertical space, the stanzas by two vertical spaces separated by a line on the left.

[5] You will find a clear presentation of my prosodic theory, a new perspective on parallelism and a proposal for a systematic strophic analysis in H. VAN GROL, *Een inleiding in de klassiek Hebreeuwse versbouw: Verkenningen in het grensgebied van versbouw en tekstsyntaxis* (Theol. Persp., 11), Bergambacht, 2VM, 2015.

Psalm 137 consists of three stanzas of two strophes each (vv. 1-2.3/4-5.6/7.8-9: 2.2/2.2/2.2).⁶ The strophes of the first and third stanza start with a tricolon (vv. 1.3a-c.7a-c.8) and continue with a bicolon.

There is no consensus about the place of verse 4 in the strophic structure:⁷ does verse 4 belong to the story, being the answer to the question of the Babylonians, or does it belong to the reflection afterwards, together with the conditional self-imprecations? Because this problem affects our interpretation, we will discuss it extensively.

One is inclined to combine verse 4 with verses 1-3 because the character WE is present in all these verses, but in that case one neglects the text-syntactically more important change from narration to discursion. The first stanza is story, the second reflection. The verbs change from *qatal*- to *yiqtol*- and jussive-forms. Of course, verse 3d-e – 'Sing us / one of the songs of Zion!' – is discursive too, but it is embedded in the story, introduced by verse 3a-c. Such an introduction is lacking in verse 4 (*and we answered them:* or the like). Verse 4 does not belong to the narrative and it is not the reaction to the order of the captors. In fact, this answer has already been given in the first strophe. The second strophe is an explanation of what is told in the first: '… on the willows in her midst / we hung up our lyres, // *for* (כי) there they asked us…'. The repetition of *there* (שם) indeed also makes this point, referring us back to verse 1b, 'there we sat…'.

One could argue that the change from first-person plural to first-person singular between verses 4 and 5 is difficult, but the same could be said of the change from second-person Jerusalem to third-person Jerusalem between cola 6a-b and 6c-d. In fact, these changes function in the chiastic build-up of the second stanza.

A			we	על אדמת נכר	איך נשיר את־שיר־יהוה
	B		I	תשכח ימיני	אם־אשכחך ירושלם
		B'	you	אם־לא אזכרכי	תדבק־לשוני לחכי
A'			she	על ראש שמחתי	אם־לא אעלה את־ירושלם

---

⁶ In this prosodic formula, a point refers to the division between strophes and a slash to the division between stanzas, while the numerals indicate the numbers of verse-lines per strophe.
⁷ See the survey of commentators in P. VAN DER LUGT, *Strofische structuren in de Bijbels-Hebreeuwse poëzie*, Kampen, Kok, 1980, pp. 437-440. According to himself, verse 4 belongs in the second stanza but as a separate strophe (division: vv. 4.5-6). J. FOKKELMAN, *Major Poems of the Hebrew Bible II* (SSN, 41), Assen, Van Gorcum, 2000, pp. 301-302 and 465) combines verse 4 with verse 3 and verse 5 with verse 6 and reads five strophes (vv. 1-2.3-4.5-6.7-8). I published an earlier but full analysis in an internal report in preparation of the Dutch *Nieuwe Bijbelvertaling* (\id NBV/19PS137.VO/20001110/ HvG/Psalm 137, 9 pp.).

The most important marker is the repetition of the *nota accusativi* את and the preposition על in exactly the same place in the verse-line. Given this linear repetition, the cola of lines A and A' are chiastic as well as that of B and B'. The chiastic connection of the cola of B and B' can be easily seen, but that of A and A' is more hidden. The first colon of A and the second of A' have the words *song* and *joy*, שיר // שמחה, which are parallel in verse 3b-c, whereas the second colon of A and the first of A' have the opposition of Babel-Jerusalem in the telling words *foreign soil* and *Jerusalem*, ירושלם // אדמת נכר.

Psalm 137 is not a communal lament, but has a unique combination of genre-motives. The first stanza contains a story, the second contains self-reflection in the form of an indignant rhetorical question and some conditional self-imprecations, and the third contains imprecations, strikingly in the form of a plea and two beatitude formulas.

The speakers are a community and an individual within that community. They mention themselves – WE and I – in the first two stanzas. The individual is not a certain anonymous individual, but stands for all individuals of the community. His 'right hand' refers to the playing of the lyre and his 'tongue' to the singing of songs.

The addressee of the story is not mentioned, but in the self-reflection it becomes clear that they are speaking to each other. The most emotional and rhetorical part of the self-reflection is directed to Jerusalem: 'If I forget you, Jerusalem…'. The addressees of the third stanza are YHWH and Babylon. The first strophe with the quote of the sons of Edom: 'Strip, strip…!' mirrors the first stanza having the quote of 'our captors' saying: 'Sing us…!' The second strophe mirrors the second stanza: both cities, Jerusalem and Babylon, are addressed in the second person.

The topic of Psalm 137 is unique. The psalm is not a complaint about the exile as such and a prayer to bring the exile to an end is missing. Likewise it is not a complaint about the misbehaviour of the 'captors'. The conduct of the שובים is noted: 'For there they asked us, / our captors, for songs, / our tormentors, for joy' (v. 3),[8] but it is not the point, as in Psalm 106,46: 'He [YHWH] made all their captors kindly disposed toward them.' The psalm is about the behaviour of the captives.[9]

---

[8] See the reading of Ps 137 by B. BECKING, *Does Exile Equal Suffering? A Fresh Look at Psalm 137*, in B. BECKING – D. HUMAN (eds.), *Exile and Suffering: A Selection of Papers Read at the 50th Anniversary of the Old Testament Society of South Africa* (OTS, 50), Leiden, Brill, 2009, 183-220; and *Exilische identiteit als post-exilische ideologie: Psalm 137 opnieuw gelezen*, in *NTT* 64 (2010), 269-283.

[9] TUCKER's evaluation: 'The object of scrutiny in Ps 137 is not Israel nor her history, but empires and their malevolence' (TUCKER, *Power* (n. 1), p. 121), may match the theme of his investigation, but does not do justice to the psalm.

Being exiled, the captives were confronted, in a ruthless way, with the choice whether to assimilate, to combine old with new, Zion with Babylon, and to go on with their lives or to refuse any assimilation whatsoever, to stick to the remembrance of Jerusalem, and to postpone their lives ('there we sat'). The story is that they did indeed make their choice. The self-reflection makes perfectly clear that the behaviour in the first strophe – sitting down, weeping, etc. – was not a primary emotional reaction but a real choice.[10] The transition from plural to singular, from WE to I, and the use of conditional self-imprecations function in this way. These kinds of choices can only be made individually, even within a strong community. The speaker-subject commits himself to stay oriented towards Jerusalem. The last self-imprecation shows the difficulty of that choice. It does not say that Jerusalem is his highest joy, but that it is *above* his highest joy. The clause suggests that a lot of joy would be possible, for example 'on foreign soil' – compare the parallel of the phrases 'above (על) my highest joy' and 'on (על) foreign soil' (see above). Why not sing with the Babylonians?!

The psalm gives a lot of attention to the characteristics of Babylon. The three first verse-lines are marked by preposed modifiers of place: 'By the rivers of Babylon, / there ...', 'on the willows in her midst / ...', and 'for there ...'. A radically different qualification is given in the second stanza: 'on foreign soil'. This phrase stands in opposition to Jerusalem (cola 4b <> 6c; see above), opposing their own and what is foreign. The same stanza defines further what is 'their own', by changing 'song of Zion' into 'song of Yhwh'. The centre of the refusal to assimilate is Yhwh. Ultimately, Yhwh is the reason why singing with the Babylonians is not such a good idea. Maybe that is the reason why, later on, the speaker addresses Yhwh, motivating him to participate in the remembrance of Jerusalem.

A text about the way to remain loyal to the own tradition while living in exile will lose its function after the exile, but the text itself is already post-exilic. The story in the first stanza is looking back. This means that the writer regarded the issue of assimilation as having actual importance in his own time, and that the exile has a typological function. The exile could stand for the diaspora or for any situation in which assimilation poses a problem.[11]

---

[10] Against Tucker, who takes verse 1 as an expression of desolation by the victims of an imperial empire (Tucker, *Power* (n. 1), pp. 123-124).

[11] In this light, the imprecations in the third stanza could be symbolic too, but the Edomites were of great hindrance during most of the Second Temple period, and the city of Babylon was not destroyed at the end of the exile.

2. The implications of a personal choice against assimilation

Psalms 138–145 are psalms of David and the part of it that is now under discussion, Psalms 138–143, is a sequence of prayers. Psalm 138 is a song of thanksgiving, Psalm 139 is a unique composition, and the other psalms are laments of the individual. The heart of the whole collection is a prayer book.

There is no inner development in the protagonist of these psalms, David the role model, but some structural aspects are important. The laments are framed by a song of thanksgiving and a hymn (Pss 138 and 145), which gives the collection a positive tone and a happy end. Moreover, David has to wait for his title *servant* until Psalm 143, where he is given this title in preparation of the climactic Psalm 144, in which this title receives a new application. Finally, within Psalms 138–143, some important motives are intertwined. The most important motive is the individual's inner struggle. Choosing for YHWH and standing up against the enemies is only possible after inner purification. Our role model is fundamentally insecure in Psalm 139, is attracted to the lifestyle of his enemies in Psalm 141, and, aware of his weakness, is praying for guidance in Psalm 143. Two other motives are combined: the need for protection by YHWH and the awareness that God protects the needy. In Psalms 138, 140, and 142 our role model is associated with the community of the poor and the righteous.[12] This identity-building is completed in Psalm 143 with the introduction of the title *servant of YHWH*.

In the next paragraphs we will select the most important passages.

a) *Psalm 138*

Role model David takes a courageous stand against the gods and YHWH will protect him until the job has been done.

The psalm brings the reader from the exile to David, but can be read as a continuation of the discourse about standing up and choosing for YHWH. The genre, a song of thanksgiving, has been chosen well, because it thanks for what God has already done, and looks forward to his future help.

---

[12] TUCKER's assessment of the function of the language of the poor is correct: 'In self-describing as one of the poor, the psalmist restructures the identity of himself and those who also identify as the poor. They are no longer simply the ones without power, but instead, the ones to whom God responds' (TUCKER, *Power* (n. 1), p. 176).

What has he done? 'When I called, you answered me, / you inspire me with courage'.¹³ One may remember the previous psalm. Anyhow, David stands up himself: 'I want to praise you with all my heart, / before the gods, sing a hymn for you, / bow toward your holy temple'. To face the other gods while choosing for YHWH makes as strong image (vv. 1-3; the first strophe). One wishes that the kings belonging to these other gods would also recognize YHWH (vv. 4-6; the second strophe). At the end of the collection, the kings have disappeared and everyone bows before YHWH : 'let all flesh bless his holy name' (Ps 145,21).

What will God do? He will protect his servant: 'When I walk amid trouble, you keep me alive, / against the fury of my foes you send your hand, / your right hand delivers me',¹⁴ until he has brought 'to an end for me' (vv. 7-8; the third strophe). The promise of protection and completion has been formulated more generally in the central strophe, in the opposition of 'the lowly' and 'the proud' (v. 6). The language of the poor will also be used elsewhere in the collection.

b) *Psalm 139*

Role model David takes a stand against the enemies of YHWH, but in an extreme way and with a lot of insecurity about himself.

Our collection is a long appeal to radically choose YHWH as God, but the last stanza of Psalm 139 contains a rather awkward version of this:

---

[13] The time frame of the last clause is difficult to assess. The *yiqtol*-clause follows a *qatal*- and a *wayyiqtol*-clause. Many translations continue the past perspective: 'you inspired me with courage' (JEWISH PUBLICATION SOCIETY, *The Book of Psalms – Sefer Tehilim: A New Translation according to the Traditional Hebrew Text*, Philadelphia PA, JPS, 1997). Moreover, the syntax and the meaning of the colon are uncertain, but most interpretations, and very old ones by that, speak about inner strength and courage. 'Du hast mich erkühnt, in meiner Seele ist Macht' (M. BUBER, *Die Schriftwerke*, Köln, Hegner, 1962). 'And (you) made me exultant, putting strength within me' (L. ALLEN, *Psalms 101-150* (WBC, 21), Waco TX, Word Books, 1983). 'Du weckst in meiner Seele Kraft' (F.-L. HOSSFELD – E. ZENGER, *Psalmen 101-150* (HTKAT), Freiburg, Herder, 2008).

[14] The division of verse 7 in BHS (and for example J. FOKKELMAN, *Major Poems of the Hebrew Bible, Volume III* (SSN, 43), Assen, Van Gorcum, 2003, pp. 312-315 and 387) is not in accordance with the Masoretic accentuation, and, more important, with Hebrew idiom. Therefore, one has to read verse 7 as a tricolon. חיה *piel* is nowhere else combined with a prepositional phrase with על, and it is used with no modifier at all in 28 passages. שלח *qal* with יד cannot stand alone and has a double prepositional object unless the object is mentioned in the following clause, which is certainly not the case in Ps 138.

> 19 If you would only kill the wicked, God –
>   you murderers, away from me! –
> 20 men who speak of you maliciously,
>   who talk falsely, your foes.
> 21 Those who hate you, YHWH, would I not hate (them),
>   those who attack you, would I not loathe (them)?
> 22 I do hate them, hate them utterly;
>   enemies they have become of me.
> 23 Examine me, God, and know my mind,
>   probe me and know my anxious thoughts,
> 24 see if I am on a way to pain,
>   guide me in the way to paradise.

The speaker stands up against the enemies of YHWH. So far so good, but he has still a lot to learn. His fanatic rejection of people who are clearly not his own enemies, his hesitations to subject himself to God's scrutiny (vv. 1-18), and his insecurity about his own behaviour (vv. 23-24),[15] betray him. Is it too far-fetched to suppose that the 'enemies' attract him in a certain way, that he is inclined to hang around with them? How otherwise to explain this mix of fanaticism and insecurity?!

c) *Psalm 140*

Role model David prays for protection against the enemies. The last strophe describes the own community in terms of being poor and righteous:

> 13 I know: YHWH champions
>   the cause of the low, the right of the needy.
> 14 Surely, righteous men will praise your name,
>   the upright will dwell in your presence.

d) *Psalm 141*

Role model David evidently has some problem with separating himself from the enemies and prays for protection against himself.

---

[15] Maybe the text contains some hints to idolatry, for example דרך־עצב, translated above with 'a way to pain' parallel to 'the way to paradise', *cf.* e.g. ALLEN, *Psalms 101-150* (n. 13), 250 and 253: 'see if I have been behaving as an idolator', and, of course, verse 20 – J. HOLMAN, *The Structure of Psalm CXXXIX*, in *VT* 21 (1971), 298-310, and *Are Idols Hiding in Psalm 139:20?*, in B. BECKING – E. PEELS (eds.), *Psalms and Prayers: Papers Read at the Joint Meeting of the Society of Old Testament Study and Het Oudtestamentisch Werkgezelschap in Nederland en België, Apeldoorn August 2006* (OTS, 55), Leiden, Brill, 2007, 119-128. Holman argues for seeing in v. 20 a reference to idolatry. He reads: 'Those who mention You (Your name) for "the lewdness", / they pronounce You for "the emptiness", your enemies', implicating that these people use the name of God for idolatrous purposes.

The strophic structure and the overall meaning of this psalm are uncertain. The text of verses 5-7 is problematic, so that any interpretation of these verses would be too hypothetical to be used in this study.

The second strophe is special. It harkens back to Psalm 139:

> 3 Set a guard, YHWH, on my mouth,
> watch at the door of my lips,
> 4 do not incline my mind to evil speaking,
> to involvement in deeds of wickedness
> with men who are evildoers –
> may I not eat of their fancy food!

The speaker is inclined to mix with the enemies. He is attracted to their lifestyle and he could participate in their evil speaking and deeds of wickedness just like that. The strophe is a prayer to protect him against himself.

The end of the psalm is a plea for protection against the enemies (vv. 8-10).

e) *Psalm 142*

Role model David prays for protection against the enemies. The last strophe describes the own community in terms of being righteous (see above, Ps 140):

> 8 Free me from prison,
> that I may praise your name;
> around me the righteous will crowd,
> when you treat me with kindness.

f) *Psalm 143*

Role model David combines prayers for mercy and guidance with pleas for protection against the enemies. He calls himself a servant of YHWH.

Whereas Psalm 139 shows the insecurity of the speaker about his own behaviour, and Psalm 141 his inclination to mix with the enemies, this psalm shows his awareness of his own weakness.

> 2 so do not enter into judgment with your servant,
> for before you no one living can be in the right.

In line with this awareness the speaker prays for guidance:

> 8 Let me hear in the morning your loving answer,
> for in you I trust;
> let me know the road I should go,
> for to you I have lifted up my soul.
> ...

10   teach me to do your will,
      for you are my God;
      may your good spirit lead me
      onto level ground.

In the last stanza we find two כי-nominal clauses, that define the relation between role model David and Y<small>HWH</small>:

10b   for you are my God   כי־אתה אלוהי
12c   for I am your servant   כי אני עבדך

These clauses will be used in the next psalm to define the identity of the present-day personages.

3. A militant spirituality

The following exposition of Psalm 144 will be divided into two parts, according to the two first-person individuals, David in the first part of the psalm, and his follower and the community he belongs to, in the second part. After the translation of the first part and a comment upon its strophic structure, we will focus on three aspects: David as royal warrior, the character of the enemies, and the 'demotization' of David.[16]

1   Blessed be Y<small>HWH</small>, my rock,
     who trains my hands for battle,
     my fingers for warfare,
2   my loyal help and my fortress,
     my stronghold and my own deliverer,
     my shield and the one with whom I find shelter,
     who subdues my people beneath me.

3   Y<small>HWH</small>, what is man that you notice him,
     a human being that you take thought for him?
4   Man resembles a breath of wind,
     his days are like a passing shadow.

---

5   Y<small>HWH</small>, spread apart your heavens and come down,
     touch the mountains so that they smoke,
6   flash lightning and scatter them,
     send your arrows and rout them.

---

[16] 'Demotization', an English neologism, is a translation of the German 'Demotisierung' (used by Otto Kaiser). 'Demotization' means that something is made available to the people (*demos*). In this case, the kingship of David is transferred to the people. See note 24.

>   7   Send your hands from on high,
>   rescue me, save me from the mighty waters,
>   from the hand of foreigners,
>   8   whose mouth speaks lies,
>   whose right hand is a perjured hand.

The first part of Psalm 144 consists of two stanzas of two strophes each (vv.1-2.3-4/5-6.7-8/).[17] The psalm has a special combination of genre-motives. The first strophe is hymnic, having a *berachah* and a litany, the second strophe is a reflection, and the second stanza consists of a prayer with some pleas and a complaint.

The David of this psalm is the same as the David in Psalms 138–143, so we could have combined these texts and we could have called our role model David *the servant of* Y*HWH,* because that title is climactically present in Psalm 143 and then again in this psalm. Instead, we took the two roles of David separately, David the supplicant and David the royal warrior, because otherwise we would play down the militant nature of this spirituality. David is a warrior-king in this psalm. He is trained for battle and has to stand his ground in war. God will protect him, save him from his enemies, and give him victory. The attention given to God's protection may not be used to caricaturize this royal warrior. David may be defended by God but he still has to stand up and fight. Most of these verses are based on Psalm 18, a song of thanksgiving in which David looks back on God's help and his own victories. Davidic spirituality is fundamentally positive and full of trust, but has its dangerous moments.

Who are the enemies? The psalm nowhere names them, but contains some descriptions. A mythological one, מים רבים, *mighty waters*, points to the dangerous character of these enemies and associates them with the primordial chaos-waters. Nevertheless, the danger and the war are primarily verbal, according to the most detailed description, which is a behavioural one: 'whose mouth speaks lies, / whose right hand is a perjured hand.' This verbal war is fought against *foreigners* (בני־נכר) and at the same time against *my people* (עמי; v. 2) – if we keep to MT and LXX, and why shouldn't we?![18] The full clause – he 'subdues *my people* beneath

---

[17] So also FOKKELMAN (*Major Poems II* (n. 7), pp. 308-310 and 469). VAN DER LUGT, *Strofische structuren*, (n. 7), pp. 477-478, suggested another division in the first part of the psalm. I published an earlier but full analysis in an internal report in preparation of the Dutch *Nieuwe Bijbelvertaling* (\id NBV/ 19PS144.VO/20010119/HvG/Psalm 144, 12 pp.).
[18] MT has עמי, *my* people, LXX τον λαόν μου; other versions have עמים, *peoples*, or the like (see BHS).

me' – is a deliberate adaptation of Psalm 18,48b, reading a singular instead of a plural – '(the God who) has made *peoples* subject to me'.[19] It makes one think of Psalm 18,44a – 'you saved me from a rebellious people', מריבי עם[20] – or, still better, of the parallel text 2 Samuel 22,44, that reads מריבי עמי, *from my rebellious people*. One could take the singular as a reference to the historical David and the civil war of Absalom,[21] but David being a role model, one has to think of a more open description. The enemy consists of members of the own people and of foreigners at the same time.

The second strophe could be a 'meditation upon human weakness', functioning 'as an attempt to arouse divine sympathy and so intervention',[22] but so far the psalm has not stated any situation requiring intervention. David presents himself as a human being, humble and transient. This anthropological reflection refers to Psalm 8,5,[23] the psalm of human kingship. Therefore, the second strophe seems to 'demotize' King David,[24] preparing the reader for the Davidic community in the second part of the psalm.

The Initiated

The second part of the exposition of Psalm 144 will start with a translation and a comment upon the strophic structure. This part is about the initiated. We will discuss the relation between the two first-person personages, the individual and the community. Is personage I the leader of the community? Another point of discussion will be the function of the beatitude in the last stanza.

> 9 God, a new song I will sing to you,
> upon a ten-stringed lute I will play to you,
> 10 the one who gives victory to kings,
> who rescues his servant David.

---

[19] The translation is taken from *The Book of Psalms – Sefer Tehilim* (n. 13).
[20] The translation is taken from the *Good News Bible: The Bible in Today's English Version*, New York, ABS, 1979.
[21] *Cf.* J.P.M. van der Ploeg, *Psalmen, Deel II* (BOT, 7b), Roermond, Romen, 1974, p. 474.
[22] Allen, *Psalms* (n. 13), p. 289.
[23] More details in Hossfeld – Zenger, *Psalmen 101-150* (n. 13), p. 781.
[24] For 'demotization/demotize' see note 16. Otto Kaiser uses the term *Demotisierung* (see K. Seybold, *Formen der Textrezeption in Psalm 144*, in R. Kratz et al. (eds.), *Schriftauslegung in der Schrift* (BZAW, 300), Berlin, De Gruyter, 2000, 281-289, p. 287). Substitution of the king by the people is found in several other places in the Bible. For example in Ps 89: 'servant' in v. 4 and 'servants' in v. 51 (whether originally or not!).

/11 From the baneful sword / rescue me,
save me from the hand of foreigners,
whose mouth speaks lies,
whose right hand is a perjured hand.

---

12 Our sons are like green trees,[25]
full-grown in their youth,
our daughters are like corner pillars,
carved to adorn a palace.
13 Our garners are full,
providing food of every kind,
our sheep increase by thousands,
even myriads, in our fields,
our oxen are well-fleshed.
14 No breach and no flight
and no wailing in our streets –
15 happy the people who have it so,
happy the people whose God is YHWH.

The second part of Psalm 144 consists of two stanzas of respectively two and three strophes (vv. 9-10b.10c-11/12.13.14-15). The special combination of genre-motives continues in the second part. The third stanza combines hymn and prayer. The fourth stanza is a beatitude.

Verses 12-15 are a reversed beatitude. Usually a beatitude starts with a beatitude formula – *happy X who Y*. Somebody (X) is called happy (אשרי) because of his behaviour (Y). The second part is a description of the happiness that will befall him. The beatitude in Psalm 144 starts with the description of happiness and has the beatitude formula at the end. The usual sequence leaves no doubt about the beginning of the beatitude, however the sequence in Psalm 144 does. The first word of verse 12 אשר marks the opening of the beatitude. In verse 12, אשר is not relational, referring to an antecedent, neither is it a conjunction. It is the marker of the beginning of the beatitude and corresponds to the word ככה in the first beatitude formula 'happy the people who have it *so*'. Happy are the people who have it like verses 12-14 describe. The word ככה refers back and can point to rather large paragraphs.[26] The markers ככה ... אשר guarantee that one will read verses 12-15 as a beatitude.

---

[25] MT has *ʾᵃsjèr*. BHS proposes *ʾasre* or *ʾasjsjer*. See our exposition.
[26] See Num 8,26; 11,15; Deut 29,23; 1 Sam 2,14; Jer 22,8; Ez 4,13.

The collection hits ground in this passage. The initiation is completed. The potential member of the Davidic community has learned from his role models, the deported in exile, David the supplicant, and David the royal warrior. Now he is a servant of YHWH himself. He will stand up against assimilation and his community will enjoy a life of progeny, prosperity, and peace.

The passage about the newly initiated individual is parallel to the one about David the royal warrior in all kind of respects (see § I), but the parallels stop abruptly after verse 11, when the initiation is completed. From the exilic individual in Psalm 137 until now everything was aimed at the learning process of the individual. Standing up against assimilation is a personal choice with severe implications, so that every individual member of the community has to make that choice himself, but surrounding him is the community. So Psalm 137 starts with the exilic community and Psalm 144 ends with the present-day community.

The parallel of Psalms 137 and 144 supports the view that the first-person individual is a member of the first-person community and not the leader, the new king. Psalm 144 is about a Davidic community and not about a new David. There are several corroborations of this view. The prosodic structure gives us a first confirmation: David the royal warrior gets two stanzas, the newly initiated individual only one. Over and against David, the individual and the community are in one package. Together they have two stanzas as David does.[27] The second strophe (vv. 3-4) substantiates our view because it presents David in a 'demotized' way (see note 16). Why 'demotize' David, if the psalm were to promote a new Davidic king? A third corroboration is found in a parallel between Psalms 143 and 144. We have already noted the two כי-nominal clauses in Psalm 143 (see above). Psalm 144 takes up these clauses, creating a chiastic sequence.

Psalm 143		כי־אתה אלוהי	A	10b
	כי אני עבדך		B	12c
Psalm 144		דוד עבדו	B	10b
	העם שיהוה אלהיו		A	15b

[27] An earlier interpretation of Ps 144 (H. VAN GROL, *De weg naar geluk: Poëzie en werkelijkheid in Psalm 144*, in B. BECKING *et al.* (eds.), *Tussen Caïro en Jeruzalem* (UTR, 53), Utrecht, UU, 2006, 31-38) contains some nice details. One of them is the fact that the writer has used the openings of the two parts of Ps 33 (vv. 2b-3a and 12a) to include the second part of his own psalm (vv. 9 and 15b).

The writer divides the two relational clauses over the two stanzas and over the two first-person personages. The community of Psalm 144 is a community of servants of YHWH.

Everything is said and the initiation is completed. After this, the initiated one, having now become a new member of the community, the community itself comes into view. Its future will be great: progeny, prosperity, and peace. It is not presented in an eschatological vision but in an extended and reversed beatitude (vv. 12-15; see above). A beatitude makes propaganda for a certain spirituality by coupling behaviour that is typical of this spirituality, to the life one may expect. The description of that life is down to earth and in the present tense. Such a description evokes the future as an already existing fact.[28] The life in this Davidic community is very attractive, to say the least.

THE EXTERNAL WRITER-READER COMMUNITY

A literary-stylistic interpretation can stand alone, but a hypothesis about the historical reference of the text certainly makes it more interesting. Our present exposition is based upon a composition-critical study, which enables us to hypothesize upon the relative time frame of the text and the possible writer-reader community.[29]

Our hypothesis about the last editorial phases of the Book of Psalms, as present in the last part of the book, departs from the observation that it consists of several collections:[30] the Song of Ascents (Pss 120–134), two hymns (135–136), the psalm about the exile (137), the Psalms of David (138–145) and the Final Hallel (146–150). The Final Hallel is part of the last edition of the book. It concludes the five books of psalms – the

---

[28] The translation or the interpretation of vv. 12-15 as a wish or even a prayer (for example TUCKER, *Power* (n. 1), pp. 133, 136 and again 189) does not do justice to the syntax and is based on a wrong assessment of the genre.

[29] The composition-critical study is found in VAN GROL, *David and his Chasidim* (n. 1). We studied the historical connection with the Hasidim in *Three Hasidisms and their Militant Ideologies: 1 and 2 Maccabees, Psalms 144 and 149*, in B. BECKING – L. GRABBE, *Between Evidence and Ideology: Essays on the History of Ancient Israel* (OTS, 59), Leiden, Brill, 2011, 93-115.

[30] Various books give a full survey of hypotheses, for example BALLHORN, *Zum Telos* (n. 1); LEUENBERGER, *Konzeptionen* (n. 78); HOSSFELD – ZENGER, *Psalmen 101-150* (n. 13); and E. ZENGER (ed.), *The Composition of the Book of Psalms* (BETL, 238), Leuven, Peeters, 2010.

first four ending in a *berachah* – with five hymns.³¹ That leaves us with Psalms 120–145. Parallel to a narrative plot, which starts with a situation and ends with a party, a sequence of psalms could feasibly start with a lament and end with a hymn. Psalms 120–145 show two of these sequences:

first sequence:	120 enmity in the diaspora	> 135–136 hymns³²
second sequence:	137 danger of assimilation	> 145 hymn

In both sequences, the first psalm poses the problem, the following psalms deal with that problem, and the hymn forms a festive conclusion.

Each sequence belongs to a redactional phase and forms the ending of an edition of the book. If one dates the last redaction at the beginning of the second century BCE, the first one could be placed in the fourth century and the second in the third century. Given this time frame, we surmise that the first sequence is about diaspora and coping with living in the diaspora,³³ and the second about Hellenization and coping with Hellenistic neighbours.³⁴

Psalm 137 confronts the reader with the exile, and, by being a post-exilic psalm, with the diaspora. The problem this psalm poses is not the deportation as such or the violence of the Babylonians, but assimilation. It promotes the choice not to assimilate, not to mix the own tradition and the foreign culture. By writing a parallel psalm (144) and combining both psalms in a collection, the editor draws a parallel between different places

---

[31] Detailed interpretations of the Final Hallel can be found in H. VAN GROL, *Sion en de Chasidim: Psalm 137-150*, in H. VAN GROL – P. VAN MIDDEN (eds.), *Een roos in de lente: Theologisch palet van de FKT* (Theol. Persp., 1), Utrecht, FKT, 2009, 83-90; and *Deconstructie van de lofzang: Psalm 146-150 als identiteitsvertoog*, in A.L.H.M. VAN WIERINGEN (ed.), *Verborgen lezers: Over tekst en communicatie in het Oude Testament* (Theol. Persp. Suppl., 2), Bergambacht, 2VM, 2011, 33-59.

[32] Ps 136 is known as the Great Hallel.

[33] A first sketch of this interpretation can be found in H. VAN GROL, *War and Peace in the Psalms: Some Compositional Explorations*, in J. LIESEN – P. BEENTJES (eds.), *Visions of Peace and Tales of War* (DCLY, 2010), Berlin, De Gruyter, 2010, 173-206, pp. 196-200.

[34] Consequently, Pss 137–145 is an editorial collection. It consists of already existing psalms, to which new material has been added, especially Ps 144. See VAN GROL, *David and his Chasidim* (n. 1).
In a recent study, TUCKER, *Power* (n. 1), proposes a much earlier date for book five of the Psalter, the Persian period. The psalms were written to construct Gods power and to deconstruct Persian power. His study is not convincing, because it proposes one theme for the whole of the book, and because its approach is too general, scanning 44 psalms on some themes. He does not write about the dynamics of the book or of a part of the book, narrative, dramatic or otherwise.

and times, between the Babylonian exile and third century Judea. Doing so, he makes the exile a *typos* for Ptolemaic Judea. The problem of assimilation is much easier to recognize within the exilic situation than in the contemporary situation at home. Moreover, the enemy is easier to define.

Psalm 144 confronts us with a strange mixture of enemies: foreigners together with fellow countrymen. This mixture could be the result of Hellenization in the third century BCE: foreign rulers and members of the own people who were attracted to their dominant culture. Hellenization brought foreigners and compatriots together and made these fellow countrymen Hellenistic, *foreign*. The message of the writer/editor is clear: a war on assimilation is required. One needs to stand up and refuse any form of assimilation.

The writer-reader community of Psalms 137–145 is a predecessor of the later Hasidim. The concluding hymn is Davidic – a remarkable fact because no other Davidic hymns are found in the Psalter; he is the man of prayers (Ps 72,20) – but is this David our role model as before or are these the words of the Davidic community that came into existence by initiation in the previous psalm? Anyhow, Gods favourites, *hasidim*, are mentioned at the centre of this psalm: 'your favourites, let them bless you!' (145,10).

Psalm 145 consists of three parts. The first one consists of two stanzas of two strophes each, the second one of one stanza of two strophes, and the third one again of two stanzas of two strophes each. Most strophes contain two verse-lines, the first and the last one three (vv. 1-3.4-5/6-7.8-9//10-11.12-13//13*-14.15-16/17-18.19-21: 3.2/2.2//2.2//2.2/2.3). The last verse-line is a tricolon (v. 21). There is no consensus about the major structure of this psalm and about the strophic division of verses 1-7.[35] The key to its structure is the distinction between the call to praise and the praise itself. There are three sequences of both. The first part of the psalm contains the first sequence. It has a call to praise in verses 1b-2 and 4-7, consisting of cohortativi and jussivi, and the praise itself in verses 3 and 8-9.[36] The second part contains the second sequence with a call to praise in verses 10-12 (jussivi) and the praise itself in verse 13a-b. The third part contains the third sequence, but now the sequence is reversed. It starts with

---

[35] VAN DER LUGT, *Strofische structuren* (n. 7), p. 478; FOKKELMAN (*Major Poems II* (n. 7), pp. 310-316 and 470). I published an earlier but full analysis in an internal report in preparation of the Dutch *Nieuwe Bijbelvertaling* (\id NBV/19PS145.VO/981106/HvG/ Psalm 145, 11 pages).

[36] One could take them as two sequences, but the cohortativi in cola 5b and 6b point to the cohortativi in verses 1-2.

the praise itself in verses 13c-20 and has the call to praise at the end in verse 21 (jussivi).³⁷

The three-part structure of Psalm 145 is important because of the different subjects of praise. Each part has a personal subject and a very general one. The personal subjects are *I* (David), *your favourites* (חסידך), and *my mouth* (David; vv. 1.10.21). At the centre of the psalm the *hasidim* are mentioned. This may be by chance, but the phrase and the message of the collection both make us think of the later Hasidim. They played a major part in the Maccabean revolt against the Seleucids and their own Hellenized and Hellenizing countrymen.³⁸

---

³⁷ The previous psalm (144) has a reversed beatitude at the end! See above.
³⁸ For detailed discussions see VAN GROL, *Three Hasidisms* (n. 29).

GOD AS THE WISE TEACHER IN JOB

Sehoon JANG
Seoul, South Korea

The book of Job has been hailed as a masterpiece of ancient literature that is concerned with the enigmatic dilemma about a righteous man's undeserved suffering. It has been understood that the book is mainly designed to respond to those who struggle with the age-old issue of theodicy. Recently, however, this traditional approach has been challenged by an increasing number of biblical interpreters who have sought to propose somewhat different options for interpreting the primary concern of the book of Job.[1] It has been pointed out that God's speeches and Job's subsequent responses play an important role in understanding the central issue of the book of Job. More significantly, a great deal of attention has been paid to the character of God whose interrogations of Job ultimately alert him to the limits of all human wisdom, which is incapable of fully fathoming the depth of the universal order of God's created world, in which chaotic realities are seemingly uncontrollable. The aim of the present essay is to articulate how God, as a wise teacher, seeks to utilize his creation as his teaching material, in order to accomplish his teaching goal of transforming his pupil's ignorance about God's inscrutable ways of ruling over his creation.

WHO IS GOD IN THE BOOK OF JOB?

The past decades have witnessed a growing interest in how God is presented as a key character in the book of Job.[2] Some scholars have argued that the central purpose of the book of Job is not to deal with the

---

[1] For a concise survey of recent trends in Joban studies, see L. WILSON, *Job* (THOC), Grand Rapids MI, Eerdmans, 2015, 1-26; L. WILSON, *Job*, in K.J. VANHOOZER (ed.), *Theological Interpretation of the Old Testament*, Grand Rapids MI, Baker, 2008, 148-150.

[2] See D. TIMMER, *God's Speeches, Job's Responses, and the Problem of Coherence in the Book of Job: Sapiential Pedagogy Revisited*, in *CBQ* 71 (2009) 286-305; J.E. PATRICK, *The Fourfold Structure of Job: Variations on a Theme*, in *VT* 50 (2005), 185-206; A.E. STEINMANN, *Structure and Message of the Book of Job*, in *VT* 46 (1996), 85-100; D. WOLFERS,

problem of suffering. Instead, several commentators have understood that the main issue of the book of Job has to do with the character of God.[3] Though the questions about the nature of God are placed at the centre of the fiery debate between Job and his three friends, God hardly appears in the poetic section of the book of Job that mainly consists of the dialogue between Job and the interlocutors, except the prologue (1,1–2,13) and God's speeches (38,1–42,7). Andrew E. Steinmann asserts:

> Satan (ii 5), Job's wife (ii 9), Job himself, his three friends, and Elihu are all concerned in one way or another about Job's suffering. But the central, and largely absent, character in the book God – is not. He never once mentions Job's suffering or suggests that he is even concerned about it (as he is about Job's death, ii 6). He makes no attempt to justify his decision to allow Job to suffer. This would suggest that Job's suffering is merely a foil for a larger issue.[4]

If the seemingly absent and invincible God is the key character in the book of Job, one may raise the question: "Who is God in the book of Job?" Many options for the character of God in the book of Job have been proposed, but no consensus has been reached as of yet. As Terence Fretheim suggests, three different types of God's image come to the fore in the book of Job.[5] Firstly, God is depicted as a stern lord or a charlatan god who somewhat belittles a suffering figure by paying no attention to the question about the problem of suffering that he keeps posing: a callous attitude that tends to frustrate the innocent sufferer completely.[6] However,

---

The Speech-Cycles in the Book of Job, in *VT* 43 (1993), 386-402; D. WOLFERS, *The Lord's Second Speech in the Book of Job*, *VT* 40 (1990), 474-499.

[3] See R.N. WHYBRAY, *Wisdom, Suffering and the Freedom of God in the Book of Job*, in E. BALL (ed.), *In Search of True Wisdom: Essays in Old Testament Interpretation in Honor of Ronald E. Clements*, Sheffield, Sheffield Academic Press, 1999, 231-245.

[4] STEINMANN, *Structure and Message*, (n. 2), p. 86.

[5] T.E. FRETHEIM, *God and World in the Old Testament: A Relational Theology of Creation*, Nashville TS, Abingdon Press, 2005, pp. 240-242. See also S.E. BALENTINE, *Job* (SHBC), Macon GA, Smyth & Helwys, 2006, pp. 30-33; J.D. LEVENSON, *The Book of Job in its Time and in the Twentieth Century*, Cambridge MA, Harvard University Press, 1972, pp. 19-29; T.N.D. METTINGER, *The God of Job: Avenger, Tyrant, or Victor?*, in L.G. PERDUE – W. CLARK GILPIN, *The Voice from the Whirlwind: Interpreting the Book of Job*, Nashville TS, Abingdon Press, 1992, 39-49. For a discussion of God's ethics in the book of Job, see K.J. DELL, *Does God Behave Unethically in the Book of Job*, in K.J. DELL (ed.), *Ethical and Unethical in the Old Testament: God and Humans in Dialogue* (LHBTS, 528), London, T&T Clark International, 2010, 170-186.

[6] As Michael Fox suggests, "this view claims, God merely intimidates Job and sneers at his ignorance and weakness. God thereby exposes himself as ... a 'charlatan god', or ... 'remote', 'unfeeling', 'unjust'." See M.V. Fox, *God's Answer and Job's Response*, in *Bib* 94 (2013), p. 2. See also M.Z. BRETTLER, *(Divine) Silence Is Golden: A New Reading of the Prologue of Job*, in J.A. AITKEN – J.M.S. CLINES – C.M. MAIER (eds.), *Interested*

one may wonder if God's appearance and address to Job in the divine speeches only play a negative role in the relationship between God and Job.

Secondly, God is presented as a loving parent who comes to Job not with criticism and censure, but with kindness and care. Even if this option has a number of strengths, it fails to demonstrate a full discussion about the creational dimension of God's ordering of the universe, in which chaotic elements seem uncontrollable.

Thirdly, God is portrayed as a creator or a sage whose message alerts Job to the recognition that, as a creature, he is incapable of understanding God's majesty and his sovereignty over his wondrous creation.

Though one may uncover a portrait of God in the book of Job, one must be cautious of claiming to have discovered "the last truth about God"[7] in the book. James L. Crenshaw aptly remarks: "the lonely voice insisting on theological complexity stands as a warning against established belief wherever it exists."[8] My position is placed in between the second and the third approach and it overlaps both. More correctly, though I partially sympathize with the thesis made by the second approach, that God's speeches focus not on condemnation, but rather on discipline, the assertion made by the last option, that God in the divine discourses (chs. 38-41) eventually awakens Job to the fact that God is in control of the universe no matter what chaotic realities seem active in the created world, is more convincing to me.

In my opinion, the divine speeches strategically serve as an unmistakable clue for understanding the nature of God in the book of Job.[9] It is significant to observe, furthermore, that God is depicted as a teacher in

---

Readers: Essays on the Hebrew Bible in Honor of David J. Clines, Atlanta GA, SBL, 2013, 19-26; J.L. CRENSHAW, *When Form and Content Clash: The Theology of Job 38:1-40:5*, in R.J. CLIFFORD – J.J. COLLINS, *Creation in the Biblical Traditions*, Washington DC, CBAA, 1992, 78-85. For an insightful postmodern approach, see D.J. CLINES, *Job's Fifth Friend: An Ethical Critique of the Book of Job*, in *BI* 12 (2004), 233-250.

[7] J.L. CRENSHAW, *Some Reflections on the Book of Job*, in *Review and Expositor* 99 (2002), p. 590.

[8] *Ibid.*

[9] R.N. Whybray correctly points out that "throughout the dialogue the principal topic that has preoccupied the participants has been neither the problem of suffering nor the nature of wisdom but the very nature of the God whom they all profess to worship. About his transcendence they have been in agreement; but the point on which they have profoundly differed has been his relationship with his human creatures. It is surely in the speeches which the author attributes to Yahweh in chs. 38-41 that the readers would naturally expect to find the solution." See WHYBRAY, *Wisdom, Suffering and the Freedom of God* (n. 3), p. 238.

the divine discourses that present several essential educational elements, such as the teacher, the teaching materials and the teaching goal. In this sense I now wish to elaborate upon how God effectively educates his pupil to reflect on what is wrong with his approach to God.

Creation as God's Teaching Material

Job wonders if he deserves all the painful ailments he is afflicted with, and complains to God that he has been dealt with unjustly. He eagerly anticipates that God will respond to him with a clear answer to the question as to why he is bitterly suffering. Ironically, Job is unexpectedly overwhelmed by a host of questions that God proposes when he finally appears out of the whirlwind, that is ironically reminiscent of the beginning of a miserable calamity that befell Job (1,19). One may ask whether these questions posed in the divine speeches could resolve Job's struggle with unprovoked suffering as well as with his scepticism about God's justice.

It ought to be noted, however, that God tends to make use of a series of rhetorical questions that are didactically designed to motivate Job to reconsider his protests and complaints to God which dominate in the preceding dialogue, including his first soliloquy in chapter 3. In this regard, I wish to elucidate how God, as a teacher, lectures Job about his ignorance and limitations by employing his teaching materials, such as the world of inanimate and animate nature, especially the marvellous image of two mythical beasts, *Behemoth* and *Leviathan* that can only be controlled by God.

1. God's Ways of Dealing with Creation as His Teaching Material

I now wish to take an in-depth look at how God deals with his created world as his teaching material in the divine discourses (38,1–42,6). The divine discourses can be divided into two speeches by God, each of which is respectively followed by Job's response. In a structural manner, the two speeches are simply parallel to Job's two responses.[10]

---

[10] Though different proposals have been suggested, there is almost universal agreement that 38:1-42:6 has these four major sections. See D.J.A. Clines, *Job 38-42* (WBC, 18B), Nashville TS, Thomas Nelson, 2011. For a discussion of other options for the structure, see J.E. Patrick, *Fourfold Structure* (n. 2), pp. 185-206; A.E. Steinmann, *Structure and Message* (n. 2), pp. 85-100.

    A. God's first speech (38,1–40,2)
       B. Job's response (40,3-5)
    A'. God's second speech (40,6–41,34)
       B'. Job's response (42,1-6)

To begin with, close attention is drawn to the first speech that can also be separated into two subsections. It is interesting to see that the first section of the speech concentrates on the wonders of inanimate nature (38,1-38), while the second focuses on the world of animate nature (38,39–39,30). In the first section, God's challenging queries begin with God's initial work of creation, when the foundation of the earth was laid (38,4-7). Then they proceed to deal with God's majestic sovereignty over the unruly waters (38,8-11), shift from the chaos of the wicked and of death (38,12–21) to God's regulation of stars and seasons (38,31-33), and end with the divine provision of rain (38,22-30.34-38). In particular, given Job's severe denunciations of the divine government of the world (9,5-12), God wonders if Job knows all about God's management of his creation, especially of the inanimate world. He challenges:

   Declare, if you know all this. (38,18)

By underscoring his incomparable wisdom, God questions:

   Who has the wisdom to number the clouds? (38,37)

God's interrogation of Job with these questions highlights that God remains sovereign over all the entire inanimate creation to which Job has no access. When Job faces these thought-provoking questions, he is urged to reflect on what is wrong with his knowledge about God's ordering of the universe. To be sure, God's questions about meteorological and astronomical aspects of creation play a pivotal role in gaining insight into a remarkable contrast between the incomparability of God's wisdom and the limits of human wisdom. It must be pointed out, therefore, that the central purpose of the questions about inanimate nature is to educate Job to be aware of his ignorance about God's control over the entire cosmic order. At this point, it needs to be emphasized that the entire inanimate creation in the first part of the speech didactically serves as God's teaching material on behalf of an unenlightened student who needs to admit his lack of knowledge about numerous domains in God's wondrous plan for creation.

In the second part of God's first speech (38,39-39,30), the questions dramatically shift their focus from the non-living physical world to the animal world, especially to five pairs of animals: lions and ravens, mountain goats and hinds, wild asses and wild oxen, ostriches and the wild horse, hawks and the eagle. It is significant to note that these animals share common features with each other. Firstly, the creatures are wild, non-domesticated beasts, a feature that indicates that they are untamed by humans. Some of them appear to be inimical to human life and often become violent. For instance, lions do harm to human beings by killing their livestock, and mountain goats and wild asses play havoc with the well-cultivated land of the farmer. Secondly, they dwell in areas uninhabited by man such as the wilderness, mountain crags and barren steppes and appear to exist in total independence of human beings, a characteristic that implies that they reside outside of human control. This suggests that God controls the entire animate creation, especially these wild creatures. Since Job only has knowledge about the regions in which he lives and the animals which are domesticated by humans, the wild creatures seem strange, absurd and even threatening to him.

Nevertheless, Job gives short shrift to the fact that God providentially cares for the wild animals, even for the dangerous beasts that are entirely controlled and maintained by their Creator. As Whybray states, "Yahweh continues to overwhelm Job, pointing out Job's ignorance of the lives and needs of a variety of animals and birds while proclaiming his own intimate knowledge of them."[11] Interestingly, here no mention is made of the role of human beings as is found in other Old Testament passages where they are described as those who are made in God's image to exercise dominion over the animal creation (Gen. 1,26-28; Ps. 8,7-9). The point made in the divine interrogation is that human beings can hardly have any intimate knowledge about the wild creatures in the world that appear to be untamed, unruly, and aggressive.

On the other hand, God not only cares for, but also manages the untameable creatures, a striking contrast that brings Job's failure to recognize God's wise but inscrutable maintenance of the animal world into relief. It ought to be pointed out, therefore, that a series of vignettes of animal life found in the second major section of the first divine speech is strategically used as teaching material to evoke Job's ignorance about God's unfathomable management of the animate realm.

---

[11] WHYBRAY, *Wisdom, Suffering and the Freedom of God* (n. 3), p. 240.

2. The portrayals of *Behemoth* and *Leviathan* as God's Teaching Material

When the first divine speech ends, Job no longer responds to God with further questions but is willing to remain silent. As Whybray states, "he [Job] has in the past tried to dispute with God ... but he now finds that he is unable to do so: there is no reply that he can make...; yet at this stage it is not stated that he has abandoned his demand for vindication."[12] It is true that this reticence alludes to Job's acknowledgement of his ignorance about God's wondrous plan for his creation that is beyond human comprehension. Still, it also suggests that some questions are still left unanswered for him. In the preceding dialogue, Job bitterly complains that God's rule is so arbitrary that he fails to govern his creation justly (9,5-12) and wonders if God really establishes His justice in the world. By decrying the injustice of God, Job desperately laments:

> The earth is given into the hand of the wicked;
> he covers the eyes of its judges—
> if it is not he, who then is it? (9,24)

Can God's justice be defended in a world where the ungodly wicked prosper while the innocent often suffer at the hands of the unrighteous? (chs. 24) Why does God fail to take action against the incorrigibly wicked? Are cosmic forces of evil that surround human beings really under God's perfect control? Perhaps Job takes it for granted that God owes him an answer to these questions. At this stage God begins his second speech with another challenge for Job to answer his unanswerable questions, a pattern that reminds us of his opening address to Job in the first divine speech. The charge God makes against Job in the second discourse is that Job imprudently seeks to discredit God's justice (40,8):

> Will you even put me in the wrong?
> Will you condemn me that you may be justified?

Given the occurrence of the Hebrew word מִשְׁפָּט, "justice," in 40,8, it comes as little surprise that the central purpose of the second discourse is to concentrate on the issue of God's justice. Is it indeed true that there is injustice with God? Is Job's insistent attempt to accuse God of injustice, legitimate?

---

[12] R.N. WHYBRAY, *Job* (Readings: A New Biblical Commentary), Sheffield, Sheffield Phoenix Press, 1988, repr. 2008, p. 19.

In order to respond to these challenging questions, God draws attention to two enigmatic beasts named *Behemoth* and *Leviathan*, representing primeval chaos, that dominate the second divine speech. It is noteworthy that the images of the mythical beasts are clearly reminiscent of a great sea monster such as *Rahab* in several passages in the Old Testament (e.g. Ps. 89,10; Isa. 51,9). Even though the identity of the beasts has been the subject of a great deal of discussion, two proposals have received much attention. Several commentators suggest that each of them is described as a mythical sea monster such as *Lotan* or *Tiamat* who are found in Ugaritic and Babylonian mythologies.

On the other hand, many interpreters argue that the beasts are nothing more than wild animals, for example a hippopotamus and a crocodile. As mentioned above, there are remarkable references to a conflict between a sea dragon (or a sea serpent) and God in several texts in the Old Testament, especially Ps. 74,13-14; Isa. 27,1, that remind us of a primordial battle between divine powers. This may lead us to side with the first option. Given the fact that no mention is made of the hostility between God and the beasts in the book of Job, however, the second proposal is more persuasive and appealing to me. Fox points out:

> Leviathan in Ugaritic and Hebrew mythology was a primordial monster who was among Baal's, then YHWH's, enemies. Perhaps Behemoth was originally of the same sort. Nevertheless, the Theophany lacks any hint of a creation battle or even of any particular hostility between YHWH and these creatures. They have been controlled and naturalized. To the author, they are majestic, powerful creatures, like the warhorse (Job 39,19-25).[13]

To be sure, these two beasts in the second speech are on no account depicted as hostile foes or threatening enemies that are ultimately vanquished by God. Instead, each of the beasts is simply presented as a monstrous form of a hippopotamus or a crocodile of the Nile.[14] At this stage, it is noteworthy that the two marvellous beasts share a common characteristic with each other. In other words, no matter how strong and ferocious these beasts are, they are not only created, but also controlled by God. God declares:

> Look at Behemoth,
>   which I made just as I made you;
>   it eats grass like an ox. (40,15)

---

[13] Fox, *God's Answer and Job's Response* (n. 6), p. 13.
[14] Some scholars such as Michael V. Fox suggest that the image of Leviathan is based on whales. See his *God's Answer and Job's Response* (n. 6), p. 12.

> It is the first of the great acts of God—
> only its Maker can approach it with the sword. (40,19)

He goes on to question:

> Can one take it with hooks
> or pierce its nose with a snare?

In the above mentioned questions, emphasis is placed upon the fact that though *Behemoth*, which may remind us of the Hebrew word בהמה, "cattle," is regarded as the greatest of all the terrestrial animals which seem to be uncontrollable, it is merely God's creation and under his control.

God's speech is now devoted to a remarkable description of *Leviathan* which is longer than that of *Behemoth*. This terrifying beast is presented as the mightiest of all the earthly creatures. Its gigantic appearance is so awesome that its menacing power is described in considerable detail. Still, God makes it clear that it is perfectly under His control:

> Can you draw out Leviathan with a fishhook,
> or press down its tongue with a cord?
> Can you put a rope in its nose,
> or pierce its jaw with a hook? (41,1-2)

God proceeds to question in order to enhance his dominion over *Leviathan*:

> No one is so fierce as to dare to stir it up.
> Who can stand before it?
> Who can confront it and be safe?
> —under the whole heaven, who? (41,10-11)

What is more, *Leviathan* is highly celebrated as God's mighty creature:

> On earth it has no equal,
> a creature without fear.
> It surveys everything that is lofty;
> it is king over all that are proud. (41,33-34)

The point made in these questions is that no matter how great and powerful it is, the beast is only one of God's creations and under his rule. The implication of the image of the two beasts for Job is obvious. God does not fail to rule over chaotic realities that seem uncontrollable in the eyes of Job, whose limited knowledge is only based on his own observations of just a part of the world, but remains sovereign over all the powers in the cosmos. In this regard, there can be no doubt that the image of the beasts is purposely intended to educate Job to acknowledge his failure to fathom God's inscrutable ways of ruling over all chaotic elements of the world.

Transforming a Pupil as the Teaching Goal

I now wish to turn to Job's last words in 42,2-6 that are one of the most controversial and confusing verses in the book of Job. In particular Job's confession in 42,6 has been the source of countless disputes due to the ambiguous meaning of the two Hebrew verbs (מאס and נחם) in the verse.[15] The majority of Joban scholars have proposed the following possible translations of the verse.

(1) Therefore I despise myself and repent upon dust and ashes
(2) Therefore I retract my words and repent of dust and ashes
(3) Therefore I reject and forswear dust and ashes
(4) Therefore I retract my words and have changed my mind concerning dust and ashes
(5) Therefore I retract my words and I am comforted concerning dust and ashes.[16]

It is clear that the first rendering focuses on Job's humiliation and the second and third denote Job's bitter mourning while the fourth and fifth interpretation highlight the human condition. Above all, the central issue of the verse is whether Job repented or not. Many decades ago, it was suggested that Job's final words in 42,6 lay special emphasis on Job's acknowledgment of his sin. In other words, this confession plays a significant role in presenting Job as a penitent who admits his sin. It should come as no surprise, therefore, that most English versions tend to deal with Job's confession in 42,6 as repentance.[17] If this were the case, one should immediately ask oneself if there is some sin for which Job ought to repent. Likewise, some may raise the question: "What kind of sin has Job committed?" It was argued that Job's complaint against and challenge to God in the preceding dialogue and monologue could be construed as being a variant of the sin of pride. It seems unreasonable, however, to favour this argument since no mention is made of Job's sin, especially the

---

[15] For a detailed discussion of these two Hebrew verbs, see D.J.A. CLINES, *Job 38-42* (n. 10), pp. 1205-1224. See also M.V. FOX, *God's Answer and Job's Response* (n. 6), p.19; C. NEWSOM, *The Book of Job*, in R. DORAN – L.E. KECK et al., *New Interpreter's Study Bible*, Vol. 4, Nashville TS, Abingdon Press, 1996, p. 629.

[16] J.L. CRENSHAW, *Job*, in J. BARTON – J. MUDDIMAN (eds.), *The Oxford Bible Commentary*, Oxford, Oxford University Press, 2001, p. 254.

[17] For instance, NIV ("Therefore I despise myself and repent in dust and ashes."), NRSV ("Therefore I despise myself, and repent in dust and ashes.") and NKJV ("Therefore I abhor myself, and repent in dust and ashes.") respectively place emphasis on Job's repentance in the verse.

sin of his pride, in the subsequent passage, where God only rebukes Job's three friends for speaking erroneously about God.

On the other hand, over the last few decades, there has been a common tendency among Joban scholars to claim that there is no room for interpreting Job's reply in 42,6 as a penitent's confession of sin. Instead, it has been asserted that Job never repents, but recants or rejects his earlier arguments or lawsuit against God.[18] Some interpreters, including John Briggs Curtis, have even advocated a far more radical approach to Job's statement in 42,6. Curtis avers that Job expresses not so much penitence or regret, but rather his antagonistic hostility toward God. He then proceeds to suggest an entirely different translation of 42,6:[19]

> Therefore I feel loathing contempt and revulsion
> (toward you, O God);
> And I am sorry for frail man.

Yet this translation is problematic since Job's words in 42,2-5 make it obvious that Job humbly admits his own ignorance about God's majestic omnipotence which is beyond human capability to fully fathom. Still, there has been growing consensus among many scholars that whatever Job confesses, he does not express contrition in 42,6.

More recently, however, several biblical experts such as Daniel Timmer and Michael Fox have insisted that the traditional rendering of 42,6, that understands Job's confession as repentance, is unproblematic. Timmer seeks to draw attention to the use and meaning of the two Hebrew verbs (מאס and נחם) in other passages, especially Jer. 8,6; 31,19, where they can possibly be rendered as repentance. Then he is willing to answer the question: "What does Job repent of?" In his opinion, Job is aware of and repents the frailty of his sinful humanity. Hence Timmer proposes his own rendering of 42,6: "Therefore I reject and repent concerning my human frailty."[20]

Having had a scrupulous look at the various meanings of the two Hebrew words (מאס and נחם) in the Old Testament, Fox also comes to the conclusion that no matter how vague and ambiguous the Hebrew verbs are

---

[18] For a concise summary of the issues, see S.E. BALENTINE, *Job* (n. 5), pp. 694-695. See also T KRÜGER, *Did Job repent?* In T. KRÜGER – M. OEMING – K. SCHMID – C. UEHLINGER (eds.), *Das Buch Hiob und seine Interpretationen*, Zürich, Theologischer Verlag Zürich, 2007, 217-229; J. BRIGGS CURTIS, *On Job's Response to Yahweh*, in *JBL* 98 (1979), 497-511.

[19] *Ibid.*, 510. For a helpful treatment of Curtis's argument, see L. NEWELL, *Job: Repentant or Rebellious?* in *WTJ* 46 (1984), 298-316.

[20] D. TIMMER, *God's Speeches, Job's Responses* (n. 2), pp.71-72.

in 42,6, the author's choice of the words are intended to convey a nuance of repentance. He remarks:

> Job is genuinely repenting – not of any sin that might have justified the calamity, but of having spoken in ignorance – as God rebukes him for doing (38,2). His ignorance was not a sin, but it was arrogant. Whatever else the Theophany means, it certainly seeks to induce humility, and it is no surprise that it has this effect on Job. Not all readers are affected that way, but that does not mean that Job was not.[21]

Still, I am reluctant to accommodate the suggestion made by Timmer and Fox that Job's words in 42,6 needs to be interpreted as contrition. I doubt whether Timmer's assertion that Job's words in 42,6 clearly refer to the frailty of sinful humanity is reasonable, since the text never says that Job's frailty results from his sinful humanity. Undoubtedly I agree with Fox that Job's ignorance was not a sin. However, I find it difficult to accommodate Fox's conclusion that Job's ignorance was arrogant. More fundamentally, I want to pose the question as to whether the rendering of the Hebrew verb נחם as "repent" is appropriate in its own context. Instead, as many scholars propose, I prefer the translation of the Hebrew word as "change one's mind". Roland E. Murphy puts it:

> The entire verse [42,6] is supposedly in support of his submission, but the exact meaning is not clear. It would be mistaken to see here repentance for all that he has said, or even merely for certain statements that he made. The repentance should be interpreted as a change of mind (as frequently the Lord is said to change his mind or "repent of the evil" he had planned to do: e.g. Jonah 3,9-10).[22]

If this were the case, it is reasonable to assume that Job is aware that he needs to change his mind. At this stage, one may pose some questions: "Why does Job need to change his mind? What goes wrong with his approach to God's dealings with his universe? Therefore I now wish to focus on what is fundamentally wrong with Job's perspective on the nature of God in the preceding dialogue between Job and the companions. One of the most challenging complaints is that God does not listen to his cry but prolongs his suffering. Job desperately bemoans:

> If I summoned him and he answered me,
>   I do not believe that he would listen to my voice
> For he crushes me with a tempest,
>   and multiplies my wounds without cause;

---

[21] M.V. Fox, *God's Answer and Job's Response* (n. 7), p. 21.
[22] R.E. Murphy, *The Tree of Life: An Exploration of Biblical Wisdom Literature*, New York NY, Doubleday, 1990, p. 43.

he will not let me get my breath,
   but fills me with bitterness (9,16-18)

What is more, Job is willing to plead his case to God:

Look, my eye has seen all this,
   my ear has heard and understood it.
What you know, I also know;
   I am not inferior to you.
But I would speak to the Almighty,
   and I desire to argue my case with God. (13,1-3)

Then Job protests against the long-lasting silence kept by God:

I cry to you and you do not answer me;
   I stand, and you merely look at me. (30,20)

Again the complainer proceeds to urge God to answer his questions as to why he is treated unjustly:

O that I had one to hear me!
   (Here is my signature! Let the Almighty answer me!) (31,35)

In the end, Job's earnest wish to have a direct encounter with God comes true. God addresses Job out of the whirlwind. Surprisingly, in contrast to his anticipation that God would appear and answer him, God instead bombards Job with a great deal of questions. God opens his first speech with a provocative question to the sceptical critic:

Who is this that darkens counsel by words without knowledge? (38,2)

He also reiterates this question later:

Who is this that hides counsel without knowledge? (42,3)

It is ironic that the critical questioner is not offered an answer, but a question about what is wrong with his words about God's dealings of creation in the earlier dialogue. It is noteworthy that the Hebrew word עצה, "counsel," is brought into prominence in the first divine speech. What is more, the reappearance of this word in 42,3 indicates that it plays a crucial role in providing a clue as to why Job is challenged by God. Since "the root of the word (עצה) essentially refers to deliberation (careful thinking and planning and the resolution arrived at by such thinking),"[23] it is evident that the Hebrew noun refers to God's wondrous plan for this world that Job does not fully fathom.

---

[23] M.V. Fox, *God's Answer and Job's Response* (n. 7), p. 3.

The occurrence of the word in this question makes it clear that Job's approach to the nature of God solely depends on his own personal experience based on his limited wisdom that is incapable of gaining a deeper understanding and appreciation of the depth of God's plan for the universe. Job's complaints about his unprovoked suffering and challenge to God's justice are seen as legitimate since, as Job claims, his afflictions are not a consequence of his sin. Still, what is wrong with Job's thinking is that he is not aware that his knowledge is merely based on observations of only a part of the world – the part that he has experienced in his life.

Indeed, God's charge is not that Job protests against the suffering of the upright but that his words about God's dealings with the world are without knowledge. It needs to be stressed, therefore, that the primary goal of the divine discourses is by no means to denounce Job for his complaints, but to transform him by demonstrating the limits of his wisdom, which is incapable of comprehending the great design of God's creation.

Concluding Remarks: Who is the Wise Teacher?

So far it has been demonstrated how God as a teacher didactically utilizes his creation as his teaching material. To be sure, God's rhetorical questions about creation play an effective role in alerting Job to the awareness that his limited knowledge is incapable of comprehending the mystery of God's unfathomable control of the universe. As a result, God's pupil is transformed from hearing of God, to seeing God and finally to changing his mind about God (42,5-6) by gaining a deeper understanding of the complexity and the profundity of God's wondrous design for creation.

It is interesting to observe that the dramatic change of Job's mind highlights the image of Job as God's idealized pupil. In other words, in Job's final reply, especially in 42,5-6, Job is cast as an exemplary pupil who, despite severe misfortune, finally comes to recognize that God has his/her suffering under his total control. On the other hand, God's rebuke of Job's three friends in 42,7-9 implies that each of the companions is depicted as a foolish pupil who "have not spoken of God what is right" (42,7-8), an image that is in stark contrast to that of Job.

More significantly, it also needs to be pointed out that the portrayal of God as a teacher is strikingly contrasted with that of Job's companions. In the book of Job, each of the four human characters (Job's four companions) is respectively presented as a wise sage who is committed to giving instructional advice on human suffering that ironically leads the righteous sufferer to enhance his own distress. In this respect, the author of the book of Job makes it obvious that the three friends' teaching about God exemplifies an entirely mistaken approach to the nature of God. This is because they try to deal with Job's unprovoked suffering from the perspective of the traditional view of the retribution principle, which was common in educated circles of the ancient Near East. It is the author's view that a strict misapplication of the doctrine of retribution appears to be intolerable.

It may be argued, moreover, that Elihu's treatment of human suffering appears to be somewhat different from that of the previous companions. It needs to be recognized, however, that no matter what contribution Elihu makes,[24] he in the end fails to alert Job to his limitations and ignorance about God's inscrutable ways of gaining control over the cosmos. To put it another way, it is reasonable to assume that his accusation against Job appears to be nothing more than a different, but more sophisticated version of the friends' accusations. This indicates that each of Job's companions is presented as a failed sage who was not able to wisely guide Job to the right way of understanding human suffering and of knowing the character of God.

The contrast between Job and his friends makes it clear that Job is the right pupil to follow. The contrast is especially important for the text-immanent reader. Job is represented as the ideal pupil who invites the text-immanent reader to become a pupil like Job. This also implies that the text-immanent reader is urged to acknowledge his own limited wisdom that is incapable of entirely fathoming God's enigmatic power and control over chaos and the cosmos. Therefore, on the level of the characters in the text, God is a wise teacher for Job, while, on the level of the text-immanent reader, God has the same function.

Significantly, unlike the previous failed sages, God is pictured as a wise teacher in the divine speeches in which the description of inanimate and animate nature and the mythical beasts are utilized as his didactic material. His teaching method is so remarkable that he never tries to focus on any polemical dispute with his pupil, but helpfully motivates him to reflect for

---

[24] The past decades have seen a growing interest in the contribution of the four speeches of Elihu in the book of Job. There is universal agreement that one of the most significant contributions of the speeches is that they play a transitional role in paving the way for the divine speeches. For an updated analysis of the Elihu speeches, see R. ANDERSEN, *The Elihu Speeches: Their Place and Sense in the Book of Job*, in TynBul 66 (2015), 75-94.

himself what is wrong with his understanding of God's inscrutable ways of ruling over his creation. In the end, his pupil comes to the realization that God is in control of all of life's circumstances, even of his own ordeal. Job may not understand why such severe misfortune befalls him, but now he does know why he should trust God whose wisdom is unfathomable and inscrutable to him. Because of the contrast between Job and his friends, this should also be the case for the text-immanent reader. He may not understand why misfortune can befall him, but he can know why he should trust God. No one but God can teach him how to cope with his misery. God alone is the wise teacher!

THE TRIPLE-LAYERED COMMUNICATION IN THE BOOK OF AMOS AND ITS MESSAGE OF NON-APPROPRIATION THEOLOGY

Archibald L.H.M. van Wieringen
Tilburg, the Netherlands

The book of Amos is fascinating. Throughout the various parts of the text, one can observe a mix of both the Northern Kingdom as well as the Southern Kingdom being addressed. Besides these two distinct addressees, the text-immanent reader is involved as well. Because of this, I consider the book of Amos as containing a triple-layered communication, directed toward the Northern Kingdom, the Southern Kingdom and the text-immanent reader.

In my view, at all these three levels, the communication in the book of Amos deals with biblical 'non-appropriation theology', a theology which implies that man is not allowed to claim God's promises and blessing for himself.[1] In this article I wish to demonstrate the connection between the triple-layered communication found in the book of Amos and the non-appropriation theology which the book of Amos expounds. At each level of the communication, the 'non-appropriation theology' is the content of the learning situation taking place.

I will first deal with 1,1-2 as initiating the triple-layered communication which is the bearer of the non-appropriation theology. Next, I will demonstrate the triple-layered communication by giving three examples: the so-called 'Oracles Against the Nations' in 1,3–2,16[2]; the narrative in 7,10-17; and the vision in 9,1-4. In my concluding remarks, I will touch upon 9,11-15 as well.

---

[1] Concerning non-appropriation theology see also: A.L.H.M. van Wieringen, *Psalm 65 as Non-Appropriation Theology*, in *Bib* 952 (2014), 179-197.

[2] Actually, the term 'Oracles Against the Nations' is not a good indication of the content of 1,3-2,16. The term 'oracle' savours of something more like ancient Delphi instead of biblical warning texts. Moreover, the texts in Amos are more about Judah and Israel than about the nations, as we will see.

TEXT AS COMMUNICATION

Texts are not only historical documents and the object of empirical historical research. In biblical studies this type of research is almost only used to discover the historical author (or authors or redactors) of the text. Texts are rather primarily carriers of communication. They wish to communicate a message to their readers. 'Readers', however, should not immediately be understood as being historically traceable readers of flesh and blood. Texts are first of all directed to the text-immanent reader, the reader who is present within the text itself.

The distinction made between the 'text-immanent reader' and the 'reader of flesh and blood' is very important in order to understand texts in general, as well as biblical texts in particular.[3] The most famous text in the Bible demonstrating this distinction is John 20,30-31. The text-immanent author, commonly referred to by the name 'John', directly addresses his text-immanent readers: he was not able to write down everything, but what he did write down, is enough to believe that Jesus is the Christ. The text-immanent reader, who is addressed in this way, cannot do anything else but believe that Jesus is the Christ. Whether a reader of flesh and blood would react in the same way, is a totally different issue. Another example found in the Bible is Isa 7,9c-d. In the middle of the narration dealing with the meeting during which the character Isaiah calls upon King Ahaz to have confidence in God, the text-immanent author of the narrative directly addresses his text-immanent reader and calls upon him to have confidence in God as well.[4]

Textual communication is always multi-layered and more complex than in the simplified description of the examples above. Actually, three distinct communication levels exist in a text. The first communication level is at the level of the characters. Characters interact with each other on the textual stage. The second level is at the level of the textual director, called 'narrator' or 'discursor' depending on the two different types of textual worlds, namely the narrative or discursive world. For a narration, the

---

[3] See already e.g.: W. ISER, *Interaction Between Text and Reader*, in S.R. SULEIMAN – I. CROSMAN (eds.), *The Reader in the Text: Essays on Audience and Interpretation*, Princeton NJ, Princeton University Press, 1980, p. 106. See also the valuable reflection in the section *analyse narrative* by COMMISSION BIBLIQUE PONTIFICALE, *L'interprétation de la Bible dans l'Église*, in *DC* 91 (1994), 18-19. *Cf.* also: A.L.H.M. VAN WIERINGEN, *The Implied Reader in Isaiah 6-12* (BIS, 34), Leiden, Brill, 1998, pp. 2-26.

[4] I have published extensively on this issue; see e.g.: VAN WIERINGEN, *Isaiah 6-12* (n. 3), pp. 51-87.

receiver's side of this communication level is called the 'narratee'.⁵ For a discursion, the receiver's side of this communication level can be called the 'discursee'. The third communication level is at the level of the text-immanent author and the text-immanent reader. These communication instances can also be indicated by the terms 'implied author' and 'implied reader'.

This distinction between three different communication levels is useful in order to understand the multiple-layered communication in the book of Amos. All the characters act within the decor of the Northern Kingdom. The Northern Kingdom, therefore, is involved at the level of the characters. The Northern Kingdom forms the first communication level. However the Southern Kingdom is also addressed, over the heads of the characters playing their parts within the decor of the Northern Kingdom. The Southern Kingdom can therefore be considered as being the narratee or discursee. Because of this, the Southern Kingdom forms the second communication level. Finally the text-immanent reader is involved. The third communication level is focussed on the implied reader of the book of Amos.⁶

AMOS 1,1-2: INITIATING THE TRIPLE-LAYERED COMMUNICATION

The three communication levels mentioned above can be found in the first two verses of the book of Amos. Verse 1 is the heading of the book of Amos; verse 2 is generally considered as being an introduction to or summary of the book of Amos.⁷

Regarding the level of the characters, the main character is introduced in the heading: the prophet Amos. He saw words על־יישראל *about Israel*, through which the communication with the Northern Kingdom is intended. In verse 2 we see this main character acting. The decor of his acts, Bethel, is not mentioned in verse 2, but becomes visible through the continuation of the *wayyiqtol*-form ויאמר much later in the *wayyiqtol*-forms וישלח,

---

⁵ See already S. CHATMAN, *Story and Discourse: Narrative Structure in Fiction and Film*, Ithaca NY, Cornell University Press, 1978, pp. 147-151; G. GENETTE, *Narrative Discourse Revisited*, Ithaca NY, Cornell University Press, 1988, pp. 130-154. For the book of Isaiah, see A.L.H.M. VAN WIERINGEN, *The Reader-Oriented Unity Of The Book Isaiah* (ACEBT Suppl. Series, 6), Vught, Skandalon, 2006, pp. 3-7.

⁶ For a first description of the multi-layered communication in the book of Amos see also: A.L.H.M. VAN WIERINGEN, *The Prophecies Against the Nations in Amos 1:2-3:15*, in *EstB* 71 (2013), 7-19.

⁷ See also: K. MÖLLER, *A Prophet in Debate: The Rhetoric of Persuasion in the Book of Amos* (JSOT.S, 372), Sheffield, Sheffield Academic Press, 2003, p. 159.

ויאמר and ויען in 7,10-17. This is the narration about the famous clash between the character Amos and the character Amaziah, the priest of Bethel, which is the sanctuary of King Jeroboam of Israel, the Northern Kingdom.[8]

Besides the communication directed to the Northern Kingdom of Israel in verses 1-2, there is also communication with Judah, the Southern Kingdom. This second communication level does not occur at the level of the characters, but takes place at the communication-level evoked by the narrator/discursor. In the heading (verse 1), the character Amos is introduced from a Judean perspective. The toponym Tekoa, the place from where the character Amos came, is located in the Southern Kingdom of Judah.[9] Moreover, the days of the Judean King Uzziah are also mentioned in the heading, and even before the days of the Israelite King Jeroboam are mentioned.[10] This shows that the Judean perspective in the heading dominates the Israelite perspective. When the character Amos starts speaking in verse 2, he therefore first of all expresses the Judean perspective: the Lord roars, using his voice, מציון *from Zion*, and utters, using his voice, ומירושלם *from Jerusalem*.

However, the Judean perspective is not only introduced into the text as the perspective from which the Northern Kingdom will be judged, but also to involve the Southern Kingdom. Jerusalem may be the religious centre, the place from which the Lord speaks, but all the same, his voice still also judges the Southern Kingdom. The effects of the Lord's words occur on הכרמל *the Carmel*, a mountain situated in the Northern Kingdom of Israel, and in the anonymous נאות הרעים *pastures of the shepherds*. In the biblical land, these pastures are located mainly in the south of Judah. In other words, the geographical indications in 1,2 should be understood as being a so-called merism, by which the northern Carmel and the southern pastures indicate the totality of the biblical land.[11]

---

[8] See Möller, *Prophet in Debate* (n. 7), p. 159. *Pace*: M. Dijkstra, '*I am neither a prophet nor a prophet's pupil*': *Amos 7:9-17 as the Presentation of a Prophet like Moses*, in J. de Moor (ed.), *The Elusive Prophet: The Prophet as a Historical Person, Literary Character and Anonymous Artist* (OTS, 45), Leiden, Brill, 2001, p. 114.

[9] See also the Tekoa-discussion in R. de Menezes, *Amos*, in W.R. Farmer (ed.), *The International Bible Commentary: A Catholic and Ecumenical Commentary for the Twenty-First Century*, Collegeville MN, Liturgical Press, 1998, pp. 1307-1317.

[10] See: W. Schottroff, *Der Prophet Amos: Versuch der Würdigung seines Auftretens unter sozialgeschichtlichem Aspekt*, in W. Schottroff – W. Stegemann (eds.), *Der Gott der kleinen Leute: Sozialgeschichtliche Bibelauslegungen*, Vol. 1, München, Kaiser, 1977; 1979, p. 40; J. Nogalski, *Literary Precursors to the Book of the Twelve* (BZAW, 217), Berlin, De Gruyter, 1993, p. 85.

[11] See in particular P. Bovati – R. Meynet, *Le Livre du Prophète Amos* (RB, 2), Paris, Cerf, 1994, pp. 28.32.

The third communication level, the one of the text-immanent reader, is also present in the verses 1-2. In verse 1, the heading locates the text-immanent reader at a position from which he is able to look back upon the past. This position of the text-immanent reader is strengthened by mentioning הרעש *the earthquake*[12] at the end of the heading. In verse 2, the narrative does not start with a traditional ויהי, but starts as it were *in medias res*.[13] Because of the fact that the narrative has no beginning, the text-immanent reader has to do a lot of reading work: who is speaking and to whom and where? These are questions which will not be answered before 7,10. From the very beginning of the book of Amos, the text-immanent reader is therefore not audience to a narration which simply passes him by, but rather to one in which he himself is involved.

The Oracles Against the Nations in Amos 1,3–2,16:
the communication with the Northern Kingdom

At the level of the characters, eight nations are acting. The order of the statements about these nations determines the communication with the Northern Kingdom. The communication with the Northern Kingdom is manipulated by means of three climaxes.

By mentioning considerably more blameworthy deeds perpetrated by Edom, than perpetrated by the other nations in the preceding statements, Edom forms the first climax.[14] In the communication with the Northern Kingdom, this rhetorical effect calls attention to someone other than the Northern Kingdom itself, as if this were a way of saying that there is nothing wrong with the Northern Kingdom, but rather with those annoying nations surrounding the Northern Kingdom, more specifically with Edom.

The Judah-statement forms the second climax.[15] After summing-up the six surrounding small nations, the rhetorical climax to be expected is the superpower Assur. However, Assur is not mentioned after the six little neighbouring nations.[16] Instead of Assur, the Southern Kingdom of Judah

---

[12] For the discussion about the meaning of the word הרעש, see: E.W. Conrad, *Semiotics, Scribes and Prophetic Books*, in R. Boer – E.W. Conrad (eds.), *Redirected Travel: Alternative Journeys and Places in Biblical Studies*, London, T & T Clark, 2003, p. 45.
[13] W. Schneider, *Und es begab sich…: Anfänge von Erzählungen im Biblischen Hebräisch*, in *BN* 70 (1993), 64-67.
[14] See also: Möller, *Prophet in Debate* (n. 7), p. 184-185.
[15] *Cf. ibid.*, p. 192.
[16] The fact that Assur is 'missing' is hardly observed in Old Testament exegesis; see however: D. Aberbach, *Imperialism and Biblical Prophecy 750-500 BCE*, London, Routledge, 1993, p. 11.

is surprisingly mentioned. Judah is therefore presented as if it were just one of the surrounding little nations; as if there were no distinction between Damascus, Gaza, Tyre, Edom, Ammon and Moab on the one hand and Judah on the other hand.

Due to Judah being an opponent of the Northern Kingdom, the rhetorical effect is great: it is not the Northern Kingdom which is wicked, but rather the Southern Kingdom, Judah. And, considering the expression uses a *qatal*-form, i.e. a verbal form with a past perspective, אשר־הלכו אבותם אחריהם *after which their fathers have walked* (2,4), the Southern Kingdom has not only recently been wicked, but has been wicked for a long time.

Next, the third and greatest climax follows by mentioning the eighth nation: this final climax is the Northern Kingdom of Israel itself. The preceding nations appear to have only been a prelude in order to put the Northern Kingdom to shame.

The communication with the Northern Kingdom is filled with non-appropriation theology. The sequence of the nations already mentioned reveals this non-appropriation theology. The first two climaxes seem to indicate the Northern Kingdom's unassailable status: every nation, even Judah, is wicked, whereas the Northern Kingdom seems to be the only nation which could expect to receive the qualification 'good'. The opposite is however the truth: the nations mentioned actually completely encircle the Northern Kingdom. Once surrounded, the Northern Kingdom receives the real blow.

The content of the communication directed from the character Amos to the Northern Kingdom also demonstrates the non-appropriation theology. Being the people of God does not guarantee an inviolable position in the world, in which the misconduct of various nations could be considered as being an automatic justification for one's own behaviour. Instead, self-criticism is required, which can be obtained by lending ear to the prophetic call of the character Amos.

Because being the people of God and being self-critical go hand in hand, no war crimes are mentioned concerning the Northern Kingdom, but rather violations against the Torah. The exploitation of the righteous and the poor (2,6-7) is central. Whereas the Torah, as in Lev 25, especially verse 39, exhorts supporting the poor and preventing them from enslavement, the power elite of the Northern Kingdom does exactly the opposite. The אביון *poor* are the victims of injustice (*cf*: Ex 23,6). Regarding the poor, the Northern Kingdom is realising exactly the opposite of what the Lord's blessing in Deut 15,4 expresses: instead of a decrease in the number of poor, an increase in the number of poor is caused by the behaviour of the Northern Kingdom. This wickedness of the Northern Kingdom is equated with adultery (*cf.* Deut 22,13-29), cynically expressed by the subject ואיש ואביו *the man and his father* (2,7) instead of 'a father and his son', which would be the normal order in education. As a result of this, the altar and the house of the Lord are distorted into כל־מזבח *every altar* and into בית אלהיהם *the house of their gods* (2,8).

The Northern Kingdom should not think that it automatically has a positive relationship with the Lord God. Its behaviour does not correspond to the acts of God in the past. Therefore, God presents himself as a contrast in an emphatic ואנכי *but I* (2,9) and sums up his own blessings as opposed to the Northern Kingdom's transgressions. In this way, the character God acts as a teacher to the Northern Kingdom. How much their relationship has been harmed, also becomes clear from the fact that God's accusation against the Northern Kingdom is formulated by using the distant third person מפניהם *away from <u>their</u> face* in 2,9 instead of the more intimate second person מפניכם *away from <u>your</u> face*.[17]

THE ORACLES AGAINST THE NATIONS IN AMOS 1,3–2,16: THE COMMUNICATION WITH THE SOUTHERN KINGDOM

Through the communication with the Northern Kingdom, the Southern Kingdom of Judah is also addressed. The Southern Kingdom has no reason to be pleased that it is the Northern Kingdom which forms the final climax to the statements concerning the nations. First of all, the fact that the Southern Kingdom is mentioned in the sequence of the nations, indicates that the Southern Kingdom is also one of the wicked parties. Even more, it is not the superpower Assur that is mentioned after the seven small nations, but rather the Southern Kingdom, which, as it were, takes the place of Assur, suggesting that Judah is as wicked as Assur. Moreover, the Southern Kingdom is dealt with just as the preceding six surrounding nations are: the Lord mentions Judah's transgressions and announces destruction.

Concerning the content of these transgressions and the destruction which is announced, the Southern Kingdom holds a special position. The

---

[17] *Pace* among other translations AMERICAN BIBLE SOCIETY, *Good News Bible. Today's English Version*, New York NY, Harper Collins, 1976, which translates 'for *your* sake' (instead of 'for *their* sake').

transgressions distinguish the Southern Kingdom from the preceding nations; the destruction equates it with them.

The transgressions of the Southern Kingdom are not war crimes, but concern the Torah of the Lord. The relation with the Lord is at stake. It is because of this that תורת יהוה *the teaching [= the Torah] of the* LORD is mentioned in the first place (2,4).[18] The Southern Kingdom is warned because, instead of being led by the *teaching of the* LORD and חקיו *his statutes*, it has been led by כזביהם *their own lies* (2,4). The word כזב *lie* is used to characterise the false prophets especially in Ez. 13: the false prophets only see lies and they prophesy based upon these lies, disguised as a נאם יהוה *utterance of the Lord*.[19] The warning against the Southern Kingdom, therefore, can be understood as a warning about not having listened to the prophets, but, instead, about listening to the false prophets; a warning about not having listened to the words of the Lord God, but, instead, about listening to their own words as if they were God's words.

In contrast to the Northern Kingdom, for which no punishment is announced, at least suggesting that it will escape without punishment, the Southern Kingdom undergoes the same punishment as the six preceding nations: a devouring fire. This fire is meant to destroy Jerusalem, the religious centre, from which the character the Lord God is acting.

This implies that the content of the communication to the Southern Kingdom also deals with non-appropriation theology: being the people of God does not mean that self-criticism is unnecessary. A critical look at one's own behaviour is required to prevent becoming like the superpower Assur. Self-criticism means that the Southern Kingdom should not listen to smooth talk, which is actually nothing else but lies, but rather to real prophets, like the narrator/discursor of the book of Amos, who is, therefore, acting as a teacher to the Southern Kingdom.

THE ORACLES AGAINST THE NATIONS IN AMOS 1,3–2,16:
THE COMMUNICATION WITH THE TEXT-IMMANENT READER

It is remarkable that, in 'the Oracles Against the Nations', the Lord addresses no one; he only speaks *about* the nations, not *to* them, not even to the Northern or Southern Kingdom. This situation changes in 2,10

---

[18] Even if the word תורה in 2:4 does not yet have the strictly technical meaning 'Torah', this does not alter the verse's communicative meaning.
[19] See also: MÖLLER, *Prophet in Debate* (n. 7), p. 192.

because of the introduction of a second person plural, which becomes visible by using an emphatic אתכם *you*. This means that the addressee of 'the Oracles Against the Nations' is not formulated before 2,10.[20] Because of the fact that the direct speech by the Lord runs as far as verse 16 and the second person plural is also present in the verses 11, 12 and 13, the verses 10-16 form a separate unit within 'the Oracles Against the Nations'.

Up to 2,10, the text-immanent reader has an ambivalent position. On the one hand, he is kept at a distance because of the narrative start of the book of Amos, using a third person in the verbal foreground form ויאמר in 1,2. On the other hand, he is involved by the lack of textual information about the addressee(s) the character Amos is speaking to in his direct speech starting in 1,2, and about the addressee(s) the Lord God is speaking to in the various statements in 1,3–2,9: the text-immanent reader is forced to think.

This situation of direct speeches without containing an explicit addressee changes in 2,10. For the first time, an addressee is formulated: אתכם *you*. The text-immanent reader can be recognized in this second person plural. This interpretation is evoked by the fact that the second person plural is first of all anonymously introduced in the text. The plural 'you' is everyone whom the speaking Lord brought out from Egypt through the desert to the promised land. Even more, these acts are continued by the Lord in calling some of their sons to be prophets or Nazirites, expressed in the text as מבניכם *of your sons* and ומבחוריכם *of your young men*. Not before this elaboration, is this general 'you' identified as the בני ישראל *sons of Israel* in verse 11d.

After this address to the general 'you' in the verses 10-11, concluded by the formula נאם יהוה *utterance of the Lord* in verse 11e, the address to the 'you' is continued in another form. In 2,12-16, neither the first person singular (= the Lord) nor the second person plural (= the 'you') occur as a separate personal pronoun. In the 'you' in 2,12-16, the presence of the text-immanent reader has decreased (without being directly marked by syntactic signs).

In 3,1-2, a second person plural occurs as well. While 2,10 indicates to whom the Lord was speaking, 3,1 indicates to whom the character

---

[20] See also: MÖLLER, *Prophet in Debate* (n. 7), p. 206. *Pace*: D.A. KNIGHT, *Tradition and Theology in the Old Testament* (BiSe), Sheffield, Sheffield Academic Press, 1990, 269; F. FÖRG, *Beobachtungen zur Struktur von Amos 2,6-12*, in *BN* 132 (2007), 13-21, p. 13.

Amos is speaking, namely to the בני ישראל *sons of Israel*, an expression which can be used to indicate the whole of God's people (Israel and Judah). In that case, the neutral expression ויאמר *and then he said* in 1,2a actually appears to be a serious communicative ויאמר לכם *and then he said to you*, a communication not at the level of the characters, but at the level of the text-immanent reader.

The warning to the 'you' in 2,10-16 concerns the rejection of the prophets. This means that the content of the communication to the 'you' runs parallel to what was communicated to the Northern Kingdom of Israel and to the Southern Kingdom of Judah. In other words: the communication at the level of the characters (Northern Kingdom – communication level 1) and at the level of the narratee/discursee (Southern Kingdom – communication level 2) is extended to the level of the text-immanent reader (the 'you' in verse 10a – communication level 3).

This implies that the same non-appropriation theology also goes for the text-immanent reader: listening to God in order to reach the promised land does not go along with ignoring God after having entered into the promised land. This means that the text-immanent author acts as a teacher to the text-immanent reader, teaching him about the non-appropriation-theology.

The narrative in Amos 7,10-17:
the communication with the Northern Kingdom

I would like to demonstrate the connection between the triple-layered communication found in the book of Amos, and the book's non-appropriation theology, using a second example, i.e. Amos 7,10-17.

At the level of the characters, the well-known narrative in 7,10-17 takes place with the decor of the Northern Kingdom of Israel as a back-drop. The sanctuary of Bethel is represented as the most important sanctuary of the Northern Kingdom, because the King himself is the owner of this sanctuary: it is a temple of the Kingdom (verse 13). The decor of the Northern Kingdom is strengthened by the movements of the character Amos. The character Amaziah wishes the character Amos to go to the land of Judah (verse 12), which implies that the narrative is located outside the land of Judah. The character Amos claims that the Lord has commissioned him to go to the people of Israel (verse 15), which is the reason for his move to the land of Israel, the Northern Kingdom. The setting within the Northern Kingdom is further strengthened by mentioning King

Jeroboam (the Northern King) by name. The contact between the priest Amaziah and King Jeroboam reveals their fear for Amos' words,[21] which actually are the words of the Lord God.

In the context of the Northern Kingdom, the announcement of the exile refers to the Assyrian exile. Amaziah lets King Jeroboam know that Amos foresees an exile taking place during Jeroboam's reign (verse 11), but Amos himself is rather less explicit about the exact moment this exile will take place (verse 17).

The communication in the narrative in 7,10-17 in fact deals with a theology of non-appropriation. At the level of the characters, this theology becomes visible with both of the main characters Amaziah and Amos. Amaziah appropriates the sanctuary for himself. The temple of Bethel is therefore described as being a sanctuary of the King, i.e. the Kingdom of Jeroboam, not of the Lord God (verse 13).[22] In Amaziah's self-appropriation of the sanctuary, there is neither place for a seer/prophet, nor is there place for a messenger from God in Bethel. This type of appropriation is rejected in the narrative.

The character Amos is also connected to a theology of non-appropriation. Before the narrative in 7,10-17, three visions are recounted in 7,1-9. In the first two visions, the character Amos takes the initiative in addressing the Lord, having shown him grasshoppers and fire, to prevent the Lord from destroying Israel (7,2.5). Amos' intercession makes the Lord repent (7,3.6). In the third vision, in contrast to the first two visions, the Lord takes the initiative in addressing Amos, showing him an instrument of destruction (7,8).[23] Amos therefore has no defence. He cannot self-appropriate the possibility of intercession. The Lord's conclusion is that he will destroy Isaac's high places, Israel's sanctuaries and Jeroboam's house (7,9). Although exile appears to be inevitable, the character Amos cannot appropriate this exile by claiming the exact moment at which the

---

[21] For the intelligence report sent by Amaziah to Jeroboam, see: DIJKSTRA, *Amos 7:9-17* (n. 8), pp. 116-119. *Cf.* concerning the verb שלח as a possible *verbum dicendi* and the absence of the so-called *Botenformel* also: S.A. MEIER, *Speaking of Speaking: Marking Direct Discourse in the Hebrew Bible* (VT.S, 46), Leiden, Brill, 1992, 121.281. *Cf.* also: H.J. STOEBE, *Noch einmal zu Amos VII 10-17*, in *VT* 39 (1989), 345-346; P.R. NOBLE, *Amos and Amaziah in Context: Synchronic and Diachronic Approaches to Amos 7-8*, in *CBQ* 60 (1998), 428-431.

[22] *Cf.* also: I. JARUZELSKA, *State and Religion in the Light of the Book of Amos and Hosea*, in M. AUGUSTIN – H.M. NIEMANN (eds.), *"Basel und Bibel": Collected Communications to the xviiith Congress of the International Organization for the Study of the Old Testament, Basel 2001* (BEAT, 51), Frankfurt, Lang, 2004, p. 162.

[23] For אנך = *instrument of destruction*, see S. BERGLER, *"Auf der Mauer – auf dem Altar": Noch einmal die Visionen des Amos*, in *VT* 50 (2000), 456-460.

exile will be implemented. It is not the historical dates of the exile which are at the centre of interest, but rather Amaziah's damaged relationship with Amos and, therefore, with God. Besides using the image of adultery, this damage is expressed in, for example, the exile.

THE NARRATIVE IN AMOS 7,10-17:
THE COMMUNICATION WITH THE SOUTHERN KINGDOM

Through the communication with the Northern Kingdom, a communication with the Southern Kingdom also arises. This communication is realised through the description of the sanctuary. If the word בית־אל *Bethel* is not understood as being a topographic proper name, but as a description meaning *house of God*, the narrative takes place in the House of God instead of in the city of Bethel. As a descriptive expression, בית־אל *house of God* indicates the temple in Jerusalem (1 Ki 8,6; 2 Ch 23,4.15.17.18). Further, the sanctuary is called מקדש־מלך *sanctuary of the King* (verse 13). This expression is unique in the Hebrew Bible. The word מקדש is never combined with the word מלך, but always with an expression indicating the Lord God (Num 19,20; Jos 24,26; 1 Ch 22,19; Ps 73,17; Lam 2,20; Eze 48,10). This suggests that the word מלך can be understood as an indication for the Lord God, which occurs elsewhere in the Hebrew Bible (1 Sam 12,12; 1 Ch 16,31; Jer 10,10; Eze 20,33; Zeph 3,15; Zech 14,9; Mal 1,14; and very often in the Psalms), especially in the book of Isaiah where God is called מלך *King* in 6,1 even before introducing several other kings.[24]

Against this background, Amaziah's title כהן בית־אל is also interesting. This title can be translated both as *a priest of Bethel* and *the priest of Bethel*. Because the word כהן is used in *status constructus*, an article cannot be used. In view of Amaziah's direct access to the King, the second translation is obvious here. As a result of this, a parallelism with the title הכהן *the high priest* (Ex 31,10), used for the main priest in Jerusalem, arises.

Due to this ambiguous decor of Bethel / the House of God, the rejection of the self-appropriation of the sanctuary of the Lord King concerns both the Northern Kingdom of Israel (Bethel) and the Southern Kingdom of Judah (Jerusalem).

---

[24] VAN WIERINGEN *The Book Isaiah* (n. 3), p. 134.

This implies that the threat of exile is transformed from the Assyrian exile (Northern Kingdom) to the Babylonian exile (Southern Kingdom). Whereas the character Amaziah uses the proper name Jeroboam in verse 11, the character Amos does not mention this name in verse 17. He only uses the proper name ישראל *Israel*, which is actually ambiguous because of the fact that it can indicate both the Northern Kingdom of Israel as well as the entire people of God, Israel and Judah.[25]

The narrative in Amos 7,10-17:
The communication with the text-immanent reader

The text-immanent reader is primarily present at the open end of the narrative. The prophet Amos announces the end of Israel by mentioning the exile (the verses 16-17). The exile, which Amaziah wants to impose upon Amos, is inverted, becoming an exile for the house of Jeroboam and for Amaziah himself. However, the narrative breaks off abruptly (verse 17).[26] The two main characters are opposed to each other; but what comes next, after both of them have spoken their direct speeches, remains untold. Exactly because of the fact that the threat of destruction and exile is not realised within the narrative, the threat still exists as a continuous open end. Therefore, the text-immanent reader has to deal with this open end. Because of the open end of the narrative, the threat of destruction remains existing at the level of the text-immanent reader. The impending threat of exile affects the text-immanent reader as well.

Against this background, some elements in the text have to be considered anew. The sanctuary has not only changed from a shrine in the Northern Kingdom to the temple in the Southern Kingdom, but also from a historically identifiable sanctuary during the monarchy, to the Jerusalem temple whenever. The text therefore becomes a warning against self-appropriation in general.

This also implies that the threat of the destruction and of the exile is continued. The Assyrian exile was followed by the Babylonian exile; a new exile cannot be excluded. The broadening of the meaning of the word ישראל *Israel* from the perspective of the communication with the narratee/

---

[25] See Van Wieringen, *Amos 1:2-3:15* (n. 6), p. 15.
[26] *Cf.* also K. Jeppesen, *'The Lord God has spoken, and who will not prophesy?'*: From Osee to Jonas in the Septuagint, in C. McCarthy – J.F. Healey (eds.), *Biblical and Near Eastern Essays* (FS K.J. Cathcart), London, T & T Clark, 2004, p. 109.

discursee (the Southern Kingdom) is continued at the communication level of the text-immanent reader.

This implies that the text-immanent author still acts as a teacher to the text-immanent reader, whereas the relation towards the Northern Kingdom and the Southern Kingdom cannot be described in terms of teaching. The focus of the text, therefore, is on the text-immanent reader, so as to learn about exile in order to avoid any possible future exile.

Against this background, an element in the answer of the character Amos to the character Amaziah's order to leave the Northern Kingdom becomes interesting. Amaziah commands Amos to go to ארץ יהודה *the land of Judah* (verse 12). In reaction, Amos does not say that he was sent to the <u>land</u> of Israel, but to עמי ישראל *my (= the Lord's)* <u>people</u> *of Israel* (verse 15). Amos' mission is not connected to a piece of land, i.e. the Northern Kingdom, but rather to a people, suggesting the entire people of the Lord God is concerned.

THE VISION IN AMOS 9,1-4:
THE COMMUNICATION WITH THE NORTHERN KINGDOM

To illustrate the connection between the triple-layered communication in Amos and its warning against the self-appropriation of God's blessings, I will give a third example, i.e. Amos 9,1-4.

The fifth vision in 9,1-4 can be considered as a continuation of the narration in 7,10-17. In the vision, the words מזבח *altar*, כפתור *lintel* and סף *threshold* occur, indicating a sanctuary. The מזבח is the liturgical centre of a sanctuary. The כפתור and סף form a merism, indicating the entire building.[27]

The description of the anonymous altar and the supposed sanctuary runs parallel to the description of the sanctuary in the narration in 7,10-17. This means that, at the communication level of the characters, i.e. the communication with the Northern Kingdom, the sanctuary has to be identified with the Bethel shrine. Just one word in 9,1-4 makes this identification explicit: in verse 3 the toponym כרמל *Carmel* is used, a mountain situated in the Northern Kingdom.

---

[27] See also: A. SCHART, *The Fifth Vision of Amos in Context*, in P.L. REDDIT – A. SCHART (eds.), *Thematic Threads in the Book of the Twelve* (BZAW, 325), Berlin, De Gruyter, 2003, 49-51.

Amos sees the Lord standing upon the altar.[28] A deity never stands upon the altar, but always resides inside the inner room of a temple (the so-called 'holy of holies'). The altar is never located inside the inner room, but always outside the inner room, out in the open air, in view of the sacrifices made upon the altar. If something is standing upon the altar, the altar can no longer be used for sacrifices. Seeing the deity standing upon the altar means that the deity has moved outside and that the altar has fallen out of use.[29] The character Amos will not have had in mind that the deity of the Bethel sanctuary has moved from the inner room to the altar in order to destroy the altar and, subsequently, put an end to the sacrifices, as well as raze the entire sanctuary-complex. The character Amos, according to 1,1-2 coming from Tekoa in the Southern Kingdom of Judah, and speaking the words of the Lord, who is located in Zion/Jerusalem, sees the Lord God standing upon the altar in Bethel. The character Amos would therefore understand that the Lord God has come from Jerusalem to Bethel in order to destroy the entire sanctuary-complex of King Jeroboam itself and to put an end to its liturgical function.

Normally, the altar should be a safe haven, to which one can flee to be subsequently rescued by the deity. The horns of the altar are a symbol of this refuge (*cf.* 1 Ki 1,50-53; Ps 119,27). However, the altar cannot be appropriated. In Amos' vision, the altar is not the starting point of rescue by the deity, but rather of destruction by the Lord.[30]

In verse 4 the threat of exile is even increased. Even if the people are deported into exile, the wrath of the Lord God will pursue them. The exile is in itself not reason enough for God not to show his power to the people that appropriated a sanctuary for themselves.

THE VISION IN AMOS 9,1-4:
THE COMMUNICATION WITH THE SOUTHERN KINGDOM

The vision seems to be favourable for the Southern Kingdom, for in it the Lord God is apparently on a punitive expedition from Zion/Jerusalem to punish the Northern Kingdom. However, parallel to the ambiguity

---

[28] The Hebrew proposition על normally means *upon*. The translation *besides* weakens the frightening image of the vision; *pace* e.g.: KJV.
[29] About the altar, the inner room, and the deity, see also: SCHART, *Fifth Vision of Amos* (n. 27), p. 49.
[30] See also: H. SCHÜNGEL-STRAUMANN, *Gottesbild und Kultkritik vorexilischer Propheten* (SBS, 60), Stuttgart, Katholisches Bibelwerk, 1972, p. 74.

regarding the sanctuary in 7,10-17 (Bethel and/or the temple in Zion/Jerusalem), the sanctuary involved in 9,1-4 can be identified with the temple in Zion/Jerusalem as well. There are some semantic clues which support this identification.

In Ex 25,31-40; 37,17-24, the word כפתור is used for one of the aspects of the sanctuary in the desert / in Jerusalem, viz. the lampstand. The word סף occurs in the description of Solomon's temple (1 Ki 7,50; 2 Ch 3,7), of Jehoash's restoration work at the temple (2 Ki 12,13), of Josiah's reformation (2 Ki 22,4; 23,4; 2 Ch 34,9), and of the entrance-guards (1 Ch 9,19.22). In the prophetic literature the word סף is always connected to the Lord's temple in Zion/Jerusalem (Isa 6,4; Jer 35,4; 52,19.24; Eze 40,6.7; 41,16; 43,8; Zech 12,2).[31]

More important than separate words, is the fact that the only combination of seeing God and a temple-building in the Hebrew Bible takes place in Jerusalem in the temple, regarding the prophet Isaiah in Isa 6.[32] Because of the role of the מזבח in Isa 6,6, the character Isaiah is located at the same place as the character Amos in Amos 9,1. Whereas the prophet Amos sees the Lord standing upon the altar, the prophet Isaiah sees the Lord sitting upon a throne (Isa 6,1). While the prophet Amos' vision is about the Lord planning destruction, the prophet Isaiah is aware of the fact that his vision could lead to destruction (Isa 6,5). In contrast to what should be expected by seeing the Lord, Isaiah's vision gives him liberation from his sins (Isa 6,7).

This not only implies that the temple in Zion/Jerusalem is also involved in Am 9,1-4, but also that the increased threat of exile can be applied to the Babylonian exile as well.

THE VISION IN AMOS 9,1-4:
THE COMMUNICATION WITH THE TEXT-IMMANENT READER

At the level of the communication with the text-immanent reader, the anonymity of the sanctuary is of importance. Because of its anonymity,

---

[31] There is only one single exception: Zeph 2,14.
[32] For the parallel between Am 9,1-4 and Isa 6 and its consequences, see: BERGLER, *Auf der Mauer – auf dem Altar* (n. 23), 457.469; M. KÖHLMOOS, *Amos 9,1-4, Jerusalem und Beth-El: Ein Beitrag zur Gerichtsverkündigung am Kultort in der Prophetie des 8. Jhs.*, in AUGUSTIN – NIEMANN, *Basel und Bibel* (n. 22), pp.173-174. *Cf.* also W.H. SCHMIDT, *Die prophetische "Grundgewissheit": Erwägungen zur Einheit prophetischer Verkündigung*, in P.H.A. NEUMANN (ed.), *Das Prophetenverständnis in der Deutschsprachigen Forschung seit Heinrich Ewald* (WdF, 307), Darmstadt, WBG Verlag, 1979, p. 543, who considers Am 7,

every sanctuary can be read into the vision in 9,1-4. The text is, therefore, not limited to the Northern or Southern Kingdom during the time of the monarchy, but to the Lord's temple whenever.

Although the text-immanent reader is not addressed directly, the anonymous opponents could be identified with anyone. The possibility that everyone can be meant is supported by the extension of the decor to all the earth's extremities, represented in two pairs ordered chiastically: the Sheol below and the heavens above (verse 3), and the summit of Mount Carmel above and the bottom of the sea below (verse 4). This extension also becomes visible in the following verses 5-6:[33] the earth and all its inhabitants (whom the text-immanent reader can consider himself as being one of) are at issue here. No-one can appropriate anything.

In this way, the text continues the learning situation of 7,10-17 and gives the text-immanent reader, although not directly present in the text, the main position in this learning process.

Concluding Remarks

The so-called Oracles Against the Nations in 1,3–2,16, the narrative in 7,10-17 and, in its wake, the fifth vision in 9,1-4 have a communicative function at three levels: regarding the Northern Kingdom, regarding the Southern Kingdom, and regarding the text-immanent reader. In all three communicative situations, the self-appropriation of God's words and of God's sanctuary is opposed. Neither the Northern Kingdom nor the Southern Kingdom and not even the text-immanent reader are allowed any self-appropriation whatsoever. The communication of the book of Amos carries a message of non-appropriation theology at all these three communication levels.

In this way, at three levels, a learning process about the non-appropriation theology can be found. The main focus in this learning process is the text-immanent reader, who is taught the non-appropriation theology in order to avoid any possible future exile.

The book of Amos pushes this to extremes. Even non-appropriation itself cannot be self-appropriated. The threat of exile, which is mentioned

---

10-17 and the so-called *Verstockungsauftrag* in Isa 6 to be parallel.

[33] *Cf.* for the position of the verses 5-6 in relation to the verses 1-4 also: A.W. PARK, *The Book of Amos as Composed and Read in Antiquity* (Studies in Biblical Literature, 37), New York NY, Lang, 2001, p. 49; *cf.* from a semantic point of view also: E. ZENGER, *Einleitung in das Alte Testament* (Kohlhammer Studienbücher Theologie, 1,1), Stuttgart, Kohlhammer, 1995, p. 390.

as an expression of the prohibition of any self-appropriation by the people of God, and, which is in the course of the book of Amos, even extended to the people of God in any place at any time, is also subject to a theology of non-appropriation. The impending destruction is itself 'destroyed' at the conclusion of the book of Amos in 9,11-15. The collapsing temple and the ruins of David's tabernacle, once fallen, are inverted by the building of a new[34] and modest building: a hut (9,11),[35] without any allusion to the divided kingdoms. Neither the Northern Kingdom nor the Southern Kingdom is in focus, but rather a new future coming after the exile.[36] The exile of God's people will be turned into a being re-planted on their own ground without any threat of a new exile (the verses 14-15).

---

[34] Concerning the aspect 'new', see also: A.L.H.M. VAN WIERINGEN, *The Theologoumenon "New": Bridging the Old and the New Testament*, in B.J. KOET – S. MOYISE – J. VERHEYDEN (eds.), *The Scriptures of Israel in Jewish and Christian Tradition* (FS M.J.J. MENKEN) (NTS, 148), Leiden, Brill, 2013, 285-301.

[35] *Cf.* also J.D. NOGALSKI, *The Problematic Suffixes of Amos IX 11*, in *VT* 43 (1993), 411-418.

[36] J.D. NOGALSKI, *Literary Precursors to the Book of the Twelve* (BZAW, 217), Berlin, De Gruyter, 1993, p. 105.

MULTIPLE TEACHERS AND DISCIPLES IN MT 8-9

Solomon PASALA
Hyderabad, India

INTRODUCTION

Matthew chapters 8-9, which narrate ten miracles, form a unit. To an ordinary reader, these miracles reveal the type of person Jesus is, how he heals the sick, relates with the poor and the needy and how he takes care of the downtrodden of society. In addition, he is also presented as a Teacher (8,19), responding and clarifying the questions and doubts of different groups of people (9,4-17). Underlying these external relationships, there is a text-immanent author communicating with the text-immanent reader, who is also known as the *Model Reader*.[1] These two (the text-immanent author and the text-immanent reader) have a teacher-disciple relationship. This relationship is effectuated in different ways. It could be through the usage of the words, the grammatical forms or structures, or the way the events have been arranged.[2]

In the present article, we would like to show the relationship between the immanent author and the immanent reader mainly from the point of the use of 'imperative' and 'indicative' moods. Secondly, we would further like to demonstrate how the events narrated in these two chapters are interconnected as a 'Drama', which brings out the discourse aspect of the events narrated, in order to show how the Teacher-disciple relationships are in focus.

---

[1] According to Howell, there are two levels of information in a text; the level of the story and the discourse. On the level of the story, characters act, speak. On the level of the narrative, however, the narrator gives information that only a model reader is allowed to know. The different levels have their own temporal sequence and are related to one another by plotting devices used to tell the story. *Cf.* D.B. HOWELL, *Matthew's Inclusive Story, A Study in the Narrative Rhetoric of the First Gospel* (JSNT.S, 42), Sheffield, JSOT Press, 1990, p. 97.

[2] S. PASALA, *The "Drama" of the Messiah in Matthew 8-9* (European University Studies Series, 23), Bern, Peter Lang, 2008, pp. 67-71.

Construction of the Model Reader through Imperatives

To communicate his message convincingly, the author uses different strategies. In Matthew chapter 8 and 9, where ten miracles are narrated, one can notice the importance the author[3] gives to the conversations or the dialogues. In a dialogue, where two or more partners are involved, there should be a question and an answer, a command and an implementation of that command or a request and a granting of the request[4]. In our two chapters, one can observe the special emphasis given to the usage of imperative and indicative moods and words like 'to follow' while using these dialogues (8,1.10.19.22.23; 9,9.19). The following are some examples.

1. The usage of Imperatives in Mt 8-9

[Mt 8,1-4] In this dialogue between Jesus and the leper, the request is in the subjunctive mood: *Lord, if you will...*, and the response is in the indicative mood: *I will, be clean*.

In the next step, Jesus takes initiative and gives four commands (imperatives) to the leper:

> *See that you say nothing to any one;*
> *but go, show yourself to the priest,*
> *and offer the gift that Moses commanded, for a proof to the people.*

However, we should take note that there is no report about the response to these commands.

[Mt 8,5-13] In the dialogue situation between Jesus and the Centurion, after the initial request and a response, there is an extended dialogue, which is not necessary, because the request has been granted. The centurion diverts from the main topic of healing and speaks about 'authority'. This he explains through *a slow motion* of words, repeating the same reality in different words:

---

[3] It is important to note which author we mean, when we say 'author'. There is the 'real' author, who wrote the work, and there is the 'text-immanent author'. We refer to the latter one, who is present in the text. *Cf.* PASALA, *The "Drama" of the Messiah* (n. 2), pp. 65-66. *Cf.* U. ECO, *Overinterpreting Text*, in S. COLLONI (ed.), *Interpretation and Overinterpretation*, Cambridge, Cambridge University Press, 1992, p. 66.

[4] PASALA, *The "Drama" of the Messiah*, (n. 177), pp. 23-27. In Conversational Analysis (CA), which is a method followed by ethno-methodologists, they speak about how a dialogue is guided by certain rules and principles. So much so, that even the silence of a dialogue partner can be interpreted. *Cf.* S.C. LEVINSON, *Pragmatics*, Cambridge, Cambridge University Press, 1983, p. 279; M.B. PAPI, *Che cos'è la pragmatica*, Milano, Bompiani, 1993, p. 271.

I say to one,	*'Go,'*	*and he goes,*
and to another,	*'Come,'*	*and he comes,*
and to my slave,	*'Do this,'*	*and he does it.*

Here, the author's focus is not only to explain the meaning of authority but also to explain the type of authority Jesus has. According to this formula, the one who has authority gives orders and uses *imperatives* and the servant or the one under authority obeys commands and his response is expressed in the *indicative* mood. Secondly, every command should have a corresponding action to show that the authority has been acknowledged and the command obeyed. The reason for *slow motion* is to offer more time to the reader, asking him to take note of the rules of the narrative. When we come to the discourse aspect of these passages, we will better understand the function of this dialogue.

[Mt 8,18] This dialogue takes place between Jesus and the crowd. Jesus gives an *order*, which is equivalent to an imperative, *to go over to the other side*, but there is no corresponding action or response. Regarding the rules established above, that for every command there should be a response, we should take note that in this case there is a lack of response on the part of the crowd.

[Mt 8,19-20] In the dialogue between a scribe and Jesus, it is important to note the use of the title "Teacher" (διδάσκαλε 8,19) by the scribe, who offers to *follow* Jesus, *where ever he goes*. Jesus' response, at first sight, does not correspond to the request (8,20).[5] Perhaps Jesus here acts rather like a Zen master, giving his disciple time to reflect.

[Mt 8,21-22] In this dialogue between Jesus and his disciple, the disciple uses an imperative in addressing Jesus: *Lord first <u>let me go</u> and bury...* (ἐπιτρέπω verb in the imperative 8,21). In response, Jesus uses two imperatives: *<u>follow me</u>, and <u>let the dead bury</u> the dead* (ἀκολουθέω and ἀφίημι 8,22). Each one commands the other.

[Mt 8,25] This dialogue takes place between the disciples and Jesus on the lake. The disciples use an imperative in their request of Jesus: *Lord, save,* (σῶσον) (8,25). Jesus' response is *Why are you afraid, O men of little faith?* (8,26), which again seems not to be the appropriate response to the request.

[Mt 8,26] In the next step, Jesus gave a *command* to the wind and the sea and the response is reported by saying that *there was a great calm* (8,26).

---

[5] In a dialogue situation, when the response does not correspond to the request, we should understand that there is something wrong in the request. It is our common experience that only the dialogue partners will understand better each other in the given context.

Here, the author takes extra effort to report the reaction of the men. They say *even wind and sea obey him* (RSV).[6]

[Mt 8,28-34] In this dialogue, which takes place between the demoniacs and Jesus, the demoniacs command Jesus in their request: *If you cast us out, send us away into the herd of swine* (ἀπόστειλον ἡμᾶς 8,31). In response, Jesus also uses an imperative: *Go* (ὑπάγω 8,32).

[Mt 9,3-5] This dialogue takes place between the scribes and Jesus, when the scribes accuse Jesus of *blaspheming* (9,3). In Jesus' response there are three verbs: *Your sins are forgiven, rise and walk* (9,5). Jesus gives two options to prove his authority: in the first option, the verb is in the indicative mood (Ἀφίενται), in the second option, the verbs are in the imperative mood (Ἔγειρε καὶ περιπάτει).

[Mt 9,6-7] In this dialogue, Jesus uses the second option to prove his authority and therefore he commands the paralytic: *take up your bed and go home* (αἴρω and ὑπάγω). While the activity of Jesus is expressed in the imperative (9,6), the response of the paralytic is expressed in the indicative mood (ἀπῆλθεν 9,7).

[Mt 9,9] In the next dialogue between Jesus and the tax collector, Jesus commands Matthew: *Follow me*. (ἀκολουθέω, the verb is in the imperative); Matthew's response is indicated in two verbs in the indicative (*rose* and *followed*: ἀνίστημι and ἀκολουθέω).

[9,30] After the calling of Matthew, the dialogue situation between Jesus and the two blind men, besides others, is noteworthy. There are two imperatives in 9,30, where Jesus sternly orders them *See that no one knows it* (RSV translation of Ὁρᾶτε μηδεὶς γινωσκέτω). Contravening these commands, we have a narrative voice reporting in the indicative mood that they did indeed do what had been prohibited (9,31).

2. Some observations

Let us take Mt 8,5-13 as our starting point. In this episode, we come across words like 'authority', 'order', 'command', 'faith' and above all a special usage of imperatives and indicative moods in the form of *slow motion* to give more time to the reader, asking him to pay attention to what is being said. As we know, this extra dialogue with the specific use of these words has nothing to do with the healing of the servant. If that is the case, what is the focus of the immanent author?

---

[6] The word ὑπακούω, has been translated as *to listen, to adhere, to obey, subject to* and so on. W. BAUER, *A Greek-English Lexicon of the New Testament and Other Early Christian Literature*, Chicago, MI, Univ. of Chicago Press, 1979, 2nd ed., p. 837.

For our purpose, let us replace the word 'authority' or the one who gives orders, with 'Teacher' and the one who 'obeys' the orders, with 'Disciple'. According to this text, it is usually the Teacher, who commands and not the disciple. The role of the disciple is to listen to the Teacher, which can be understood as willingness to learn. A follower or disciple should have the aptitude of openness to listen to the Teacher and learn from him. Only when there is openness to the Teacher, does a disciple acquire knowledge. Though the words used in this regard appear to be of 'military' discipline, there is a close relationship between the centurion and his servant, which is close to that of a 'father-son' relationship. If there had been no such relationship, the centurion would not have come in person to plead for his servant.[7] This openness leads towards deeper relationships and the communion of persons. We could call this type of relationship a 'Teacher-Disciple' relationship. Let us look into other episodes and dialogue situations from this perspective.

In 8,18, when Jesus gives an order to the crowd, which is depicted as following (8,1) him, there is, however, no response. In view of the narrative rules, when a command is obeyed, it is reported.[8] This is therefore an indication that, at this stage, there is no Teacher-Disciple relationship between Jesus and the crowd.

On the other hand, in the dialogue between the scribe and Jesus (8,19-20), the scribe rightly calls him the 'Teacher' and offers to follow Jesus *wherever he goes*. At this self-offer, Jesus' response should be *come and join*. Instead, his response does not correspond to the request, which is a sign that there is something wrong about this self-offer by the scribe.

Interestingly, in the next dialogue, his disciple commands the Teacher to permit him *to go away* or turn away (ἐπιτρέπω verb in the imperative 8,21) from following Jesus, to bury his father. Instead of giving permission, Jesus, the Teacher, uses two imperatives to show what a disciple should do.

---

[7] The word παῖς has different meanings such as servant, child or son. BAUER, *A Greek-English Lexicon of the New Testament* (n. 6), p. 604. There is also a theological significance for this word. While showing the immanent reader in the text, Van Wieringen argues that Abraham offered his son Isaac as 'the servant' and thus he becomes 'his son'. *Cf.* van A.L.H.M. VAN WIERINGEN, *The Reader in Genesis 22,1-19*, in *EstB* 53 (1995), 289-304.

[8] This idea will be made clear, when we come to the next part, where we speak of 'Drama' or the discourse aspect of the narrative.

In the scene of the tempest, the disciples use an imperative instead of a subjunctive (8,25) in their request. If the author has used the subjunctive mood to express a request by the leper (8,2), why does he not do the same in both the case of the disciple who wants to bury his father (8,21) and of the disciples in the boat (8,25)? It appears that he uses the imperatives purposely to communicate the attitude of the disciples or the followers. In the same episode, the use of the word ὑπακούω, which means *to obey* or *to listen*, by the men in the boat (8,27), could be an indication that a transformation is taking place and they are beginning to recognize what is expected of them.

In the next episode, which takes place at the tombs with the demoniacs (8,28-34), the demoniacs use an imperative in their request. Jesus uses another imperative to grant their request. The outcome is death and destruction (8,32). This scene helps the model reader to understand what happens to a disciple when he does not obey, or decides for himself and acts as he wants.

In the next dialogue situation, when Jesus gives two commands to the paralytic (9,6-7), there is a positive response to these commands. The response is expressed in the indicative mood to show that what has been commanded has been fulfilled. Jesus the Teacher uses commands (imperative mood) and the paralytic does as he is commanded (indicative mood).

In the call of the tax collector (9,9), this type of relationship is further re-established. Jesus the Teacher uses the imperative with regard to the tax collector Matthew, commanding him *to follow*, and Matthew implements the command.

In the call of Matthew, we have a model reader or a text-immanent reader. As a model reader he tells that a disciple is the one who is in relationship with the Teacher and who is able to understand and accept what is being communicated.

However, we agree that not everything has been clarified with our explanation. Above all, the presence of 'disobedience' in 9,30-31 raises questions. How do we explain this disobedience to Jesus' command towards the end of the unit?

CONSTRUCTION OF THE MODEL READER FROM THE DISCOURSE ASPECT

To better understand the text-immanent reader who is present in the text, we have called upon the assistance of 'Drama' or the discourse aspect of the narrative.[9] According to Aristotle's description,[10] drama is a representation of an action, where the emphasis falls, not so much on the magnitude of the work, but rather on the completeness of the work. A complete work has three parts: a beginning, middle and end. These three parts are not independent units but consequences that flow one from the other.

In contemporary thinking, scholars[11] follow the subdivision of drama into different *moments* such as exposition, inciting moment, complication, climax or turning point, resolution or transforming action, denouement and the final situation.[12] In doing so, they give more emphasis to the 'discourse' aspect of the drama, where plot emerges with clarity. Therefore, while taking into consideration different moments of the drama, it is possible to keep to the three-part division proposed by Aristotle.

1. Mt 8,1-17: Exposition of the drama

The exposition is the presentation of indispensable pieces of information about the state of affairs that precede the beginning of the action itself. The function of the exposition is to provide the reader with the background information about the setting, about the characters and their relationship

---

[9] In this article, our main concern is not to show that there exists a dramatic structure in these two chapters. This we have already demonstrated in our book. *Cf.* PASALA, *The "Drama" of the Messiah* (n. 2), pp. 96-99. However, here I will provide the basic information necessary to understand our discourse.

[10] ARISTOTLE, *Poetics*, in R. MCKEON (ed.), *The Basics of Aristotle* (Modern Library Classics), New York NY, Random House, 1941, § 7: *We have laid it down that tragedy is a representation of an action that is whole and complete and of certain magnitude, since a thing may be a whole and yet have no magnitude. A whole is what has a beginning and middle and end. A beginning is that which is not a necessary consequent of anything else but after which something else exists or happens as a natural result. An end on the contrary is that which is inevitably or, as a rule, the natural result of something else but from which nothing else follows, a middle follows something else and something follows from it. Well constructed plots must not therefore begin and end at random, but must embody the formulae we have stated. Cf.* PASALA, *The "Drama" of the Messiah* (n. 2), pp. 96-97.

[11] Here, I refer to Ska, and Chatman. *Cf.* PASALA, *The "Drama" of the Messiah* (n. 2), pp. 96-97; J.L. SKA, *'Our Fathers Have Told Us'. Introduction to the Analysis of Hebrew Narratives* (SubBi, 13), Rome, GB Press, 1990, pp. 21-25; *Cf.* S. CHATMAN, *Story and Discourse. Narrative Structure in Fiction and Film*, Ithaca NY, Cornell Press, 1978, pp. 9 and 19-37.

[12] *Cf.* SKA, *'Our Fathers'* (n. 11), pp. 20-21; Also, according to Marguerat and Bourquin, there are five divisions: 1) initial situation or exposition; 2) complication; 3) transforming action; 4) denouement and 5) final situation. *Cf.* D. MARGUERAT – Y. BOURQUIN, *Pour lire les récit bibliques*, Paris, Cerf, 1998; Eng. tr. *How to Read Bible Stories*, London, SCM Press, 1999, pp. 40-44.

(who, what, and where). Eventually, it should give a key to understanding the narrative.[13]

The narration in our two chapters begins with the cleansing of a leper (8,2-4), the healing of a pagan centurion's servant (8,5-13) and the healing a woman (8,14-15). After narrating three miracles (8,1-15), there is a change of the rhythm and tone where a summary statement is inserted (8,16) and a quotation from the prophet Isaiah is given (8,17). By means of this quotation, the author gives a twist[14] to the entire narration.

In chapters 5-7, Jesus is presented as the 'Teacher with authority' (7,28-29).[15] The same theme is continued in chapter 8-9 but now from a narrative perspective. The centurion certifies Jesus as the man of authority (8,5-9), in continuation of what has been said at the end of chapter 7 (7,28-29). He further clarifies what it means to have authority (8,9). According to his explanation, the orders of the man of authority have to be obeyed. In the given context, the orders mean listening to and accepting the teachings of Jesus. Now Jesus has to prove his authority as a Teacher.

2. Mt 8,18–9,17: Complication of the drama

In dramatic terms, the word 'complication' refers to all the moments of dramatic action, in which there is narrative tension and suspense, and as to how the initial problem is solved, whereby one draws nearer to the truth.[16]

---

[13] *Cf.* SKA, *'Our Fathers'* (n. 11), pp. 21-25. This last point, namely that 'exposition provides a key', is very important for our purpose. In the episode of the centurion (8,5-13), we have a key to understand the narrative. As we have said earlier, we find extra information about the meaning of authority and the servant. We will see how this key will be used in the episode of the paralytic.

[14] In historical-critical or redactional studies, these types of insertions are often understood as *glosses* or *redactional insertions* and as such they are neglected. In Sheeley's view, they are addressed to the audience directly and they have a bearing on the major thematic plot devices. These asides often intensify the events in their context, thus adding impetus to the movement of the plot. *Cf.* S. M. SHEELEY, *Narrative Asides in Luke-Acts* (JNST.S, 72), Sheffield, 1992, pp. 19,148. M. Tenny also asserts that these explanatory comments, interjected into the running narrative of the story, are intended to illuminate or to explain how some important statement should be understood. *Cf.* M. TENNY, *The Footnotes of John's Gospel*, in *BSac* 117 (1960), 350.

[15] As for our understanding, Mt 4,23-9,37 forms a unit with two main parts: 'Halakhah' (5-7) and 'Aggadah' (8-9). They are considered to be two sides of the same coin. *Cf.* PASALA, *The "Drama" of the Messiah* (n. 2), pp. 268-279.

[16] *Cf.* SKA, *'Our Fathers'* (n. 11), pp. 25-26.

2.1. *The complicating episodes in the second part*

In the second part of the drama (8,18–9,17), there are six scenes which constitute complication. To unify all these events, except in the first episode (8,18–22), the author has used the phenomena of questions (8,26.27.29; 9,4.5.11.14.15) not only to demonstrate the complicated nature of this section but also to project Jesus as the Teacher, who has to prove himself as 'Teacher' by answering these questions.

In this section (8,18–9,17), Jesus encounters different groups who have problems in understanding him and in accepting him as the Teacher.[17] The scribe addresses Jesus as teacher (διδάσκαλε 8,19) and offers to follow him wherever he goes (8,19; *cf*. 5,20), but Jesus says that he has no place to go (8,20). One of his disciples wants to *turn away* to bury his father, but Jesus orders him to follow (8,21-22). In the scene of the tempest, the prayer of the disciples, *save us Lord*, is described as 'littleness' of faith (8,26). After the healing of the Gadarene demoniacs (8,28-34), the townspeople throw Jesus out of their territory instead of asking him to stay with them. In the scene of the paralytic (9,1-8), when Jesus forgives sins (9,2; *cf*. 1,21), the scribes call it a blasphemy and they question his authority.[18] Further, the Pharisees question his eating with sinners and the outcastes of the community (9,9-13)[19]. And finally, the disciples of the Baptist also come to interrogate Jesus as to why His disciples do not fast (9,14-17). Therefore, in all these episodes we can perceive how the identity of Jesus as the Teacher is tested. Given so many questions, how does Jesus prove his authority as the Teacher?

2.2. *Dramatic moments in Mt 8,18–9,17*

In encountering different groups of people, our focus will be on how the author creates the dramatic tension, and in doing so, how he constructs his model reader at the discourse level, so that the real reader can come closer to the truth about Jesus, the Teacher.

---

[17] In Qumran literature, the messiah is treated as a Teacher of the law and mediator of God's will. His role may be compared to that of the Teacher of Righteousness. *Cf*. M. DE JONGE, *Messiah*, in *Anchor Bible Dictionary*, Vol. 4, New York NY, Doubleday, 1992, p. 783.

[18] They contest because according to their understanding, this authority is reserved only to God (Ex 34,6-7; Ps 25,18; 32,1-4; Isa 43,25) and it is performed only on the day of *Yôm kippûr* through a complex ritual (*cf*. Lv 4-5; 16). According to the scribes, in the act of forgiving, Jesus is taking for himself the prerogative reserved to God.

[19] When the Pharisees interrogate Jesus about eating with sinners, they have a problem with the teacher who associates with them, and not with the righteous (*cf*. 5,20).

2.2.1. Mt 8,18-22 as inciting moment

The first episode (8,18-22) begins with a *command* by Jesus *to go to the other side* (εἰς τὸ πέραν 8:18)[20]. This command is directed to the crowd, which is depicted as following him (8,1). However there is no report about the implementation of this command. According to the rules of the narrative, the authority of Jesus as a Teacher is not accepted at this stage, as expressed in 8,9. Instead, there is a scribe who comes up with a good proposal to follow him *wherever he goes* (8,19) and a disciple, who wants to *return* home (8,21). Though it is not clear what exactly the problem is with these two requests, Jesus' response does not give the impression that he is happy with them (8,19-22). In view of the key provided in the first part of the drama (8,5-13), a disciple, while addressing his master as *Lord* should not give him orders. If Jesus is a Teacher with authority (διδάσκων αὐτοὺς ὡς ἐξουσίαν ἔχων *cf.* 7:29) and if a man of authority commands obedience (*cf.* 8,9), his disciple should listen to him. However, in this episode, the disciple does not want to listen to his teacher, but rather, he wants his teacher to listen to him. We could say that they do not yet know him and that they do not yet know what it means to be a disciple.[21] We can say that there is ignorance on the part of those who want to be his disciples. This ignorance constitutes the *inciting moment*.[22]

2.2.2. Mt 8,23-9,1 as preparatory scenes for the climax

With no obedience having been given to his command, in the next scene, Jesus himself gets into the boat *first*, followed by his disciples (8,23). The disciples' reaction to the danger at sea makes the reader realize what the problem was with the request of the scribe, who stated that he would follow Jesus *where ever he goes*. Now on the sea, when faced with mortal danger, instead of trusting their Lord and Teacher, they command

---

[20] In my opinion εἰς τὸ πέραν (8,18) is a technical term, which reappears in 9,2 as διεπέρασεν. Besides referring to the geographical situation, it recalls the people of Israel 'crossing over' the Reed-sea, and 'crossing over' the river Jordan. It is only in this context that Jesus' order becomes significant.

[21] According to Sternberg, if there is no ignorance there is no conflict, and if there is no conflict, there is no plot. *Cf.* M. STERNBERG, *Poetics of Biblical Narrative*, Bloomington IN, Indiana University Press, 1985, pp. 172-179.

[22] The inciting moment is the moment at which the conflict or the problem appears for the first time and arouses the interest of the reader. Often it is the 'what' of the exposition of the story. In many cases, it is difficult to distinguish it from the exposition or the complication. *Cf.* SKA, *'Our Fathers'* (n. 11), p. 25.

him (see the imperative σῶσον in their request). With this background in mind, the reader is enabled to notice the ignorance of the 'followers'[23] in the boat (8,23). With Jesus' act of calming the sea, the disciples slowly begin to recognize who he is and why they need to obey his orders (see the presence of the word ὑπακούω in the reaction of the disciples in 8,27, which confirms the matter of obedience as being the problem).

In the scene of the Gadarenes (8,28–9,1), the focus is on the demoniacs and their dialogue with Jesus. They not only use the imperative (*send us*, ἀπόστειλον ἡμᾶς) in their request, but they also decide upon their destiny. Jesus' response consists of just one word Ὑπάγετε, in the imperative. The result is that the demoniacs and the herd of swine are destroyed. These two scenes make the followers realize who Jesus is and what happens to them if they do not obey his orders. Because of this, we call these two episodes *preparatory scenes* for the climax.[24]

2.2.3. Mt 9,2-8 as the turning point or the climax

If what have gone before are preparatory scenes, then there must be a reaction in the next scene (9,2-8). The reader can notice the reaction of the people in the act of the carrying of the paralytic (9,2).[25] The central issue in this episode is whether Jesus has authority or not (9,3-5). If we wish to understand and appreciate the dramatic tension and the beauty of the argument, we need the help of the model reader, who is a textual construct. As we have noted before, in the miracle of the centurion's servant, the author has taken extra time to explain the relationship between the authority (Teacher) and the servant (disciple) and how this relationship is equated with having faith (8,9-10).[26] According to this argument, a Teacher's authority necessarily invites acceptance of his teaching, and

---

[23] It is also important to note the use of the word *to follow*, which helps the text-immanent author to construct the text-immanent reader.

[24] To heighten the narrative tension and prepare the climax of a narrative, the Bible also uses 'preparatory scenes'. *Cf.* SKA, *'Our Fathers'* (n. 11), pp. 25-26.

[25] It is important to take note of the word διεπέρασεν, which is used in 8,18. It is not just a geographical shore that they cross, but they do so also in the biblical sense (see note 20). By using the same expression at this point, we are shown the continuity of the narrative flow and the construction of the text-immanent reader. Jesus, therefore, does not need any information about the man who is brought to him, not even a request for healing.

[26] The centurion, after acknowledging the authority of Jesus to heal his servant from afar (8,8), in the next step goes on to explain what it means to have authority. According to him, authority by its very nature commands obedience (8,9). In the third step, Jesus synthesizes this understanding between authority and obedience as faith (8,10).

to accept a Teacher means to have faith in him. In short, faith is manifested in the act of acceptance or obedience.

With this in mind, the scene of the paralytic receives a dramatic tension. According to the above understanding (8,9), the authority of Jesus can be proved only if someone obeys him. Jesus' command has already been disobeyed in 8,18. Will Jesus take another opportunity to prove his authority? Yes, he will, because he has seen a sign of change in the act of the carrying of the paralytic (9,2). Therefore, when Jesus gives a command to the paralytic to get up and walk (9,6b see the imperatives), there is a positive response (9,7), whereby he proves his authority.

There is a trick in the argument and the author kills two birds with one stone. While proving the authority of Jesus, the emphasis equally falls on the realization and the insight gained by the people (9,2). For in obeying Jesus' command, the paralytic demonstrates his knowledge about Jesus and his authority. In other words, he has faith in Jesus. Because the paralytic has obeyed the command of Jesus, he has proved not only Jesus' authority but also his own new insight into the identity of Jesus and his faith in him. The presence of the word περιπατέω in 9,5, which is a technical term in dramatics,[27] is a sign that there is drama in these two chapters and a *turning* has taken place in the drama.

2.2.4. Mt 9,9-17 as the final suspense

To offer further confirmation that a turning has taken place, in the next episode the author introduces the calling of Matthew. The calling is presented in the imperative mood *follow me* ('Ακολούθει μοι) and the response is in the indicative mood: *he got up and followed him* (ἠκολούθησεν αὐτῷ 9:9). By this stage, the disciple has learned to obey his Teacher. By inserting the calling of Matthew at this stage of the drama, the author of Matthew demonstrates the continuity of the theme from the previous scenes and the thematic development. The character Matthew, who got up and followed Jesus, is not only a real person but also a model reader, who has followed what has happened so far. To follow Jesus or

---

By faith, we mean a relationship of total trust, which leads towards the communion and transformation of persons.

[27] Classically, the word *peripeteia* is used to mark the "turning point" or the "climax" of a story or a drama. It can be the moment of greatest tension, or the appearance of a decisive element or character. In a plot of action, the resolution is called *peripeteia*. It is the change from one state of affairs to its exact opposite. In a plot about gaining knowledge or discovery, the resolution is the passage from ignorance to knowledge. *Cf.* S. CHATMAN, *Story* (n. 11), p. 85.

become his disciple, one should know him. In the case of Matthew, we hear about him for the first time in the Gospel of Matthew. So the reader can have legitimate doubts. It is in this context that the text-immanent reader comes to our aid to help us make sense of it all. Here the character Matthew represents the text-immanent reader, who has followed all that has happened so far and who is in the position to respond to Jesus' command. In immediately getting up and following Jesus, he demonstrates the change that has taken place in the dramatic action. By the use of the word *to follow* at this juncture, we can also see the continuity with the theme of discipleship. In responding to the call, Matthew enters into a Teacher-Disciple relationship.

However, after the turning point, the author introduces another two groups of people with another two questions in order to prolong the suspense of the drama.[28] The Pharisees address Jesus as *Teacher* (διδάσκαλε) and they ask why he eats with sinners (9,11). In Jesus' answer (9,12-13), which consists of three sentences, there is a logical development. In the first place, there is the universal truth about the need of the sick for a doctor. In the second step, quoting the prophet Hosea, Jesus throws a challenge in the form of an imperative: *go and learn* (πορευθέντες δὲ μάθετε τί ἐστιν· ἔλεος θέλω καὶ οὐ θυσίαν· οὐ γὰρ ἦλθον καλέσαι δικαίους ἀλλὰ ἁμαρτωλούς).[29] For Hosea, YHWH's essential quality is mercy and fidelity and it surpasses human mercy and sacrifices (*cf.* Hos 1-6)[30]. Based on the above propositions, Jesus affirms in the final sentence, that in line with YHWH, he has come (on a mission) for sinners. Jesus' choice for sinners is an unmerited gift for the sinners. God's merciful action is manifested in the calling of a sinful man named Matthew, whose name signifies a 'gift of God'. With this, Jesus manifests not only his new teaching, but also his teaching authority.

By introducing the disciples of the Baptist with another question, the dramatic suspense takes another twist. In the previous episode, the problem was 'why' with regard to the sinner. In this episode, the question is 'how' sinners can be saved without fasting or good works.[31] In Jesus'

---

[28] According to Ska, between the climax and the final conclusion, there can be a moment of delay or retardation (final suspense). *Cf.* SKA, *'Our Fathers'* (n. 11), p. 28.

[29] The use of the imperative *learn* at this juncture is very fitting because it explains and summarizes the meaning of the word *obedience* as a learning process. Once again, in this episode, Jesus manifests his teaching authority.

[30] For further details please see. PASALA, *The "Drama" of the Messiah* (n. 2), pp. 185-195.

[31] The presence of τότε in 9,14 helps us understand the consequential nature of the previous argument A.H. McNeile argues that Matthew's use of τότε as a connective particle to introduce a subsequent subject or event, represents the force of *"waw"* consecutive

answer, which consists of more than seventy five words, there are some symbolic images, which need to be interpreted in the right perspective in order to get the point.

In the answer of Jesus, fasting is not totally abolished for the disciples (cf. 4,2; 6,16-18) but rather it is postponed to a *future* event, namely till the death of the Bridegroom (ὅταν ἀπαρθῇ ἀπ' αὐτῶν ὁ νυμφίος 9:15).[32] By recalling the covenantal symbols[33] like 'old', 'new', 'wine', 'wineskins' and 'cloth' (cf. Gen 3,7; 9,15-27; Jos 9,4-27; Eze 16,1-63, Hos 2,9-10) the author may be indicating the Last Supper (see the presence of καινός in 9,17 and 26,29), where Jesus will offer his blood as the sign of the new covenant for the forgiveness of sins (26,20-35). After his death, Jesus, by calling his disciples 'my brothers' (28,10), will manifest his forgiveness[34] concretely for those who have negated and betrayed him. This means that his disciples will be forgiven or saved, not because of their fasting, but by Jesus' merciful action. In short, in answer to the question as to how his disciples are saved without fasting, Jesus' reply is once again the same and a continuation of what was said before quoting Hosea. It is not because of their fasting or sacrifices that sinners are saved, but by the merciful action of Jesus on the cross, which illumines or saves sinners. In other words, Jesus the Teacher is the one, who lays down his life for his disciples and not the one, who demands their life for his sake. His love and mercy have the power to transform the disciples. All that they need to do is to be open to him, listen to him and enter into a loving relationship with him.

---

in Hebrew idiom. *Cf.* A.H. MCNEILE, Τότε *in St. Matthew*, in *JTS* 12 (1911), 127-128, p. 127.

[32] When the Baptist says that he is not worthy to touch his sandals, he makes a reference to Jesus as the Bridegroom upon whom the Spirit has descended in the form of a dove (3,16). Jesus, by speaking about his violent death as a Bridegroom (9,15), recalls the levirate law, which says that when a man dies without leaving children, his brothers must take up the widow to raise the children for the dead brother (Deut 25,5-10). In a way, this reference prepares for the future action of Jesus, who will call his disciples 'my brothers' (28,10).

[33] R. Meynet in his article on Luke 5,17-6,11, which is a parallel text to that of Mt 9,1-17, says that all these symbolic expressions have something to do with the covenantal theme. *Cf.* R. MEYNET, *A vino nuovo, otri nuovi!*, in *StRBS* 13 (2002) 1-27, pp. 24-27; repr. in R. MEYNET, *Il vangelo secondo Luca* (ReBib, 7), Bologna, EDB, 2003, 2nd ed., 229-255.

[34] According to Meynet, the description of the disciples as 'my brothers' recalls the forgiveness granted to Cain, who killed his brother (Gen 4,1-16) and the forgiveness granted by Joseph to his brothers, who sold him into slavery (Gen 45,4-5; 50,20). *Cf.* R. MEYNET, *Morto e Risorto secondo le Scritture*, Bologna, EDB, 2002, p. 51.

Now the reader is in a better situation to understand why the author has prolonged the complication by introducing two more interlocutors. If Jesus was identified as a Teacher with authority (7,28-29; 8,8-9), the last two episodes explain the type of Teacher Jesus is. If in the inciting moment the problem was ignorance about the Teacher, towards the end of the second section the reader has an answer.

2.3. *Mt 9,18-34: Resolution or the final situation of the drama*

If in the second part of the drama (8,18–9,17) ignorance is removed, then in the final part one must see the results. Accordingly, we have three other scenes (Mt 9,18-34) where the results are demonstrated.[35] As it has been noted by Luz, in the final section (9,18-34), there are particular and remarkable linguistic and thematic reminiscences of 8,1-9,17[36]. It is also possible to see how the author has worked out different moments in the third or the final part of the drama.

2.3.1. Mt 9,18-26 as resolution

If resolution is the solution to the initial problem,[37] then in the final part, we have a solution. In the leader (ἄρχων) who comes to Jesus, we have a man who recognizes in Jesus, a Saviour (ζάω or σῴζω: 9,18.21.22). He is similar to the leper and the centurion as to the aspects of kneeling and imploring (*cf.* 8,2.5), but he is different in his request (9,18). He requests salvation for his daughter who has died (9,18; *cf.* Mark 5,23; Luke 8,42).[38]

In a similar way, the woman with a haemorrhage is presented as a model or paradigm of faith (9,22; *cf.* 8,11).[39] In spite of the hopelessness of her

---

[35] The function of the final part of the drama is to show the results or the consequences of the main action in the central part. The consequential nature of this section can be seen from the way the author has depicted the action of Jesus in the central part and in the final part. While in the central part, it was Jesus who takes the initiative (*cf.* 8,18.23.28; 9,1.9-10), in the final part it is the leader, the woman and the people (9,18.20.27 and 32) who take the initiative to go to Jesus.

[36] *Cf.* U. Luz, *The Miracle Stories of Matthew 8-9*, in *Studies in Matthew*, Grand Rapids MI; Cambridge, Eerdmans, 2005, pp. 221-242, esp. p. 225.

[37] The resolution is the solution to the initial situation. It is a transforming action, which aims at removing the difficulty or the disturbance announced by the story. The transforming dynamic action can consist of a particular action or a long process of change. *Cf.* Ska, 'Our Fathers' (n. 11), pp. 27-30.

[38] Klostermann sees in the words of Jairus an incredible faith. *Cf.* E. Klostermann, *Das Matthäusevangelium* (HNT, 4), Tübingen, Mohr, 1927, 2nd ed., p. 82.

[39] M. Grilli, *Vangelo secondo Matteo*, in V. Mancuso – P. Pellezari (eds.), *La Bibbia Piemme*, Bologna, EDB, 1995, pp. 2326-2327.

suffering, she *lays* all her burden on Jesus in the symbolic gesture of touching Jesus' garment (9,20-21; see the mention of garments in 9,16-17). She is seeking not just physical healing, but an encounter with the Messiah, who can save her (*cf.* 1,21). For this reason, in this section we do not find words of healing (καθαρίζω 8:2.3, ἰάομαι 8:8.13, θεραπεύω 8:7.16) as in the first section, but rather words like ζάω or σῴζω (9,18.22), by which Jesus comes to be accepted as the Saviour. The use of these words indicates a changed situation.[40]

2.3.2. Mt 9,27-31 as denouement

In the episode of two blind men in 9,27-31, we come across the words *to follow* (9,27) *faith* (9,28) and two imperatives: *See that no one knows it* (Ὁρᾶτε μηδεὶς γινωσκέτω 9,30). As we have noted before, there is something strange in the use of these imperatives: the first one is in the second person plural and the second one is in the third person singular. Usually the imperatives are in the second person singular or plural, but by using γινωσκέτω in the third person singular while addressing the people who are present, we are asked to pay attention to this word and its use. The problem with this command is that the blind men, who are depicted as *following Jesus* (ἠκολούθησαν 9,27), disobey the commands of Jesus after receiving their sight. If up until now we have stated that there is a gradual development of the theme of learning, their disobedience at this stage makes our arguments null and void. In other words, if we have maintained that the disciples in the course of the drama have learned to obey the Teacher, why this disobedience towards the end of the drama?

The purpose of the third part of the drama is to indicate the results or the transformation that has taken place as a result of Jesus' action.[41] If that is the case, the function of this episode is to show what the outcome of this drama is, or what type of transformation has taken place in the life of the disciples. In their cry to Jesus *have mercy on us, Son of David*, the two blind men manifest a renewed understanding about Jesus as a merciful Teacher (*cf.* 9,11-13), who can forgive their sins (9,14-17). The result of their faith is not merely *sight* but rather *insight*[42] about Jesus.

---

[40] In the view of Luz, in a narrative, *courses of events are presented in such a way that an initial situation gives way to a changed final situation. Cf.* LUZ, *The Miracle Stories* (n. 36), p. 226.

[41] PASALA, *The "Drama" of the Messiah* (n. 2), pp. 233-261.

[42] Here, the sight that the blind men have received is not merely physical 'sight' but above all it is 'insight' (see the presence of the word γινώσκω in 9,30), which could

Therefore, they cannot keep it hidden, just like the light (*cf.* 5,14-16).[43] Hence, the disobedience in this case becomes a symbol of *denouement*,[44] in which the effects of salvation are manifested in their life (*cf.* Isa 52,13; 53,11).

Therefore, the disobedience to the command of Jesus in this episode should not be considered as disobedience, but rather as a positive development of what happens to a disciple when he/she enters into a filial relationship with Jesus (9,2). Jesus does not take away the disciples' freedom, but he rather enhances it. They are filled with the light, which cannot be hidden.[45] This disobedience of the two blind men, when compared to that of the leper in 8,4, demonstrates the difference. The leper was cured of his disease, but he did not become Jesus' disciple. On the contrary, the two blind men, because of their faith, come to be transformed and they cannot keep their knowledge hidden. Hence they go and proclaim the Good News about Jesus, their Teacher. In short, the disciples have become 'teachers'.

2.3.3. Mt 9,32-34 as conclusion

In the episode of the dumb (and deaf) demoniac (9,32-33), the dumb and deaf are not only those who cannot speak and hear (11,5; 12,22) but figuratively they are people "without knowledge" (*cf.* Deut 29,3-4; Wis 10,21). If, in the previous miracle narrative, the sight the two blind men have received is compared to light or wisdom, then, wisdom opens their mouths. The last miracle, in the form of healing the deaf and dumb demoniac, completes this process of the final stage of the drama.[46] Thus the outcome of the drama is connected to next phase of the narration, where the twelve are nominated and are instructed to be sent out to

---

be compared to light or wisdom. The 'light' is a fundamental concept of divine revelation. The light is identified with peace and prosperity and the salvation of men. *Cf.* B. MARCONCINI, *I canti del servo*, in B. MARCONCINI *et al.* (eds.), *Profeti e Apocalittici* (Logos 3), Torino, Leumann, 1994, 275-294, p. 285.

[43] PASALA, *The "Drama" of the Messiah* (n. 2), pp. 250-256.
[44] The literal sense of the word 'denouement' means untying or precipitating the final action, where the mystery is solved or the understanding becomes clear. *Cf.* SKA, *'Our Fathers'* (n. 11), pp. 27-30.
[45] In the view of Grasso, an encounter with Jesus cannot be hidden. *Cf.* S. GRASSO, *Il ciclo dei miracoli*, in *RB* 54 (2006), 159-183, p. 180.
[46] The final situation is a type of conclusion to the narrative and contains the results and the sequels. It describes the effects of the transforming action on the people concerned, or the way in which the situation is re-established. *Cf.* SKA, *'Our Fathers'* (n. 11), pp. 28-29.

preach (Mt 10,5). Thus, in the course of the drama, the *Teacher with authority* (7,28-29) has transformed his followers (8,1), who have learned to obey him (9,9) as teachers and preachers (10,5).

Conclusion

In the above pages, we have seen how the immanent author has constructed his immanent reader. Firstly, we saw how the immanent author built up his model reader through the use of imperatives and indicative moods. Consistency and connectivity may be found in all this. To give further confirmation, we studied the same matter from the discourse aspect of the 'Drama'. In both cases, there is a gradual development of the theme. It begins with the ignorance of the disciples concerning the Teacher. The Teacher takes initiative and begins the process of educating and transforming those who follow him (8,1.23.27). In the calling of Matthew, we have a text-immanent reader, who follows the instructions of the text-immanent author. By getting up and following Jesus without any hesitation, he demonstrates the continuity of the discourse. The next two episodes, further explain in depth, the teaching authority of Jesus.

Hence, we could call Matthew, the tax collector, a model reader, because, he has followed the instructions of the text-immanent author and understood what has happened so far and is now in a position to respond to the call. In other words, the tax collector Matthew, whom we encounter, is not simply a man who got up and followed Jesus without knowing who Jesus is, but the text-immanent reader who knows what it means to follow him. He follows Jesus with determination, knowing who Jesus is and what type of Teacher he is. That is the reason why the response is instantaneous and without hesitation. Thus by repeating the 'imperatives' and the dramatic structure, the immanent author has beautifully constructed his immanent reader in these two chapters.

Though we have translated the word ὑπακούω with *obedience* or *openness*, it should be understood as a type of filial relationship, based on mutual trust and confidence, which leads to the communion of persons. The commands of Jesus which are in the imperative mood, should be taken in this sense: as an invitation to the disciple or the reader to open himself/herself up to a greater reality. Only an open-minded attitude will help a disciple to learn and to grow towards deeper communion with the Teacher, and thus in turn become a teacher (Mt 28,20).

MULTIPLE COMMUNICATION LAYERS AND THE ENIGMA OF THE LAST JUDGMENT (MATT 25,31-46)

Lauri Thurén
Joensuu, Finland

Different layers of interaction pose a challenge for understanding the stories told by Jesus. He addresses his hearers, typically disciples, antagonists, or Galilean people at the textual level. By telling about this, the evangelist persuades his own recipients. Within the story, the characters speak to each other. Beyond the text, the historical Jesus may have delivered a different tale. In front of the text, modern pastors address their congregations based on the story. Each communicator delivers a different message, prompted by different exigencies.

One text, the reading of which suffers from confusion as a result of these many communicative layers, is the narrative about the judgment in Matt 25,31-46. In addition to Jesus and his hearers, the text includes at least 14 different individuals or groups interacting on at least 6 different levels.[1] In addition, there are various historical and theological meta-levels to be considered.

In this contribution, I identify the various levels of communication in Matt 25,31-46 and ask how Matthew[2] and his protagonist use them in their argument. This enables us to understand the message and function of the story as story and within its context. The historical and hermeneutical problems remain outside the reach of my methodology. However, focusing on the textual level may also yield material for these perspectives. In the first part, Traditional Interpretations, some common ways of reading the story will be discussed. In the second part, Interaction at the Textual Level, I will scrutinize it by using modern narratology and argumentation analysis.

---

[1] For a closer description, see below Figure 4.
[2] I use the traditional name without taking a stand on the identity of the historical author.

Traditional Interpretations

The complex narrative has given impetus to a large number of interpretations.[3] Below, I discuss three main perspectives before suggesting a new approach.

1. The Dogmatic Reading

In churches, but also in academia, soteriological interests have dominated the interpretation of this text as Jesus appears to reveal the basis by which people are eventually doomed either to eternal punishment or eternal life. The story attracted the early fathers: in the East, John Chrysostom, for example, refers to it hundreds of times;[4] in the Western liturgical tradition, it is often connected to the Last Sunday,[5] resulting in numerous attempts to find mercy within the story.

The dogmatic reading consists of two levels only: in the text, Jesus is informing his disciples, us, or any reader about the forthcoming judgment (II). Beyond this message one can assume a higher ideological viz. theological level (I), where the conditions of salvation are defined.

FIGURE 1. DOGMATIC INTERPRETATION OF MATT 25,31-46

Level	Sender	Recipient	Genre
I	God	Any reader	Theology
II	Jesus (many aliases)	Any reader	Prophecy

Using the story as a source for theological information involves three challenges. First, it fails to mention Jesus, God, Heaven, Hell, Christians,

---

[3] In Matthew, only the Sermon on the Mount has been examined more often. S.W. Gray, *The Least of My Brothers: Matthew 25:31-46, A History of Interpretation* (SBLDS, 114), Atlanta GA, Scholars, 1989, presents essential interpretations of the story starting from the fathers of the third century. D.A. Hagner, *Matthew 14–28* (WBC, 33B), Nashville TN, Thomas Nelson, 1995, pp. 737-739, lists 40 important academic articles. See also G.N. Stanton, *A Gospel for a New People: Studies in Matthew*, Louisville KY, Westminster John Knox, 1993, pp. 207–209; K.R. Snodgrass, *Stories with Intent: A Comprehensive Guide to the Parables of Jesus*, Grand Rapids MI, Eerdmans, 2008, pp. 551-552; and U. Luz, *Matthew 21–28* (Hermeneia), Minneapolis MN, Fortress, 2005, pp. 267-274. The variety of religious interpretations is even wider.

[4] Snodgrass, *Stories* (n. 3), p. 562, finds 400 references, Luz, *Matthew 21–28* (n. 224), p. 272, only 170 cases.

[5] For example, in Finland since 1686 (XIV §VI), see O. Kurvinen, *Evankeliumikirjan synty ja sisällys* (STKSJ, 54), Helsinki 1951, p. 48.

Church or Jews, not to speak of *diakonia*. Thus, a substantial re-interpretation is required, which should not, however, be allowed to distort the story. Secondly, as the text contains so many characters discussing with each other on various communicative levels, dogmatic explanations have tended to conflate them. The characters are forced to interact across their boundaries. For example, despite recognizing a "puzzling change" of identity in the protagonist from the Son of Man to a king in verses 31 and 34,[6] these two characters are usually seen as one person, who moreover is identical with Jesus, the shepherd and the judge.[7] However, the narrator must have had a reason for using so many different characters instead of one. In order to solve the puzzle, each character should be studied in his or her own right.

The third challenge comes from the story itself. The religious or ideological reading of Matt 25,31-46 presupposes a transcendent communicative level, where God reveals to the readers how and on what basis the last judgment will take place. Since the story leaves little soteriological leeway, it has inspired numerous ingenious attempts to shift it in a more merciful direction. For this purpose, external aid has been brought in from other gospel passages, Paul, or from the early fathers.

Popular religious attempts to soften the exacting message of the story include the following: although good deeds guarantee salvation, they cannot be regarded as a matter of human merit because they are created by God himself;[8] one should refer to Jesus' deeds, not to one's own; and good works will only be counted if they are forgotten. According to Calvin, good deeds but witness of prior election.[9] Accordingly, one may argue that since the sheep and the goats are born like that, human beings

---

[6] W.F. ALBRIGHT – C.S. MANN, *Matthew* (AB, 26), Garden City NY, Doubleday, 1971, p. 306; R. SCHNACKENBURG, *Matthäusevangelium* (Die neue Echter Bibel), Vol. 2, Würtzburg, Echter, 1987, p. 248; J. GNILKA, *Das Matthäusevangelium*, Vol. 2, Freiburg, Herder, 1988, p. 372.

[7] *Ibid.*, p. 377, not only identifies Jesus with the king and the judge, but uses a conglomerate expression "Völkerhirte". See also J. SCHNIEWIND, *Das Evangelium nach Markus und Matthäus* (NTD, 1/1), Göttingen, Vandenhoeck & Ruprecht, 1937, p. 247; F.V. FILSON, *A Commentary on the Gospel according to St. Matthew* (BNTC), London, Black, 1960, p. 266; HAGNER, *Matthew* (n. 3), p. 743; and LUZ, *Matthew 21–28* (n. 3), p. 264, according to whom the "World Judge" is "designated as 'king'". According to a more precise description, the king is a metaphor for the Son of Man (C. MÜNCH, *Der Hirt wird sie scheiden Mt 25,32f*, in R. ZIMMERMANN (ed.), *Kompendium der Gleichnisse Jesu*, Gütersloh, Gütersloher, 2007, pp. 504-509, esp. p. 504).

[8] For example J. SCHNIEWIND, *Markus und Matthäus* (n. 7), p. 247, referring to John 3,21 and Acts 10,35.

[9] LUZ, *Matthew 21–28* (n. 3), p. 273.

are also, therefore, predestined to their eternal fate. In a Lutheran vein, the whole story can be counted as law, only to be annulled by the gospel.[10]

Even academic scholars have strived to alleviate the harsh soteriology of the story.[11] It is sometimes attributed to the evangelist alone in order to separate it from the more merciful Jesus or Paul.[12] In this way, Pelagianism and other un-Pauline theology would be avoided.[13] Another common solution is to argue that only the Gentiles are judged based on their deeds. Christians are the "little brethren", who will in turn be saved by their faith.[14] Such an explanation is artificial. As Ulrich Luz points out, neither the disciples nor Matthew's readers would have been able to identify with the brethren as they only appear at the end of the story. When "all the nations" are gathered together, nobody is meant to be excluded.[15] Donald Hagner's doctrinal reading is even more difficult to understand: "The deeds of mercy in the present passage are symbolic of a deeper reality, and as Gray notes, 'the main point of the parable is the acceptance or the rejection of the Christian faith'".[16] How could the recipients perceive such a "deep reality" or "faith" not mentioned in the story? For Dick France, it "surely" emphasizes "the sovereignty of the Son of Man as the universal judge" and the identity of Jesus.[17] Such a message would make the final discussion between the king and his astonished subjects unnecessary.

No doubt, dogmatic interpretations are meaningful when the goal is to retell the story in a new situation in order to meet contemporary religious needs.[18] However, their exegetical value is debatable as they are based

---

[10] LUTHER argues that in the Bible, the law tells what to do in order to be justified. However, thereby nobody is saved. The only way to be justified is by faith alone. See M. LUTHER, *Werke* (WA, 36), Weimar, Böhlaus, 1909, at https://archive.org/stream/werkekritischege36luthuoft#page/n5/mode/2up (March 2017), 17-26, p. 25). Correspondingly, R.T. FRANCE, *The Gospel of Matthew* (NICNT), Grand Rapids, MI, Eerdmans, 2007, p. 959, refers to systematic theologians' ability to combine judgment according to works with justification by grace. However, he reminds that Matthew is not one of them.

[11] See FRANCE, *Matthew* (n. 231), pp. 957-960, and SNODGRASS, *Stories* (n. 3), pp. 558-563.

[12] For discussion and typical exegetical solutions, see FRANCE, *Matthew* (n. 10), pp. 957-959. *Cf.* GNILKA, *Matthäusevangelium*, p. 378, and LUZ, *Matthew 21–28* (n. 3), pp. 290-296.

[13] See FRANCE, *Matthew* (n. 10), p. 957.

[14] SNODGRASS, *Stories* (n. 3), p. 552. For the discussion concerning the phrase πάντα τὰ ἔθνη, see HAGNER, *Matthew* (n. 3), p. 742.

[15] LUZ, *Matthew 21–28* (n. 3), pp. 274-276.280-282.

[16] HAGNER, *Matthew* (n. 3), pp. 747, referring to GRAY, *The Least* (n. 3), pp. 353.359.

[17] FRANCE, *Matthew* (n. 10), pp. 957-959.

[18] In the New Testament, corresponding techniques abound: Israeli and Jewish stories are retold in order to deliver new messages. For example, Abraham's story is circulated in Rom 4; Gal 3; Heb 6,13–7,10; Jas 2,21-24.

on external factors and these interpretations are therefore inconceivable for the hearers referred to in Matthew's text. In addition, altering any story or adding external data to it weakens the ability to understand the narrator and the author.[19]

2. The Historical Perspective

Academic research focusing on the historical reality behind Matt 25,31-46[20] has also been blurred by the story's manifold nature. In the search for its original historical version, the scholar shifts from the level of the communicators in the text to a time before it – to the historical Jesus and his real hearers, or to the historical author and his community. The story is assessed to reflect the ideas of the author, for whom the codename Matthew is used, rather than the historical Jesus, whose version – if it ever existed – ought to be reconstructed. Perhaps the current version illustrates the strict rules for salvation in Matthew's community;[21] at the very least, they have redesigned Jesus' historical opinions. Unfortunately, for many scholars it has proved difficult to differentiate between the historical and textual partners in communication.

Scholarly interpretations can be divided into universalistic and particularistic readings, depending on whether the story relates to anyone who is thirsty, hungry, etc., or only to Christian brethren in need.[22] Alternatively, the story may relate to Jews who are neglected by the Christians.[23] The text has also been read as Matthew's encouragement to an idle congregation, as a warning of the destruction of Jerusalem, as a sign of God's sovereignty, and as a guideline for the righteous life.[24] Such historical assumptions are justifiable as long as the aim is to reconstruct either Jesus' or the author's thoughts, or their historical setting. However, since this approach tends to pay insufficient attention to the narrative features of the existing text, historical results, too, may be compromised.

---

[19] See L. THURÉN, *Parables Unplugged – Reading the Lukan Parables in Their Rhetorical Context*, Minneapolis MN, Fortress, 2014, pp. 5-9, 23-26.
[20] For studies of the tradition history behind the story, see GNILKA, *Matthäusevangelium*, pp. 368-370; LUZ, *Matthew 21–28* (n. 3), pp. 264-267.
[21] See SNODGRASS, *Stories* (n. 3), p. 553.
[22] See STANTON, *New People* (n. 3), pp. 208-209; FRANCE, *Matthew* (n. 10), pp. 957-958, and HAGNER, *Matthew* (n. 3), pp. 744-745. For him, the brethren mean the disciples only.
[23] LUZ, *Matthew 21–28* (n. 3), p. 269; HAGNER, *Matthew* (n. 3), p. 744; SNODGRASS, *Stories* (n. 3), p. 552.
[24] SNODGRASS, *Stories* (n. 3), p. 543.

FIGURE 2. HISTORICAL INTEPRETATION OF MATT 25,31-46

Level	Sender	Recipient	Genre
A	Historical Jesus	Original audience	History or fiction
B	Historical author ("Matthew")	Historical recipients (Matthew's community)	History, real
[C	Jesus in the text	Disciples	Fiction]

Focusing on levels A and B involves two difficulties. First, if each interpreter leaves the Matthean Jesus and begins by reconstructing his or her own historical version of the story, the results are hardly compatible with other reconstructions. Secondly, the historical reconstructions are of little use when the goal is to understand the text (level C), but may only serve the scholars' own interpretations.

3. Guidelines for Charity?

A third option is to focus on the practical purpose of the story. Whereas exhortation to self-amputation in the Sermon on the Mount is usually overlooked as hyperbolical,[25] the story of the judgment (like the parable of the Samaritan in Lk 10,30-37) is read as practical advice for the Christian community, a manual for those willing to do good, or a handbook for *diakonia*.[26] The narrative provides information on the behaviour expected and persuades its recipients to act accordingly. The last judgment serves as a motivating factor. The scope is not doctrinal; Jesus aims at strengthening the charitable work done by his followers. This reading is applicable for contemporary Christianity and it is not bound to any spiritual tradition. It fits both textual and historical analyses equally.

FIGURE 3. DIACONAL INTEPRETATION OF MATT 25,31-46

Level	Sender	Recipient	Genre
a	Jesus/God	Disciples/We	Ethical instruction
b	Son of Man/King	Nations/Subjects	Prophecy

---

[25] U. Luz, *Matthew 1–7* (Hermeneia), Minneapolis, Fortress, 2007, pp. 246-247; France, *Matthew* (n. 10), p. 205.

[26] C.E.B. Cranfield, *Diakonia: Mt 25,31-46*, in *LQHR* 30 (1961), 275-281; Luz, *Matthew 21–28* (n. 3), pp. 268-269.

Verses 35-45 include several examples where the king's subjects have met him in disguise. The characters he has played have needed six types of sustenance: food, drink, lodging, clothing, and support in sickness or while imprisoned. Those who have recognized the need, even if not the person, and who have acted accordingly, will be rewarded. The rest will be punished.

How should an ideal recipient respond to such a story? A simple interpretation would read: One must help anybody matching the description of the king's cameo roles. A collective reaction, such as an organized and long-lasting campaign for helping those groups, would be even better.[27] Since no-one can create a safety net for all those in need, co-operation and perseverance are required to ensure that the king will not be left alone. Indeed, the narrative has served as one of the most important biblical cornerstones and guidelines for *diakonia* or *caritas* – organized charitable work by Christian communities.

The list of good works is not meant to be exclusive.[28] The king's cameo roles as someone who is hungry, thirsty etc. should not be interpreted allegorically as God's only check-points.[29] More likely, the three pairs of people in need (hungry/thirsty; strangers/poor; sick/in prison) are simply intended as examples.[30] Most are also mentioned in other early Jewish lists of good works.[31] In addition, although these lists typically urge followers to take care of orphans and bury the dead, in the context of the narration, these tasks have been left out. The king could hardly claim that he was dead and that his non-observant servants failed to bury him.[32] Thus, these two tasks are substituted with references to an imprisoned individual (see also *T. Jos.* 1,6).

The diaconal interpretation focuses on the practical function of the story, urging followers to act as allegedly told by Jesus. This has several advantages:

---

[27] *Cf.* LUZ, *Matthew 21–28* (n. 3), pp. 268-269; SNODGRASS, *Stories* (n. 3), p. 551.
[28] Such an interpretation gives an almost opposite aim to the demand for all-encompassing aid.
[29] Clearly, the parable of the Samaritan does not seek to claim that good deeds should only be performed on the way to Jericho. See P. OLLIKAINEN: *The Boss Out of Sight – Matt. 25,31-46 from the viewpoint of narration and argumentation*, MTh. Thesis, University of Eastern Finland, 2015, pp. 67-68.
[30] So also HAGNER, *Matthew* (n. 3), p. 744.
[31] For OT and Early Jewish resemblances, see J. SCHMID, *Das Evangelium nach Matthäus* (RNT, 1), Regensburg, Pustet, 1965, pp. 351-356; LUZ, *Matthew 21–28* (n. 3), pp. 278-279, esp. n. 132.
[32] However, in Catholic tradition, burying the dead has been added to the list, probably in order to reach a total of seven good works.

- The simplest explanation is usually the best. Stories told by Jesus were designed to make an impact when heard on certain one-off occasions. Thus, they probably have some plain purpose that fits the need described or implied by the author in the framework story. Accordingly, one should focus on the context provided by the evangelist and set aside complicated theological trains of thought that can only be secondary.[33]
- The diaconal explanation does not exclude other readings. Although often limited to a particularistic view of the story, as if Jesus was speaking to or of the Christians only, diaconal explanation also suits a universal interpretation. It can even be combined with a soteriological message.[34]
- Matthew's ethics are often assessed as aiming at practical love of one's neighbour, irrespective of religion.[35] Luz emphasizes that the ideals presented are realistic guidelines that are not impossible to fulfil.[36] Accordingly, Snodgrass maintains that the story is not so much concerned with the afterlife; rather, its sole aim is to make people compassionate towards each other: "All else is ancillary".[37]

4. Problems with the Interpretations

Dogmatic, historical and diaconal interpretations are all rewarding, as they meet the particular demands of the respective interpreters. The narrative can reveal Jesus' plan for human relations, his soteriology, or his or Matthew's historical reality. However, such tailor-made results may be due more to the interpreters' expectations than curiosity at what the narrative actually aims at in its context. These interpretations typically draw on external ideas and information. In the worst case, these ideas are used to determine the message of the text. To prevent this, the message within the text should never be overlooked, even when focusing on some other goal.

When striving to understand what Matthew, the author and Jesus, the narrator, aim at with the story, traditional dogmatic and diaconal interpretations appear problematic:

---

[33] THURÉN, *Parables Unplugged* (n. 19), pp. 26-27.
[34] For example, good works may prove one's humility, whereas omissions indicate "the lack of insight on the part of the righteous" (LUZ, *Matthew 21–28*, n. 3, p. 272).
[35] LUZ, *Matthew 21–28* (n. 3), pp. 268-270. According to Luz, the story fits with Kantian ethics as well as Catholic *caritas*, liberation theology and even atheism. Correspondingly, for GNILKA, *Matthäusevangelium*, p. 377, the story is a "Gerichtsparänese".
[36] LUZ, *Matthew 21–28* (n. 3), p. 293.
[37] SNODGRASS, *Stories* (n. 3), p. 564.

- If grace alone is decisive for salvation, rather than good works,[38] why did Jesus say the opposite? His words scarcely suggest giving a second chance to those doomed to eternal fire.
- If a combination of good works and divine grace is meant, or if Matthew just wanted to intensify the efforts of his idle congregation, why the emphasis on only two alternatives, life or death, based only on human behaviour?
- If everybody is predestined to his or her fate like the sheep and the goats, why specify good deeds to those in need and why emphasize their crucial importance?
- If judgment does not apply to the disciples, or if Jesus wanted to victimize his opponents, or to predict the fall of Jerusalem, why specify good deeds to those in need?
- If Christians are excluded from the judgment or if they are the little brethren, how are the disciples in the story supposed to understand the message? They were hardly Christians themselves.
- If any group is excluded, why emphasize universality (πάντα τὰ ἔθνη)?
- If Jesus wanted to refresh the concept of neighbourly love, why did he not provide any new guidelines? Correspondingly, in the parable of the Samaritan (Lk 10,30-37), the question is not what one should do, but to whom.[39]
- If Jesus wanted to found a system of organized neighbourly love, to give his disciples practical hints, or at least to encourage them to give fresh water to the thirsty, why the gloomy storyline emphasizing the absolute divergence of the nations and the eternal nature of the judgment? Did nothing else suffice?

In general, damage is done to the story when its eschatological character and the exclusive importance of good works for salvation are overlooked, where the main message is narrowed down to practical guidelines, or where the main message is explained by something not found in the text, such as faith, grace, or predestination.

However, to read the story merely as information about the crucial importance of good works does not fit the storyline either. The *clou* or message of a good parable or story typically comes as a surprise,[40] but the good works principle does not shock anybody in this text. The king's subjects do not oppose it. Instead, they are very surprised at the effectiveness of the king's close scrutiny of their behaviour.

---

[38] See, for example, HAGNER, *Matthew* (n. 3), p. 747.
[39] THURÉN, *Parables Unplugged* (n. 19), pp. 56-59.
[40] THURÉN, *Parables Unplugged* (n. 19), pp. 112-113.

Interaction at the Textual Level

To understand the story, one should read it from the audience's perspective and focus on what is happening inside the text.[41] The first step to do this is to assess the genre of the story. Then I identify the different layers of interaction. Matthew does not make this any easier, as his text contains simultaneous signs of two genres: prophecy and parable. Finally, I read the story with the help of narrative and argumentation analysis. In this way, I hope to discover the simple meaning of this complex text and its function both for Matthew, the author, and his protagonist, Jesus the narrator.

1. The Genre

Traditionally, the story is referred to as a parable, but most modern commentaries state that only verses 32b-33, which talk of a shepherd, fit this definition.[42] The story as a whole appears to speak of real future events. Annoyingly, there are a number of signals that also suggest the parable form throughout the story.[43] Thus, a common alternative genre has not been found. France labels the story as "majestic visions of divine judgment" corresponding to the Apocalypse.[44] Hagner calls it "apocalyptic revelation discourse",[45] but Luz notes that no vision is included.[46] For him, the story is merely a "depiction of judgement".[47] However, such descriptions do not belong to any known literary genres. Hagner further claims that the story describes a "very real, though future event", but this does not fit the discussion between the king and his subjects – it is difficult to imagine all the nations having the described conversation together with the Son of Man. What would be the practical arrangements for such a discussion?

One cannot avoid the impression that the story contains both prophetic claims regarding the future and features that apply to the parable form. For a better understanding, both these two genres should be defined and

---

[41] One of the few scholars paying heed to this aspect is LUZ, *Matthew 21–28* (n. 3), pp. 274-275.
[42] Thus e.g. LUZ, *Matthew 21–28* (n. 3), p. 264.
[43] SNODGRASS, *Stories* (n. 3), first states: "This is not really a parable" (p. 543), but then categorizes it as "among the most influential parabolic texts" (p. 562).
[44] FRANCE, *Matthew* (n. 10), p. 960.
[45] HAGNER, *Matthew* (n. 3), p. 740.
[46] LUZ, *Matthew 21–28* (n. 3), p. 264.
[47] *Ibid.*

recognized in the text. While both prophecy and parable attempt to influence the audience and may include symbolic speech, the essential difference lies in their functions regarding the audience.

Based on recent developments in parable research, I have defined the genre as follows: "A parable is a narrative, non-historical, and metaphoric saying by Jesus, appealing to an audience. It illustrates a general principle to be applied in a particular context."[48] In comparison with prophecy, two features are of importance: first, a prophecy refers to divine authority, whereas a parable appeals to the hearer's reason and emotions; secondly, a prophecy claims to describe (possibly future) reality, whereas a parable is non-historical.

The story about the last judgment is a rare hybrid, where two parables are wrapped into a prophetic framework. Matthew's choice may have a rhetorical purpose: the combination of methods attempts to influence the audience with both divine authority in a prophecy and by appealing to reason and emotion with two parables.

The narrative opens as a prophecy (Matt 25,31-32a), predicting what the Son of Man, the eschatological human-like heavenly ruler (Dan 7,13-14) and judge of the nations (1 Enoch 62,2-5; 69,27-29), will do when he arrives in his glory.[49] He will meet all the nations and separate them from each other. The end of the story (Matt 25,46) returns to this theme: the bad are sent to eternal punishment and the good to eternal life. The big question is: What is the purpose of this prophecy? How is it designed to influence the recipients? It surely does not aim solely at sharing information about future events.

The shepherd sorting his livestock (Matt 25,32b-33) is clearly a parable. But how about the king and his subjects (Matt 25,34-46)? The interpreters axiomatically identify the king with the Son of Man, but are simultaneously perplexed by this change of identity.[50] This riddle ought to be taken seriously as it reveals how the text has often been read too hastily.

As argued above, the complete story does not contain all these different characters for no good reason. Instead of talking only about the Son of Man and the nations, the narrator refers to numerous other individuals or groups that resemble each other to a certain degree. However, they are not identical and should not be treated as such. They are all separate characters with their own functions.

---

[48] THURÉN, *Parables Unplugged* (n. 19), p. 369.
[49] LUZ, *Matthew 21–28* (n. 3), p. 264; HAGNER, *Matthew* (n. 3), 1995, pp. 740-741.
[50] See above n. 226.

Although the story about the king talking with his subjects has something in common with the prophecy about the Son of Man judging the nations, there are also differences. The king is presented as being flesh and blood – starving, sick, imprisoned, etc. – unlike the heavenly Son of Man, not to speak of any theological levels. In Jesus' parables, the king is but one of his fictive colleagues, who deal with their servants (Matt 18,23-34; 22,2-13) or go to war (Lk 14,31-32). The translations misleadingly use a capital letter for the king's father (25,34) – it was common for kingship to be inherited.

There may be some theological colouring within the parable, as the kingdom has existed "from the foundation of the world" (v. 34) and its opposite, the eternal flame, is prepared for the Devil and his angels. However, such exaggeration is not unusual: in royalist propaganda, many empires have claimed to be eternal, and many curses refer to the Devil.

A natural explanation for the common and different features of the three powerful men in Matt 25,31-46 is that the stories of the shepherd and the king are parables that are connected to the prophecy about the Son of Man. The shepherd sorting his livestock (Matt 25,32b-33) and the king rewarding and punishing his subjects are neither apocalyptic visions nor descriptions of reality. These men and other details in their stories are not to be axiomatically identified with anyone in the prophecy, let alone at other levels within or outside the text. The Old Testament images (Son of Man, shepherd, king) are not automatically cover-names for the Divinity. Each must be seen operating in its own right to serve Matthew's general narrative.

Christian Münch makes an important observation when he argues that the text first speaks about the Son of Man and only then about the king, yet that the king should actually come first in order for the story to be a good parable that explains the prophecy of the Son of Man.[51] But what if this order is exactly the point? Perhaps the prophecy supports the parable, not vice versa. Then the main message of the text is to be found in the parable of the king: anyone neglecting those in need will be severely punished. The eschatological prophecy simply gives this message extra weight.

2. Levels of Communication

It is remarkable that in Luke's parables, the highest number of separate individuals or groups is nine (the Great Banquet, Lk 14,16-24), whereas

---

[51] C. MÜNCH, *Der Hirt* (n. 7), p. 504.

Matthew's story of the judgment contains no less than 14 actors. The whole group of actors – the Son of Man, the angels, the nations, the shepherd, the sheep, the goats, the king, his subjects, his father, the righteous and the unrighteous people, Devil, his angels and the king's younger brothers – consist of characters within the story-world created by Jesus. Their exact connection to the "real world" of Matthew's gospel is mostly difficult to prove, not to mention any references to later Church history.

According to the classical model by Wayne Booth and Seymour Chatman, several levels of communication can be found within a narrative.[52] The senders and recipients can be real, implied, ideal, etc., but they communicate on their own level only. In Matt 25,31-46, the levels shown in Figure 4 can be identified.[53]

FIGURE 4. NARRATIVE LEVELS OF INTERACTION IN MATT 25,31-46

Level	Sender	Recipient	Genre
[1	Real author	Real Reader	History, real]
2	Implied author (Matthew)	Implied reader	History, literary
3	Jesus	Disciples	History, literary
4	Son of Man	Nations	Prophecy
5	Shepherd	Animals	Parable basic
6	King	Subjects	Parable narrative
7	King in disguise	Subjects	Parable narrative

The levels can be explained as follows:

1. The actual physical author sends a message that was or is read by real people.
2. The explicit and implicit signals in the text yield an image of its writer (the "implied author"), who sends a message to his putative recipients (the "implied readers").
3. The author tells a framework story, where his protagonist, Jesus, tells his disciples other stories (levels 4–7).
4. In Jesus' narrative, the heavenly Son of Man interacts with all the nations. This level is often read as an accurate description of forthcoming reality. Yet some difficulties in time and space occur. The encounter is further illustrated by two parables.

---

[52] S. CHATMAN, *Story and Discourse: Narrative Structure in Fiction and Film*, Ithaca, Cornell UP, 1978, pp. 148-151.253–254.267.
[53] The structure is partly based on OLLIKAINEN, *Boss* (n. 29).

5. In the first parable, a shepherd interacts with his animals. This illustrates a principle which is followed from the previous level.
6. In the second parable, a king talks with his subjects, also illustrating a principle used on level 4.
7. Embedded within the parable, the king tells his subjects yet another story about their previous encounters.

The first stages of interaction (1 and 2) remain at the meta-level. Not until level 3 do we reach the framework story described by Matthew. Communication at each higher level contains all the levels below it. Only levels 3, 6 and 7 display explicit interaction, via discussion between the partners. Yet even at levels 1–2 and 4, the partners implicitly influence each other. The author modifies his presentation based on the development of the audience he has in mind. The parables allude to a discussion between the Son of Man and the nations. Only level 5 remains one-sided.

All these levels must be kept apart so that their functions do not become intertwined. The Son of Man does not separate the goats, and Jesus is not in prison. Instead, the impact of each level on those above must be adequately assessed.

Narration and Argumentation

1. Guidelines for a New Approach

Now the argument must be recognized as a whole. How is the entire story designed to appeal to its recipients? What kinds of reactions do Matthew and his Jesus expect from their audiences?

In order to answer these questions, the historical communication level 1 is omitted, as are any other historical and theological levels,[54] involving messages from God to humankind and from the historical Jesus to his real hearers. This is because the text as such does not serve such ventures. Instead, I focus on levels 2–7: I ask about what Matthew says to his envisioned recipients (level 2), what his protagonist Jesus conveys to his disciples when they approach him on the Mount of Olives (level 3, *cf.* Matt 24,3), and what the individuals in his story say to each other (levels 4–7).

The story opens – and perhaps also ends – with a prophecy about the Son of Man and all the nations (Matt 25,31-32a [and 46]; level 4). It is

---

[54] Figure 1, level I; Figure 3, level a; and Figure 2, level AB.

illustrated by two parables, which tell stories about a shepherd and a king. In the following paragraphs, the story is analysed according to my novel approach to parables. The main idea is to read the plain text and to search for its general message with the help of narratology and modern argumentation analysis.[55] The method builds on three main rules:

1. Nothing should be inserted or excluded from the text. The author usually provides all the information he reckons is necessary for understanding his message.[56]
2. A parable always seeks to influence its recipient by first distancing them from the issue under discussion. Using a different context, the parable illustrates a general principle that should then be applied to the original issue.[57]
3. The principle illustrated by a longer, narrative parable should be sought in the surprise of its message, typically appearing at the end. In order to perceive it, one should avoid applying any details of the parable to reality by using allegory.[58]

2. The Shepherd

The description of a shepherd (Matt 25,32b-33; level 5) belongs to the "simple rule" parable category.[59] It nevertheless fulfils the minimum requirements of a parable.[60] In contrast to a static metaphor, some action can be found, and in contrast to the preceding prophecy, no particular real occasion is referred to. It is important to keep levels 4 and 5 separate: the individual dividing the sheep and the goats is not the Son of Man (level 4), nor is he Jesus (level 3) or God (level I in Figure 1).

The parable illustrates absolute divergence as the animals are divided into exactly two groups. The Jewish *qal wahomer* principle applies: if an ordinary shepherd follows this principle, how much more will the divine judge do so? There will be only two alternatives for all the nations: eternal life or eternal punishment. This tiny parable exemplifies that no third option exists. Only the perfect and blessed (οἱ εὐλογημένοι), and the completely bad or cursed (οἱ κατηραμένοι) will exist.

---

[55] THURÉN, *Parables Unplugged* (n. 19), pp. 22-40.
[56] Clearly, our general knowledge is not identical with that of Matthew's implied readers, but whenever we want to narrow that gap with any text-external information, great caution must be used and the consequences assessed.
[57] THURÉN, *Parables Unplugged* (n. 19), p. 369.
[58] See THURÉN, *Parables Unplugged* (n. 19), pp. 19-22.
[59] For a definition, see THURÉN, *Parables Unplugged* (n. 19), p. 202.
[60] See the previous section.

Figure 5 displays the parable's role in the argumentation structure of Matt 25,32b-33. It applies Stephen Toulmin's model, according to which any human reasoning can be broken down into certain functional elements. A specific opinion put forward (a claim) is supported by specific information (data). Their connection is ensured by a general rule (a warrant), supported by general information (the backing).[61] A parable always serves as the backing for some reasoning.[62]

FIGURE 5. ARGUMENTATION IN MATT 25,32b-33

Backing: A shepherd divides his animals into two groups
▼
Warrant: Absolute divergence is a common procedure
▼
Data: The Son of Man will judge ▶ *Claim*: The nations will be divided
the exactly nations

3. The King

The second parable tells of the communication between a fictive king and his subjects (Matt 25,34-45; level 6). Within this narrative, they remember past encounters, during which the king was acting undercover (level 7). The connection between this parable and the prophecy is often blurred in the interpretation. Indeed, verse 46, speaking of eternal punishment and eternal life, can simultaneously be seen as an *inclusio* of the whole story in vv. 31-46, bringing together the opening prophecy and the parable.

This parable sounds more realistic than the opening prophecy. It portrays a limited number of individuals, perhaps featuring noble men in the court. It can be characterized as a fictive narrative rather than a description of reality. Contrary to the prophecy on level 4, not all the nations but only a few individuals capable of helping others are judged. The poor, the hungry, the thirsty, etc. are not judged at all.

A longer parable typically contains a surprise. Here, nobody is astonished when the king's subjects are rewarded or punished according to their actions. The king's subjects do not criticize this principle. The connection

---

[61] See S.E. TOULMIN, *The Uses of Argument*, Cambridge, Cambridge University Press, 1958, and THURÉN, *Parables Unplugged* (n. 240), pp. 30-32.
[62] THURÉN, *Parables Unplugged* (n. 240), pp. 33-34.

between righteous behaviour and high reward would hardly be a new idea, either for Jesus' disciples or for Matthew's audience if they knew the basics of contemporary Judaism.[63]

However, all the king's men are shocked to hear that he has observed their behaviour so closely. More precisely, they were not aware of where he had been during his surveillance of their behaviour. They are to be judged according to their actions in situations where they did not think they could be observed. The king has acted undercover. Of course, even those on his left would have helped him if only they had been able to recognize him.[64]

FIGURE 6. ARGUMENTATION IN MATT 25,34-45

Backing: A king monitoring his subjects in unpredicted situations

▼

Warrant: One cannot know when one's performance is being observed; thus, it is best to do good to everyone at all times ◄ (+ *qal wahomer*: If this applies to an earthly ruler, how much more to the heavenly one)

▼

Data: You meet people in need ► *Claim*: They must be helped without exception

The claim is also supported by the parable of the shepherd, and even by the prophecy about the Son of Man: anyone failing to comply completely will be severely punished.

THE CONTEXT

Next, the story needs to be seen in its larger context, Matt 24–25, as well as in the context of the whole book. One should also seek corresponding messages within the same piece of text. A completely unique idea is hardly credible.

---

[63] For example, in Matt 5,20 Jesus assures his audience: "For I tell you, unless your righteousness greatly exceeds that of the scribes and Pharisees, you will never enter the kingdom of heaven!" In both texts, the sanction is eternal fire (Matt 5,22 and 25,41), *cf.* Luke 10,25-28.

[64] A modern version of the parable would be the TV series "Undercover Boss", or a driver receiving a speeding ticket even though he has remembered to slow down before each known traffic surveillance camera.

1. The Requirement is Eschatological

For Matthew, the story is of great importance, as he presents it as Jesus' last parable, completing not only his eschatological speeches, but his whole teaching (Matt 26,1).[65] Any interpretation of Matt 25,31-46 must match its weighty position.[66]

The text could merely aim at intensifying neighbourly love, motivated by a reference to the judgment. Yet the compilation (Matt 24–25) is thoroughly eschatological. It is introduced by the disciples' question: "Tell us, when will these things take place, and what will be the sign of your coming and of the end of the age?" (Matt 24,3). Thus, the eschatological signals are not irrelevant. I have suggested above that the eschatological prophecy aims to make the parables that follow more effective.

2. Absolute Control Requires Blameless Performance

The main section of Matt 24–25 contains four major narrative parables, all describing decisive meetings of masters and their servants. They all emphasize that not only do the servants' preceding actions determine their destiny, but also that the master has an unprecedented oversight of these actions. As a result, no excuses or exceptions are allowed.

Each story has its own emphasis. The first narrative parable (Matt 24,45–51) tells of a servant, who is cut into two pieces (διχοτομήσει) when his master arrives unexpectedly, due to his bad behaviour. Thus, one should always act correctly, even in the master's absence.

The parable about the virgins (25,1-12), which follows, also suggests that something needs to be done in order to be ready for the master's arrival, but that the timing is less important.[67] No clearer guidelines for being properly equipped are presented. In the climax (vv. 11-12), the virgins are crying in vain for mercy.

The parable of the talents (25,14-30) emphasizes that one must be brave enough to act. The amount of profit is not important: the master would have been satisfied with minimum interest from the bank; doubling his

---

[65] See also Luz, *Matthew 21–28* (n. 3), p. 264.

[66] For the historical Jesus and his historical hearers, the literary context has a small role. Thus, it is important to be cognizant of the level under discussion, and not to mix them.

[67] The late entrance of the bridegroom or the sleeping of the girls makes no difference, since the torches of the "foolish" girls would have gone out anyway; the only thing they did wrong was that they were not properly equipped in the first place.

capital was not required (25,26). What irritated the rich man was the third servant's passivity.[68] Again, there is no mercy in sight.

The final parable of the judgment (25,34-45) is based on the servants' inability to recognize the king in disguise. Only those who treat everybody well will prevail.[69]

The theme of Matt 24–25, God's all-encompassing scrutiny with regard to the eternal judgment, has already been introduced in Matt 5–6. There, God will reward those who give alms (Matt 6,1-4), pray (6,6), or fast (6,16-18) in secret, for he watches over them at all times. According to Matt 5,28-29, even secret thoughts are assessed in the same way as actions, and will be punished or rewarded accordingly. Since people cannot avoid judgment by any excuse, neighbourly love should be followed universally and without restriction as to time, or the identity or behaviour of the people in need. They should treat friends and enemies, those who love them and those who have sinned against them, in exactly the same way (5,43-48).

The final section (Matt 24–25) adds kings and beggars to the examples of people deserving similar treatment, but stays on a general level. It no longer focuses on particular excuses, but on general consistency in observance. This section consists mostly of parables rather than direct speech. The motivation is the same: God is checking one's behaviour when least expected.

Since both Matt 5–6 and 24–25 emphasize the all-encompassing and unrestricted requirements of the Torah and God's surprising ability to enforce his demands, these ideas must be crucial for Matthew and his protagonist.

FIGURE 7. OBSERVANCE OF THE TORAH SHOULD NOT BE RESTRICTED IN ANY WAY

MATT 5–6	DIMENSION OF OBEDIENCE	OVERRULED EXCUSE	MATT 24–25
5,17-21	Extent of the commands	Any excuse pertaining to any single commandment	

---

[68] So also Luz, *Matthew 21–28* (n. 3), p. 252. According to him, the problem with the servant was not laziness but fear (p. 255).

[69] Although unknown for Matthew's implied readers, Luke's parable of the Samaritan (Luke 10,30-35) carries a corresponding message. There, too, eternal life is at stake when deciding whether to help an unknown patient when nobody is watching (THURÉN, *Parables Unplugged* (n. 19), pp. 53-75).

MATT 5-6	DIMENSION OF OBEDIENCE	OVERRULED EXCUSE	MATT 24-25
5,21-22	Mode of surveillance	Words less serious than deeds	
5,27-30	Mode of surveillance	Intentions less serious than deeds	
5,31-32	Marriage	Writing of divorce	
5,33-37	Mode of speech	Not being under oath	
5,43-48	Quality of other person	Enmity or friendship	
6,1-6.16-17	Others' surveillance	Being watched or not	(time) 24,48-51 (identity) 25,31-46
6,12-14	Others' behaviour	Being violated by others Being afraid of the master	25,14-30

CONCLUSIONS

Careless transgression of the different communicative levels blurs the message of Matt 25,31-46. Axiomatic identification of Jesus as the Son of Man, the shepherd and the king, together with allegorical references to them, prevents the natural understanding of the story as a whole. They are all independent figures with distinctive functions.

The story reveals neither novel criteria for obtaining salvation[70] nor does it yield new information about whom to help or how. Instead, it reminds the readers that everyone in need must be helped without exception and it motivates the readers to obey the command in an extreme way. What does this exacting message aim at?

According to Luz, the story does not proclaim the law in the Pauline sense of the word, not to speak of the Reformation's. Although it might be correct to reject such interpretations coming from other contexts, I cannot follow Luz's assessment that the story instead presents viable requirements.[71] The narrative structure and the argument point elsewhere. Jesus not only rephrases the command of neighbourly love but strongly emphasizes that the recipients can never tell when and where they are being observed. All omissions will be noted and they lead to the company of the Devil and his angels. This parable and its predecessors in Matt 24–25, all

---

[70] Threats of eternal fire (Matt 25,41) and punishment (25,46) correspond to earlier references to the judgment (5,21), the *synedrion* (5,22) and the (fire of) *gehenna* (5,22.29).
[71] LUZ, *Matthew 21–28* (n. 3), p. 293.

end by describing the punishment ordered by a powerful man for those who have failed his expectations. Most stories culminate with a comment on the powerful man's cunning and ruthless surveillance.

To be sure, each parable displays people who succeed – the wise bridesmaids, the brave investors and those who helped the king – but the recipients do not resemble them, because they need encouragement (Matt 25,13). The absolute requirement, motivated finally by the eschatological division of all the nations, indicates that no slight improvement of one's ethical level will do. Only an impeccable record will be sufficient. In each case, the final discussion (Matt 25,11-12.24-27.44-45) emphasizes that the transgressors have no hope; their pleas for clemency will not be heard.

If the attitude of the parables' powerful men resembles that of God, the recipients should realize that fulfilling all his demands at all times is not only necessary but impossible. Correspondingly, in Matt 5, Jesus makes victims of all his hearers. According to his reasoning, eternal punishment cannot be avoided, for who has not sometimes spoken or thought something bad? Nevertheless, the final purpose of the Sermon on the Mount is not to suggest that the audience should amputate their limbs to avoid punishment.

Likewise, the big question about the final purpose of Matt 25,31-46 remains. How do Matthew and his Jesus want their recipients to respond to these unrealistic requirements? An interesting reaction from the disciples is presented in Matt 19,21-26. Jesus requires that a rich young man should be perfect.[72] Then he comments on his own requirement to the disciples, using a rhetorical technique called *adynaton* in modern literary research:[73] "It is easier for a camel to go through a needle's eye" (19,24). The disciples reply: "Who then can be saved?" and Jesus answers: "For humans it is impossible (ἀδύνατον) (19,26).[74] The addition "for God all things are possible" remains unfortunately without further clarification.

Matthew's text does not end with chapters 24–25. They prepare his readers for the climax in chapters 26–28, which describe Jesus' last days, death and resurrection. There, Jesus predicts that his blood will be poured out for many people for the forgiveness of sins (Matt 26,28). Although this divine pardon could offer a glimpse of hope to the desperate individuals in the previous chapters, its position in the text should not be moved backwards. These stories are not to be altered; the nations, the

---

[72] This is the goal of Matt 5,48 as well.
[73] S. CUSHMAN et al., *The Princeton Encyclopedia of Poetry and Poetics*, 4th ed., Princeton NJ, Princeton University Press, 2012, p. 9.
[74] In Heb 6,4-6 the same term is applied to those who have fallen away from their faith.

goats and the king's subjects are not forgiven. Even the disciples are left without any third option.[75] It is only Matthew's audience (level 2) that can proceed to the narrative of the passion and there find a solution to the soteriological dead-end.

Chapters 24–25, and especially the story about the judgment, play a key role in the structure of Matthew's gospel. In the literary context, Jesus' final plea to his disciples is not to behave better. Instead he creates the need for an incomparable forgiveness that cannot be provided by any earthly master or even the eschatological judge. In this way, Matthew prepares his readers for the final section of the book, which tells about the pouring out of Jesus' blood for the forgiveness of sins. Thus, the emphasis on strict requirements for salvation is not due to some dogmatic structure, but rather due to a literary one. In order to serve this function, Matthew and his Jesus put great effort into making the story of the judgment as exacting and watertight as possible. The right solution is not to soften it in any way, but to perceive its full force. Whether or not this was the aim of the historical Jesus is another question.

I hope to have shown that recognizing the levels of interaction is essential for an understanding of the complex story told in Matt 25,31-46. Only by differentiating the dogmatic, historical, and textual perspectives, and separating the different genres within the text, can their proper function be observed. This does not make historical or theological questions irrelevant, but enables a new way of approaching them.

The story of the judgment exemplifies Jesus' daring model of teaching. Instead of giving mature, balanced instruction, which would illuminate the case from many sides and suit people in different situations,[76] he tends to utter hyperbolical and extreme ideas and slogans.[77] While later theologians have desperately attempted to domesticate them, Jesus' hearers on the level of the text cannot be but shocked by such statements. This may be due to Matthew's or his protagonist's pursuit of maximal rhetorical effect, even at the risk of being misunderstood.

---

[75] Of course, the solution is anticipated in the Sermon on the Mount, where the disciples are urged to pray for forgiveness for what they have neglected (τὰ ὀφειλήματα, Matt 6,12-15). In the same prayer, God is asked to deliver them from the πειρασμός, the final test. Such omissions and tests are then described in Matt 24–25.

[76] First Peter shows how such a sensible and well-adjusted presentation was possible in Early Christian writings (see THURÉN, *The Rhetorical Stragegy of 1 Peter*, Åbo, Åbo Academy Press, 1990, 181-185).

[77] For example: "Let the dead bury their own dead" (Matt 8,22); "Who is my mother, and who are my brothers?" (12,48); "It is not right to take the children's bread and throw it to the puppies" (15,26).

A TALE OF TWO TEACHERS
Jesus about Jesus and John the Baptist
(Luke 7,18-35)

Bart J. KOET
Tilburg, the Netherlands

In an article long ago, the German author W. Moock wrote that there was probably not enough wine at the wedding in Cana, because Jesus and his disciples were there.[1] Is it possible that he is hinting at Luke 7,34 or Matt 11,19 where Jesus is depicted as οἰνοπότης?[2] Although Matthew and Luke put this description on the lips of Jesus, it remains remarkable that such a term is used in gospel narratives.

In this article we shall look at how Jesus is presented in Luke 7,18-35 and at how his habit of drinking and eating fits his defence of his own teaching, as well as that of John the Baptist. We shall start with a critical review of a recent monograph and this will lead to our research-question. After defining and describing the unity and context of Luke 7,18-35 we shall, in the following section, describe our method. After our methodological reading of the periscope we shall, in the last sections, sketch how our analysis contributes to a profile of Jesus and John the Baptist as teachers.

INTRODUCTION. IS LUKE 7,18-35 AN INDICTMENT OF THE RELIGIOUS LEADERS?

Luke 7,18-35 has a parallel in Matt 11,1-19 and therefore belongs to what is usually called Q. These passages are often studied using historical-critical methods. In his recent study, Roberto Martinez approaches the Lukan passage from a narrative-critical perspective, arguing that many commentators have conflated the Matthean and Lukan passages and thus

---

[1] W. MOOCK, 'Zu Jo 2,1-11', in *TGl* 30 (1938), 313-316, p. 313.
[2] LSJ, *sub verbo*, 1207, gives as the only possible translation: 'wine-bibber'. For the negative connotation, see also Proverbs 23,20.

bypass the important differences between them. He assumes that a narrative-critical analysis will shed new light on the coherence of Luke 7,18-35.[3]

In a short introduction to his method, Martinez explains that his analysis takes into consideration literary aspects such as characterization, point of view, setting and plot.[4] He claims that Luke has inserted the question of the Baptist into the narrative's implicit acceptance of a promised prophetic figure. It is within the context of this assumption that the gradual revelation of Jesus in the first chapters of Luke occurs.[5] It seems to me that this is one of Martinez' most important observations.

Martinez' interpretation of 7,30 as the frustration of God's plan by the religious leaders is the most extensive of all the sections in his book. This indicates that it is this motif which he will present as one of the more important messages of this passage.[6] I am not so sure that the reproach of the religious leaders in 7,30 is as important for the interpretation of the whole pericope as Martinez suggests, and I doubt whether Luke 7,31-35 is an indictment of the Jewish leaders.[7] An argument against Martinez' interpretation is that the addressees of verses 29-30 are not, at first sight, clear.[8] Is it the crowds, mentioned in 7,24, who are listening to Jesus? Or is it possible that all the people, mentioned in 7,29, are doing so? While the answer to these questions is not so obvious, it is evident, that there is no indication that it is the religious leaders who are the audience.[9] In Luke 7,33 Jesus does not say that the religious leaders call him a 'glutton and drunkard'. While according to Matt 11,19 Jesus argues that a

---

[3] Cf. R. MARTINEZ, *The Question of John the Baptist and Jesus' Indictment of the Religious Leaders: A Critical Analysis of Luke 7:18-35*, Cambridge, James Clarke & Co, 2012, pp. 47-48 and 50. One can also find an assessment of Luke 7,18-35 in J. RINDOŠ, *He of Whom It Is Written: John the Baptist and Elijah in Luke* (ÖBS, 38), Frankfurt am Main, Peter Lang, 2010, pp. 165-192.

[4] *Ibid.*, pp. 80-83, esp. 81.

[5] *Ibid.*, pp. 97 and 101.

[6] *Ibid.*, pp. 141-151. *Cf.* the title of his book. The indictment of the religious leaders is already mentioned at the beginning of his research (see 62), for example when he tries to describe the immediate context of Luke 7,18-35. This could indicate that this judgement is not only the result of Martinez's research, but probably also part of his presuppositions.

[7] Furthermore MARTINEZ does not differentiate enough between the various roles of Jewish leaders. For this, see D.B. GOWLER in his review of Martinez in *JTS* 64 (2013), 559-662, p. 661: "Martinez sometimes conflates the Lukan Pharisees with 'the religious leaders'".

[8] Is it a parenthetical remark by the narrator, a redactional summary, or are these verses part of what Jesus says? See e.g. RINDOŠ, *He of Whom It Is Written* (n. 3), p. 185, footnote 656.

[9] Pace MARTINEZ, *The Question of John the Baptist* (n. 3), p. 153.

non-specified "they" typifies him as such, in Luke 7,34 Jesus engages his audience: he refers to the fact that "you say [λέγετε]" that he is such a person, and in doing so, he addresses somebody more or less directly.[10] In this way, the Lukan Jesus is not as clear in defining his opponents as Martinez tries to argue.[11]

It therefore becomes necessary to look more closely at those to whom Jesus' words are directed and to look into what these words convey to their audience. The research-question becomes: who are the audiences involved in this passage and to whom does Jesus address his remarks? In order to answer these questions it necessary to analyse the whole interaction and communication pattern of this passage.

The thesis of this article is that the special attention we will give to the pattern of communication will help us not only to answer the question about the addressees of Jesus' comparison, but also to understand some other elements in this passage, such as the relation between Jesus and John the Baptist and the characterization of the children. I would like to examine Luke 7,18-35 from a communication-oriented approach in order to shed light on the question of Jesus' addressees. Before providing an analysis of this passage it will be helpful to sketch its context and (literary) unity.

CONTEXT, UNITY AND STRUCTURE OF LUKE 7,18-35

The preface of the Lukan Gospel (1,1-4) is followed by two introductory chapters presenting the birth narratives with their careful parallel structure between John's and Jesus' stories in (1,5-2,52).[12] Although there is some discussion about details, like identifying the beginning of the section, the

---

[10] Earlier MARTINEZ, *The Question of John the Baptist* (n. 3), p. 58, rightly argues that the statement of Luke's Jesus becomes a direct address to the crowd and that Jesus is, therefore, *not* addressing the religious leaders.

[11] Another argument against Martinez's thesis that Luke 7,31-34 is an indictment of the Jewish leaders, is that it is never clever to preach against those who are not present. Because the Jewish leaders are not addressed, it is at least probable that they are not present. Alternatively, if they were, it was not important enough for Luke to mention it.

[12] See B.J. KOET, *Simeons Worte (Luke 2,29-32.34c-35) und Israels Geschick*, in F. VAN SEGBROECK et al. (eds.), *The Four Gospels 1992* (FS F. NEIRYNCK) (BETL, 100), Leuven, Peeters, 1992, pp. 1549-1569, repr. in B.J. KOET, *Dreams and Scripture in Luke-Acts: Collected Essays* (CBET, 43), LEUVEN, Peeters, 2006, 99-122; B.J. KOET, *Holy Place and Hannah's prayer: A Comparison of LAB 51 and Luke 2,22-39 à propos 1 Sam 1–2*, in A. HOUTMAN et al. (eds.), *Sanctity of Time and Space in Tradition and Modernity* (JCPS, 1), Leiden, Brill, 1998, 45-72, repr. in *Dreams and Scripture in Luke-Acts*, 123-146.

Lukan narrative about Jesus, found in the body of the Gospel, is divided into three phases by most scholars.[13] The first phase is Jesus' mission in Galilee (and Judaea; Luke 3,21/4,14[16]-9,50). The second stage is his going up to Jerusalem (9,51-19,27/28).[14] The final part of this Gospel is formed by reports about Jesus' entry into that city, his teachings in the Temple and the last supper, followed by the story about his death and the resurrection narratives (19,28/29-24,53).

Luke 7,18-38 is thus part of the first phase of Jesus' ministry. Adelbert Denaux argues that the καὶ ἐγένετο formula is one of the important elements for the structure of the Gospel of Luke.[15] In the first part nearly all the larger subsections are marked by καὶ ἐγένετο: *3,21-4,44*; *5,1-6,11*; *6,12-49*; 7,1-50; *8,1-21*; *8,22-56*; *9,1-17*; *9,18-27*, *9,28-36* (those verses where we can find this form are in italics).[16]

Luke 7,18-38 is often seen as part of the subsection 7,1-50.[17] After what Jesus has said in Luke 6,20-49, Jesus goes into Capernaum. There is therefore a clear-cut change of place and action. In 8,1-3, there is a new subsection, again indicated by καὶ ἐγένετο, a change of place and a *summarium*.[18]

---

[13] See e.g. F. BOVON, *Das Evangelium nach Lukas* (EKKNT, 3), Zürich, Neukirchen 1989, pp. 14-17. BOVON uses the word 'Abschnitt' as a designation for such a part. For the sake of convenience I use 'section' or 'phase' and 'subsection' for a smaller unit. A subsection can consist of several scenes. Quite often the different subsections are linked by summaries. These summarize the preceding scenes, and at the same time prepare for the following subsection; see e.g. S.J. NOORDA, *Scene and Summary: A Proposal for Reading Acts 4,32-5,16*, in J. KREMER (ed.), *Les Actes des Apôtres: Traditions, rédaction, théologie* (BETL, 48), Leuven, Leuven University Press, 1979, 474-483. For a survey of the tripartite division see A. DENAUX, *The Delineation of the Lukan Travel Narrative within the Overall Structure of the Gospel of Luke*, in C. FOCANT (ed.), *The Synoptic Gospels. Source Criticism and the New Literary Criticism* (BETL, 110), Louvain, Peeters, 1993, 359-392; repr. in A. DENAUX, *Studies in the Gospel of Luke: Structure, Language and Theology: Collected Essays* (TTS, 4), Berlin, LIT Verlag, 2010, 3-37, pp. 33-34. For multipartite divisions, see pp. 34-37.

[14] For some scholars, Jesus' entry into Jerusalem belongs to this part. See the discussion in DENAUX, *Delineation* (n. 13, in repr.), pp. 29-32.

[15] DENAUX, *Delineation* (n. 13, in repr.), pp. 22-23. He argues that, in itself, the formula is not sufficient to indicate a new beginning, but that other factors like content, change of time, place, etc., should be taken into account.

[16] DENAUX, *Delineation* (n. 13, in repr.), p. 23. In 7,11 καὶ ἐγένετο is used. It is quite often an indication of a new beginning. It is interesting that in *Codex Bezae* we find καὶ ἐγένετο in 7,1 and not in 7,11 (but again in 7,12). See for text and English translation J. READ-HEIMERDINGER – J. RIUS-CAMPS (eds.), *Luke's Demonstration to Theophilus: The Gospel and Acts of the Apostles according to Codex Bezae*, London, Bloomsbury, 2013.

[17] See e.g. MARTINEZ, *The Question of John the Baptist* (n. 3), 153.

[18] Some scholars see Luke 7,1-8,3 as a subsection: J.A. FITZMYER, *The Gospel according to Luke I-IX* (AB, 28), Garden City, New York, 1981, p. 137; L.T. JOHNSON, *The Literary Functions of Possessions in Luke-Acts* (SBLDS, 39), Missoula, Scholars Press, 1977, p. 96.

Although in this section Luke combines material from the double tradition (7,18-35; for Luke 7,1-11, see Matt 8,5-13 and John 4,43-54) with *Sondergut* (7,12-17; *cf.* 8,1-3), the materials are shaped by him into a certain unity.[19] There are quite a few connections between the passages which link them together and there are some details which are shared by the different episodes. In Luke 7 the overarching theme is a presentation of what Jesus is doing and of who he is.

There is a quite strong connection between Luke 7,1-17 and 7,18-35. In each episode or scene of this subsection, the audience is typified as ὄχλος (7,9.11.12.24). In Luke 7,1-10 the communication between Jesus and the ἑκατοντάρχης takes place through intermediaries, and that is also the case regarding the communication between John the Baptist and Jesus (7,18-35).[20] While in 7,4 Jewish elders come to Jesus and in 7,6 some friends of the centurion appear, in Luke 7,20 it is the two disciples from John the Baptist who come to him.[21] Michael Goulder remarks that this repetition is a Lukan feature.[22]

In Luke 7,1-17 we hear about two miracles: Jesus heals the slave/boy (see 7,1.2.7) of a commander of one hundred (ἑκατοντάρχης/*centurion*) and raises the son of a widow from the dead.[23] The disciples of John the Baptist tell the Baptist about "all these things". Quite probably this refers to everything that happened during Jesus' ministry as described in Luke, but certainly it refers to these last miracles. The reason for the Baptist's message to Jesus is his hearing about these 'things'. In his answer to John's messengers, Jesus refers to what he is doing in terms reminiscent of prophetic language.

In Luke 7,1-17 as well as in 7,22 there are possible echoes of Luke 4,16-30. Johnson sees in the two stories in 7,1-17 a rough correspondence to

---

[19] See e.g. JOHNSON, *Literary Functions* (n. 18), pp. 96-103. MARTINEZ, *The Question of John the Baptist* (n. 3), 64, argues that the narrative logic and the literary function of this passage are smoother and less abrupt than those of its Matthean counterpart.

[20] *Cf.* ἀποστέλλω in 7,3.20; πέμπω in 7.6.10.19 and παραγίνομαι (8× in Luke) in 7,4.20.

[21] In the parallel in Matt 8,5-13 it is the *centurion* himself who has a communication with Jesus. Thus, Luke enhances the parallels between Luke 7,1-10 and Luke 7,18-24.

[22] See M. GOULDER, *Luke: A New Paradigm* (JSNT.S, 20), Vol. 1, Sheffield, JSOT Press, 1989, pp. 388-389: "Two make a normal Lucan embassy (10.1; 19.29; 22.8). John tells them to say 'Are you the coming one...', and in v. 20 they say it, just as the centurion told his embassy what to say and they said it in 7.3-5". FITZMYER, *Luke, I-IX* (n. 18), p. 650, refers to it as 'double delegation'.

[23] These stories recall miracles of Elisha and Elijah. For Luke 7,11-17 and its relation to 1 Kings, see e.g. T.L BRODIE, *Towards Unravelling Luke's Use of the Old Testament: Luke 7,11-17 as an* Imitatio *of 1 Kings 11.17-24*, in *NTS* 32 (1986), 247-267.

the stories of Elijah and Elisa in Luke 4,25-27.[24] Elisha heals a Gentile commander, through the intercession of a Jewish girl (2 Kings 5), while Jesus cures the beloved 'boy' of the Roman commander of a hundred through the intercession of Jewish elders. The literary relationship between Elijah's raising of the son of a widow (1 Kings 17) and Jesus' raising of a widow's son in Nain is even closer. When in Luke 7,22 Jesus informs the messengers that they can tell John that the dead are raised up, in the Lukan narrative this is of course connected to the preceding story about the widow and her dead son. His references to evangelizing the poor echo his announcement in Nazareth (Luke 4,18; cf. 8,1 and 20,1).[25]

The description of Jesus' ministry in Luke 7,22 is also reminiscent of the language of Isaiah and concurs to a certain extent with the mixed-quotation in Luke 4,18-19.[26] There is also a connection between Luke 7,33-34 and Luke 7,36-50.[27] David Neale, for example, argues that Jesus's remark in 7,34 serves a pivotal function in connecting the parable of the children in the market to the story of the sinful woman.[28] In Luke 7,30 there is a reference to the Pharisees in general, while in 7,34 there is one

---

[24] See e.g. JOHNSON, *Literary function* (n. 18), 97-98.

[25] See B.J. KOET, *"Today this Scripture Has Been Fulfilled in your Ears" : Jesus' Explanation of Scripture in Luke 4,16-30*, in B.J. KOET, *Five Studies on the Interpretation of Scripture in Luke-Acts* (SNTA, 14), Peeters, Leuven, 1989, 24-55.

[26] There is quite a discussion about the Isaianic background of Luke 7,22. The resurrection of the dead recalls Isa 26,19. The healing of the "deaf" and the "blind" evokes Isa 29,18 (see also Isa 42,7, where the "blind" are accompanied by those who are relegated to the darkness of prison). R. MEYNET, *Traité de Rhétorique Biblique*, Paris, Cerf, 1939; Eng. transl. by Leo Arnold, *Treatise on Biblical Rhetoric* (ISHR, 3), Leiden, Brill, 2012, p. 269-270, argues that it is only in Isa 35,5-6 that we find a list which will be echoed by Luke: "Behold, this is your God. This is the vengeance that is coming. This is the recompense of God. It is he who comes, your saviour. Then the eyes of the blind will be opened; the ears of the deaf will be opened. Then the lame will leap like a deer and the tongue of the dumb will cry for joy (Isa 35,4-6)".
This is the only one of all these texts in Isaiah that adds "the lame" to "the blind" and to "the deaf". Still more importantly, the words of Jesus are uttered in reply to John the Baptist's question: "Are you the one who is coming or are we to wait for another?" (Luke 7:19; this question is repeated in the next verse by those sent by John). The two verses from Isa 35,5-6 are preceded by a bimember, announcing, twice also, that the Lord is "coming". Hence it may be concluded that this last text of the prophet is the most relevant for clarifying Luke's wording in its context.

[27] *Cf.* ἁμαρτωλός in 7,34 and 7,37.39. Luke 7,36-50 is an example of those scenes which show that Jesus indeed is somebody for whom eating together is important. For Jesus as the guest at table, see R.F. COLLINS, *The Man Who Came to Dinner*, in R. BIERINGER et al. (eds.), *Luke and his Readers* (FS A. DENAUX) (BETL, 182), Peeters, Leuven, 2005, 151-172.

[28] D.A. NEALE, *None but the Sinners, Religious Categories in the Gospel of Luke* (JSNT.S, 58), Sheffield, JSOT Press, 1991, p. 137.

to Jesus as a friend of sinners. In 7,36-50 we are given concrete examples of the attitudes mentioned in 7,30-34: the Pharisee Simon is an instance of the first, while in the sinful woman we encounter a case of the second. The verb χαρίζομαι occurs three times in this chapter, once in the first passage (7,21), and twice in the last (7,42.43). It is not used elsewhere in Luke. This could indicate that this passage is a unity.

The theme of πίστις (11× in Luke) is a clue to the first scene or episode (7,9) as well as to the last (7,50).[29]

However, probably one of the most important themes shared by the different episodes of this subsection is the question of whether the audience indeed recognizes Jesus as a prophet, as is obvious that he is from the keyword προφήτης in 7,16.26.28.39.[30]

COMMUNICATING IN LUKE 7,18-35

We have seen above that one of the key problems in assessing these passages is the identity of the one to whom the last verse is directed: to the readers of Luke-Acts, to Jesus' audience or, as suggested by Martinez, to the religious leaders who possibly may not even be there? Luke wishes to communicate a message to his readers.

Yet, who were his 'readers? Texts are first of all directed to the text-immanent reader, the reader who is present within the text itself. The distinction made between the 'text-immanent reader' and the 'reader of flesh and blood' is quite important in order to understand texts in general, as well as biblical texts in particular.[31] The text-immanent author, who is

---

[29] It is well known that Luke has an *Episodenstil*. See already J. DE ZWAAN, *The Use of the Greek language in Acts*, in F.J. FOAKES JACKSON – K. LAKE (eds.), *The Beginning of Christianity; The Acts of the Apostles 2, Prolegomena II Criticism*, London, Macmillan & Co, 1922, p. 65: 'As a reaction against the compact uninterrupted style, pathetic effects and an *episodic composition* (Italics BJK), meant to give a dramatic movement to the whole, were preferred'. DE ZWAAN is followed by many scholars in defining Luke's style as episodic.

[30] This concurs with the whole of Luke 4,16-9,50. R. MEYNET, *L'Évangile selon saint Luc: Analyse rhétorique* (RB,1), Paris, Cerf, 1988, p. 405, argues that the question of the identity of Jesus is the *Leitmotiv* of the whole section (Luke 4,22; 4,36; 5,21; 7:19.20; 7,49; 8,25; 9,9.24, until the last sequence of the section (9:1-50) with Peter's confession in reply to Jesus' question right in the centre of the passage 9:18-22: "He said to them: 'And you, who do you say that I am?'. Peter replied: 'The Christ of God!'" (9,20). We have to note that in 7,6b.13 as well as in 7.19 Jesus is addressed as κύριος (however, 7,13.19 not in D).

[31] See e.g.: W. ISER, 'Interaction Between Text and Reader', in: S.R. SULEIMAN – I. CROSMAN (eds.), *The Reader in the Text: Essays on Audience and Interpretation*, Princeton

according to tradition Luke, directly addresses the most famous text-immanent reader in the Bible, Theophilus (Luke 1,1 and Acts1,1). He is addressed in such a way, that he cannot do anything else but know the certainty of the things wherein he has been instructed (Luke 1,4).

In his article on Amos in this volume Archibald van Wieringen argues that textual communication is always multi-layered. He distinguishes three communication levels in a text. The first one is at the level of the characters. Characters interact with one another on the textual stage (in Luke 7,18 for example Jesus and the disciples of John). The second level is at the level of the textual director, called 'narrator' or 'discursor' depending on the two different types of textual worlds, namely the narrative or discursive world. For a narration, the receiver's side of this communication level is called the 'narratee'.[32] For a discourse, the receiver's side of this communication level may be called the 'discursee'. The third communication level is at that of the text-immanent author and the text-immanent reader. These communication instances may also be indicated by the terms 'implied author' and 'implied reader'.

1. Text-linguistic Analysis and Domain Analysis

The text-linguistic analysis of Old Testament texts is based upon the work of the linguist Harold Weinrich.[33] There are two basic principles according to Weinrich.

1) A text is considered to be communicative;
2) The linguistic signs in a text derive their meaning from the entity of the text in which they occur.

Discussing the verbal tenses, Weinrich distinguished several fundamental aspects of communication within texts. Here is not the place to discuss them.[34] There is, however, one element of his theory, which without much change may also be used for an analysis of the Greek text of the New Testament. I think that an analysis of the communication of Luke 7,18-35

NJ, Princeton University Press, 1980, p. 106. *Cf.* also A.L.H.M. VAN WIERINGEN, *The Implied Reader in Isaiah 6-12* (BIS, 34), Leiden, Brill, 1998, pp. 2-26.

[32] See: S. CHATMAN, *Story and Discourse: Narrative Structure in Fiction and Film*, Ithaca NY, Cornell University Press, 1978, pp. 147-151; G. GENETTE, *Narrative Discourse Revisited*, Ithaca NY, Cornell University Press, 1988, pp. 130-154. For the book of Isaiah, see A.L.H.M. VAN WIERINGEN, *The Reader-Oriented Unity Of The Book Isaiah* (ACEBT Suppl. Series, 6), Vught, Skandalon, 2006, pp. 3-7.

[33] H. WEINRICH, *Tempus: Besprochene und erzählte Welt*, München, Beck, 1964.

[34] But see VAN WIERINGEN, *The Implied Reader in Isaiah* (n. 31), pp. 6-12.

can help to get a clearer view of the problems about the audience as mentioned above. Weinrich argues that there are two different possible worlds of a text: A text is part of the world in which something is dealt with (*discoursed*) and a text can be part of the world where something is told (*narrated*). It is possible that this distinction can help to interpret Luke 7,29-30.

An important aspect of this method is that one can distinguish certain domains in a text. Whatever is said in a text, it always somebody's domain. The question at stake here is: who says, thinks or perceives something and at which point in the text? These domains can be made visible in a diagram.

A text consists of a basis domain which is the whole of the text(-fragment) which one wants to analyse. This text is the domain of the implied author. As described by Van Wieringen, one can depict the different domains in a schema: the basis domain with dependent sub-domains.[35] Within the basis domain, dependent sub-domains may occur with new textual realities. Subordinated domains are evoked by a domain builder: a non-factive verb. These verbs indicate speaking, thinking or perception. A clear example of such a subordinated domain is direct speech, but domains may also contain indirect speech and perceptions of feelings and thinking.

2. Luke 7,18-35: a domain analysis[36]

In Luke 7,18-35 the creator of the domains is the implied author, which tradition calls Luke. Each time that there is a new speaker, we can describe what the new speaker says as a subdomain. It is exactly this way of analysing that can help us to get a better insight into the audiences involved in this passage. There are several domain-owners in this passage. 'Luke' is the owner of the basic domain (Luke 7,18-35). There are several subdomains. The first subdomain-owners are the disciples of John (7,18), who '*report all these things to him*'. John the Baptist is the next domain-owner (7,19). He sends two of his disciples to Jesus, saying: '*Are you the one, who is to come? Or do we expect another?*'

These two disciples of John, who are sent by him to the Lord, are the next domain owners. In their domain ('*John the Baptist has sent us to you*') another domain is opened: '*Saying: "Are you the one, who is to come?" Or do we expect another?*'

---

[35] *Ibid.*, pp. 11-22.
[36] See the chart at the end of this article.

Luke is again the domain-owner of 7,21-22a. He describes some activities of Jesus' ministry. In his answer to John's question, which he addresses to the disciples of the Baptist, Jesus opens another subdomain in his own subdomain ('*Go and announce to John, what you see and what you hear*'). Here, the disciples are supposed to be domain-owners: '*The blind see, the lame walk, lepers are cleansed and the deaf hear, the dead are raised, the poor are evangelized*'.

But what happens in 7,23? Who is the domain-owner here? Again, it is quite probably Jesus who is the domain-owner: '*And blessed is the one who is not offended in me*' (ἐν ἐμοι). This ἐν ἐμοι refers to Jesus as the speaker.

In 7,24 Luke is back as domain-owner, introducing a new subdomain with Jesus as domain-owner. Jesus addresses the crowd with three consecutive rhetorical questions ('*What did you go out to see in the desert?*' [7,24], and '*What did you go out to see?*' [7,25.26]). Each question is followed by a possible answer in the form of another rhetorical question. The first two, as argued by Martinez, are almost hyperbolically a false portrayal of John.[37] The final answer is the right one: a prophet.

However, after these three questions Jesus opens another subdomain in his own subdomain: *I tell you*. The second subdomain which opens here is a reference to Scripture. It is quite probably a combined allusion to Malachi 3,1 and Exod 23,20.[38]

A problem arises in 7,29. Is it Jesus who is the domain-owner, or is it Luke? There are no clear-cut indications that a new subdomain has been opened: there is no *verbum dicendi*. There are suddenly new characters: all the people and the tax collectors. It comes as no surprise that commentators have discussed the question whether these verses are a continuation of Jesus' statements or a narrative commentary.[39] An indication that it is a new domain may be found in the fact that, formally, there are new characters: the people and the tax collectors. However, οὖν in 7,31 seems to connect Jesus' new pronouncement with the preceding statements.[40] It seems to me that the ambiguity of this passage contains a clue to its

---

[37] MARTINEZ, *The Question of John the Baptist* (n. 3), p. 113.

[38] *Cf.* Mal 3,1: ἰδοὺ ἐγὼ ἐξαποστέλλω τὸν ἄγγελόν μου and Exod 23,20: καὶ ἰδοὺ ἐγὼ ἀποστέλλω τὸν ἄγγελόν μου πρὸ προσώπου σου. In this article I cannot deal with the form and origin of this reference to the Old Testament, but see e.g. R. RUSAM, *Das Alte Testament bei Lukas* (BZNW, 112), Berlin-New York, 2003, pp. 163-164.

[39] MARTINEZ, *The Question of John the Baptist* (n. 3), p. 131; see also FITZMYER, *Luke I-IX* (n. 18), pp. 670-671.

[40] The word οὖν quite clearly refers to something which precedes: *therefore, consequently, accordingly*: Also FITZMYER, *Luke I-IX* (n. 18), p. 678, sees this connection.

interpretation. Although it is more probable that Jesus is the domain-owner, his opinion can now also be seen as echoing the voice of the domain-owner Luke.

It is quite clear that in 7,31 Jesus is once again the domain-owner. However, in 7,32b he introduces children sitting in the marketplace as new domain-owners: Their domain is quite clear as indicated by the first and second person plural.

Jesus is again the domain-owner in 7,33 and in 7,34, introducing his audience as domain-owners twice (λέγετε). This detail is crucial for the interpretation of this passage. But who is the domain-owner in 7,35: Jesus or Luke? Quite a few commentators attribute this aphorism to Jesus.[41] One of the reasons is that there is a link between the children in the marketplace and the children of wisdom.[42]

3. The positions of 7,23.29-30 and 7,35

The most difficult verses to assess are Luke 7,29-30 and 7,35, but we saw above that the position of 7,23 is also not so clear. We have to note that all these verses describe a reaction to a prophetic activity.

Luke 7,17 is also a reaction to a prophetic lesson of Jesus, but there it is quite clearly part of Luke's own domain (like in 7,11-12 or in 4,28-30). I tend to see Luke 7,23; 7,29-30 and 7,35 as part of Jesus' domain. In these verses, he reflects on the effect of the audience's reaction to the prophetic gestures and styles of both himself and John the Baptist. While in 7,23 he says that those who do not react negatively to his own prophetic healing are blessed, he identifies two different reactions to John's ministry: a positive one (7,29) and an indifferent and thus negative one (7,30). Jesus concludes with a remark about the reactions of the children of Wisdom personified.

If these asides are part of the domain of Jesus, this has consequences for their function. In the first instance this seems to be aimed at Jesus' audience as described by Luke. The saying *'Blessed is the one who is not offended by me'* (7,23), of course has as a possible audience the two disciples and also, via their mission, John the Baptist. It is not mentioned in 7,18-23 that there were other people present, but considering the context,

---

We have to note that in Matt 11,16 we do not have οὖν, but δὲ. However, Luke 7,29-30 is Lukan *Sondergut*.

[41] MARTINEZ, *The Question of John the Baptist* (n. 3), p. 162.

[42] MARTINEZ, *The Question of John the Baptist* (n. 3), p. 165; FITZMYER, *Luke I-IX* (n. 18), p. 681: "the connection is not by catchword bonding, but by sense".

there must have been an audience: in 7,24 Jesus begins to speak about John the Baptist to the crowds and thus they are not only the first recipients of Jesus remarks in 7,24b-28 and 7,31-34, but also of those in 7,29-30.35.

In all these verses there is a reference to a positive relation between human beings and God.[43] In 7,23 it is said that somebody is μακάριός when he does not take offense in Jesus. Μακάριός is quite clearly a description of somebody who has a good relation with God and his Torah (see only for example Psalm 1,1; 2,12; 32,2, Psalms of Solomon 4,23; see also Luke 1,45; 6,20; 11,28).

In 7,29 there is another instance of positive relations between human beings and God: all the people when they heard, and the publicans, justified God, by being baptized with the baptism of John.[44] Luke 7,30, however, refers to an indifferent reaction: the Pharisees and the legal experts set aside God's purpose.

In Luke 7,35 there is a positive relation between Wisdom and her children (like in 7,29 typified by a form of the verb δικαιόω). Although the identity of Wisdom is not totally clear, there are enough reasons to assume that it refers in one way or another to God or one of his attributes.[45] The connection between Luke 7,29-30 and 7,35 shows that personified Wisdom is connected to accepting the baptism of John and opposed to the rejection of God's will/design (βουλή).[46] Thus, Wisdom is to a certain extent here a symbol of divinity.[47] So we have to conclude that in this passage there is a clear voice that tells the listeners that a positive attitude to God and divine Wisdom is possible.

---

[43] We have to note that σκανδαλίζω is to a certain extent the opposite of δικαιόω and that there is therefore much in common in 7,23-7,29-30 and 7,35.

[44] According to FITZMYER, *Luke I-IX* (n. 18), p. 324, 'All the people' is a typical Lukan rhetorical exaggeration.

[45] Quite a few commentators refer to F. CHRIST, *Jesus Sophia: Die Sophia-Christologie bei den Synoptikern* (ATANT, 57), Zürich, Zwingli, 1979, pp. 63-80. He argues (p. 79) that in Luke 7,35, like in the Q logion and Matt 11,19, Jesus is depicted as personified Wisdom. I think that CHRIST overemphasizes the evidence. See e.g. FITZMYER, *Luke I-IX* (n. 18), p. 679, who notes that Wisdom is personified and that Jesus and John are her children.

[46] See RINDOŠ, *He of Whom It Is Written* (n. 3), pp. 187-189. RINDOŠ [188] argues that the book of Wisdom contains several elements which are pertinent to the texts concerning John the Baptist in Luke (e.g. ἡ βουλή τοῦ θεοῦ only in Wisdom 6,4; 9,13 and in Luke 7,35, Acts 2,23; 13,36 and 20,27).

[47] F. CHRIST, *Jesus Sophia* (n. 45), p. 77, rightly argues that especially in Luke the context (Luke 7,29-30) helps to interpret 7,35 (he typifies this logion as 'das Rechtfertigungswort'), but he neglects the fact that this parallel makes his identification of Jesus as personified Wisdom difficult.

4. How can the listeners effect a positive relationship with God and divine Wisdom?

As we have said above, the first addressees of the pronouncements in this passage are Jesus' audience. An important argument for this is that Jesus refers to them twice (λέγετε). In this passage Jesus challenges his listeners to make a choice. The interesting part is that there are two choices possible, which are clearly not the same but are complementary.

It is remarkable that in the Lukan passage we encounter quite a few pairs (binarity). Two disciples of John are sent to the Lord with a question (7,18; diff. Matt 11,2). Luke mentions this question twice (7,19.20; diff. Matt 11,3). In Luke 7,29 we hear about the combination of the people and tax collectors, while in 7,30 it is the combination between Pharisees and the legal experts. In the children's song we hear about those who dance and pipe and about those who wail and weep.

However, the most important combination in this passage is that of John and Jesus. Although the disciples have a question about the identity of Jesus, after giving his answer, Jesus discusses the identity of John. Already in Luke 1-2 John and Jesus are presented as a kind of couple and here again they are presented as a pair.

It seems to me that in these passages this binarity underscores two contrary movements which are even more important: the contrast between the two teachers John and Jesus *and* between the two different attitudes towards such teachers.

While Luke 7,18-23 deals with John's question about Jesus' ministry, in 7,24 Jesus' assessment of John's ministry is at stake. In 7,31-35 the reaction of the men of this generation to these two prophets is discussed. Although in 7,29 it is said that all the people – even including the tax collectors – reacted positively to John, now we hear about a negative reaction. Jesus argues that his audience, referring to the Baptist's ascetic lifestyle, accuses him of having a demon, while his own lifestyle gives rise to their accusation that he is glutton and a wine drinker (7,33).[48] In a chiastic structure Jesus opposes two lifestyles.[49]

---

[48] The two opposite characterizations of John as somebody who teaches fasting and Jesus as somebody who enjoys drinking and eating as if he were at a wedding, should not come as a surprise. In the context of a great banquet (Luke 5,27-32; see 5,29; this is a Lukan element; *cf.* Mk 2,15 // Matt 9,10) unnamed persons ask Jesus, why he does not teach his disciples to fast like those of John and those of the Pharisees (5,33-39; See also the parallels in Mk 2,18-22 // Matt 9,14-17; the references to eating and drinking instead of fasting is also Lukan, like the reference to praying).
[49] FITZMYER, *Luke I-IX* (n. 18), pp. 678-679, gives a survey of the different interpretations of the parable.

7,31-32ab	The men and women of this generation resemble children at a marketplace
7,32c	A Flute playing and dancing
7,32d	B Wailing and weeping
7,33	B' Not eating, not drinking, assessed as having a demon[50]
7,34	A' Eating and drinking, accused of being a drinker and an overeater

Children sitting at the marketplace invite each other to dance and to weep. It is remarkable that Luke uses the same word (προσφωνέω, 7 × NT; 1 × Matt; 4 × Luke and twice in Acts) for the childrens' invitation to one another, as for the calling of the disciples/apostles in Luke 6,13. This could be an indication that this invitation to play is more than just that. It could also be a reminder of an invitation to engage with the lessons of a teacher and to follow him. The Hebrew Bible contains nearly a dozen Hebrew verbs which can describe quite different dancing activities. There are two very well-known passages: Miriam's dance after the crossing of the Red Sea (Ex 15,20) and David's dance before the ark in Jerusalem (see 2 Sam 6,5.14.15 and 1 Ch 15,29). Here is not the place to develop a theology of dancing and singing, but it is clear that music and dance were regarded as an expression of joy, often about what God had done for Israel.

It is probable that flute playing is seen as a sign of feasting and dining.[51] This seems to concur with one of Jesus's favourite activities in the Gospel of Luke: sharing a meal.[52] The wailing and the weeping seems to be connected with the fasting of John (For a discussion of the relationship between weeping, being hungry and mourning, see e.g. Luke 6,25). Wailing, weeping and fasting are connected and often a sign of repentance.[53] And of course, there is a time to mourn and a time to dance (Eccl 3,1.4).

---

[50] In Luke 1,15 the angel says to Zechariah about John: 'He must never drink wine or strong drink.' So here Luke's depiction of John is presented as the fulfilment of this command. That is to say, John's lifestyle, when it comes to drinking/fasting is as much about living according to the angel's prescription as it is about choosing asceticism for itself.

[51] In the LXX, but also in the writings of Josephus, there are only very few references to flutes and flute-playing. Ambrose in his commentary on Luke 7,35, refers to several prophetic figures who sang or danced: Moses, Isaiah, Daniel and his companions, Habakkuk and Ezekiel. See (in French translation) AMBROSE, *Traité sur l'Évangile de saint Luc* (SC, 45), ed. G. TISSOT, Paris, Cerf, 1956, here Book 6,7-10, pp. 230-231. Ambrose stresses that they did so in a modest way. However, there is a connection between singing and Jesus as a bridegroom. For a negative association of playing flute and drinking wine, see for example Isa 5,12. For the combination of flutes and dancing, see the description of the inauguration of King Solomon in *Jewish Antiquities* 7,358.

[52] See COLLINS, *The Man Who Came to Dinner* (n. 27).

[53] For an example of the combination of mourning and fasting, see Joel 2,12.

As so often in a case such as this, the significance of every detail in the parable of the children in the marketplace is not clear. However, the main point seems to be that the children invite other children to engage with each other, either in weeping together or in dancing together. The children who are invited to join are comparable with the men and women of this generation. These folk are disapproving of John's as well as of Jesus' ministry, albeit for quite contrary reasons.

However, the analysis of the communication shows that in 7,35 there is a reference to the fact that all ('all', a typical Lukan 'overemphasizing of the evidence') the people and even all the tax collectors choose the baptism of John and that therefore there is a possibility for the audience to become children of Wisdom by joining one of the teachers.

MODELS OF TEACHERS IN LUKE 7,18-35

The analysis of the communication helps us to understand some important elements of this passage. Focusing on the communication in Luke 7,18-35 teaches us that it is too easy to depict this text as an indictment of the religious leaders of Israel. There is only one, more or less negative, statement about Pharisees and legal experts (7,30), while there are three statements of a more positive nature regarding the teaching of John (7,29.35) or of Jesus (7,23.35). It is remarkable that again and again New Testament texts are used to attack Jewish persons and of course especially their leaders.[54] Martinez seems to be one example of this approach. An indictment of the religious leaders is not so obvious, because neither the audience in the passage, nor the text-immanent reader, are supposed to be Jewish religious leaders. In this passage there is less a contrast between Jesus and the Jewish religious leaders, than between indifferent people (like the Pharisees) and those who are ready to become a follower of a teacher.[55] In Luke 7,18-35 the most important element is the invitation to Jesus' audience to get involved and to follow a teacher, whether it be John or Jesus. This is probably also an invitation to the text-immanent reader.

---

[54] For Luke's view on Israel, see B.J. KOET *Five Studies* (n. 25), pp. 150-153.
[55] Note that only in 7,30 does the Lukan Jesus mention a negative reaction to John's preaching. The other reactions to his or to John's preaching are positive: 7,23.29.35.

1. John the Baptist and Jesus as complementary teachers

This text tells how Jesus answers John the Baptist's question of. Via two disciples he reveals to John, and also to the listeners, something about Jesus' own ministry. Jesus is a prophet who performs prophetic gestures as described, for example, in Isaiah. The phrasing of the first part of his answer is reminiscent of prophetic, especially of Isaianic, language.

For the benefit of his audience, Jesus portrays John's identity as 'the greatest of the prophets'. He asks them three rhetorical questions. In answering the last question himself, he also describes the prophetic mission of John in language which especially refers to the prophet Malachi.

However, the narrative does not only answer the question about the identity of Jesus and of John. It also depicts their relation in a special, and possibly even in a unique way, compared to other places where John and Jesus are paralleled. Jesus invites his audience to engage either with John's teaching *or* with his own. Both John and Jesus are presented as teachers having their own disciples, and although their teachings and lifestyles appear contrary to each other, Jesus presents them as being complementary.

This could be surprising because often the relationship between them is portrayed as being unequal. Quite a few scholars stress that there is a carefully composed parallel between Jesus and John the Baptist in Luke 1-2.[56] Often it is argued that in these parallels the Jesus-side comes off better.[57] However, Karl Allen Kuhn stresses that the cooperative rather than the competitive tone dominates Luke's portrayal of the two figures in Chapters 1-2. The parallels between them and their missions serve to underscore the shared objective of their respective, and in many cases similar, roles.[58]

It is less noted that the parallel between John and Jesus in Luke 3-4 is also quite substantial. In a recent article, Joop Smit argues that at the

---

[56] See for example FITZMYER, *Luke I-IX* (n. 18), pp. 313-316; E. SCHWEIZER, *Zum Aufbau von Lukas 1 und 2*, in D.Y. HADIDIAN (ed.), *Intergerini Parietis Septum (Eph 2,14)* (FS. M. BARTH), Pittsburgh PA, 1982, 309-335; repr. in E. SCHWEIZER, *Neues Testament und Christologie im Werden*, Göttingen, Vandenhoeck & Ruprecht, 2011, pp. 11-32.

[57] FITZMYER, *Luke, I-IX* (n. 18), p. 315. See also K.A. KUHN, *Deaf or Defiant? The Literary, Cultural, and Affective-Rhetorical Keys to the Naming of John (Luke 1:57-80)*, in *CBQ* 75 (2013), 485-503, p. 493: "Commentators frequently note that one of the clear implications of Luke's parallel accounts of John and Jesus, and the specific parallels he draws between their person and mission, is that they are comparative, with the result that Jesus emerges as the more exalted of the two."

[58] KUHN, *Deaf or Defiant?* (n. 57), pp. 493-494.

beginning of his Gospel Luke describes the relationship between John and Jesus not with two but with three diptychs: the announcement of their birth (1,5-56), their birth (1,57-2,52) *and* their public appearance (3,1-4,30).[59] Smit stresses the fact that at the beginning of John's preaching, as well as at the beginning of Jesus' mission, Luke uses a quotation from the prophet Isaiah: Isa 40,3-5 in 3,4-6 and Isa 61,1-2 (mixed with 58,6) in 4,18-19.[60]

We have to say that in Luke 1-4 the cooperative relationship between John and Jesus is quite possibly accompanied by a competitive element. However, in Luke 7,18-35 the relationship is even more complementary.[61] According to Luke, Jesus himself presents *both* figures as essential to the accomplishment of God's awaited salvation. John is an ascetic teacher and Jesus teaches at table and while drinking wine, but Jesus discloses to his audience that both teaching styles can be seen as positive and that his audience can choose, like the children in a marketplace, between weeping and dancing, between the ascetic John and the feasting Jesus.[62]

2. Learning from children

The analysis of the communication suggests that in Luke 7,23.29-30 and 7,35 Jesus makes an appeal to his audience. His reference to the playing children as well as these hints, combine to create a receptive attitude to John's as well as his own teachings as possible concretizations of a positive relationship with the divine.

---

[59] J. SMIT, *The Function of the Two Quotations from Isaiah in Luke 3-4*, in B.J. KOET – S. MOYISE – J. VERHEYDEN (eds.), *The Scriptures of Israel in Jewish and Christian Tradition* (FS M.J.J. MENKEN) (NTS, 148), Brill, Leiden, 2013, 41-55; for an overview of the parallels, see p. 48.

[60] J. SMIT, *The Function of the Two Quotations* (n. 59), p. 55: "The quotations are adapted to each other, but they are not of the same weight. They fit in with the pattern of surpassing parallelism between John and Jesus which Luke applies in each of the three diptychs".

[61] But see Luke 7,28.

[62] The fact that Jesus and John are to a certain extent a pair, recalls a tradition depicted in *Pirke Avot* 1,4-15, where one can find five pairs of complementary teachers; *cf.* A. TROPPER, *Wisdom, Politics, and Historiography, Tractate Avot in the context of the Graeco-Roman Near East* (OOM), Oxford, Oxford University Press, 2004, pp. 22-23. In Jewish tradition there is also a difference between these teachers. Hillel for example is considered to be the president of the Sanhedrin, while Shammai was *Av Beth Din*, a kind of chief of Justice. There is also the traditionally cited difference in character between Hillel and Shammai. Hillel is considered to have been lenient and forthcoming, as opposed to Shammai, who is known to have been strict and aloof. We can see in these differences, parallels to the dissimilarities between Jesus and John.

In 7,31-32 Jesus uses children and their playing and singing as a model to typify the people of his generation, but also as the first step of an invitation to his audience to engage with a teacher. In his appeal to them, Jesus twice refers to children and this suggests that his disciples are able to learn from children.[63]

We can also find this idea elsewhere in the Gospel.[64] Luke is the only one who tells his readers something about Jesus and John the Baptist as children. In Luke 1,16-17 Zachariah has to turn his heart to his son in order to get his voice back.[65] According to Luke Jesus himself (Ἰησοῦς ὁ παῖς; Luke 2,43) is seated in the midst of the teachers, listening to them and asking them questions, and all who heard him were astounded at his understanding and his answers (2,46-47). Jesus is an example of how teachers can learn something from a youngster.

Reference to children as an inspiration and a model for discipleship is not only a Lukan theme.[66] It is depicted in two stories which all the three synoptic gospels share. In Luke 9,46-48 (parr. Mk 9,33-38 // Matt 18,1-5), Jesus shows his ambitious disciples that they have to be 'attuned' to children. In Matt 19,13-15 // Mk 10,13-16 // Luke 18,15-17, Jesus makes children into a model for entering the reign of God.[67]

3. Eating and learning

Another theme in Luke 7,18-35 is quite typical of Luke. Frequently Jesus' teaching takes the form of table-talk. In Luke 7,34 Jesus mentions

---

[63] There are some differences between the Greek words used here. Παιδίον refers normally to a very young child, an infant (see e.g. Luke 1,59.66.76.80; 2,17.27.40 and 9,47.48), while τέκνον mostly to one's own child (see e.g. Luke 1,7; 11,13; 14,26; 15,31; 18,29; 19,44; 20,31).

[64] See e.g. J.T. CAROLL, *What Then Will This Child Become? Perspectives on Children in the Gospel of Luke*, in M. BUNGE – T.E. FRETHEIM – B. ROBERTS GAVENTA (eds.), *The Child in the Bible*, Grand Rapids MI, Eerdmans, 2008, pp. 177–94.

[65] See B.J. KOET, *Elijah as Reconciler of Father and Son: From 1 Kings 16:34 and Malachi 3:22-24 to Ben Sira 48:1-11 and Luke 1:13-17*, in J. CORLEY – H. VAN GROL (eds.), *Rewriting Biblical History: Essays on Chronicles and Ben Sira in Honor of Pancratius Beentjes* (DCLS, 7), Berlin, De Gruyter, 2011, 173-190.

[66] For a connection between the disciples and children, *cf.* The Gospel of Thomas Logion 21: "Mary said to Jesus, 'What are your disciples like?' He said, "They are like little children living in a field that is not theirs. When the owners of the field come, they will say, 'Give us back our field.' They take off their clothes in front of them in order to give it back to them, and they return their field to them".

[67] For a very young child teaching lessons in life, see The Gospel of Thomas, Logion 4: "Jesus said, 'The person old in days won't hesitate to ask a little child seven days old about the place of life'".

that he is seen as a glutton and winebibber (φάγος καὶ οἰνοπότης).[68] However, this negative or ironic characterization is not without reason. The presentation of Jesus as somebody who likes to eat and drink with all kinds of people is in line with the Lukan theme that Jesus is often depicted as dining together with all kinds of different people.[69] Not only with sinners, but also with Pharisees! Here we can only note that this theme also tells us something about Jesus as a teacher. He combines eating with healing and teaching (See for example Luke 14,1-6.7-11; *cf.* Luke 10,38-42).[70]

Conclusions

In his book on Augustine and the catechumenate, William Harmless notes that not only the 'what' but also the 'how' of the message is important for Augustine.[71] The bishop of Hippo did not only seek clarity of thought, but also crispness of formulation. What applies to Augustine also applies to Jesus. It is not only important to investigate *what* Jesus teaches, but also to notice *whom* he teaches and *how* he does so.

Where can we find a great wisdom teacher who uses children's rhymes to depict his teachings? According to this article, we can meet such a teacher in Luke 7,31-35, where Jesus explains his own teaching and that of John the Baptist and at the same time, defends their teachings, albeit so very different from each other, by referring to a children's song. Jesus addresses his audience and presents them with two complementary teachers: John the Baptist as a sober teacher and Jesus himself as somebody who connects teaching with joyful eating together. Sitting together at table is for Jesus an important way of teaching. His reference to children highlights a theme, which is also present in the other synoptic gospels, but most prominent in the Gospel of Luke: whoever does not receive the kingdom of God like a child, shall not enter into it. It is as simple as that.

---

[68] Φάγος only in Luke 7,34 and parr. The vulgate is quite suggestive: *manducans*. For οἰνοπότης (1× LXX; in NT only here and in the Matthean parallel) as winebibber, see Prov 23,20: 'Be not among winebibbers; among gluttonous eaters of flesh'.
[69] We have to note that Luke does not mention that John the Baptist eats locusts and wild honey (Mk 1,6 // Matt 3,4). He does mention that John will not drink wine (1,15).
[70] Collins, *The Man who Came to Dinner* (n. 27).
[71] W. Harmless, *Augustine and the Catechumenate* (rev. ed.), Collegeville MN, Liturgical Press, 2014, p. 409.

Domain-Analyse Luke 7:18-35 (with thanks to Lars Koks)

> Domain-owner = author of the Gospel 'Luke'
>
> 18 Καὶ ἀπήγγειλαν Ἰωάννῃ οἱ μαθηταὶ αὐτοῦ
>
> > Domain-owner: his disciples
> > περὶ πάντων τούτων
>
> καὶ προσκαλεσάμενος δύο τινὰς τῶν μαθητῶν αὐτοῦ ὁ Ἰωάννης
> 19 ἔπεμψεν πρὸς τὸν κύριον λέγων
>
> > Domain-owner = John
> > σὺ εἶ ὁ ἐρχόμενος
> > ἢ ἄλλον προσδοκῶμεν;
>
> 20 παραγενόμενοι δὲ πρὸς αὐτὸν
> οἱ ἄνδρες εἶπαν
>
> > Domain-owner = the men
> > Ἰωάννης ὁ βαπτιστὴς ἀπέστειλεν ἡμᾶς πρὸς σὲ
> > λέγων
> >
> > > Domain-owner = John
> > > **σὺ εἶ ὁ ἐρχόμενος**
> > > ἢ ἄλλον <u>προσδοκῶμεν</u>;
>
> 21 ἐν ἐκείνῃ τῇ ὥρᾳ ἐθεράπευσεν πολλοὺς ἀπὸ νόσων
> καὶ μαστίγων
> καὶ πνευμάτων πονηρῶν
> καὶ τυφλοῖς πολλοῖς ἐχαρίσατο βλέπειν.
> 22 καὶ ἀποκριθεὶς εἶπεν αὐτοῖς
>
> > Domain-owner = he (Jesus)
> > πορευθέντες ἀπαγγείλατε Ἰωάννῃ
> >
> > > Domain-owner: you (the men)
> > > ἃ εἴδετε καὶ ἠκούσατε
> > >
> > > > Domain-owner = you
> > > > τυφλοὶ ἀναβλέπουσιν,
> > > > χωλοὶ περιπατοῦσιν,
> > > > λεπροὶ καθαρίζονται
> > > > καὶ κωφοὶ ἀκούουσιν,
> > > > νεκροὶ ἐγείρονται,
> > > > πτωχοὶ εὐαγγελίζονται
> >
> > 23 καὶ μακάριός <u>ἐστιν</u>
> > ὃς ἐὰν μὴ σκανδαλισθῇ <u>ἐν ἐμοί</u>.

24 Ἀπελθόντων δὲ τῶν ἀγγέλων Ἰωάννου
ἤρξατο λέγειν πρὸς τοὺς ὄχλους περὶ Ἰωάννου

> Domain-owner = he (Jesus)
> τί ἐξήλθατε εἰς τὴν ἔρημον θεάσασθαι;
> κάλαμον ὑπὸ ἀνέμου σαλευόμενον;
> 25 ἀλλὰ τί ἐξήλθατε ἰδεῖν;
> ἄνθρωπον ἐν μαλακοῖς ἱματίοις ἠμφιεσμένον;
> ἰδοὺ οἱ ἐν ἱματισμῷ ἐνδόξῳ καὶ τρυφῇ ὑπάρχοντες
> ἐν τοῖς βασιλείοις εἰσίν.
> 26 ἀλλὰ τί ἐξήλθατε ἰδεῖν;
> προφήτην; (...) λέγω ὑμῖν,
>
> > Domain-owner = I (Jesus)
> > ναὶ (...) καὶ περισσότερον προφήτου.
> > 27 οὗτός ἐστιν περὶ οὗ γέγραπται
> >
> > > Domain-owner = Malachi (3,1)
> > > ἰδοὺ ἀποστέλλω τὸν ἄγγελόν μου πρὸ
> > > προσώπου σου,
> > > ὃς κατασκευάσει τὴν ὁδόν σου ἔμπροσθέν
> > > σου.
>
> 28 λέγω ὑμῖν,
>
> > Domain-owner = I (Jesus)
> > μείζων ἐν γεννητοῖς γυναικῶν Ἰωάννου οὐδείς ἐστιν
> > ὁ δὲ μικρότερος ἐν τῇ βασιλείᾳ τοῦ θεοῦ μείζων αὐτοῦ
> > ἐστιν.

> Domain-owner = Luke or Jesus?
> 29 Καὶ πᾶς ὁ <u>λαὸς</u> ἀκούσας καὶ οἱ <u>τελῶναι</u>
> ἐδικαίωσαν
> βαπτισθέντες τὸ βάπτισμα Ἰωάννου
> 30 οἱ δὲ <u>Φαρισαῖοι</u> καὶ οἱ <u>νομικοὶ</u> τὴν βουλὴν τοῦ θεοῦ
> ἠθέτησαν εἰς ἑαυτοὺς
> μὴ βαπτισθέντες ὑπ' αὐτοῦ
>
> > Domain-owner = people, publicans
> > τὸν θεὸν

> Domain-owner: he (Jesus)
>> Domain-owner = I (Jesus)
>> 31 Τίνι οὖν ὁμοιώσω τοὺς ἀνθρώπους τῆς γενεᾶς
>> ταύτης καὶ τίνι εἰσὶν ὅμοιοι;
>> 32 ὅμοιοί εἰσιν παιδίοις
>> τοῖς ἐν ἀγορᾷ καθημένοις
>> καὶ προσφωνοῦσιν ἀλλήλοις
>> ἃ λέγει
>>> Domain-owner = the children
>>> ηὐλήσαμεν ὑμῖν
>>> καὶ οὐκ ὠρχήσασθε,
>>> ἐθρηνήσαμεν
>>> καὶ οὐκ ἐκλαύσατε.
>> 33 ἐλήλυθεν γὰρ Ἰωάννης ὁ βαπτιστὴς
>> μὴ ἐσθίων ἄρτον
>> μήτε πίνων οἶνον,
>> καὶ λέγετε
>>> Domain-owner = you
>>> δαιμόνιον ἔχει.
>> 34 ἐλήλυθεν ὁ υἱὸς τοῦ ἀνθρώπου
>> ἐσθίων
>> καὶ πίνων,
>> καὶ λέγετε
>>> Domain-owner = you
>>> ἰδοὺ ἄνθρωπος φάγος καὶ οἰνοπότης, φίλος
>>> τελωνῶν καὶ ἁμαρτωλῶν.

35 καὶ ἐδικαιώθη ἡ σοφία ἀπὸ πάντων τῶν τέκνων αὐτῆς.

EDUCATION AND TEACHING IN JOHN'S GOSPEL[1]

Jan VAN DER WATT
Nijmegen, the Netherlands

INTRODUCTION

The Gospel of John[2] is known for its use of figurative language, including larger metaphorical networks related to the concepts of family[3], temple[4], and kingship/kingdom[5]. These networks *inter alia* serve as structuring devices in John. It has been similarly argued that the central and determinative concept of ancient mission should also be interpreted as a metaphor[6]. Central to the idea of mission is the idea of preparing the one sent for his/her mission. This is the case in John 5,19-23, where an educational metaphor is used to describe the identity of Jesus as the Son who may do what his Father does[7]. This raises the question of the significance of the concept of education in John, especially in light of the fact that Jesus claims that his Father taught him (8,28) and that his disciples indeed call him 'Teacher' (13,13-14).

The aim of this essay is to determine the dynamics of education or educational processes in John by investigating the use of relevant educational terminology, and thereafter analysing the conceptual references to education.

---

[1] Similar research was published in Afrikaans in *Stellenbosch Theological Journal* (2016) under the title "'Julle noem My Leermeester... en julle is reg, want Ek is dit' (Joh. 13,13). Onderrig in die Johannesevangelie". See *STJ* 2 (2016), 441-461, http://ojs.reformedjournals.co.za/index.php/stj/article/view/1341.
[2] For convenience sake the word 'John' is used to refer both to the Gospel as well as to the author, depending on the context.
[3] J.G. VAN DER WATT, *Family of the King: Dynamics of metaphor in the Gospel according to John*, Leiden, Brill, 2000.
[4] See U. BUSSE, *Tempelmetaphorik als ein Beispiel von implizitem Rekurs auf die biblische Tradition im Johannesevangelium*, in TUCKETT, C.M. (ed.), *The Scriptures in the Gospels*, Leuven, Peeters, 1996, 395-428; M.L. COLOE, *God dwells with us: Temple symbolism in the Fourth Gospel*, Collegeville, MN, Liturgical Press, 2001.
[5] U. BUSSE, *Metaphorik und Rethorik im Johannesevangelium: Das Bildfeld vom König*, in J. FREY – J.G. VAN DER WATT – R. ZIMMERMANN – G. KERN, *Imagery in the Gospel of John*, Tübingen, Mohr Siebeck, 2006, pp. 279-317.
[6] VAN DER WATT, *Family of the King* (n. 3), pp. 296-303.
[7] *Ibid.*, pp. 266-275.

The word διδάσκ- and derivates (both the verbs and the nouns) are used in John to refer to teaching or teachers. Other related terms like ῥαββί, γράμματα and the μαθ- word group are also used, but with a lower frequency, with the exception of ῥαββί.[8] Notable is that the words ῥαββί and διδάσκαλος are used only in the first section of the Gospel (up to chapter 12), with the exception of 20,16 where Mary calls Jesus ῥαββουνί and in 13,13-14 where Jesus mentions that his disciples call him διδάσκαλος. The same applies to the verb, with one or two exceptions (14,26; 18,19. 28).

a) The use of ῥαββί, ῥαββουνί and διδάσκαλος

The noun διδάσκαλος as well as the transcribed Hebrew words ῥαββί and ῥαββουνί (רַב, רַבִּי) translates as 'teacher' in John. The Hebrew term ῥαββί is translated into Greek as διδάσκαλος (1,38 – ῥαββί en 20,16 – ῥαββουνί) which indicates that John sees these two terms as equivalent[9]. Turning our attention to the occurrences of διδάσκαλος in John: the term is consistently used as a functional description (of Jesus: 3,2; 11,28; 13,13-14; of Nicodemus 3,10), with the exception of the two times it is used to translate ῥαββί/ ῥαββουνί (1,38; 20,16) and the text-critically problematic 8,4 where it is used as vocative.[10] The word is used to refer to a person who teaches and is acknowledged as such.[11]

Nicodemus starts his discussion with Jesus by acknowledging Jesus as teacher from God (ἀπὸ θεοῦ ἐλήλυθας διδάσκαλος – 3,2). The reason he gives for identifying Jesus as teacher of God relates not to what Jesus said, but to what he did, namely, his signs (τὰ σημεῖα), also referred to in 2,23-24. Functionally the concept of teaching includes not only words, but also deeds, in this case specifically revelatory deeds. In the process of teaching they are interrelated. This is evident from the use of the word

---

[8] Derivates that are also used are διδακτοὶ (6:45 – learned people); διδαχὴ (7,16.17; 18,19 – teachings) and γράμματα en μεμαθηκώς in 7,15 (cf. also 5,47). Terms like παιδαγωγός and its derivates are not used in John.

[9] F. FOULKES, *Rabbi, Rabboni*, in J.D. DOUGLAS (ed.), *The New Bible Dictionary*, Downers Grove IL, IVP, 1996, p. 996.

[10] Due to the problematic text-critical nature of 8,4, it is not going to be considered any further.

[11] Cf. W. ARNDT– F.W. DANKER – W. BAUER, *A Greek-English lexicon of the New Testament and other early Christian literature*, Chicago, University of Chicago Press, 2000, p. 241. According to H.G. LIDDELL – R. SCOTT, *A Greek-English Lexicon*, Oxford, Oxford University Press, 1996, p. 421, the word may also be translated as master, trainer of a chorus, or producer of a play. These latter possibilities are not applicable to our contexts.

just eight verses on (3,10), where Jesus notes that Nicodemus is a teacher of Israel, but does not know what Jesus' teaching refers to. Here the term teacher suggests cognitive knowledge. Nicodemus displayed theological knowledge in his argument about Jesus as coming from God, linking the deeds of Jesus to the presence of God, but he lacks further knowledge about what the presence of Jesus is all about. The use of διδάσκαλος suggests that being a teacher involves having cognitive knowledge as well as expressing that in deeds.

Martha refers to Jesus as the teacher when calling Mary (11,28). The implication is that they both know who 'the Teacher' is. Although Jesus 'taught' Martha about the eschatological things during their discussion (11,23-27), both Martha and Mary confront Jesus on a different level, namely, the level of his ability to act, by saying that if he had been present, their brother would not have died (11,21-22.32). The healing abilities of Jesus form the conceptual background to these remarks by the two sisters calling Jesus 'Teacher'. Again the cognitive teaching and special deeds of Jesus are combined in the context where Jesus is called 'teacher'.

After washing the feet of his disciples, Jesus refers to the example he set (13,15). As part of his argument why the disciples should also wash one another's feet, Jesus remarks that the disciples call him 'Teacher and Lord' and that he is indeed their teacher (13,13). Noteworthy is that Jesus is explaining to the disciples the significance of his deed (washing feet) which should be imitated, 'mimicked', by them.[12] Mimesis in ancient times formed an important basis for the effectiveness of the teaching process. In this case they should mimic his loving service of which washing one another's feet is an example. The deeds actually support the message (teaching) about love (13,15.34-35).

Several aspects are combined: the teaching of Jesus of his disciples in private, his deeds (both revelatory and ethical), which should serve as an example for the disciples, and the well-known concept of mimesis, a central concept in ancient educational practices. The functional use of the word διδάσκαλος suggests a comprehensive teaching process that combined words and deeds, both which should be accepted, understood, and mimicked.

---

[12] *Vorbildcharacter* as Gielen calls it, see M. GIELEN, *Tradition und Theologie neutestamentlicher Haustafelethik*, Bonn, Anton Hain, 1990, p. 147. See also A.J. BLASI, *Early Christian culture as interaction*, in A.J. BLASI – J. DUHAIME – P.-A. TURCOTTE (eds.), *Handbook of early Christianity: Social science approaches*, New York NY, Altamira, 2002, 291-308, pp. 302-303; J.G. VAN DER WATT, 2014 *Navolging van Jesus, mimesis in 1 Johannes*, in *In die Skriflig/ In Luce Verbi* 48 (2014), no. 1, art 1819, http://dx.doi.org/10.4102/ids.v48:1.1819; C. BENNEMA, *Mimesis in John 13: Cloning or creative articulation?* in *NT* 56 (2014), 261-274.

This echoes the ancient teaching practices and is not unique to Jesus[13]. That is why not only Jesus, but also Nicodemus could be called a teacher. General expectations of what an ancient teacher should do, lie behind the descriptions of Jesus or Nicodemus being teachers.

In John the Hebrew word ῥαββί has a different rhetorical function than διδάσκαλος. *Rabbi* was an honorific title (see *M. 'Abot* 4,12) with an authoritative undertone, but evidence from the first century seems to indicate that the word was not exclusively used to refer to 'teacher', but was also used in a more general meaning of 'sir'[14]. Köstenberger[15] on the other hand opines that the term rabbi identifies Jesus as 'Jewish religious teacher'. It is doubtful whether one should push the argument that rabbi may also be used to refer to 'sir' too far. Contextual arguments argue against the idea of 'sir': for instance, the link to διδάσκαλος that clearly refers to a teacher, the verb that refers to Jesus' teaching, or Nicodemus noting Jesus' works, that can only signal his relationship to God, which identifies him as teacher.

It is remarkable that nowhere in the Gospel of John is Jesus actually addressed by his disciples with the Greek title διδάσκαλος, although Jesus maintains that in 13,13-14. The disciples do call Jesus teacher (vocative) in the Gospel, but the transcription of the Hebrew (ῥαββί) is consistently used (ῥαββί: 1,38; 1,49; 3,2.26; 4,31; 6,25; 9,2; 11,8; ῥαββουνί: 20,16). The question is: why is the Greek διδάσκαλος not used in the vocative at all[16], while the Hebrew ῥαββί is consistently used in the vocative, even though it needs translation (1,38; 20,19)? The author knew the Greek word, but nevertheless chose to consistently use the Hebrew transcription to address Jesus. This use of the words cannot be by chance.

Using the transcribed Hebrew word ῥαββί within a narrative unfolding in a basically exclusive Jewish space has a strong socio-cultural impact. With this Jewish title, Jesus is identified as a specific type of figure in this Jewish context, namely, as specifically a Jewish teacher. The title refers to those people in Jewish society who would have been regarded using the word ῥαββί, and being addressed with it.

---

[13] *Cf.* A. LEMAIRE, *Education*, in D.N. FREEDMAN (ed.), *Anchor Bible Dictionary*, New York NY, Doubleday, 1992, 301-317; J.G. VAN DER WATT, *Family of the King: Dynamics of metaphor in the Gospel according to John*, Leiden, Brill, 2000, pp. 266-284); VAN DER WATT, *Family of the King* (n. 3), pp. 266-284.

[14] See R. RIESNER, *Teacher*, in *Dictionary of Jesus and the Gospels*, Downers Grove IL, IVP, 1992, 807-810, p. 807; H. LAPIN, *Rabbi*, in D.N. FREEDMAN (ed.), *Anchor Bible Dictionary*, New York NY, Doubleday, 1992, 600-602, p. 600.

[15] A.J. KÖSTENBERGER, *Jesus as Rabbi in the Fourth Gospel*, in *BBR* 8 (1998), 97-128, pp. 100-102.

[16] Except for 8,4, as has already been mentioned.

This runs against the opinion of Hengel[17] who argues that in John Jesus is not presented as a Jewish rabbi and therefore stands outside the uniform Jewish tradition. Hays[18] even remarks that 'Jesus is represented in John not as a teacher...'. This is to emphasize that what Jesus teaches stands in opposition to typical Jewish teachings. The use of the term in John should therefore simply be interpreted as a sign of respect. Hengel is of course correct that the teachings of Jesus oppose that of the Jewish leadership in several (not all) respects. However, this downgrading of the rhetorical use of ῥαββί in John overlooks the semantic contribution of the word. The word ῥαββί does not refer to the message of the person, but to his function. As others taught in Jewish society, Jesus also taught. In the narrative, Jesus fulfils the function expected of a ῥαββί in that society. As Köstenberger[19] remarks, the term rabbi identifies Jesus as a 'Jewish religious teacher'.

That the functional use of the word ῥαββί is intended, is also evident from the fact that the word is not used exclusively of Jesus. In 3,26 John (the Baptist) is addressed as ῥαββί by his disciples, which confirms a more general use of the term (not limiting it to Jesus). Notable is also the people who address Jesus as ῥαββί in John. Apart from his disciples (4,31; 9,2; 11,8), of course, there are other cases where Jesus is addressed as ῥαββί by people who are (not yet) his disciples, which implies a more objective and less personal use of the title. In 1,38.49 Jesus is addressed as ῥαββί by his future disciples – at that point they are not yet his disciples, but recognize him as teacher. The same applies to Nicodemus who has just met Jesus and addresses him functionally as ῥαββί, as well as Mary who calls Jesus ῥαββουνί in 20,16. True, the disciples are not limited to the Twelve in John (*cf.* 6,61.66) and the above mentioned figures are all (later) related to Jesus in a special way, but nevertheless the more general use of the term ῥαββί indicates a functional use.

The fact that Jesus is identified as a Jewish teacher, is also apparent from other references to teaching which are ironically expressed. For instance, πῶς οὗτος γράμματα οἶδεν μὴ μεμαθηκώς; (7,15; 'How does this man know letters[20] having never learned?'). The Scriptures (τοῖς ἐκείνου γράμμασιν) are identified in 5,47 with Moses (*cf.* also 5,39-40) and his Jewish heritage.

---

[17] M. HENGEL, *The Charismatic leader and his followers*, Edinburgh, T&T Clark, 1981, pp. 42-45.
[18] R.B. HAYS, *The moral vision of the New Testament: A contemporary introduction to New Testament ethics*, San Francisco, Harper, 1996, p. 138.
[19] KÖSTENBERGER, *Jesus as Rabbi* (n. 15), pp. 100-102.
[20] ARNDT et al., *Greek-English lexicon* (n. 11), ad loc.

Having established that Jesus is presented as a Jewish teacher in the Gospel, a brief overview at a rather high level of abstraction could help in understanding the framework within which John presents his narrative. John mentions the disciples (οἱ μαθηταί[21]) of both Jesus and John (the Baptist). A teacher obviously needed, or had, disciples or followers. Due to restrictions of space, this aspect of the teaching process will not be treated in this essay, but discipleship in John is thoroughly discussed in secondary literature.[22]

Disciples formally followed their teacher (ῥαββί) and learned from him by carefully observing what he did and said, and continued their education by asking him in private discussions what his actions or words meant (Köstenberger[23] mentions the following sources in support: *b. Ber.* 23a-b, 24a, 60a; *b. Šabb.* 12b, 108b, 112a; *b. Erub.* 30a; *b. Roš Haš* 34b; *y. Hag.* 2,1; *y. B. Mesi* 2,3).[24] This was possible, since the relationship was characterized by an openness, as Aberbach[25] remarks: 'In spite of the extraordinary reverence in which rabbis were held by their students, the relations between them were usually very close and far from formal. It was ... essentially a paternal-filial relationship transcended and surpassed by the intense love master and disciple bore to each other (*Cant. Rab.* 8:7; *b. Ber.* 5b; *b. Sanh.* 101a)'[26]. Because of this intimate relational bonding, the groups and their members could be identified as such. These groups

---

[21] ARNDT et al., *Greek-English lexicon* (n. 11), *ad loc.*, describes the lexicographical meaning in the following way, 'one who engages in learning through instruction from another, *pupil, apprentice*... one who is rather constantly associated with someone who has a pedagogical reputation or a particular set of views, *disciple, adherent*'.

[22] *Cf.* for instance, F.F. SEGOVIA (ed.), *Discipleship in the New Testament*, Philadelphia PA, Augsburg Fortress Press, 1985, 103-126; J.A. DU RAND, *'Perspectives on Johannine discipleship according to the Farewell Discourse'*, in *Neot.* 25 (1991), 311-325; D.F. TOLMIE, *Jesus' farewell to the disciples: John 13,1–17,26 in narratological perspective*, Leiden, Brill, 1995; R.N. LONGENECKER (ed.), *Patterns of discipleship in the New Testament*, Grand Rapids MI, Eerdmans, 1996; D.G. VAN DER MERWE, *Towards a theological understanding of Johannine discipleship*, *Neot.* 31 (1997), 339-359; R.M. CHENNATTU, *Johannine discipleship as a covenant relation*, Peabody MA, Hendrickson, 2006; N. FARELLY, *The disciples in the Fourth Gospel*, Tübingen, Mohr Siebeck, 2010.

[23] KÖSTENBERGER, *Jesus as Rabbi* (n. 15), p. 119.

[24] Reference to later rabbinic literature may be problematic, but the broad informed assumption is that within the ancient Jewish practices of preserving tradition, this material may shed some light on earlier practices, of course not concentrating on detail, but assuming a higher level of abstraction.

[25] M. ABERBACH, *Relations between master and disciple in the Talmudic age*, in H.J. ZIMMELS et al. (eds.), *Essays presented to chief rabbi Israel Brodie*, London, Soncino, 1946, 2-126, p. 101.

[26] *Cf.* also KÖSTENBERGER, *Jesus as Rabbi* (n. 15), p. 122.

were usually formally organized with different members having different responsibilities in order to ensure the effective functioning of the group. Obviously the relation between the teacher and his followers could be intense or less intense – a centre and a periphery could be identified.

The teacher-disciple relation was aimed at education. Gerhardsson[27] notes, 'the Rabbi's didactic symbolic actions... concrete, visible measures whereby they capture the attention of their pupils, after which they either explain what they have done or leave it to the pupils to work it out for themselves'. The openness of the relationship allowed for free discussions within the group in which the teacher could even be challenged. 'Students would not hesitate to question their teacher when his actions seemed to contradict his teachings or when his behaviour appeared unseemly (cf. m. Ber. 2,6-7; y. Sot. 1,4)', as Aberbach[28] remarks. These open discussions usually took place when the group was on its own in order to prevent the teacher from being shamed[29]. The purpose of the teaching process was to prepare the disciples to become teachers themselves (knowing the 'letters' – 7,15) and thus continuing the teachings and tradition. The perfect disciple was that person who 'fully absorbed his master's teaching' and 'was drawing on it to spread it abroad'[30].

Drawing upon the above brief description of the typical Jewish teacher-disciple profile, John utilizes this profile to characterize the relation between Jesus and his followers. Jesus' disciples are called to follow him (1,39.43), they form a loyal group whose identity is characterized as loving one another (13,34-35), even being willing to follow their teacher to the death (11,16; 13,36-38). Obedience was an essential requirement (13,34-35; 15,1-8.14-17). As a group they are described as being well organized, with different disciples having different tasks: some carried swords for safety (18,10), there was a treasurer (13,29), some were responsible for food (6,5; cf. also 4,8), or controlling access to their teacher (12,20-21). The Twelve were close-knit as friends of their teacher (15,9-17) and were required to love and serve one another (13,34-35); they ate together (13-16). The teaching process also corresponds to the tradition, with the disciples learning from Jesus by engaging in (private) discussions (9,2-4; 14,6-10) and even arguments (cf. Peter – 13,6-10, 36-38; the disciples 11,5-16). In 17,6-8 Jesus claims that the disciples have accepted the words

---

[27] B. GERHARDSSON, *Memory and Manuscript: Oral Tradition and Written Transmission in Rabbinic Judaism and Early Christianity*, Uppsala, Gleerup, 1961, p. 185.
[28] ABERBACH, *Relations* (n. 25), p. 94.
[29] *Ibid.*, pp. 95-99 – he refers to b. Šabb. 3b; m. Abot 5,7; Der. Er. Zut. 1.
[30] *Ibid.*, p. 94; b. Yoma 28a.

of the Father and are thus equipped for their task of carrying the message further (17,18; 20,21-22). Apart from the Twelve, Jesus also had other more peripheral disciples, for example those who eventually left him and went home (6,66). These characteristics of the relation between Jesus and the disciples run parallel to those of Jewish teachers and their followers.

In sum, when it comes to teaching in John, Jesus (and his followers) are placed squarely within the contexts of Jewish religious education, namely, of a formal teacher or ῥαββί with his disciples.

b) The use of the verb διδάσκω

From the preceding discussions it has become clear that the two words ῥαββί and διδάσκαλος, although overlapping, each make a specific contribution within the narrative of the Gospel. What is the case concerning the verb διδάσκω?

The verb focuses mainly on teachings somehow related to Jesus (6,59; 7,28.35; 8,20; 9,34 [present tense]; 8,28; 18,19.28 [aorist]; 14,26 [future tense]). For instance, if Jesus motivates why he healed a man on the Sabbath, he describes how the Father taught him and showed him everything (5,17-23), apart from giving everything into his hands (3,31-36). In another case, people wonder about his learnedness in theological matters (7,15), which prompts Jesus to implicitly reply that God is his teacher, whom he mimics. He was indeed taught by the Father, placing him in a special revelatory and ethical position (8,28). These references indicate what John had in mind as the content of the teachings of Jesus. According to John, these teachings mainly take place in the temple or synagogues (6,59; 7,28; 8,20; 18,20), which confirms that John uses the word in the context of formal Jewish teaching by a ῥαββί, not only to the narrow circle of his disciples, but also to the Jewish people in general.

Taking the use of the verb διδάσκω in different contexts as a cue, the following emerges as the content of Jesus' teachings.

- The use of the verb διδάσκω in 6,59 refers to the teachings about Jesus as bread of life whose body and blood should be consumed (eat = a metaphor for faith[31], in order to have eternal life. This touches upon the essence of the intended message of Jesus (*cf.* 20,30-31) as well as the willingness of the people to believe in Jesus.

---

[31] VAN DER WATT, *Family of the King* (n. 3), pp. 223-224.

- Discussions about the way in which the law should be interpreted and understood underlines that Jesus is the legitimate interpreter of the law (7,28), and is therefore implicitly a 'teacher of God's law'.
- In 8,13 the Pharisees challenge Jesus' right to witness to himself. An 'aside' or narrator's comment in 8,20 however confirms that the discussion in Chapter 8 should be understood as the teaching of Jesus. The Jewish opponents' inability to acknowledge Jesus for whom he is or to listen to his words, serve as an undeniable illustration of their lack of knowledge of God (*cf.* also 8,54).
- In his defence in front of the High Priest, Jesus claims that he taught openly and not in secret, an indication that his message is not subversive but honest and true (18,20). His teaching is intended for everybody.

The above information confirms that when, by using the verb διδάσκω, John refers to the teaching of Jesus, he does not limit it to one aspect or place. He taught everywhere in Jewish public religious spaces and the content of his teaching included the essence of his message about the acceptance of Jesus as the one sent by the Father, about faith, life, correct behaviour because of a changed identity, about the correct interpretation of the Law and so on. The generic character of this teaching is further confirmed by the use of the verb διδάσκω in 7,35 where the Jewish crowd speculates where Jesus is going. They are of the opinion that he is going to teach the Greeks, implying teaching activities in general. The same is true of the use of the word διδαχή (teaching) in 18,19 where the High Priest enquires about the teaching of Jesus in general (*cf.* also 7,16-17 where Jesus claims his teaching – in general – comes from God).

There are other occurrences of the διδάσκ- word group in the Gospel that do not refer to Jesus. In their debate with the blind man in chapter 9, the Jewish leaders accuse him of being born in sin but nevertheless he tries to teach them about religious issues (ἐν ἁμαρτίαις σὺ ἐγεννήθης ὅλος καὶ σὺ *διδάσκεις* ἡμᾶς; – 9,34). The debate focuses on the ability of somebody to heal without the assistance of God, something that seems theologically impossible. This theological argument of the blind man is indeed interpreted by the Jewish opponents as 'teaching', which illustrates the conceptual framework of the use of the word. Two other figures that teach are the Father (8,28) and the Spirit-Paraclete (14,26). We shall return to them.

In the light of this information we may conclude that the verb διδάσκω is used to refer to the teaching activity of Jesus when dealing with issues of religious significance. The use of the word is not restricted to Jesus, neither is it used to refer to only one aspect of Jesus' teaching.

The argument above illustrates that John uses the typical Jewish (higher) formal 'educational system' to explain Jesus' religious teaching activity. This forms a socio-cultural frame against which Jesus' educational activities should be understood.

THE SCENE CHANGES FROM FORMAL RABBINIC TEACHING TO FAMILIAL EDUCATION

In 8,28 Jesus states that the Father taught him (ἐδίδαξέν με ὁ πατὴρ). Conceptually this educational practice of a father, who teaches his son, is metaphorically developed in relation to the Father and his Son in 5,19-23.[32]

Jesus heals a cripple on the Sabbath (*cf.* 5,1-18). When his Jewish opponents question him about this, his reply is that just as his Father has worked up until now, he also works, identifying what he does with the works of his Father. How this could be is then explained in terms of a metaphor with education as its source. Within a loving relationship the Father shows his Son all he is doing (5,20). The Son does nothing of his own accord, but observes what the Father does and then does likewise (5,19). This is typical of a father teaching his son his trade. The 'trade' or work the Father teaches the Son is to give life, something that only the creator God can do (*cf.* also the argument of the healed blind man in 9,28-34). The Father also hands him the right and power of eschatological judgment (8,22).

In order to appreciate the metaphorical dynamics of this educational language, the main characteristics of the relevant ancient manner of education should receive *brief* attention.

The education of children, both morally and vocationally, was a central issue in the ancient world, although no standardized, common, or overarching system existed.[33] For our purposes two broad approaches should be noted, namely, a more formal system where children were educated

---

[32] It is known that metaphorical imagery in John is developed in networks that correspond to ordinary earthly situations and events; see J.G. VAN DER WATT, *Family of the King* (n. 3); this is also the case with the references to teachers and education, especially the description of the familial educational system.

[33] 'Natural education' of infants or smaller children does not come into focus here. In any case, PLATO (*Laws* 7.792e) argues that because of the power of habit, education must

by pedagogues in a more formal context and a system where the children were educated at home, mainly by living with their family and partaking in the events of the family. In some cases these two systems could also overlap. It was the primary task of the parents to educate their children or to have them educated[34]. Kurz remarks, 'The father was responsible for the total education of his children in the "way" that leads to a long, happy life'[35]. He notes that 'the most common use for the image of fatherhood is the comparison of teaching activities to parental duties. It envisages not merely formal teaching but the total formation...' (Prov. 1,8; 6,20; 23,22; Deut. 6,6-25. *Cf.* also 1 Chr. 4,14; Philo LA II,90; Greek world: Plato *Crit.* 17,25; Roman world: Plutarch *Marc. Cat.* XX 4–7; Dixon 1991,118).[36]

The first, more formal, approach was well known in the Greco-Roman context. Children partaking in this more formal educational process were educated by pedagogues in subjects like rhetoric, music, or grammar.[37] *Mimesis* or following the example set by the pedagogue or other figures of authority played an essential role in this process[38]. Apart from being obedient, the child had to observe the example set by the pedagogue or his father for that matter, and follow their moral style 'to the degree that in some cases the student and teacher could exchange places'.[39]

In the other system children were educated at home, mainly by their parents, but of course the extended family also played a role in this educational process. This type of education was typical of Jewish society,

---

 begin at birth, or even before birth, since what happens to the pregnant woman also influences the child (*cf.* S. Dixon, *The Roman Family*, London, Hopkins, 1991, p. 118).

[34] J.-A. Shelton, *As the Romans did; A source book in Roman social history*, Oxford, Oxford University Press, 1988, p. 104; *cf.* also Plutarch *Vit. Cato* XX.4-7; Tacitus *Dial. Or.* 28-29.

[35] W.S. Kurz, *Kenotic imitation of Paul and of Christ in Philippians 2 and 3*, in F.F. Segovia (ed.), *Discipleship in the New Testament* (n. 22), 103-126, p. 107. See also A.J. Malherbe, *Paraenesis in the Epistle of Titus*, in J. Starr – T. Engberg-Pedersen, *Early Christian paraenesis in context*, Berlin, De Gruyter, 2004, 297-317, p. 315.

[36] W.S. Kurz, *Kenotic imitation* (n. 35), p. 107.

[37] Plutarch, *Moralia* 8f.; Dionysius of Halicarnassus, *Antiquitates Romanae* XX.13,3; Quintilian, *Institutio Oratoria* I.iii.13-14; Flavius Josephus, *Ant.* IV.260-264; Philo, *De Spec. Leg.* II.236, 240-241.

[38] R. Hunter, *Plato and the traditions of ancient literature*, Cambridge, Cambridge University Press, 2012, p. 20.

[39] S. Eastman, *Imitating Christ imitating us: Paul's educational project in Philippians*, in J.R. Wagner – A.K. Grieb – C.K. Rowe (eds.), *The Word leaps the gap: Studies in Scripture and Theology in honor of Richard B. Hays*, Grand Rapids MI, Eerdmans, 2008, 427-451, pp. 432-433.

besides the expectation that every male child should be educated in the Torah (Ps. 119,1; Gen. 18,19; Deut. 30,16; Prov. 2,6). The ethos of the family, including their traditions, values and moral expectations, was conveyed through example, as well as discussion, from the fathers to the children[40]. This ethos was something to be respected and obeyed (1 Macc. 1,54-58; 2,15-28; 4,36-43; Josephus *Ant.* 1.3.1 §72). Josephus (*Ad Ap.* 2.204) describes the process by remarking that the children should not only be taught, but also exercised in obeying the laws. They should be introduced and exposed to the behaviour of their predecessors in order to mimic them (*cf.* also *Ant.* 1.2.3, 68-69; *b Qid* 82a-b) and thus continue the honourable name of the family. In ancient times the social status and honour of a person were co-determined by his education[41]. Neyrey further remarks, 'young men were only as good as their teachers and those who formed them in the social values enshrined in their past culture'.[42]

The usual practice was that the son grew up at home and from approximately his sixth year started his 'education' by accompanying and observing his father, not only vocationally but also morally (*cf.* Philo *De Spec Leg* II.236). This did not only involve simple observation, but also practising what was observed and taught through repetition and memory[43]. The process was based on the expectation of obedience and loyalty (Ex. 20,12; Prov. 1,8; 4,1ff.; 6,20; 23,22-25)[44], which implied that a 'good' son would display the teachings of his father faithfully. Apart from this, sons could also broaden their knowledge by joining a rabbi or the more formal Hellenistic educational system, as has been explained above. It goes without saying that levels of education also differed between boys and girls, social status and financial abilities.

Based on the above description, it may be concluded that the education of the Son by the Father is described in terms of a father teaching his son, and not of a rabbi teaching his disciples or a pedagogue teaching his pupils. The education of the Son is metaphorically expressed in familial terms, suggesting a loving relationship (1,18; 5,19-20). Thus John prefers to use a second form of education to explain Jesus' knowledge of the Father (8,28).

---

[40] *Cf. Tos. Qid.* I, 11b; J.H. NEYREY, *The trials (forensic) and tribulations (honor challenges) of Jesus: John 7 in Social Science Perspective*, in *BTB* 26 (1996), 107-124, p. 120.
[41] NEYREY, *The trials* (n. 40), p. 119.
[42] *Ibid.* p. 120.
[43] See A. LEMAIRE, *Education* (n. 13), pp. 305-312; C.K. BARRETT, *The Gospel according to St John*, London, SPCK, 1978, pp. 259.
[44] See J.F. MCGRATH, *A rebellious son? Hugo Odeberg and the interpretation of John 5,18*, in *NTS* 44 (1998), 470-73, p. 472.

In 7,15-16 the 'systems' of rabbinic and familial education that are both used by John, are contextually linked. The use of terminology by the crowd in 7,15 (πῶς οὗτος γράμματα οἶδεν μὴ μεμαθηκώς;) seems to refer to Jewish (rabbinic) education that would enable Jesus to teach on religious matters like the Torah. Jesus' reply situates his teaching (ἡ ἐμὴ διδαχὴ) within the relational context with the Father, as is suggested in 5,19-23. This obviously places his knowledge, honour and status on a completely different level (5,23) and distinguishes him as ῥαββί from the other Jewish teachers (cf. Hengel)[45].

The Son does not only say what he heard from the Father, but he was also given the power to act like the Father (5,17-23; 3,32-33; 7,15-16). He was taught in both words and deeds[46]. The words and deeds of the Father and the Son are inseparable in kind and nature (10,28-30; 14,9-10). Jesus underlines this point when the crowds question the level of his education that stands in contrast to his knowledge (7,15).[47]

A theological theme directly related to the filial education of the Son is the *mission* of the Son. This personal knowledge and power to act like the Father enable Jesus to perform his mission (5,23). This aspect will not be explored any further here.

In sum, the education of Jesus is metaphorically described in terms of a process in which the Father taught his Son. This is the first-hand knowledge and power Jesus possesses in order to perform his mission.

Jesus Teaches

In the first section of this essay, where the word group διδάσκ- and its derivates were discussed, it was shown that the teaching (διδαχή) of Jesus is described in terms of a ῥαββί teaching in public in synagogues and the temple (18,20-21; cf. 7,14.28; 8,20; 10,23; in public in Jerusalem – 5,2; cf. also 11,54), while his disciples follow him and indeed learn

---

[45] HENGEL, *Charismatic Leader* (n. 17), pp. 42-45.
[46] See J.A. BÜHNER, *Der Gesandte und sein Weg im 4. Evangelium*, Tübingen, Mohr Siebeck, 1977, p. 245.
[47] S. EASTMAN, *Imitating Christ imitating us*, (n. 39), p. 431: 'Paul's educational project in Philippians, in J.R. WAGNER – A.K. GRIEB – C.K. ROWE (eds.), *The Word leaps the gap: Studies in Scripture and Theology in honor of Richard B. Hays*, Grand Rapids MI, Eerdmans, 2008, 427-451, p. 431, remarks, 'education... functioned as a means of enculturation into a "system of hierarchical difference" that differentiated the educated from the uneducated by training young men (mainly) to be partners of the elite culture... to be educated was to distinguish oneself from those who were not and to secure one's identity on the "correct" side of the social polarities that structured Greco-Roman society'. This also applied to Jewish social life.

from him in observing what he does. His teaching is presented in a variety of forms, for instance: mono- or dialogues (*cf.* 3,3-36; 13-16); arguments (7,16-24); private discussions with his followers (4,31-38); or revelatory teachings (11,20-27). His deeds are also portrayed as being of educational significance, as is evident from his signs (*cf.*, for instance, 2,1-11; 5,1-17 etc.); illustrative actions (13,1-17) and, of course, his death (18-20; 10,17-18; 11,24-26). This will not be discussed any further here, since it has already been discussed in the first part of this essay.

THE PARACLETE TEACHES

The Spirit-Paraclete is also functionally described as teaching the disciples of Jesus.[48] In this regard Hays[49] remarks, 'the Paraclete is to provide not only God's continuing presence within the community but also a source of continuing revelation'[50]. Bennema explains the presence of the presence of the Spirit-Paraclete as follows, 'However, by nature they are not able to do so, and further divine help is needed. What is needed is a cognitive agent "from above" who can assist people in thinking "from above" and consequently in accessing the realities "from above". This cognitive or epistemic divine agent is *the Spirit*'[51]. These aspects of the work of the Spirit and also his educational functions are especially developed in John 14-16 under the title *Paraclete*.

According to 14,26 (*cf.* also 16,13-15) the task of the Spirit-Paraclete is to teach the disciples and remind them of what Jesus taught: 'The Paraclete… will teach you everything (ἐκεῖνος ὑμᾶς διδάξει πάντα), and remind you of all that I have said to you'. Within the unfolding realisation of Johannine eschatology[52] the Spirit-Paraclete plays a central role

---

[48] For more details, *cf.* R. BULTMANN, *Das Evangelium des Johannes*. Göttingen, Vandenhoeck & Ruprecht, 1978, p. 485; R. SCHNACKENBURG, *The Gospel according to St. John*, Vol. 3, London, Burns & Oats, 1982, p. 83; U. SCHNELLE, *Johannes als Geisttheologe*, in *NT* 40 (1998), 17-31, pp. 20-21.

[49] Hays, *Moral Vision* (n. 18), p. 151.

[50] *Cf.* C.G. LINGAD, *The problems of Jewish Christians in the Johannine community*, Rome, 2001, pp. 226-227.

[51] C. BENNEMA, *Christ, the Spirit and the knowledge of God: A study in Johannine Epistemology*, in M. HEALY – R. PARRY (eds.), *The Bible and epistemology: Biblical soundings on the knowledge of God*, Milton Keynes, Paternoster, 2007, 107-133, p. 116.

[52] VAN DER WATT, *Family of the King* (n. 3), pp. 435-436; J.G. VAN DER WATT, *Eschatology in the Gospel according to John*, in J.G. VAN DER WATT (ed.), *Eschatology of the New Testament and some related documents*, Tübingen, Mohr Siebeck, 2011, pp. 109-140.

in keeping the disciples connected to the Jesus tradition (14,26 – ὁ δὲ παράκλητος, τὸ πνεῦμα τὸ ἅγιον... ἐκεῖνος ὑμᾶς διδάξει πάντα καὶ ὑπομνήσει ὑμᾶς πάντα ἃ εἶπον ὑμῖν [ἐγώ][53]. As Schnelle[54] remarks, 'Der Geist wird also keine neuen Offenbarungen über das Wirken Jesu hinaus bringen, sondern er vergegenwärtigt und erschließt die Jesus-Offenbarung. Hinter dieser Aussage stehen Erkenntnis-, Lehr-, und Lernprozesse der johanneischen Schule'. Apart from this, the Spirit-Paraclete bears witnesses in this world together with the disciples (15,26-27; cf. also 14,15-17) and in this sense the Spirit-Paraclete partakes in the mission of the disciples. The Spirit-Paraclete facilitates the Jesus tradition as well as the unfolding of the tradition (15,26-27), keeping it alive. This aspect of Johannine theology suggests the movement of the group towards a tradition-orientated society.

How does this teaching take place? The exact way in which the Spirit-Paraclete will 'teach' is not developed in any detail in the Gospel and remains uncertain. One way of explaining it is by associating the Beloved Disciple with the Spirit-Paraclete, at least functionally[55]. The main reason is that the functions of both figures overlap considerably, facilitating the tradition. This implies that the Gospel itself (i.e. the witness of the Beloved Disciple) becomes part of the teachings of the Spirit-Paraclete in the sense that it preserves and bears witness to the words and deeds (teachings) of Jesus.

Do the disciples teach?

An interesting observation is that nowhere it is said that the disciples of Jesus teach, although John knows the wider application of the term, as has been argued (9,34; cf. also 3,10.26). This might not be by chance. The disciples are sent by Jesus to continue his teaching and tradition (14,6-25), which seems to suppose some sort of educational function. Nevertheless, it is not described as such, although the work of the Spirit-Paraclete is explained in this way (17,18; 20,21-22).

---

[53] Cf. F. MATERA, *New Testament ethics: The legacies of Jesus and Paul*, Louisville, KY, Westminster John Knox, 1996, p. 110.
[54] SCHNELLE, *Johannes als Geisttheologe* (n. 48), p. 19, emphasizes the continuity of what the Spirit-Paraclete does: 'Der Paraklet ist bei der Gemeinde für "ewig", d.h. die Verbindung der Glaubenden mit Jesus und durch Jesus mit Gott ist für alle Zukunft offen'.
[55] See J.H. CHARLESWORTH, *The Beloved Disciple: whose witness validates the Gospel of John?* London, Trinity Press International, 1995; R. BAUCKHAM, *The Testimony of the Beloved Disciple*, Grand Rapids MI, Baker, 2007.

It could be a possibility that διδάσκ- and its derivates are not used for the disciples, because the teaching remains the 'teaching (διδαχή) of Jesus', as the reference to the Spirit-Paraclete suggests (14,26). The actions of the disciples are nevertheless terminologically described in terms of 'witnessing' (μαρτυρ- and its derivates – 15,26). The disciples witness to what they have seen and heard from their teacher. The word group is not used exclusively of the disciples, but does refer to their activities connected to the Spirit (15,26-27).

Although the followers of Jesus are not called teachers in John, they nevertheless continue his mission, as witnesses to, as well as being on a mission (17,18; 20,21-23).

Some Concluding Remarks

In John a central theological emphasis is the mediation of divine knowledge to the *kosmos* (1,14-18). References to educational systems serve as central structural means in clarifying the mediation and presence of this knowledge. Two educational systems are utilized. The one system refers to the typical rabbinic education system, as is evident from the references to, for instance, Nicodemus or the healed blind man as teachers.

Jesus is indeed presented in the narrative as a Jewish ῥαββί who teaches the Jews about divine things, but who might also teach others, for instance the Greeks. By way of metaphor, familial education is applied to explain why and how the Son can and may speak and act like his Father. This is related to the mission of Jesus that will be continued through the teaching and witness of the Spirit-Paraclete as well as through the witness of his followers. His followers will not 'teach' but will witness to the 'teaching' of Jesus.

A last point is in order. In John, the theme of teaching proves to be a central concept in the Gospel's theological structure. Without this information, it would not be clear where Jesus got his teachings from or how, which would be problematic in a document that deals with significant dogmatic issues related to the presence of God. Jesus is described as ῥαββί, which colours the narrative significantly. His journeying and movement, together with disciples, frames him as an authoritative figure on a mission and also ensures the continuation of his message through the mission of these disciples. This is inherently part of the narrative structure of the Gospel. Taking these aspects out of the structure of the narrative would cause it to collapse.

PAUL AS A RECIPIENT AND TEACHER OF TRADITION

Peter J. TOMSON
the Netherlands

Learning and teaching always involve tradition. Such is the lesson of the paradigmatic anecdote that rabbinic literature attributes to the legendary 'pair' of sages, Shammai and Hillel.[1] Someone asked Shammai, 'How many Torahs do you have?' He was dismissed angrily. Then he went to Hillel who invited him to sit down, wrote out the first letters of the alphabet, and asked him to read. 'A, B, C...' the man read, so Hillel asked him how he knew. The man said he had 'accepted this on faith'. Then Hillel taught him: similarly, you must 'accept on faith' that the written Torah only comes with an oral Torah. Scripture presupposes teaching and tradition.[2]

This lesson is likely to be lost on those Protestants who stress 'scripture' or 'revelation' rather than the Catholic predilection for 'tradition'. Possibly due to the dominance of Protestant exegesis in nineteenth and twentieth century scholarship, a similar inhibition is also seen in some Catholic exegetes. Therefore an invitation from the Tilburg School of Catholic Theology to write on 'Teachers and disciples in biblical texts' is a choice occasion for a scholar who is also a Protestant. In the given biblically-oriented perspective, it invites him to review some elements of Protestant thought, especially since the appearance of the volume will likely coincide with the fifth centennial of the Reformation.

Protestant doctrine made Paul the central biblical author, and Romans and Galatians, with their prominent 'justification' theme, his 'most canonical' letters.[3] We shall have to ask questions about such preoccupations,

---

[1] On the 'pairs' (זוגות) *cf. m. Peah* 2,6 and *m. Avot* 1,4-12, on which *cf.* BICKERMAN, n. 446.
[2] Paraphrasing *Avot de-Rabbi Natan* B 29 (ed. Schechter, 31a-b). *Cf.* G. STEMBERGER, *Einleitung in Talmud und Midrasch*, 8th ed., Munich, Beck, 1992, p. 41, on 'Oral and Written Tradition'.
[3] *Cf.* E. KÄSEMANN (ed.), *Das Neue Testament als Kanon, Dokumentation und kritische Analyse zur gegenwärtigen Diskussion*, Göttingen, Vandenhoeck & Ruprecht, 1970, in particular Käsemann's *Zusammenfassung*, 399-410, and H. KÜNG, *Der Frühkatholizismus im NT als kontroverstheologisches Problem*, ibid., 175-204.

while trying to read Paul's letters afresh within their Jewish and Greco-Roman environs and thus uncover hitherto overlooked aspects and elements. We should not be surprised to meet a rather different Paul, a man who taught and imparted traditions and who even seems to have held a 'school', the curriculum of which featured modified elements of Jewish tradition in the fields of halakha and mysticism.

Paul's Letters as Didactic Communication

Paul's letters are precious documents in many respects. Those we may consider authentic are supposedly one-off letters, each reflecting a unique historical situation usually not otherwise documented. In light of this, Philipp Vielhauer – himself also a Protestant – observes in his remarkably perceptive *Geschichte der altchristlichen Literatur* that Paul's letters were meant and read as 'a stand-in for oral delivery' aimed at such situations, recording on paper the live voice of the apostle dictating his messages to his churches.[4] Already this insight suggests that Paul would have used traditional elements.

Indeed, paying close attention to literary form, Vielhauer distinguishes four types of traditional elements in Paul's letters.[5] (1) The frequent formal quotations from 'Scripture', which obviously reflect the methods of Jewish exegesis. (2) 'Pre-Pauline Christian texts', sometimes introduced by 'the technical tradition terminology of παραλαμβάνειν / παραδιδόναι'. (3) Parenetical passages involving familiar ethical and sapiential material from the Greco-Roman and Greco-Jewish worlds.[6] (4) The typical Pauline 'Einlagen' or excursions, self-contained pieces of argument that sit rather loosely in their context and are often considered insertions. But, Vielhauer warns, interpolation theories are inadequate here for two reasons: similar digressions on favourite themes are frequent also in Cynic-Stoic popular teaching, and these 'excursions' by vocabulary, style, and content are not at all un-Pauline. Vielhauer refers to a study by Hans Conzelmann which is worth quoting:

---

[4] Ph. Vielhauer, *Geschichte der urchristlichen Literatur: Einleitung in das Neue Testament, die Apokryphen und die Apostolischen Vätern*, Berlin, De Gruyter, 1985, 4th ed., pp. 56 (re. 1 Thess 4,1), 59.
[5] *Ibid*, pp. 68-70.
[6] *Cf.* the useful survey in Vielhauer, *Geschichte*, 49-57.

> Their make-up [i.e. of these excursive units] evinces a typical school-like character. Undoubtedly, this is expressive of Paul's formal education as a *Jewish* theologian. It is the more likely since we can observe a corresponding relation of his with the *Jewish* wisdom tradition. We could even go one step further and suppose that in the background, we can make out a schooling system that Paul intentionally organized, a 'school of Paul'...[7]

Thus Vielhauer, following Conzelmann's lead, presents Paul as an apostle of Jesus who has also remained a teacher of wisdom and traditional tradition, in line with his Jewish or Pharisaic training. They even intuit a Pauline 'school'.

Addressing the overall theme of the present volume, we can now conclude that, practically speaking, there is a single level of communication in Paul's authentic letters. There is only the implied teacher-disciple relation, i.e., the relationship between Paul and the church he addresses. Paul did not write for external readers of the 'corpus' of his letters. This is different for the Deutero-Paulines, insofar as those were edited, rewritten or written by a collaborator of Paul's, creating a 'classical' apostolic character.[8] It is certainly different for the Gospels, where traditional material is presented in a redactional framework that at times considerably differs in outlook from the tradition units it integrates. By contrast, the authentic letters put us face to face with Paul, the teacher of Greco-Roman, Jewish, and Christian tradition. But then again, it is precisely the traditional elements embedded in the epistolary argument that have a more general, 'didactic' import.

Protestant Preoccupations

We must be reminded, however, that we are not Paul's first-hand addressees. Twenty-first century readers are largely outsiders to the world of Paul and his churches, certainly as regards the unique situations he was addressing. Consequently it is crucial to monitor the way we read and appropriate these documents. In particular, it has become almost unavoidable to read them in the framework of latter-day, Christian and especially Protestant theology. Thus the letter to the Romans, with its extended arguments, is the favourite quarrying ground for construing Paul's supposed

---

[7] H. Conzelmann, *Paulus und die Weisheit*, in *NTS* 12 (1966), 231-244, p. 233 (my translation, italics as in original).
[8] See Vielhauer, *Geschichte*, pp. 223-225 on style and vocabulary.

'theology'. Already Melanchthon (1520) called Romans a *doctrinae christianae compendium*, albeit a rather limited one, but also Rudolf Bultmann (1948-53) and more recently James Dunn (1997) based their descriptions of Paul's thought primarily on that letter.[9] However other Protestant exegetes, notably Ferdinand Christian Baur (1836) and Krister Stendahl (1976), have emphasized that Romans should not be read as a timeless theological treatise, but as another ad hoc letter addressed to the unique situation of the Roman church around 58 CE.[10]

A cherished Protestant idea also concerns the genesis of Paul's message. Probably indirectly in reaction to the Catholic emphasis on authorized tradition, a typically Protestant emphasis can be heard in the concentration on Galatians, where Paul asserts about his 'gospel': 'I did not receive it (παρέλαβον) from a human source, nor was I taught it (ἐδιδάχθην), but I received it through a revelation of Jesus Christ' (Gal 1,12). As we have seen, the technical terminology of παραλαμβάνω signals formal teaching of tradition; similarly does διδάσκω. For such pillars of Protestant liberal theology as Baur and Harnack who took Galatians as the standard for interpreting Paul, it would follow that Paul's gospel was not based on tradition. And given the polemic with Judaizers that typifies this letter, this would mean that his gospel specifically opposed Jewish tradition.[11] In the school of *Religionsgeschichte* (Wilhelm Bousset), this was further developed into the antithesis between the primitive Palestinian church and the 'Hellenistic church' that was the cradle of Paul's beliefs, and from there the idea gained a crucial significance in Rudolf Bultmann's

---

[9] On Melanchthon: J.A. FITZMYER, *Romans: A New Translation with Introduction and Commentary* (AB, 33), New York NY, Doubleday 1992, pp. 74-80. See further R. BULTMANN, *Theologie des Neuen Testaments*, Tübingen, Mohr Siebeck, 1965, 5th ed., 187-353. J.D.G. DUNN, *The Theology of Paul the Apostle*, 1997, 3rd ed., Grand Rapids MI, Eerdmans, 1999, p. 25: Romans is less bound to a particular church and offers 'the most sustained and reflective statement of Paul's own theology'.

[10] On Baur and Stendahl see P.J. TOMSON, *Romans 9–11 and Political Developments in Rome and Judaea with Some Thoughts on Historical Criticism and Theological Exegesis*, in *Zeitschrift für dialektische Theologie* 33 (2017) 48-73.

[11] F.C. BAUR, *Die Christuspartei in der korinthischen Gemeinde, der Gegensatz des petrinischen und paulinischen Christentums in der ältesten Kirche, der Apostel Petrus in Rom*, in *Tübinger Zeitschrift für Theologie* 4 (1831), 61-206; repr. in F.C. BAUR, *Ausgewählte Werke in Einzelausgaben*, Vol. 1, K. SCHOLDER (ed.), Stuttgart, Frommann, 1963, 1-146, esp. pp. 108-114; 136. For Harnack (as quoted by K.H. RENGSTORF, art. διδάσκω in G. KITTEL et al., *Theologisches Wörterbuch zum Neuen Testament*, Vol. 2, Stuttgart, Kohlhammer 1960, 138-168, p.150), the Old Testament was no basis for Paul's moral teaching. Basically similar: A. LINDEMANN, *Die biblischen Toragebote und die paulinische Ethik*, in W. SCHRAGE (ed.), *Studien zum Text und zur Ethik des Neuen Testaments* (FS H. GREEVEN), Berlin, De Gruyter, 1986, 242-265.

Theologie des Neuen Testaments. In this approach, the few 'cult traditions' concerning Jesus cited by Paul (1 Cor 11,23-25; 15,3-8) must derive from the 'early Hellenistic Church', not from the 'early Palestinian Church', let alone from Jesus.[12]

We insist, however, on the principle laid down by Baur himself: Galatians as well should be read in view of the specific situation it addresses. Attention should be given both to its rhetorical structure and to its historical context.[13] In his commentary on Galatians, Hans-Dieter Betz gives an enlightening analysis of the rhetorical structure of the letter. He finds the 'hermeneutical key' to the letter in the autographed postscript that functions as *peroratio*.[14] Here Paul writes: 'It is those who want to make a good showing in the flesh that try to compel you to be circumcised – only that they may not be persecuted for the cross of Christ' (Gal 6,12). This exposes Paul's adversaries and their message that he designated at the beginning as 'another gospel' (1,7). We are being informed that their campaign for circumcision of male gentile Galatians aimed to boost their own reputation and thus to avoid being 'persecuted'.

The much-debated question is: who were these adversaries and what caused them in turn to be 'persecuted'? Betz seems to understand them simply as 'Jewish Christians' who propagated the 'gospel of the circumcision' mentioned in Gal 2,7.[15] It must be stressed, however, that Paul uses the latter expression to indicate Peter's mission to the Jews, which in the apostles' agreement (Gal 2,7-10) was juxtaposed to Paul's own 'gospel of the foreskin' as being of equal value.[16] It is more likely that *certain* Jewish

---

[12] Compare the main structure of Bultmann's *Theologie* with that of W. BOUSSET, *Kyrios Christos: Geschichte des Christusglaubens von den Anfängen des Christentums bis Irenäus*, Göttingen, Vandenhoeck & Ruprecht, 1965, 5th ed. See already B. GERHARDSSON, *Memory and Manuscript: Oral Tradition and Written Transmission in Rabbinic Judaism and Early Christianity* (ASNU, 22), Uppsala, 1961; repr., with foreword by J. Neusner, Grand Rapids MI, Eerdmans, 1998, p. 297 n. 4; and *cf.* P.J. TOMSON, *Rudolf Bultmann, Theologie des Neuen Testaments*, in *NTT* 69 (2015), 137-147.

[13] M.M. MITCHELL argues that rhetorical analysis should be one of the tools of historical criticism: *Paul and the Rhetoric of Reconciliation: An Exegetical Investigation of the Language and Composition of 1 Corinthians* (HUT, 28), Tübingen, Mohr Siebeck, 1991; repr. Louisville KY, Westminster John Knox, 1993, p. 6.

[14] H.-D. BETZ, *Galatians: A Commentary on Paul's Letter to the Churches of Galatia* (Hermeneia), Philadelphia PA, Fortress Press, 1979, p. 313. More elaboration in P.J. TOMSON, *Sources on the Politics of Judaea in the Fifties CE – A Response to Martin Goodman*, in *Journal of Jewish Studies* (forthcoming).

[15] BETZ, *Galatians* (n. 9), pp. 313f. (on Gal 6,12), 49f. (on 1,7). However he does not present this interpretation in the commentary on 2,7-9, pp. 95-101. On p. 315 he finds the persecution 'an extremely difficult problem'.

[16] *Ibid.*, pp. 98, 100.

Christians had begun to violate the agreement, being influenced by a *development* among Jews in Judaea that made itself felt also in adjacent lands. Such a development appears to be reflected in successive stages in Galatians, most visibly in what Betz views as the *expositio*, i.e., Paul's narrative of preceding events (1,13–2,21).[17] The aggravated state of the development at the moment of writing in the mid-50s CE is reflected in the 'other gospel' that is indicated in 1,7 and 6,12 and that urges the circumcision of male gentile Christians. This meant an outright violation of the apostolic agreement. As such, it was a radicalization away from the position adopted some years earlier by Cephas/Peter and Barnabas during the conflict at Antioch (Gal 2,11-14). The development as a whole apparently involved a growing emphasis on circumcision and law observance, coupled with a revulsion against pagan cult and as such is reminiscent of the Maccabaean revolt. Since Paul indicates that the conflict at Antioch was triggered by 'men from James' (Gal 2,12), it is likely that the current crisis in Galatia was also fanned by agitators from Judaea, who apparently were ready to 'persecute' those missionaries to Galatia if they did not actually 'preach circumcision'.[18]

A similar interpretation on the basis of a development among Jews in Judaea and elsewhere also allows us to better explain the different emphases of Galatians and Romans. Galatians neither opposes Jewish Christians in general, nor the 'gospel of the circumcision' headed by Peter. On the contrary, its argument is explicitly based on the apostolic agreement that recognizes Paul's mission to the gentiles and Peter's to the Jews as equal in value. What Galatians fights against tooth and nail is precisely the violation of this agreement by 'those who preach circumcision' (6,12f, *cf.* 5,11), i.e., those who cross the line and impose the 'gospel of the circumcision' on *gentile* Christians. It is in this configuration that Paul claims he did not receive his gospel from tradition, contrasting his position as much as possible from that of the agitators in Jerusalem.[19]

The argument of Romans is very different.[20] It also addresses gentile Christians, not in order to keep them away from circumcision and Jewish observance this time round, but urging them to re-accept Jewish Christians

---

[17] More in TOMSON, *Sources on the Politics of Judaea* (n. 14).
[18] Thus already R. JEWETT, *The Agitators and the Galatian Congregation*, in *NTS* 17 (1971), 198–212.
[19] BETZ, *Galatians* (n. 14), 62f., concludes that the material pertaining to Gal 1,12 requires 'new investigation'. *Cf. ibid.* 63-66 the valuable excursus 'Conversion, Revelation, and Tradition'.
[20] See TOMSON, *Romans 9–11 and Political Developments* (n. 434).

in their midst. The likely historical setting is the relaxation of Claudius' decree that had banned Jews or Jewish Christians from the city, while rumours about radicalizing Jews in Judaea may have been rumbling in the background. Hence the extraordinarily cautious argument of Romans, moreover addressing a church Paul had never visited before. Romans carries the exceptional message that the gospel addresses 'the Jew *first and also* the Greek' (Rom 1,16f.; 2,10f), and chapters 9–11, about the place of the Jewish people in God's history, are not marginal but central. It is not a dogmatic treatise about various topics, but a diplomatic letter that carefully and resourcefully addresses a complex situation involving various opposed interests.

Teachers, Disciples, and Tradition among Greeks and Jews

The above diversion about Galatians and Romans was necessary to clear the ground for the reiterated assertion that Paul was indeed also a teacher of tradition, not in opposition to Judaism, but following a particular strand within it. For a correct understanding, we must also view the phenomenon of teaching by tradition in the perspective of the larger Greco-Roman world.

As Elias Bickerman has shown, the idea of a 'chain of tradition' as a guarantee of authenticity and authority did not originate with the rabbinic tractate *Avot*, but was found centuries earlier in Greek philosophical schools, and was also adopted in the discipline of Roman law. 'Like the philosophy of the Greeks, the Torah of the Pharisees was transmitted from master to disciple, not from father to son.' Moreover for the Greeks this concerned 'not some kind of technical knowledge which can become obsolete, but rather a way of living, an *ars vivendi*, which the founder of the school had discovered'.[21] Not unlike Bickerman, Loveday Alexander has studied the characteristics of the Hellenistic schools, in particular as represented by the pagan philosopher Galen (late second century CE). These schools were not 'academic' in the modern sense but had much to do with 'faith', and they compare well with what Galen called the 'school of Moses' and the 'school of Christ'.[22] Similarly, in his wide-ranging

---

[21] E. Bickerman, *The Chain of the Pharisaic Tradition*, in E. Bickerman, *Studies in Jewish and Christian History* (AJEC, 68.1-2), Vol. 1, Leiden, Brill 2007, rev. ed., 528-542, pp. 542 and 535 (cited in the original French by Gerhardsson, *Memory*, n. 12, p. 193).

[22] L. Alexander, *Paul and the Hellenistic Schools: The Evidence of Galen*, in T. Engberg-Pedersen (ed.), *Paul in His Hellenistic Context*, Minneapolis MN, Fortress Press, 1995, 60-83, p. 83.

'Prolegomena to the Study of Oral Tradition in the Hellenistic World', David Aune makes particular mention of the oral tradition of the Pythagoraeans and other philosophical schools and of the *chreia* or 'anecdote' as a favourite form of Greek popular teaching.[23]

Orality in teaching, studying, and even transmitting tradition was typical especially of the ancient academies that produced the classic rabbinic documents, beginning with Mishnah and Tosefta. Such is the conclusion of the ever unsurpassed standard work on the textual history of the Mishnah by Jacob Nahum Epstein (1948). Scrupulously taking stock of the data scattered across rabbinic literature, he adds that this did not exclude the use of written letters, notes, and aide-mémoires, even by the *tannaim*, 'repeaters', i.e. the specialists of memorization who retained the tradition and performed it orally in the regular rabbinic study sessions: 'In conclusion, while it is obvious that the 'tannaim' did write down and record their mishnayot and halakhot, these texts were not meant as study books, because they taught orally.'[24] This conclusion is adopted by Günter Stemberger in his *Einleitung in Talmud und Midrasch*.[25] Without elaborating on the use of written records by the rabbis as noted by Epstein, Shmuel Safrai has given an illuminating description of the processes of oral creation, composition, redaction, and transmission that are characteristic of classic rabbinic literature.[26]

Worthy of mention is also the pioneering study by Birger Gerhardsson (1961) of oral and written tradition in rabbinic Judaism and early Christianity.[27] The first and larger part of the work meanders across the various methods by which the rabbis preserved and transmitted their oral teachings, paying detailed attention to the terminology and techniques of oral tradition. On that basis, the second part studies the way in which the followers of Jesus recorded their master's words, and this includes an important section on Paul. While Paul had distanced himself from his adherence

---

[23] D.E. AUNE, *Prolegomena to the Study of Oral Tradition in the Hellenistic World*, in D.E. AUNE, *Jesus, Gospel Tradition and Paul in the Context of Jewish and Graeco-Roman Antiquity: Collected Essays II*, Tübingen, Mohr Siebeck, 2013, 220-355, here pp. 345-348 and p. 251f.

[24] J.N. EPSTEIN, *Mavo le-nosah ha-Mishna: Nosah ha-Mishna ve-gilgulav lemi-yemei ha-Amoraim ha-rishonim ve-ad defusei R. Yomtov Lippmann Heller*, Jerusalem, private ed., 1948; repr. 1963-1964 (Hebrew), 692-706, quote at p. 702 (my translation).

[25] STEMBERGER, *Einleitung in Talmud und Midrasch* (n. 2), p. 47.

[26] S. SAFRAI, *Oral Tora*, in S. SAFRAI (ed.), *The Literature of the Sages, part 1: Oral Tora, Halakha, Mishna, Tosefta, Talmud, External Tractates* (CRINT, II/3a), Assen, Van Gorcum, 1987, 35-119, esp. pp. 60-77.

[27] See GERHARDSSON, *Memory* (n. 12).

to the contents of Pharisaic tradition, he did transmit specific traditions of Jesus and the earliest church using a terminology similar to that of rabbinic literature, and he based his own instruction on those traditions. Gerhardsson roughly distinguishes three 'sections' of Pauline instruction: doctrinal (e.g. 1 Cor 15), ethical (1 Thess 4,1ff.), and 'ecclesiastical' (1 Cor 11 and 14), and he also sees Paul 'delivering decisions of halakhic nature' such as in 1 Cor 7.[28]

Gerhardsson was severely criticized, first of all by Jacob Neusner, for 'anachronistically' using rabbinic literature in studying the New Testament. A re-emerging interest in oral tradition, however, caused the book to be reprinted in 1998 – this time round with a remarkably positive introduction by Neusner, who explained that 'paradigmatic' comparison as practised by Gerhardsson should not be confused with causal historical explanation.[29] The point is worth considering. Rabbinic legend claims that 'oral Torah' harks back to time immemorial. This is impossible to prove of course, but is likely in a general sense. As we learned at the outset, written texts always presuppose oral interpretation and hence a schooling system. The similarities with the Greco-Roman 'schools' we have reviewed enhance the likelihood. Further confirmation could be found in terminological similarity. Such is indeed the case.

As shown by Gerhardsson, Paul's terminology for handling tradition parallels that of the rabbinic 'schools'.[30] A case in point is the way he uses διδαχή for traditional teaching. This is also the word used for the apostolic tradition in the early Church from Didache and Barnabas onwards.[31] Thus Paul can remind the Romans that they 'have become obedient ... to the form of teaching to which you were entrusted' (εἰς ὃν παρεδόθητε τύπον διδαχῆς, Rom 6,17) and warn them to avoid offenses that oppose 'the teaching that you have learned' (τὴν διδαχὴν ἣν ὑμεῖς ἐμάθετε, Rom 16,17). Similarly, using the passive of the verb διδάσκω, he can encourage the Colossians to 'continue to live your lives ... just as you were taught' (καθὼς ἐδιδάχθητε, Col 2,7), and the Thessalonians to 'hold fast to the traditions that you were taught by us (παραδόσεις ἃς ἐδιδάχθητε),

---

[28] *Ibid.*, pp. 303-305, 311-314.
[29] J. NEUSNER, *Foreword*, in GERHARDSSON, *Memory* (n. 12), xxv-xlvi. *Cf.* D.E. AUNE, *Jesus Tradition and the Pauline Letters*, in D.E. AUNE, *Jesus, Gospel Tradition and Paul* (n. 23), 303-327, here pp. 6-13.
[30] GERHARDSSON, *Memory* (n. 12), pp. 288-302.
[31] E.g. Did 1,3; 6,1; Barn 18,1.

either by word of mouth or by our letter' (2 Thess 2,15).[32] Again, Paul praises the Corinthians who 'maintain the traditions (παραδόσεις) just as I handed them on to you' (1 Cor 11,2).

We conclude that Conzelmann's and Vielhauer's intuition of a 'school of Paul' – in the non-academic, 'life-style' sense of the Greco-Roman world – finds confirmation. In similar vein, Acts consistently calls the early followers of Jesus μαθηταί, disciples (once μαθήτρια: Tabitha, Acts 9,36).[33] Although this is not Paul's own usage, it does continue the usage in the Gospels, where Jesus' followers are called 'disciples' of a master who sticks to another tradition than 'the tradition of the elders' (Mk 7,5). And even though Paul did not follow Jesus' teaching in person, he did 'receive' his tradition, as we shall presently see, and in that sense he certainly was his disciple.

In the remainder of this article, we shall discuss two types of Jesus tradition cited by Paul: ethical teachings, usually dealt with under the caption of parenesis that, in view of their background in Judaism, we shall call halakhic traditions, and teachings of Christological character that appear to have developed from esoteric traditions about Jesus' true nature.[34]

Halakhic Jesus Traditions

An obvious and much-discussed aspect of Paul's handling of tradition concerns his attitude to the Jesus tradition. The conditions in which nineteenth- and twentieth-century scholars began to find it hard to imagine that Paul had received traditions from Jesus have been sketched above. More or less in line with the dominant Baur-Bultmann paradigm, many modern exegetes take a sceptical attitude.[35] Thus Frans Neirynck, having painstakingly surveyed previous research, stated in 1986, '[T]here is no

---

[32] For AUNE, *Jesus Tradition* (n. 29), p. 325, παραλαμβάνω and διδάσκω [διδάσκομαι?] are synonyms in Paul, therefore παραλαμβάνω is not a technical term for institutionally transmitting oral tradition. But Pauline παρέλαβον and ἐδιδάχθην are just as synonymous as rabbinic מקובל אני (I have received) and למוד אני (I am instructed).

[33] *Cf.* ALEXANDER, *Paul and the Hellenistic Schools* (n. 22), p. 79. Cf. also R. RIESNER, *Paulus und die Jesus-Überlieferung*, in I. ÅDNA – S.J. HAFEMANN – O. HOFIUS (eds.), *Evangelium – Schrift – Auslegung – Kirche* (FS P. STUHLMACHER), Göttingen, Vandenhoeck & Ruprecht, 1997, pp. 347-365, esp. p. 361: ... Paulus (fügt sich) in das Bild von einer bewussten ... schulmässigen Weitergabe der Jesustradition ein ...

[34] Out to investigate the relation of Paul and Jesus, D. HÄUSSER, *Christusbekenntnis und Jesusüberlieferung bei Paulus* (WUNT, 2.110), Tübingen, Mohr Siebeck, 2006, p. 39 concentrates on 'a decisive area of Pauline theology... Christology', overlooking the importance of ethical or halakhic Jesus traditions.

[35] See Häusser's survey of research on Jesus traditions in Paul, *ibid.*, pp. 1-38. On Paul and oral tradition see AUNE, *Jesus Tradition* (n. 29), pp. 7-20.

trace ... in the Pauline letters of a conscious use of a saying of Jesus'. Ten years later, noting that some find him a 'minimalist', he kept insisting that 'there are only two explicit references', 1 Cor 7,10 and 9,14.[36]

Some years earlier, Dale Allison had come to a different conclusion, while referring to trends in nineteenth and early twentieth century theology, notably the Bultmann school: '[T]he theological situation has continued to discourage the search for the ways in which Paul is dependent upon the historical Jesus.' In contrast, Allison finds multiple allusions to the Jesus tradition in Paul, though most of the time not by way of citation.

> With the exception of 1 Cor. 11.23-26 and 15.1-7, his letters contain only free renderings of or allusions to individual sayings. But in his correspondence Paul merely *refers* to the Jesus tradition; he never *hands it down*. ... The epistles were simply not the place for its transmission.

Appreciative of Gerhardsson's work, Allison infers: 'It is likely that the Paul who in person nurtured infant churches on tradition would, if we could but behold him, appear more conservative than the Paul known by his letters.'[37]

We do not need to pursue the discussion further. More recently Harm Hollander, building among others on Neirynck, established:

> In summation, we may conclude that in the letters of Paul there are no more than three instances of an explicit reference to a saying of the Lord, namely, in 1 Cor. 11,23-25, 7,10-11, and 9,14. ... It cannot be accidental that they all occur in 1 Corinthians, a letter that primarily deals with Christian ethics.[38]

While stipulating that this does not prove 'with any certainty' that Jesus actually said such things, Hollander concludes that it does confirm his own hypothesis that, '[T]he first oral and written early Christian traditions were sayings attributed to Jesus which dealt with community rules, directions for Christians as to how to live in a new age.' Although Hollander has little appreciation for Gerhardsson's approach, he thus finds himself not far from the latter's conclusion that Paul's letters do contain 'decisions of halakhic nature' attributed to Jesus.[39]

---

[36] F. NEIRYNCK, *Paul and the Sayings of Jesus*, in A. VANHOYE (ed.), *L'Apôtre Paul: personnalité, style et conception du ministère* (BETL, 76), Leuven, Peeters 1986, 265-321, p. 320; F. NEIRYNCK, *The Sayings of Jesus in 1 Corinthians*, in R. BIERINGER (ed.), *The Corinthian Correspondence*, Leuven, Peeters, 1996, 141-176, pp. 141 and 176.
[37] D.C. ALLISON, *The Pauline Epistles and the Synoptic Gospels: The Patterns of the Parallels*, in *NTS* 28 (1982), 1-32, pp. 21-24.
[38] H. HOLLANDER, *The Words of Jesus: From Oral Tradition to Written Record in Paul and Q*, in *NT* 42 (2000), 340-357, p. 349.
[39] *Ibid.*, p. 344, on GERHARDSSON pp. 342f.

These considerations bring us to a point easily overlooked in Protestant theology, namely that 1 Corinthians is important precisely because, rather than Paul's 'theology', it contains primarily practical injunctions, including some deriving from the Jesus tradition. Let us revisit some of the halakhic Jesus traditions in this letter.[40]

Most important for our discussion is 1 Cor 7. The chapter deals in an orderly way with a number of questions written by the Corinthians (περὶ δὲ ὧν ἐγράψατε, 7,1).[41] They all have to do with related subjects: sexual abstinence, divorce, celibacy, and widowhood, all for the sake of σχολάζειν τῇ προσευχῇ, 'devoting oneself to prayer' (7,5), or μεριμνᾶν τὰ τοῦ κυρίου, 'caring about the things of the Lord' (7,32-35). In all cases, Paul is explicit about his source of authority, always preferring the more ascetic option without prescribing it, and giving as a basic rule that marriage and sexual relations are good. Thus he addresses six different situations:

(1) 1 Cor 7,1-7. 'By way of concession, not a commandment' (κατὰ συγγνώμην οὐ κατ' ἐπιταγήν), Paul allows married partners to desist from intercourse, but only for a limited period and by mutual consent.

(2) 7,8-9. 'I say (λέγω δὲ) to the unmarried and widowed: it would be good if they remained as I also am, but if they cannot contain themselves, let them marry, for it is better to marry than to burn.'

(3) 7,10-11. 'To the married I order, not I but the Lord (παραγγέλλω, οὐκ ἐγὼ ἀλλὰ ὁ κύριος): the wife is not to depart from the husband – and if she did depart, she must remain single or return to her husband – and the husband is not to dismiss his wife.'

(4) 7,12-16. 'To the others I say, not the Lord' (λέγω ἐγὼ οὐχ ὁ κύριος) – this appears to concern those bound to an unbelieving partner by an informal marriage, in which exceptional case Paul allows divorce if the unbelieving partner wishes so.[42]

---

[40] For the following see P.J. TOMSON, *Paul and the Jewish Law; Halakha in the Letters of the Apostle to the Gentiles* (CRINT, 3.1), Assen, Van Gorcum, 1990, chapters 3 and 5.

[41] See GERHARDSSON, *Memory* (n. 23), p. 311; P. RICHARDSON, *"I Say, not the Lord": Personal Opinion, Apostolic Authority and the Development of Early Christian Halakah*, in TynBul 31 (1980), 65-96; P.J. TOMSON, *Paul's Jewish Background in View of His Law Teaching in 1 Cor 7*, in J.D.G. DUNN (ed.), *Paul and the Mosaic Law; The Third Durham-Tübingen Research Symposium on Earliest Christianity and Judaism (Durham, September, 1994)*, Tübingen, Mohr Siebeck, 1996, 251-269, esp. P. 259.

[42] See TOMSON, *Paul and the Jewish Law* (n. 40), pp. 117-119. Under the name of *privilegium paulinum*, the ruling became a loophole for dissolving marriages in Roman Catholic canon law: canon 1143.

7,17-24 is a digression which states Paul's 'rule for all churches': it is better 'to remain in the calling in which you were called'.
(5) 7,25-38. 'Now about the virgins, I have no commandment of the Lord, but I give my opinion' (ἐπιταγὴν κυρίου οὐκ ἔχω, γνώμην δὲ δίδωμι) – which follows after an exhortation about devotion to the Lord: 'He who marries his virgin does well, and who does not marry her does better.'
(6) 7,39-40. Widows apparently require further specification, and a general rule is followed by Paul's own opinion: 'A woman is bound as long as her husband lives; but if the husband decease, she is free to be married to whom she wishes, if only in the Lord; but she is happier if she stays so, in my opinion' (κατὰ τὴν ἐμὴν γνώμην).

Here we see Paul teaching the Corinthians on the basis of tradition and occasionally adding his own apostolic 'opinion'. The approach is casuistic, in each case distinguishing between 'commandment' (ἐπιταγή), 'opinion' or 'judgment' (γνώμη), or 'concession' (συγγνώμη).[43] A 'commandment of the Lord' (ἐπιταγὴ κυρίου) has highest authority and for the Corinthians apparently was a known category – they had at least received Paul's basic instruction on the matter at hand. In the case of the 'virgins', Paul does not have such a commandment, in that of the married, he does: 'I order, not I but the Lord'. We obviously do not know what specific questions the Corinthians had written, but the question of the 'virgins' is likely to have been among them, possibly asking whether there was a commandment of Jesus on the matter.[44]

Paul did possess such a commandment concerning divorce, however, and as Neirynck and others have established, 1 Cor 7,10-11 is an obvious reflection of the divorce prohibition in the synoptic Jesus tradition.[45] From various sources it appears that this prohibition represents a particular Jewish interpretation that differs from Pharisaic-rabbinic tradition and is rather similar to Qumran Essene opinion.[46] However Paul probably

---

[43] See BDAG, *s.v.* γνώμη and συγγνώμη.
[44] The introduction, περὶ δὲ τῶν παρθένων, seems to announce a new, separate subject, as in 7,1, 8,1, 12,1, see M.M. MITCHELL, *Concerning PERI DE in 1 Corinthians*, in *NT* 31 (1989), 229-256. Also, the diversion that precedes (7,17-24) and the long parenetic middle section (7,26-35, producing the A-B-A' structure Paul often uses) seem to reflect the importance of this question.
[45] NEIRYNCK, *The Sayings of Jesus* (n. 36), pp. 158-174.
[46] See e.g. J.A. FITZMYER, *First Corinthians: A New Translation with Introduction and Commentary* (AB, 32), New Haven CT, Yale UP, 2008, pp. 287-292, *cf.* 328f.; TOMSON, *Paul and the Jewish law* (n. 40), 97-124; P.J. TOMSON, *Divorce Halakhah in Paul and*

adapts Jesus' commandment to suit the situation of gentiles by mentioning the woman's initiative, which is also done in Mk 10,12 and addresses the case of a Hellenistic common law marriage.⁴⁷ Moreover the stipulation that a widow 'is free to be married to whom she wishes if only in the Lord' must be an accepted traditional law, for Paul gives his own more stringent opinion as an alternative. The expression μόνον ἐν κυρίῳ shows that it is an early Christian law, or in other words, an apostolic halakha. Paul quotes the same rule by way of a 'law' known to the Roman church in Rom 7,1-2.⁴⁸ We conclude that in 1 Cor 7, Paul teaches his Corinthian church on the basis of the Jesus tradition, apostolic tradition, and his own apostolic authority.

Another Jesus tradition is cited in 1 Cor 9,14, in the context of three chapters devoted to the question of idol offerings, 1 Cor 8,1–11,1. The chapters have the triple structure mentioned before: (A) 8,1-13, introduction of the subject; (B) 9,1–10,22, digression exploring motives in a wider perspective; (A') 10,23–11,1, definitive treatment of the subject. Our passage of interest is in the digression, where Paul presents his own person as an example, arguing that even though he has certain privileges as an apostle, he needs not necessarily make use of them, certainly if that would harm others. So, Paul argues, Christians who believe they may eat any meat, may refrain from doing so when 'weaker' brothers believe they should not.

> Am I not free? Am I not an apostle? Have I not seen Jesus our Lord? ... If I am not an apostle to others, at least I am to you... Do we not have the right to our food and drink? Do we not have the right to be accompanied by a believing wife, as do the other apostles and the brothers of the Lord and Cephas? ... Do you not know that those who are employed in the temple service get their food from the temple ...? In the same way, the Lord commanded that those who proclaim the gospel should get their living by the gospel. But I have made no use of any of these rights...

---

in the Jesus Tradition, in R. BIERINGER – F. GARCIA MARTINEZ – D. POLLEFEYT – P.J. TOMSON (eds.), *The New Testament and Rabbinic Literature* (JSJ Suppl., 136), Leiden, Brill, 2010, 289-332. Fitzmyer studiously avoids bringing in rabbinic evidence (*cf.* p. 289f., 329), depriving himself of important sources in assessing Jesus' place in Judaism.

47. TOMSON, *Paul and the Jewish Law* (n. 40), p. 109 n. 76; TOMSON, *Divorce Halakhah in Paul* (n. 46), p. 304 and footnotes 46-47; Fitzmyer, *First Corinthians* (n. 46), p. 289f.

48. P.J. TOMSON, *What did Paul mean by "Those Who Know the Law"? (Rom 7.1)*, in *NTS* 49 (2003), 573-581.

The mention of 'the other apostles and Cephas' is interesting, because they may be supposed to heed the teachings of Jesus. Their right to be sustained by the church surely implies that they were seen as 'those who proclaim the gospel' and as per the 'command' of the Lord 'should get their living by the gospel'. This inference from the context confirms the identification scholars have proposed with the rule preserved in the synoptic tradition that 'the labourer is worthy of his wages' or, presumably closer to the Jewish sources, with the rule which relates to the rights of field labourers (*cf.* Deut 25,24f.), 'the labourer is worthy of his food'.[49] The wide-spread documentation of the rule and its links with the supposedly well-entrenched laws pertaining to field labourers suggests that the saying was adopted from general Jewish tradition, either by Jesus or by his disciples. In any case 1 Cor 9,14 is another instance where Paul teaches by means of tradition.

The third instance in which Paul explicitly cites the Jesus tradition, 1 Cor 11,23-25, is a narrative embedded in a parenetic context. The narrative wording strikingly contrasts with the surrounding exhortative language:

> ...What shall I say to you? Shall I commend you in this? No, I will not. For I received from the Lord what I also delivered to you, *that the Lord Jesus on the night when he was betrayed took bread, and when he had given thanks, he broke it, and said, This is my body which is for you. Do this in remembrance of me. In the same way also the cup, after supper* ... For as often as you eat this bread and drink... Whoever, therefore, eats...

The introductory formula, 'I received from the Lord what I also delivered to you', produces a formal tone that appears to be intentional and meant to contrast with the informal exhortative style of the whole passage. The narrative that follows and that is italicized here had been already 'delivered' to the Corinthians and therefore was known to them. No, Paul is not going to 'commend' them. Instead he will use the familiar tradition of the Lord to commend them. The narrative is cited with a didactic, parenetic purpose: once again Paul teaches by means of tradition. The most plausible explanation of the situation at hand, it seems, is that according to Paul's information, the Corinthian church's meals proceeded in an unruly

---

[49] Matt 10,10; Did 13,2 (ἄξιος τῆς τροφῆς αὐτοῦ); Luke 10,7; 1 Tim 5,18 (ἄξιος τοῦ μισθοῦ αὐτοῦ). Fitzmyer, *First Corinthians* (n. 46), 365f., Neirynck, *The Sayings of Jesus* (n. 36), pp. 174-176. For discussion and documentation of the larger halakhic complex see Tomson, *Paul and the Jewish Law* (n. 40), pp.125-131.

way, and he presents the example set by Jesus as the way to begin and terminate a festive meal. The probable intention then is not, as it is often read nowadays, to remind the Corinthians of the institution of 'the Lord's Supper' by citing the foundational words of Jesus, but to teach them how to demarcate the beginning and end of a meal by breaking the bread and lifting the cup. In that sense, it concerns another halakhic Jesus tradition.

In this reading, the introductory formula does signal formal delivery of tradition:[50] Paul uses it to mediate the authority of Jesus, thus underscoring his lesson to the Corinthians. Further implications are that in this exceptional instance, Paul cites gospel tradition in a form similar to the one known to us from the canonical Gospels, and that at that moment, supposedly years before written Gospels existed, Paul was familiar with parts of the oral gospel tradition. In all other cases, he only gives a brief paraphrase of the tradition. Allison's explanation that 'epistles were simply not the place for its transmission' seems satisfactory. Paul may be citing verbally in this case precisely because the text supposedly was exceptionally well-known among the Corinthians and would generate more authority.

Mystical Jesus Traditions

The other type of Jesus traditions in Paul we want to deal with may, in view of their origin, be called 'mystical-apocalyptic'. Here we find ourselves on poorly laboured ground, due to both the rationalist reservations of modern scholars and to the inherent secrecy of ancient apostles and rabbis about this material. First to be mentioned is the pioneering work of Gershom Scholem who, in the mid-twentieth century, almost single-handedly claimed a recognized place for Jewish mysticism in modern scholarship. He showed that both in Antiquity and in the Middle Ages an esoteric tradition existed among Jews, including rabbis and early Christians, notably Paul in his famous disclosure in 2 Cor 12,2-4.[51] Earlier still, coming from another direction, Albert Schweitzer had already offered an interpretation of Paul's 'mysticism' on the basis of comparison with the ancient Jewish apocalypses, which he understood as eschatological

---

[50] *Pace* AUNE, see n. 29 and n. 32. My position is similar to RIESNER, *Paulus* (n. 33).
[51] G. SCHOLEM, *Major Trends in Jewish Mysticism*, New York NY, Schocken, 1941; repr New York NY, Schocken 1991. For *Antiquity*, see chapter 2. On 2 Cor 12, see G. SCHOLEM, *Jewish Gnosticism, Merkabah Mysticism, and Talmudic Tradition*, New York NY, JTSA, 1965, pp. 14-19.

writings.⁵² Later in the twentieth century, Peter Schäfer produced important studies and scholarly editions of esoteric rabbinic works, while claiming against Scholem that rabbinic mysticism developed too late to be of any significance for the New Testament.⁵³ A different understanding was advanced by Christopher Rowland. Not unlike Schweitzer, basing himself on ancient apocalyptic texts, now including writings from Qumran, he described early Jewish apocalypticism as 'knowledge of the divine mysteries through revelation', implying that this includes both eschatological secrets of the future and cosmological mysteries in heaven, or, formulated differently, it includes both a temporal and a spatial axis.⁵⁴ In other words, apocalypticism closely relates to mysticism. As such, Rowland claimed, the phenomenon was found both among early rabbis including Yohanan ben Zakkai and Akiva, and among early Christians including Paul. Together with Christopher Morray-Jones, Rowland published *The Mystery of God* (2009), in which the authors take stock of the Jewish mystical materials, including rabbinic ones, that appear to be reflected in the New Testament.⁵⁵

The early Jewish apocalypses give the suggestion that their creation and reading were associated with esoteric sessions and rituals, and some of the Qumran scrolls reinforce that impression. Rabbinic literature, however, is just to give explicit reports about the initiation into and transmission of mystical traditions. The rabbis were very reticent about this and ruled that the respective subjects; notably the 'creation story' and the 'chariot' were to be rehearsed only with one or two individuals of mature age and understanding (*m. Hag.* 2,1). In this connection a story is told of Yohanan ben Zakkai who, when travelling with his mature disciple Elazar ben Arakh, allowed the latter to give an exposition of 'the Chariot' (Eze 1). When he began to speak, the master descended from his donkey, wrapped his head in his cloak and sat down with him under a fig tree, 'and fire descended from heaven and encircled them.' In the continuation, a chain of tradition is given:

---

[52] A. SCHWEITZER, *Die Mystik des Apostels Paulus*, Tübingen, Mohr Siebeck, 1930; repr. UTB-Mohr Siebeck, 1981.

[53] P. SCHÄFER, *New Testament and Hekhalot Literature: The Journey into Heaven in Paul and in Merkavah Mysticism*, in P. SCHÄFER, *Hekhalot-Studien* (TSAJ, 19), Tübingen, Mohr Siebeck, 1989, 234-249. *Cf.* P. SCHÄFER et al. (eds.), *Übersetzung der Hekhalot-Literatur* (TSAJ, 17, 23, 29, 46), 4 Vols., Tübingen, Mohr Siebeck, 1987-1994.

[54] The latter formulation is that of J.J. COLLINS, *Towards the Morphology of a Genre*, in *Semeia* 14 (1979) (= J.J. COLLINS (ed.), *Apocalypse: The Morphology of a Genre*, Missoula MT, SBL, 1979, 1-20, pp. 6-7).

[55] C. ROWLAND – C.R.A. MORRAY-JONES, *The Mystery of God: Early Jewish Mysticism and the New Testament* (CRINT, 12), Leiden, Brill, 2009.

Yoshua 'performed before' Yohanan ben Zakkai, Akiva before Yoshua, Hananya ben Hakinai before Akiva.[56] Significantly, most of these are leading figures of the early rabbinic movement and have a central place in the Mishnah. The conclusion follows that the early rabbis not only formulated halakhic and midrashic traditions in their public sessions, but that at least some of them also cultivated apocalyptic-mystical traditions in private.[57]

Keeping in mind the close association of apocalypticism and mysticism, we can observe that the phenomenon plays a crucial role throughout the New Testament. This is particularly clear in the narrative of Mark. Jesus has an apocalyptic vision at his baptism: 'He saw the heavens torn apart and the Spirit descending like a dove on him, and a voice came from heaven: You are my son, the beloved...' (1,11). The heavenly secret imparted to him is that he is the Son of God. Then he starts proclaiming the kingdom of God, teaching, and healing. When the disciples ask him to explain the parable of the seed, he answers: 'To you has been given the secret (μυστήριον) of the kingdom of God, but for those outside, everything comes in parables' (4,11). The disciples are worthy to receive esoteric knowledge.[58] Indeed, three of them are initiated into the heavenly secret of Jesus' true nature: '(Jesus) was transfigured before them, and his clothes became dazzling white... From the cloud there came a voice, This is my Son, the Beloved...' (9,2-7). Meanwhile, Jesus has begun to teach them 'that the son of man must undergo great suffering, and be rejected by the elders...' Peter protests, but 'he rebuked Peter and said, Get behind me, Satan!' (8,31-33). 'Son of man' is the phrase from the apocalypses of Daniel and Enoch that Jesus adopts to describe his career on earth. He keeps teaching about his suffering: 'The son of man came not to be served but to serve and to give his life a ransom for many' (10,45). When tried before the Sanhedrin, he says, 'You will see the son of man seated at the right hand of the Power and coming with the clouds of heaven' (14,62, *cf.* Ps 110,1 and Dan 7,13). Finally, mourning his death already on the third day, women are addressed by angels who tell them, 'You are looking for Jesus of Nazareth, the crucified one? He has been resurrected, he is not here' (Mk 16,6). In this apocalyptic perception of the world, as with the early rabbis, angels impart heavenly truths to humans.

---

[56] *T. Hag.* 2,1; *y. Hag.* 2,1 (77a); *Mekhilta de-R. Shimon ben Yohai*, ed. Epstein-Melamed, 158f. In the story, Yohanan ben Zakkai cites the rule found in *m. Hag.* 1,1, suggesting the rule existed by the mid-first century BCE.

[57] *Cf.* SCHOLEM, *Major Trends* (n. 51), chapter 2.

[58] For a similar reading of the passage see J.R. KIRKLAND, *The Earliest Understanding of Jesus' Use of Parables: Mark IV 10-12 in Context*, in *NT* 19 (1977), 1-21.

Thus, as proposed by Jack Kingsbury in his enlightening *Christology of Mark's Gospel*, Mark's narrative consists in a gradual unfolding of the secret of Jesus' true identity, not first of all as Messiah, but as Son of God.[59] In other words, following Mark, what we used to call 'Christology' is in fact a mystical subject that involves esoteric knowledge of Jesus' true nature, both before as well as after his death. His resurrection belongs in this domain and in this light is only a passage from this life to eternal life, where he sits 'at the right hand of God' (*cf.* also Mk 12,36). These are the elements of what was to become the 'creed', the hymnic summary of main events of Jesus' true existence, among which his suffering and crucifixion 'under Pontius Pilate' remind the believers that he lived this hidden life among us on earth. An early form of such a summary of Jesus' true existence can be found in the tradition Paul quotes in 1 Cor 15, which we shall discuss in a moment.

We still need to stipulate that what was said above about 'poorly laboured ground' only concerns the esoteric, mystic-apocalyptic aspect of the traditions involved, not their contents. These belong to what is widely considered to be the central theme of Christian theology: *Christology*. Its originally esoteric character probably was less strange for the ancients than for modern eyes. Secrecy was a regular feature of both the Jewish sect of the Essenes and the Greco-Roman mystery cults, and the teachings of such prominent Christian theologians such as Clement of Alexandria and Origen had a clear esoteric component. Similarly, the early declarative creeds probably had their origin in the pre-baptismal catechetical setting, which implies confidentiality.[60]

Thus let us hear how in his great chapter on resurrection, Paul repeats once again the tradition he had 'received' himself and had imparted to the Corinthians at an earlier stage:

---

[59] J.D. KINGSBURY, *The Christology of Mark's Gospel*, Philadelphia PA, Fortress, 1983, repr. 1989, referring to W. WREDE, *Das Messiasgeheimnis in den Evangelien*, Göttingen, Vandenhoeck & Ruprecht, 1901, repr. 1963. One does not need to follow Kingsbury's acceptance of the reading υἱοῦ θεοῦ in Mk 1,1 (p. 14) to admire the persuasiveness of his thesis

[60] On the Essenes see FLAVIUS JOSEPHUS, War 2:142; for mystery cults see W. BURKERT, *Ancient Mystery Cults*, Cambridge MA, 1987, pp. 7f. For Clement see A. VAN DEN HOEK, review of A.C. ITTER, *Esoteric Teaching in the "Stromateis" of Clement of Alexandria* (VC Suppl., 97), Leiden, Brill, 2009, in *VC* 64 (2010), 414-418; for Origen, the introduction and selected readings in R.A. GREER (ed.), *Origen*, Mahwah NJ, Paulist, 1979. On the creeds see J.N.D. KELLY, *Early Christian Creeds*, Harlow, Longman, 1979, 3rd. ed., 49-52.

> For I handed on to you as of first importance what I in turn had received: that Christ died for our sins in accordance with the scriptures, and that he was buried, and that he was raised on the third day in accordance with the scriptures, and that he appeared to Cephas, then to the twelve. Then he appeared to more than five hundred brothers at one time... Then he appeared to James, then to all the apostles. Last of all... he appeared also to me... (1 Cor 15,3-8)

As in the case of 1 Cor 11,23-25, it is clear that Paul runs through gospel tradition, not, however, in a verbatim quote but in a series of summary statements that could serve well to instruct neophytes.[61] Many parallels with the canonical Gospels can be identified. The repeated phrase 'in accordance with the scriptures' strikingly recalls the emphases of Luke 24.[62]

As we know from his letters and is confirmed by Acts, Paul himself had ecstatic 'revelations' at pivotal moments in his life. The most explicit account is in 2 Cor 12,1-5, which seems to speak of himself in the third person, reflecting the reticence typical of mystics. Remarkably, it does not mention an encounter with Jesus, nor does the other example in the retrospective account in Gal 2,1.[63] Gal 1,11-16, however, indirectly narrates Paul's calling vision of Jesus, in which he 'received' his gospel 'not from a human source ... but through a revelation' (Gal 1,12, δι' ἀποκαλύψεως). We have argued that with this emphasis he distances himself from the agitators in Jerusalem, not necessarily from the apostles. On the contrary, Gal 2,1-10 claims basic unity with Peter. It seems Gerhardsson is right in stating that Paul here presents himself not as an 'apocalyptic' as opposed to Peter, but as 'his *apostolic equal*'.[64]

In 1 Cor 15,3-8, however, Paul shows that he is also a recipient of apocalyptic tradition. As with the halakhic injunctions from the Jesus tradition, so also in the case of this resurrection narrative Paul 'hands on' what he has himself directly or indirectly 'received' from the disciples of Jesus. Thus interestingly, Paul's example shows how what we have been calling

---

[61] See KELLY, *Early Christian Creeds* (n. 60), pp.16f. ('manifestly drawn up for catechetical purposes'); GERHARDSSON, *Memory* (n. 12), pp. 297f. ('a logos fixed by the college of Apostles' – *cf.* doubts by AUNE, *Jesus Tradition*, n. 29, pp. 9f.); FITZMYER, *First Corinthians* (n. 470), pp. 536-544 (discussion of traditional character).

[62] See HÄUSSER, *Christusbekenntnis* (n. 34), pp. 106-141; 124fp. on Luke 24.

[63] See on Paul's visions and their similarities with rabbinic esoteric experiences C. MORRAY-JONES in ROWLAND – MORRAY-JONES, *The Mystery of God* (n. 55), 341-419, who interestingly links Gal 2,1 with Acts 22,17-22.

[64] GERHARDSSON, *Memory* (n. 12), 268f. (emphasis in original), stressing the phrase σὰρξ καὶ αἷμα also found in 1 Cor 15,50 and Matt 16,17.

the 'Jesus tradition' has come to include both *statements attributed to* Jesus and *narratives about* him, in particular traditions about his death and resurrection that reveal his 'true nature'. In other words, 'Christology' is an integral component of the early Jesus tradition, and it did not originate in 'Hellenistic Christianity' but in the first churches in Jerusalem (Luke 24, Acts 1) and Galilee (Mk 16).

We can speculate about who was Paul's source for the Jesus tradition. On the basis of our scarce information, Cephas/Peter is the most likely guess. The prominence of Peter in 1 Cor 15,5 (ὤφθη Κηφᾷ) is suggestive,[65] and the fortnight spent with him in Jerusalem to 'get to know' or 'to get information from him' (ἱστορῆσαι Κηφᾶν, Gal 1,18f.) would be an ideal opportunity early in Paul's career.[66] At least we cannot exclude that Peter was one of Paul's sources. But there is much we do not know and there might certainly have been others. In any case, in addition to being one of the great visionary theologians of Christianity, Paul was a recipient and teacher of traditions deriving from Jesus and his disciples.

---

[65] HÄUSSER, *Christusbekenntnis* (n. 34), pp. 127-129.
[66] Thus GERHARDSSON, *Memory* (n. 12), pp. 297-299. The meaning of ἱστορῆσαι as 'getting information' is stressed by J.D.G. DUNN, *The Relationship between Paul and Jerusalem according to Galatians 1 and 2*, and *Additional Note*, in J.D.G. DUNN, *Jesus, Paul, and the Law: Studies in Mark and Galatians*, London, SPCK, 1990, 108-128, as against O. HOFIUS, *Gal. 1.18: ἱστορῆσαι Κηφᾶν*, in ZNW 75 (1984), 73-85.

HILLEL AS A TEACHER:
SAYINGS AND NARRATIVES

Eric OTTENHEIJM
Utrecht, the Netherlands

Hillel the Elder was a teacher who lived in the last part of the Second Temple Period, and who is accredited with having engendered a movement that would become known after 70 CE as Rabbinic Judaism. His teachings, scattered throughout Rabbinic literature, reflect a covenantal theology prioritizing inter-human relations, including a version of the Golden Rule as the summary of the Law.[1] His sayings display a remarkable religious pedagogy that combines a high sense of self-awareness with humility and religious trust. A remarkable feature in his sayings and narratives is his strategy to draw people nigh to the study of Torah. This study seeks to flesh out the practice and social setting of Hillel's teaching. We will concentrate in particular on the relation between form, spatial setting and rhetorical function.[2] Moreover, we will detect what editorial strategies were operative in the way Hillel traditions were preserved in the sources. In doing so, we seek to formulate a typology of Hillel's way of teaching, and distinguish this from the Rabbinic 'Hillel tradition'. Here, a methodological caveat is in order. Contrary to the Gospels, Rabbinic literature, being a literature of tradition with anonymous editors, presents Hillel's teachings as a part of a collective Rabbinic discourse on the Torah.[3] Moreover,

---

[1] Hillel's negative version of the Golden Rule is presented in the narrative of a non-Jew who wanted to know the Torah while standing 'on one foot' (*b. Šabb.* 31a). This summary echoes an ethic broadly known ('Vulgarethik') in Judaism, Christianity, and pagan sources: P.S. ALEXANDER, *Jesus and the Golden Rule*, in J. CHARLESWORTH (ed.), *Hillel and Jesus: Comparative Studies of Two Major Religious Leaders*, Minneapolis, MN, Fortress Press, 1997, 363-388. The curious motif of 'on one foot' (על רגל אחת) may actually mean 'in one rule', Hebrew רגל being a loanword derived from Latin *regula*: R. JOSPE, *Hillel's Rule*, in *JQR* 81(1990), 45-70.

[2] Space is, beyond its physical dimensions ('l'espace perçu'), the socially and culturally defined dimension of human activity and human experience: H. LEFEBVRE, *The Production of Space*, Oxford, Blackwell, 1991, pp. 16-18, labels the social dimension of space as 'l'espace vécu', lived space, and the representation of space (as in our literary sources) as 'l'espace conçu'. Both dimensions are mutually informative and cannot be separated.

[3] This is the major objection to any comparative approach based on biographical readings of the sources, as voiced by Goshen Gottstein and argued in his contribution to the abovementioned volume.

Hillel traditions are framed in narrative settings similar to the Late Antique genre of the *chreia*, where a sage's saying is embedded in a short narrative on his life.[4] Even if these imagined contexts might not reflect accurate historical events of the historical Hillel, they do reflect settings dearly associated with his way of teaching. Oral traditions preserve a more or less coherent memory of a style of teaching rather than a sage's biography does. In this study we will take this approach, in the form of probes of Hillel's non-ethical sayings and teachings. In assessing the ways in which Rabbinic comments reflect connections between spatial and rhetorical settings associated with Hillel, we distinguish between forms of discipleship connected to Hillel and the later developments and rhetoric of Hillel's lore in Rabbinic settings.

Biography

While scholars question the possibility of deriving a biography from rabbinic sources, some features may reflect the actual life of Hillel.[5] He was of non-Palestinian origin, coming from Babylon to Jerusalem.[6] All sources make it clear that Hillel's rise to power came as a result of him solving legal issues.[7] He is consistently portrayed as combining a great

---

[4] C. Hezser, *Die Verwendung der hellenistischen Gattung Chrie*, in *JQR* 27 (1996), 371-439.

[5] N. Glatzer, *Hillel the Elder: The Emergence of Classical Judaism*, New York NY, Schocken Books, 1956, pictures Hillel as a religious philosopher, proximate in some of his teachings to the middle-Stoa, and as reviving early Chassidic values in a non-Essene context of Jerusalem. J. Neusner, *The Rabbinic Traditions about the Pharisees before 70: Part 1. The Masters*, Leiden, Brill, 1971, 294-302, argues that a lot of the 'biographical' traditions were produced in later generations to connect Hillel to other Tannaitic sages. With W.S. Green, *What's in a Name? The Problematic of Rabbinic "Biography"*, in: W.S. Green (ed.), *Approaches to Ancient Judaism BJS 1*, Missoula MT, Brown University Press, 1978, 77-96, the problem of Rabbinic pseudepigraphy is associated with some Hillel traditions as well. The epochal study delineating the problems in a biographical reading of Rabbinic literature (not aimed at Hillel, unfortunately) is A. Goshen Gottstein, *The Sinner and the Amnesiac*, Princeton NJ, Princeton University Press, 2000.

[6] This is attested in Tannaitic sources: *Sifrei Deut.* 357, ed. Finkelstein 429; *T. Negaim* 1,16. Hillel refers to what he 'heard' as being a tradition from Shemaya and Abtalyon' in *p. Pes.* 6,1; *p. Šabb.* 19,1, but compare T.Pisha 4,13 (ed. Lieberman, 165-166). The tale in b.Yoma 35b about Hillel's poverty as a student may reflect legendary accretion more than reality.

[7] He solves the issue before the 'sons of Bathyra' whether bringing the Pesah sacrifice overrides the Sabbath: *T. Pisha* 4:13, ed. Lieberman 165-166; p.Pes. 6:1. D.R. Schwartz, *Hillel and Scripture: From Authority to Exegesis*, in Charlesworth, *Hillel and Jesus*

sense of self-awareness with a deeply practiced humility.[8] Hillel probably died around the year 10 CE, while his colleague Shammai outlived him for more than two decades. Amoraic Rabbinic traditions tell us that Hillel had 70 pairs (sic!) of students (ARN a 14, ed. Schechter 29a; p.Ned. 5:6), but this probably reflects the Rabbis aligning themselves with this Torah scholar more than it reflects historical accuracy.[9] Actually, even the discipleship of Rabban Yohanan ben Zakkai may be doubted, since he does not follow Shammai and Hillel in the 'chain of tradition' (m.Avot 1), and nowhere quotes traditions from his alleged master.[10] On the other hand, since Hillel holds that 'a fool (בור) cannot be a pious person (חסיד)' (*Avot* 2,5), and 'one should not separate oneself from the community' (*ibid.*), the ideological link of the Pharisaic teacher with the Rabbinic elite trying to unite the people of Israel after the demise of two catastrophic wars (66-70 CE and 132-136 CE) is not farfetched. The link between Hillel and Rabbinic Judaism after 70 CE is, however, primarily based on the heirs of Hillel as being the house of the patriarch, e.g. Rabban Gamliel the Elder, Rabban Gamliel of Yavne, and R. Juda haNasi, the editor of the Mishna.

Two Sayings

The numerous sayings of Hillel in the Mishna reflect his philosophy.[11] While his sayings are reminiscent of the form and rhythm of Biblical proverbs, they take a new turn by creating paradoxes:[12]

> If I am not for myself, who will be?
> And if only for myself, what am I?
> And if not now, when?
>
> (m.Avot 1:14, following Ms. Kaufmann)

(n. 2), pp. 346-350, shows how the oldest versions of the story picture Hillel as a legal thinker and how he develops into a skilful Scriptural exegete.

[8] Hillel's humbleness is proverbial (see further) and he is the only one who is worthy to receive the holy spirit (*T. Sota* 13,3). In *T. Peah* 4,10, Hillel buys a horse and a slave for an impoverished man, so he would not lose his sense of pride; in the Babylonian version (*b. Ket* 67b) he even ran before a man because he could not find a slave.

[9] NEUSNER, *Rabbinic Traditions* (n. 5), p. 252.

[10] E. OTTENHEIJM, *Disputen Omwille van de Hemel: Rol en betekenis van intentie in de controverse over sjabbat en reinheid tussen de Huizen van Sjammai en Hillel*, Amsterdam, Amfora, 2004, 64-69.

[11] For a classification of sayings, C. SAFRAI, *Sayings and Legends in the Hillel Tradition*, in CHARLESWORTH, *Hillel and Jesus* (n. 2), pp. 306-320.

[12] All translations are mine, unless indicated otherwise, and are based on the editions mentioned.

The saying signals a high sense of self, albeit a self that is necessarily also related to the other. However, who is this other, and how could I be only for myself? By implication, sayings involve metaphorical language, but Hillel expands a metaphor into sayings which share features of a riddle. Riddles offer an elaborate metaphor which has to be decoded by the listener or reader in order to solve a problem in his or her situation.[13] What is meant by the three lines? The classical commentaries of the Mishna (Rashi, Bertinoro) connect the saying to the issue of merits: if I do not perform the commandments, who else will do so? And if I take it only upon myself, then an even greater responsibility lies upon my shoulders. Also the momentary character of my observing the commandments fits in this view: one should act today, since tomorrow may be the day of your death, which attitude is compared to the preparation for the Sabbath (Rashi, Bertinoro). Their explanations draw on the older, Palestinian comment on this saying:

> He used to say: 'If I am not for myself, who will be?': if I do not gain merit in my life, who will gain merit for me? 'And if only for myself, what am I?': if I do not gain merit for myself, who will gain for myself? 'And if not now, when?': If I do not gain merit in my life, who will gain merit after I die?
>
> (Avot de-Rabbi Nathan a 12, ed. Becker 138-139)[14]

It is, however, the question whether this saying was originally aimed at the system of commandments and the accompanying accruing of merits. Hillel's saying does not hint at it, and the Palestinian comment does not connect it to a biographical setting of his teaching. A similar Rabbinic interpretation of a riddle-like saying of Hillel occurs in the form of a midrash:

> To the place which my heart loves, there my feet lead me. If you will come to my house, I will come to your house. If you will not come to my house, I will not come to your house. As it is said: 'In every place where I shall cause my name to be mentioned I shall come to you and bless you.' (Ex. 20,24)
>
> (T. Šukkah 4,3, ed. Lieberman 272; transl. Neusner)[15]

---

[13] D. PAGIS, *Toward a Theory of the Literary Riddle*, in G. HASAN-ROKEM and D. SHULMAN (eds.), *Untying the Knots: On Riddles and Other Enigmatic Modes*, Oxford, Oxford University Press, 1998, p. 81: a riddle combines a social aspect of competition with a literary form. While the social aspect is absent in the case of the Hillel sayings, like in a riddle, his enigmatic sayings contain the elements to solve their meaning for the readers. Rabbinic tradition took up this challenge in their fashion, as we will see.

[14] The explanation is followed by a quote from Qohelet 9,4, embedding Hillel's saying in a midrashic context.

[15] The manuscripts of the parallel in Avot deRabbi Nathan a 12 (ed. Becker, 138-139) show minor variations.

The Tosephta presents the saying in the context of discussing *Beith Hash'evah*, the nocturnal ritual of pouring out water over the altar during the festival of Sukkoth, thus providing these sayings with an imagined 'Sitz im Leben'.[16] We do not have any decisive evidence that this was the intended meaning. This spatial setting is fit, however, for the editors of the Babylonian Talmud to locate a second saying in it as well:

> It was taught: they told about Hillel the Elder that when he was participating in the joy of the celebration of the water he said thus: 'If I am here, all is here; and if I am not here, who will be here?' He used to say thus: 'To the place which my heart loves, there my feet lead me. If you will come to my house, I will come to your house. If you will not come to my house, I will not come to your house.' As it is said: 'In every place where I shall cause my name to be mentioned I shall come to you and bless you.' (Ex 20,24). (...)[17]
>
> (b. Šukkah 53a)

This narrative locates two sayings in a proper religious context with the concurring practice of common liturgical celebrations, developing a saying into a fully-fledged *chreia*. The first saying, 'If I am here, all is here, and if I am not here, who is here?' (אם אני כאן הכל כאן ואם איני כאן מי כאן) is similar to the saying discussed above, but now with a locative focus ('here'). This could be featured in many settings. However, the Talmudic editors' strategy embeds Hillel's religious outlook in current Rabbinic practice. The contextualizing allows the reader to understand the allusive references of Hillel's presence as the presence of God ('your house'/'my house', 'all is here') while Hillel is performing the commandments of the Sukkah celebrations in the sacred space of the Temple. God's blessing, bestowed upon any pilgrim from the Temple, is a religious commonplace with biblical roots, and in this line Hillel's saying is transformed into a divine promise: if man comes to the Temple of God, God will bestow His blessing.[18] Hillel's enigmatic saying has become a hymn, expressing Temple theology instead of a highly exalted self-awareness.[19] Simultaneously, these ritual celebrations, albeit relegated to a lost past, now receive an

---

[16] See: *m. Šukkah* 5,1: בית השואבה, a word probably direved from Isa 12,3.
[17] The *baraita* also recounts the saying on the floating skull (*m. Avot* 2,6), but the connection with the festival can only be explained via reference to the water, since any connection of a human body part with the Temple precincts would be strange indeed.
[18] S. SAFRAI, *The Sayings of Hillel: Their Transmission and Reinterpretation*, in CHARLESWORTH, *Hillel and Jesus* (n. 2), pp. 330-334, argues that the repeated 'I' in the saying is referring to Hillel himself, and not, as the 'hypercorrection' (p. 331) of the Bavli according to some manuscripts, God.
[19] On this self-awareness, D. FLUSSER, *Hillel's Moderation*, in D. FLUSSER, *Judaism of the Second Temple Period*, Volume 2: The Jewish Sages and their Literature, Grand Rapids MI, Eerdmans, 2009, pp. 210-215.

idealized and mystical quality, picturing Temple times as an ideal era (and location) for individual piousness and religious exaltation. In this setting, Hillel's awareness becomes approachable for the regular reader, albeit at the cost of losing its philosophical panache, with Hillel's elevated state reflecting every human being's destiny.[20] Finally, Hillel becomes a teacher of an idealized and mystical past, since the Temple has been lost, and the implementation of his sayings has become an almost impossible avenue to follow. Contrary to this, the Palestinian tradition records a different exposition that links the saying to the core space of the Rabbinic world, the synagogue and the learning house, before addressing the issue of Temple pilgrimage:

> 'To the place which my heart loves, there my feet lead me': How? These are the people who rise up early and go to bed late in order to enter the synagogues and learning houses[21] of the Holy One blessed be He, as is said: 'In every place where I shall cause my name to be mentioned I shall come to you and bless you.' (Ex 20,24)
>
> 'If you will come to my house, I will come to your house': How? These are the people who leave their money and gold and perform pilgrimage to receive the face of the *Shekhinah* in the Temple. The Holy one blessed be, He will protect them in their dwellings, as it is said: 'No one shall covet your land when you go up to appear before the LORD your God three times in the year.' (Ex 34,24).
>
> (Avot de-Rabbi Nathan a 12, ed. Becker 138-139)

The explanations of the saying of Hillel are introduced by the introductory term כיצד, 'how', a technical term in Rabbinic discourse to explain a legal statement or accepted principle.[22] Moreover, like in the example of the comment on the saying 'If I am not for myself', the comment shows how Rabbinic tradition approached Hillel's sayings as if it were Scripture itself. In addressing the several lines of the saying separately, as communicating different messages for the reader, the comment operates according to the logic of midrash. This form of Rabbinic exegesis, which separates the parts of a Biblical verse and comments upon each of these, as providing additional information, is regular hermeneutical practice.

---

[20] *Ibid.*, p. 214: '(...) it is clear that the 'I' in question is not God but Hillel himself, who represents man as such.' I am not sure whether, as Flusser states, the 'you' is 'anyone that Hillel encounters, particularly in the context of Torah study', and could not include the possibility of God as well.

[21] MS. New York Rab. 25 omits 'of the Holy One blessed be He' but explains how the blessing comes about: '(...) and they recite Shema and say prayers and the Holy One blessed be He blesses them, as it is said: etc.'

[22] Missing in ms.Oxford Heb. C 24 (ed. Becker, 138).

Here we detect a shift from Hillel's audience to the readers of Rabbinic lore on Hillel. This is buttressed by the fact that Hillel's saying itself becomes part of a midrash, since it is adduced to comment on the Biblical commandments to show yourself before God three times a year (Ex. 34,24). This double Rabbinic hermeneutic of Hillel's saying entwines its mystical philosophy within the framework of Rabbinic exegesis, embedding Hillel in the ideological rhetoric of the Rabbinic world.

The rhetoric of the text is also highly fraught with Rabbinic theology. Just as in the Talmud, the saying is fused with spatial imagery. However, in following the sequence of 'learning house/synagogue' and 'Temple', the reader may find himself in continuity with a lost past, and enable himself to connect to his own religious practice, which is visiting the synagogue and the Rabbinic academy, a practice closely associated to Temple pilgrimage. Now the accessibility of the Hillel tradition is greatly enhanced. Its theological rhetoric is evident: the study of Torah and communal prayer are a substitute for the lost Temple service, and provide an alternative way of fulfilling Hillel's mystical sayings on bodily encounters of the divine and imploring divine blessings. Both the hermeneutical strategy of the Rabbinic expositions on Hillel's sayings and their spatial imagery firmly entrench Hillel's outlook in the Rabbinic world. In short, while three of his enigmatic sayings have become rabbinized, so has Hillel himself.[23] Hillel's intended audience for this saying shifts towards the reader of the Rabbinic text.[24]

Man as Image of God

The rabbinized strategy of explaining Hillel's sayings does not concur with the sparse, imagined or real, spatial settings of Hillel traditions: Hillel's teachings are never related to a synagogue or to an academic atmosphere, even in later sources.[25] One tradition places him in 'the house

---

[23] Safrai, *Sayings of Hillel* (n. 18), discusses other sayings as examples of a similar strategy.

[24] Remarkably, the contents of his sayings remain rather easily distinguishable from latter additions and comments. Despite the repeated performances of Hillel-traditons in later generations, this beautifully illustrates the tensions between (following Foley) the 'register' of Hillel's teaching and the 'economy' of early and late performances of his teaching; cf. the discussion in: E. Eve, *Behind the Gospels: Understanding the Tradition*, Minneapolis, Fortress Press, 2014, p. 105.

[25] The story of Hillel as a poor young pupil, lying on the roof of the academy of Avtalyon and Shemaya in Jerusalem to listen to their teachings is only attested in the Babylonian Talmud (*b. Yoma* 35b). Nowhere does Hillel appear as teaching in an academic setting.

of Gurya in Jericho' (*T. Sota* 13,3), where a divine voice announces that in his generation only Hillel is fit to receive the divine Presence, because of his modesty, but this is an attempt to explain his religious authority after the fact.[26] Most common in the Hillel traditions is the location of the city and the Temple as the place of his teachings. Hillel decided the debate on whether it was permitted to carry slaughter knifes for the Passover sacrifice, which had to be brought by each individual to the Temple Mount, when the eve of Passover concurs with the Sabbath, by observing how the people perform the practice, since 'if they are no prophets they are the disciples of prophets' (*T. Pisha* 4,13; *p. Šabb.* 19,1). Indeed, 'when he saw the deed he was reminded of the Law'! This 'looking' presupposes the proximity of this practice, and indeed, we find Hillel associated with the Temple Mount, as discussed above. However, the city also provides the natural context for Hillel teaching his students. Two traditions in the fourth century CE homiletical midrash Leviticus Rabbah tell about Hillel teaching while walking with his students in an urban context, presumably Jerusalem:

> 'Those who are kind (a pious man) reward themselves, but the cruel do themselves harm.' (Prov. 11,17 NRS) 'Those who are kind reward themselves': this is Hillel the Elder. At a certain moment that Hillel the Elder departed from his disciples he was walking. His disciples asked him: Master, where are you going? He said to them: to perform a commandment. They said to him: well, what commandment will Hillel do? He said to them: to wash in the bathhouse (לרחוץ במרחץ). They said to them: is this a commandment? He said to them: yes. If it applies to the statues (איקוניות) of the kings that he erects in his theatres and in his circuses, that he who is appointed over them to cleanse and rinse, that they put a turban on him, and not only that, but he is raised among the important ones of the kingdom, to us, who are created in the image and likeness of God, as it is said: 'for in the image of God He made man' (Gen. 9,7), does it not all the more apply so?
>
> (Lev.R. Behar 34:3, ed. Margalioth 775-777)

The narrative does not presuppose the institutional settings known in the Rabbinic word, the academy and the synagogue. It starts while Hillel has 'departed from his pupils', suggesting a departure from Jewish space (Prayer? Study?), into urban space and walking to a place where they evidently do not expect him to be. There is an underlying assumption in this opening: pupils stay with their teacher, wherever he is going or whatever he is doing, in order to emulate his acts or derive teachings from

---

[26] NEUSNER, *Rabbinic Traditions* (n. 5), pp. 238-239, rightly points to the tension with Hillel's own teaching that all Israelites receive the holy spirit (*T. Pisha* 4,13; *p. Šabb.* 19,1).

details of his praxis.²⁷ However, the staging of a wandering teacher and his disciples evokes a non-institutional context of Hillel's teaching methods. The ensuing dialogue brings us to the core of the matter: can acts like washing and the anointing of the body be perceived as fulfilling divine commandment? The legal logic underlying this story is weak, since the quoted text is neither admonitory nor prohibitive, but the philosophical debate on the implications of Biblical anthropology dominates the stage. Hillel nonetheless subsumes the act of visiting a bathhouse as falling under the range of fulfilling a commandment. The hinge for his equation of the public care for the Imperial statues to the private care by a human being for his own body is presented in the motif of honour, the form of reward implied in fulfilling these actions. Whereas the public servants responsible for cleaning the statues receive public honour, visualized by them wearing a turban, the honour imparted upon man while washing his body is both visible (= social) and invisible (= merits). Implicitly, Hillel urges his disciples to walk in the public sphere like images of God and to radiate their divine destination even in the public sphere. The loanword איקוניות, 'statues', is derived from Greek εἰκών (image, statue), a word used by the LXX in Genesis 1,27 and Genesis 9,7 for the Hebrew צלם, *tselem*.²⁸ *Eikoon* ('statue') signifies the visible statue of the Emperor while it hints at the Biblical *tselem*, underlined in the quote from the divine prohibition (Gen. 9,6-7) of the spilling of human blood in the story of Noah. Altogether, Hillel's reference constitutes an ironical comment on the statue as embodying a cultural and political reality: if the statue of the emperor, who symbolizes Roman order, the Imperial cult, as well as Roman bloodshed, already gains honour for those who clean it, all the more so does the washer of the body of a single Jewish human being deserve attention in the eyes of God, since not the emperor but rather every man represents the real image of God.²⁹ The quote may also allow for a second association. The narrative comments upon living as a Jew in the cultural-political life in a Romanized city: while visiting a bath house might have been understood outwardly as a form of assimilation into Roman culture, Hillel redefines it as an act of keeping to the Jewish law. This reading is strengthened

---

[27] The teacher is embodied Torah and his practice reflects the memorized text: M. JAFFEE, *Torah in the Mouth: Writing and Oral Tradition in Palestinian Judaism 200 BCE - 400 CE*, Oxford, Oxford University Press, 2001, p. 155.

[28] The morphology differs: ARN b 31, ms.Vatikan 303 has אוקיינות, Ms.Parma, de Rossi 327 איקוניות.

[29] This may reflect Rabbinic ideology, since Scriptural references reflect Rabbinic redaction: C. SAFRAI, *Hillel fulfils Scripture*, in H.J. BARKENINGS et a. (eds.), *Tun und Erkennen: Theologisches Fragen und Vermitteln im Kontext des Jüdisch-Christlichen Gesprächs*, Duisburg, 1997, 99-112.

if we look at the continuation of the text, since Leviticus Rabbah adds a second narrative, following a similar plotline, where Hillel teaches the soul to be a guest in the body:

> 'Those who are kind reward themselves': this is Hillel the Elder. At a certain moment that Hillel the Elder departed from his disciples he was walking. His disciples asked him: Master, where are you going? He said to them: to repay goodness to this guest who is in the house. They said to him: all day you have guests? He said to them: is not this poor soul a guest in the body, for this day it is here and tomorrow it is not here.
>
> (Lev.R. Behar 34:3, ed. Margalioth 777-778)

This narrative legitimates physical care as taking care of the eternal soul, as serving spiritual needs. An echo of the stoic *topos* on the body as being the temporary abode of the eternal soul is noticeable in the Aramaic proverbial saying: למגמול חסד עם הדין אכסניא דאית גו בייתא, 'to repay goodness to this guest who is in the house'.[30] Leviticus Rabbah tells these two teachings of Hillel as a comment on Proverbs 11,17, showing Hillel's behaviour to be an illustration of the reciprocation of goodness. However, a parallel version makes it clear that the story on washing the body also circulated as a separate tradition, without the second story of the soul as a 'guest' in the body. Moreover, in this version, the students' question is brought into relief: they react to Hillel going to a place (למקום) where they would not have expected him to go to a place which was definitely not naturally associated with the Jewish code of Torah, prayer, or commandments.

> 'And let all your deeds be for the sake of Heaven'. When Hillel the Elder was going to a place (למקום) they asked him: Master, where are you going? He said to them: I am going to perform a commandment. They said: what commandment, Hillel? He said: to the toilet (לבית הכיסא) I am going. They said to them: is this a commandment? He said to them: yes. In order not to ruin the body.
>
> He went. They said: where are you going Hillel? I am going to perform a commandment. What commandment, Hillel? To the bath house (לבית המרחץ) I am going. Is this a commandment? He said to them: yes. To clean the body. Know that thus it applies to the statues that are erected in the palaces of the kings, that he who is appointed over them to pour and clean them, that the kingdom grants him a salary every year, and not only that, but that he is raised among the important ones of the kingdom. We, who are created in the image and likeness of God, as it is said: 'for in the image of God He made man' (Gen. 9,7), does it not all the more apply so?
>
> (Avot de-Rabbi Nathan b 30, ed. Becker 364)

---

[30] GLATZER, *Hillel the Elder* (n. 5), p. 37.

This version is less focussed on Hillel as a pious person and more on how to deal with Roman cultural domination. The two spatial images, bath house (לבית המרחץ) and public toilet (לבית הכיסא), refer to public facilities that were part of civic culture, imbued with Imperial symbolism and emblematic for Roman culture.[31] The story follows as a comment on a saying of R. Jose (*m. Avot* 2,12), that 'all your deeds must be for Heaven'. This principle is Hillel's, according to a later source (Pesiqta Rabbati 23, ed. Friedman 116). Hillel's philosophy of enlarging religious devotion and divine service to encompass even spheres of human culture not associated with Judaism, in spatial contexts understood as being an outer world, is part of his overall view, as recorded in a discussion on how to observe the Sabbath:

> They said about Shammai the Elder that he would eat all his days in honour of the Sabbath. When he found an animal, he would say: 'this is for the Sabbath!' But when he found a better one, he would leave the second one and eat the first one. But Hillel has a different measure, for all his actions were for the sake of Heaven, as it is said: 'Blessed be the LORD day by day' (Ps. 68,19)

(*b. Beitsa* 16a).

While it is only a Babylonian source that has preserved this dispute, the ideological outlook appears to be in line with the sayings attested in older sources: Hillel did not limit the sphere of religious devotion to the formalized system of commandments or Jewish institutional practices.[32] So it is within this ideological framework that we encounter Hillel again, in the city, walking to a certain place, which evokes a question from his pupils. However, whereas Leviticus Rabbah presented a balanced view on man as being compounded of body and soul, this version fully concentrates on the bodily aspect of man as the Biblical 'image' of God. While the first event explains visiting the toilet as preventing the body being ruined, since not going to the toilet may lead to serious obstipation, the second event portrays bodily care in a positive and honorary fashion as a way of honouring God's image, and, in doing so, God himself. Here, the logic does not follow the rhetoric of 'body and soul', but the Biblical distinction between positive and negative commandments, expanding this

---

[31] J. ZANGENBERG – D. VAN DER ZANDE, *Urbanization*, in C. HEZSER (ed.), *The Oxford Handbook of Jewish Daily Life in Roman Palestine*, Oxford, Oxford University Press, 2010, p. 171; material culture attests how bathhouses are disseminated in the Land from the first century CE onwards and Rabbinic sources discuss them as well, Y. ELIAV, *Bathhouses as Places of Social and Cultural Interaction*, in: *ibid.*, pp. 609-611.

[32] OTTENHEIJM, *Disputen* (n. 10), pp. 187-191.

logic to include every action pertaining to physical care. There is a medical aspect in this version: visiting the toilet is recommended as a preventive measure, with the religious value of honouring the image of God. Moreover, while it is clear that both versions contain a shared tradition, their rhetorical setting is different. Hillel's narrative stresses how this is applicable even to actions that could be deemed as derogatory, such as hygiene and defecation. It stresses how man's taking responsibility for his body fulfils a negative and a positive commandment: not causing any damage to his body as well as keeping it clean. While these actions are evidently not explicit commandments, Hillel embraces them as such. Finally, these tales share some characteristics of a parable. First, they compare two situations on a metaphorical level, playfully varying on the possible meanings of the word '*eikoon*', as either referring to the statue or to the biblical definition of man. Secondly, the imagery of the narrative (statue, king, honour, cleaning) finds a parallel in the application: man's body, God, merit, washing. However, no Rabbinic introductory terminology ('with what may we compare it?', 'it is like', 'like') nor any introduction of the *nimshal* (thus, likewise) mark them as such. Moreover, the 'I-centred' and 'action-based' perspective, as well as the explicit legal principle of 'heavy and light' (*qal wahomer*), makes them appear to be a legal analogy. While there may be political undertones of an ironical comment on Roman public culture and Imperial worship, these undertones are not spelled out in either sources. Our example shows how a Hillel tradition is applied to different contexts, either exegetical or rhetorical, and adapted to fit a Rabbinic discourse.

Tutoring new disciples

Three famous narratives contrast the patience of Hillel with the hot temperedness of Shammai the Elder.[33] In all versions Hillel winds up being a pedagogical genius. In the first narrative, Hillel is approached by a man who wants to put him to the test on the eve of the Sabbath, after having made a bet with his friend. Of course, he loses the bet. In the second story Shammai and Hillel are approached by individuals (only the Bavli labels these consequently as pagans). Crucial in this two-tiered story is that both individuals want to become proselytes on specific conditions. The first person opts for the highest position in the Temple-centred form of Judaism:

---

[33] Avot de-Rabbi Nathan b 29; Avot de-Rabbi Nathan a 15; *b. Beitsa* 30b-31a.

the High Priest. Of course this is a sheer impossibility, if only due to the fact that the priesthood is patrilineal in Judaism. While Shammai rebukes them and sends them away, Hillel receives them and teaches one of them to read the book of Leviticus. When the would-be proselyte reads the verse 'And the common man that draws nigh shall be put to death.' (Numbers 1,51)', Hillel comes with classic Rabbinic a fortiori reasoning, the *qal wahomer*, and deduces that if this applies to King David, then this would apply to him all the more so. The second story tells of a person who only accepts the value of the written Torah, not the oral Torah. Again Shammai rebukes him and sends him away, while Hillel places the person before him, as a student, and teaches him the Hebrew letters:

> He came before Hillel. He said to him: Master, how many *toroth* have been given from heaven?[34] He said to him: One written and one oral. He said to him: Only the one given written I believe on your account but the one given oral I do not believe (איני מאמינך). He wrote out the aleph-bet for him. He said to him: This, what is it? He said to him: A bet. He said to him: Who has informed you that this is an aleph and this a bet? He said to him: So I took it on faith. He said to him: Just as you took this on faith so take that on faith.
>
> (Avot de-Rabbi Nathan b 29, ed. Becker, 362)

The crucial element in his response is the hardly translatable expression, איני מאמינך, 'I do not believe it on your account' (German 'glaube ich dir nicht' is closer to the point). The pointe of Hillel's answer is that there is an intrinsic connection between having faith in the core asset of Rabbinic theology, the revelatory value of the oral Tora, and having faith in the teacher. Moreover, while Hillel teaches this individual that he already has entered a master-pupil relationship based on trust, he connects this leap of faith with the faith the pupil is supposed to have in the divine nature of the oral Tora. Moreover, by inviting the person to start studying, Hillel draws the person into the sphere of oral Tora, without him yet being aware of it. The only thing for the individual to do here is to draw this own conclusion.

Scholars have valued these stories as highly fabricated, and ideologically Hillel biased.[35] However, it may be noted that the imagined situation of Hillel is not the ingathering of large numbers of disciples, but in individual tutoring. Apart from the clear Rabbinic terminology 'oral Tora', which surely will have had a different connotation in the era of these late

---

[34] Version a and the Bavli omit 'from Heaven'.
[35] HEZSER, *Die Verwendung* (n. 3).

Pharisaic teachers, we do not encounter Rabbinic institutions.[36] And the issue of oral traditions labelled by the later Rabbis as 'oral Tora' was a disputed one in Second Temple circles, as is manifest both from the New Testament and Josephus.[37] Finally, there is no 'reaching out' by Hillel; rather, he responds to people approaching him. Even in these legendary stories extolling the virtues of Hillel, we encounter an imagined reality that was close to his ways of teaching.

Market and Eternity

Let us return to the imagined social setting of Hillel's teaching as recounted in the story of his visiting the Temple Mount. These are highly consistent. Following the exposition on the sayings of Hillel discussed above, the Palestinian tradition records a second beautiful story depicting Hillel while walking in Jerusalem:

> He used to say: If I am here, all is here. If I am not here, who is here? Turn in it and turn around in it. For all is in it. And in all is applicable: the wage is according to the travail.
>
> It happened that Hillel the Elder was walking on the road and he came upon some men carrying wheat. He said to them: How much for a *sea*? They said to him: two denarii. And he came across some others. He said to them: how much for a *sea*? They said to him: three denarii. He said to them: did not the first ones say: two? They said to him: stupid Babylonian, if you only knew that according to the travail runs the wage! He said to them: fools and empty heads. On what I have said to you, you return me thus? What did he do, Hillel the Elder? He turned them to good!
>
> (Avot de-Rabbi Nathan a 12, ed. Becker 140-141)

Here we have a rare instance of the Rabbinic tradition providing for a social setting of three sayings of Hillel, especially the last proverb.[38] Again, the spatial rhetoric is not institutional, not even associated with the presence of disciples, but narrating common city life. Hillel appears like

---

[36] While there must have been a connection between the Pharisaic *'paradosis'* and the Rabbinic Oral Tora, the two should not be identified: JAFFEE, *Torah in the Mouth* (n. 27), pp. 39-61.
[37] Acts 22,3; Mk 7,3; Josephus, *Ant* 13.297.
[38] The second saying is attributed in m.Avot 5:22 to a sage named Ben Bag Bag, identified by the Talmud as one of the disciples of Hillel; see E. OTTENHEIJM, *Belichaamde Tora: Toramystiek in Avot 5:22 volgens de versie in ms. Kaufmann*, in *NTT* 63 (2009), 51-66, and literature cited there.

a wandering philosopher, who addresses common folk concerning their economic behaviour and starts a Socratic dialogue in order to draw them away from the rules of economy towards the rules of religious economy. The irony of the story is obvious: the two merchants defend their higher price for wheat by citing the Aramaic proverb attributed to Hillel: 'the wage is according to the travail' (לפום צערא אגרא). While it makes perfect sense in a literal reading, and the merchants indeed apparently misunderstood it by explaining the saying in its literal dimension, it reflects a principle operative in an economic system of invested value (by labour) and the concurring fluctuation of prices. This level, however, is applied to the laws of religion, where a man's toil in Tora study and performing commandments earns him a wage as well, although on a different level. Again, the story confronts us with the riddle-like character of some of Hillel sayings, since a plain economical reading would make the saying as sound as a metaphorical reading does, but on a radically different level. Hillel's reaction is commented upon by the final gloss of the narrator telling us that Hillel turned these people back to a better understanding, presumably a religious one. We are left, nonetheless, with the impression that Hillel actually could be misunderstood, or insulted, and the motif of the 'stupid Babylonian' may reflect an accurate appreciation of Hillel's initial status in Jerusalem. Nonetheless, the spatial imagery is one of immersion in civic economic life and featuring a foreign sage raising the bar of religious understanding. While his way of teaching can be characterized as the astute observance of daily economic behaviour, his religious language emulates this economic sphere in order to comment upon a different level.

In a similar vein, Hillel addresses the common folk going to their work, in order to consider their daily plight in light of their destination:

> 'And bring them close to the Torah' (= *m. Avot* 1,12c). It happened that Hillel was standing at the gate (פתחה) of Jerusalem while people went off to work. He asked them: 'How much will you earn today?' One says: a denarius. Another says: two denarii. He said to them: 'These wages, what do you do with them? They responded: 'we use them to sustain ourselves for the time (לחיי שעה).' He said to them: 'why don't you come and inherit (תבואו ותנחלו) Torah and inherit this world and the next world'? Thus did Hillel do all his days, until he would gather them under the wings of Heaven.
>
> (Avot de-Rabbi Nathan b 26, ed. Becker 357-8)

Commenting on Hillel's dictum 'Be as the disciples of Aaron: loving peace and pursuing peace, loving mankind, and bringing them nigh to the Law' (*m. Avot* 1,12, transl. Danby), the tradition illustrates this by Hillel's manner of teaching the common folk in Jerusalem. The motif of Hillel standing at the gate is noteworthy, since city gates are places of local markets but also the exit for people earning their wages as day-labourers outside the city.[39] The workers' answer echoes similar realism: they have to live by the day (לחיי שעה). Hillel does not deny their plight, but invites those who go out 'to come and inherit' (תבואו ותנחלו) not only daily sustenance but also eternal life. So Hillel redefines their work as both for the day ('this world') and for the 'world to come'. While we encounter some of the motifs discussed earlier (city, workers, denarii, wages), the tone is different: there is less tension in the scene, and economic life forms a stepping-stone for religious work. Here, again, the Socratic nature of Hillel's teaching comes to the fore.[40] He gets in touch with people by showing them how to complement the religious dimension of daily life by means of study, without negating the needs of their physical existence.

Conclusions

The spatial contexts in which Rabbinic lore locates Hillel traditions, whether these are historical traditions or settings associated with him, are coherently limited to city life: streets, markets, gates, bathing facilities, public toilets, where he walks and confronts either his own disciples or people passing by. It is here that we may also actually encounter the teaching style of the historical Hillel. His teaching takes place by means of his physical presence in situations suggestive of a shared social space by Jewish and non-Jewish culture alike, and it is this social practice which evokes questions. In some cases individuals, either from a Jewish or non-Jewish origin, seek to put him to the test as a teacher.

Moreover, Hillel roams the streets and picks up the cultural or economic signals he sees as instructive for his views on religious life; daily life provides all the metaphors for his sayings: city gates, streets, bathing installations, parks, Temple, public toilets. There is a correlation in the way in which Rabbinic lore locates him in the social context of city life, and the metaphors used by Hillel to appeal to his audience in his sayings and diatribes. A statue reminds him of the state of man as image of God, a

---

[39] While in urban contexts, markets were located on squares and along colonnaded streets, in the Galilee, which is the cultural context of the Rabbis editing these sources, gates could serve as the sites of the markets: P. RICHARDSON, *Building Jewish in the Roman East*, Waco TX, Baylor University Press, 2004, p. 60.

[40] FLUSSER, *Hillel's Moderation* (n. 19), p. 211.

toilet of not doing harm to one's body, carrying food to the market lends him to comment on religious labour, silly questions by an individual seeking new social-religious connections 'in town', is a device for teaching this person humility while accepting him within the sphere of discipleship.

These traits offer us a coherent typology of Hillel's style of teaching. The rabbinizing aspect, offering a Hillel suited to meet the needs of the readers of Rabbinic lore, is visible in the way some of Hillel's enigmatic sayings are dramatized to explain these by connecting them to the regular biblical practice of Temple era conditions. The Rabbinic reception of Hillel traditions shows how the Rabbis wrestle to locate the sayings within their own world view. In the case of the mystic sayings, which are expressive of a high awareness of his presence as representing the sublime, the rabbinic interpretations even seem to neutralize their possible *hubris* by locating the individual within the realm of Torah study and the performance of commandments. Here, Hillel really becomes the founder of Rabbinic Judaism.

However, while Rabbinic tradition embraces Hillel's heritage and frames its message according to dominant Rabbinic ideology, Hillel never appears in the context of typical Rabbinic institutions such as the academy, or classic communal institutes of Rabbinic Judaism like the synagogue.[41] Remarkably also, the scarcity of direct Biblical exegesis differentiates Hillel from the later Rabbis. This feature of Hillel traditions has been analysed by Daniel Schwartz and more recently by Paul Mandel, and both conclude that the exegetical operations inserted into the Hillel material stem from early Rabbinic generations. Hillel himself most probably merely relies on legal logic. He reads Scriptural texts in plain fashion and without the refined hermeneutics attributed to him.[42] We may add that this also

---

[41] Whether and to what extent the synagogue was a Rabbinically controlled institution is a hotly contested issue among scholars. I tend to follow the cautiously formulated conclusion by L. LEVINE, *Between Leadership and Marginality: Models for Evaluating the Role of the Rabbis on the Early Centuries* CE, in L.I. LEVINE – D.R. SCHWARTZ (eds.), *Jewish Identities in Antiquity: Studies in Memory of Menahem Stern*, Tübingen, Mohr-Siebeck, 2009, p. 205: 'Indeed, the synagogue of the first centuries CE can best be seen as an institution in which rabbinic presence is visible but with undefined and incomplete authority.'

[42] SCHWARTZ, 'Hillel and Scripture' (n. 7), p. 360. This approach is strengthened and expanded in P. MANDEL, *Legal Midrash between Hillel and Rabbi Akiva: Did 70 CE make a Difference?*, in D.R. SCHWARTZ – Z. WEISS (eds.), *Was 70 a Watershed in Jewish History?: On Jews and Judaism before and after the Destruction of the Second Temple*, Leiden, Brill, 2012, 343-370: Hillel was a Pharisee who was less expounding Scripture but more elaborating (Oral) Law. The hermeneutical rules are not Hillel's: G. STEMBERGER, *Einleitung in Talmud und Midrasch*, Munich, Beck, 2011, 9e Aufl., p. 28.

accounts for the favoured genre of the Rabbis religious pedagogy, and the one we are acquainted with through Jesus' teaching according to the synoptic Gospels: parables. Whereas Hillel refers to real life conditions in order to illustrate religious values and perspectives, he never does so in the form of the short fictive tales which compare daily life with the religious realm.[43] The example closest to a narrative parable is the story of Hillel going to the bath house, but the analogy drawn here, in combination with the a fortiori argument, is more of a legal analogy (*cf.* Matt. 12,10). This finding is remarkable and needs further explanation in a diachronic perspective. Did Hillel's Babylonian descent and Jerusalemite residence not predispose him to a form of teaching that developed in the context of the Galilee?[44] In any case, Rabbinic literature teaches us that Hillel is an enigmatic teacher, expressing at the same time a humble and sublime vision of man, and teaching how to live as a representation of the divine in the city.

---

[43] Narrative parables process motifs of daily life and social reality, both in Rabbinic parables and Jesus' parables: D. FLUSSER, *Die rabbinischen Gleichnisse und der Gleichniserzähler Jesus: 1. Teil Das Wesen der Gleichnissen*.(Judaica et Christiana, 4), Bern, Peter Lang, 1981; L. SCHOTROFF, *Die Gleichnisse Jesu: Forschungen zur Religion und Literatur des Alten und Neuen Testaments*, Göttingen, Vandenhoeck & Ruprecht, 2005.

[44] The earliest known teacher to whom a fully-fledged narrative parable is attributed is the Galilean based Rabban Yohanan ben Zakkai (b.Shabbat 153a), but the parallel in Qohelet Rabbah 9,8 to R. Juda, and Massekhet Semachot de R. Hiya 2:1 to R. Juda in name of Yohanan ben Zakkai. The saying of Antigonos of Sokho 'be not like slaves who serve their master to receive their wage, but be like slaves who serve their master not in order to receive wage' (*m. Avot* 1,3) is a simile. Among the approximately 275 disputes between the Houses of Hillel and Shammai, only one parable is known: *p. Hag.* 2,1 (77c); *b. Hag.* 12a; Bereshit Rabbah 1,21; Leviticus Rabbah 36,1. The diachronic development of parables is addressed in the NWO funded Research Project 'Parables and the Partings of the Ways'.

RELIGIOUS TEACHERS AND STUDENTS ON BIBLICAL TEACHING AND DISCIPLESHIP
An Account of a Recent Exploration

Toke ELSHOF
Tilburg, the Netherlands

In the contributions of this volume one can find several models of teachers and students. How can these models serve as an inspiration to prospective pupils and teachers? This article describes how prospective teachers of Religious Education (RE) reflect on Jesus as a teacher. This offers – albeit modestly – a possibility to gain some insight into processes that may arise when prospective teachers are faced with Scriptural models.

It should be said that not all the models that are presented elsewhere in this volume are addressed. One aspect that could be of influence is that most aspiring teachers are from a Catholic environment. Their knowledge of the Old Testament is often lacking and Paul's writings are barely known to them. This does not mean that insights on how to deal with models of teaching and discipleship cannot be obtained.

A premise of the contributions in this volume regarding teacher-student relationships in biblical texts is that these relationships are complex and layered. These relationships can play a role at multiple textual levels: at the level of the characters, at the level of the textual director and at the level of the text-immanent author and the text-immanent reader.[1] However these relationships may take shape and are historically anchored, they are primarily text-oriented. As one of the contributions clarifies that the relationship between God and Job could be described as being a relationship between teacher and pupil, so a second one clarifies that the relations of the Northern Kingdom of Israel to the Southern Kingdom of Judah are carriers of the communication between the text-immanent author and reader, which rise above the concrete historicity. In other words, the text also increasingly acts as a teacher itself.

---

[1] See the contribution of A.L.H.M. van Wieringen in this volume.

This contribution is based on written material in which future teachers of RE explore the significance of Bible stories about Jesus for their work. Which kind of models of the roles of teachers and students do they propose? Do biblical stories about Jesus play a role in this, and if so, to what extent? The students' papers, which have been used with their permission for this contribution, point out that stories about Jesus' role as a teacher continue to be relevant for the school subject of Religious Education, even when this school subject is not aimed at the Christian initiation of pupils, but rather at the development of their personal (religious) worldview.[2] Their papers also express a limited familiarity with the Bible and even with the Biblical stories about Jesus. This lack of familiarity turns out to be interwoven with a selective and idealistic approach to both Jesus' role as a teacher as well as their own role as a teacher. For this reason it is desirable to introduce them to a wider range of scriptural models of teaching and discipleship.

The first section of this chapter discusses the present situation concerning: religious education in the Netherlands, the prospective teachers and their professional roles. The second section describes the significance of Bible stories about Jesus for prospective teachers and their professionalism, including a reflection upon this from a religious pedagogical perspective. The third section endeavours to build connections with the commitment of this volume.

RELIGIOUS EDUCATION IN THE NETHERLANDS:
THE PROFESSION AND THE PROFESSIONAL

For a growing group of pupils in the Netherlands, the school-subject Religious Education is the first occasion they can, in a more or less structured way, come into contact with religions and world views.[3] The reason

---

[2] For an insight into how Catholic education thinks about religious identity, socialization and education, see: P. VERMEER, *Religious Education and Socialization* in *Religious Education* 105 (2010), 103-116; T. ELSHOF, *Catholic Schools and the Embodiment of Religiosity: The Development of Religiosity towards the Common Good*, in *Religious Education* 110 (2015), 150-161.

[3] See B. ROEBBEN, *Seeking Sense in the City: European Perspectives on Religious Education*, Berlin, LIT Verlag, 2013; P. VERMEER, *Meta-concepts, thinking skills and religious education*, in *BJRE* 34 (2012), 333-347; M. SCHAMBECK, *Mystagogisches Lernen: Zu einer Perspektive religiöser Bildung* (STPS, 62), Würzburg, Echter Verlag, 2006, pp. 1-7. M. SCHAMBECK, *Mystagogisches Lernen*, in G. HILGER – S. LEIMGRUBER – H.G. ZIEBERTZ (eds.), *Religionsdidaktik: Ein Leitfaden für Studium, Ausbildung und Beruf*, München, Kosel 2010, pp. 400-415.

why familiarity with religions and world views has decreased correlates with the decreasing significance and recognisability of Christian religion within family life[4] and social life, due to three processes. The process of detraditionalization implies people's changed relation to the religious traditions: this relation is now less apparent or more fragmented. Furthermore, personal preferences and choices now play a larger role due to the process of individualization. In addition, this relation to religious traditions is taking shape against the background of other traditions with their own truth-claims: i.e. pluralization.[5] The religious illiteracy of pupils (their lack of knowledge about religious language, practices, symbols and communities) is closely linked to the post-secular and post-Christian society in which they grew up.[6] The school subject faces the challenge of having to install religious literacy into its pupils. It is generally assumed that this literacy, and thus the pupils' personal and social development, is promoted when they receive knowledge about religions and world views, when they learn to reflect and communicate about their meaning, and when they gain experience with them.[7]

These goals require high levels of professionalism of RE teachers. Typically, there are three distinct, but interrelated, roles which are deemed essential: the so-called WSM roles.[8] The role of Witness refers to the personal inspiration of the teacher and the teachers' personal commitment

---

[4] T. ELSHOF, *Diskussion und Deutung der Gottesfrage: Über die beziehungsreiche Kraft der religiösen Tradition*, in *Bibel und Liturgie* 89 (2016), 51-61; T. ELSHOF, *Religious Heritage: The Development of Religiosity and Religious Socialization over three Generations of Roman Catholic Family Life*, in D. OWETSCHKIN (ed.), *Tradierungsprozesse im Wandel der Moderne: Religion und Familie im Spannungsfeld von Konfessionalität und Pluralisierung*, Essen, Klartekst, 2012, pp. 165-180.

[5] L. BOEVE, *Religious Education in a post-secular and post-Christian context*, in *JBV* 33 (2012), 143-156.

[6] ROEBBEN, *Seeking sense* (n. 3).

[7] Within RE there are different views on the meaning of each of these goals and their interrelationships.

[8] D. POLLEFEYT, *Belgium: the Hermeneutic-communicative Model; a Feasible Option?*, in H.G. ZIEBERTZ & U. RIEGEL (eds.), *How Teachers in Europe Teach Religion: An International Empirical Study in 16 Countries*, Berlin, LIT Verlag 2009, 31-43; ROEBBEN, *Seeking sense* (n. 535).

These terms come from Catholic education in Flanders but are used more extensively: in the Netherlands and within Protestant Christian education. The realization that theological knowledge, personal spirituality and pedagogical and didactical qualities collectively contribute to professionalism, is widely recognized internationally. See for example A. ADAMS, in his contribution *Religious Education teacher: profession-person-competence* to the recently published religious educational standard work M. ROTHGANGEL, T. SCHLAG & F. SCHWEITZER (eds.), *Basics of Religious Education*, Göttingen, Vandenhoeck & Ruprecht, 2014, pp. 279-295.

to the Christian faith. The role of Specialist refers to the teachers' knowledge of Christian tradition, and the role of Moderator includes their pedagogical and didactic qualities that promote the religious development of pupils.[9]

When we study the above-mentioned papers of future teachers, we find an area of tension concerning these three professional roles. This tension, as we shall see, not only plays a role among future teachers; it can be recognized among experienced religious teachers as well.

To explain this, we need to be aware of the diversity expressed within the papers of the future teachers.[10] This diversity firstly includes their family background: whether or not they are socialized in a Christian-religious way and, by extension, whether or not they attended religious education at a Catholic-Protestant Christian school. In addition, there are differences in the attitudes towards the Christian faith and church. Along with involvement and openness there is also rejection and resistance: the Christian faith and Church are sometimes considered to be detrimental to religious freedom and authenticity. Finally, there are big differences in terms of religious knowledge. Many papers show unfamiliarity with Bible stories, Church life, the history of the church, liturgy, rituals, sacraments and symbols. Familiarity with other religions is even lower.[11] The term "religious

---

[9] Due to the aforementioned processes of religious detraditionalization, individualization and pluralization, the notion that the role of Specialist should not solely be filled mono-religiously has gained ground. Teachers should be familiar with a broad religious / ideological palette: for example POLLEFEYT, *Belgium* (n. 8), p. 37. Gradually, it is being recognized that such processes are also relevant to the role of Witness: the spirituality of teachers can have different sources. See B. ROEBBEN, *Inclusieve godsdienstpedagogiek: Grondlijnen voor levensbeschouwelijke vorming*, Leuven/Den Haag, Acco, 2015, pp. 147-148. The significance of these processes for the role of moderator is not yet recognized. This chapter briefly talks about this in the conclusion.

[10] This study followed a group of fifteen students (four women and eleven men) between 25 and 50 years of age during the Spring of 2016 at Tilburg University, School of Catholic Theology (the Netherlands), where they were following the course *Historic Catechetics*. Some of them were already working as a religious teacher. They followed the training to obtain a higher degree of education. They wrote the papers and the final report on which this contribution is based, after following six lectures and seminars in *Historic Catechetics*. Most of their comments on Jesus come from their notes taken during the lectures on the Bible. Yet also the reports on other historical periods contain relevant remarks on biblical texts in which Jesus is mentioned. This also applies to the final reports. In total, I consulted 105 reports: seven reports by each of the 15 course-participants. The view on the contemporary relevance of biblical texts about Jesus, is based on these 105 papers.

[11] The prospective teachers, who are well versed in Christianity, also appear to have the most knowledge of other religions.

illiteracy" thus appears not only to be applicable to pupils but also to many prospective teachers of Religious Education.[12] Another significant finding concerning religious illiteracy refers to the sometimes assumed connections between religious illiteracy and religious neutrality and religious openness.[13] In these papers, religious illiteracy is regularly interwoven with an unfavourable or ambivalent standpoint towards religions.[14]

When this data, in particular the findings about religious attitude and religious knowledge, is related to the roles of a professional teacher a tension can be observed, particularly when observing the roles of Witness and Specialist. This does not solely affect teachers in training, but also poses a problem to those already working as a teacher. The advocated consistency between the three professional roles appears to be unstable. Research in the field shows that RE teachers, similar to the aspiring teachers from my research, have difficulty with the roles of Witness and Specialist.[15] They primarily give meaning to the role as Moderator and see themselves as coaches of the personal development of their pupils in the religious and world view domains. Neither their personal religiosity or spirituality, nor the social and cultural significance of religions and world views are often discussed and treated. The inadequate implementation of the role of Witness and Specialist not only undermines the importance of Religious Education for the formation of students,[16] but also detracts from the weight of Religious Education as a school subject to be taken seriously.[17]

---

[12] Although these results are obviously not representative of prospective RE teachers in a broader sense, they are not isolated. In England a similar lack of knowledge was perceived by D. CARR, *Post-secularism, religious knowledge and religious education*, in *JBV* 33 (2012), 157-168.

[13] VERMEER, *Meta-concepts* (n. 3).

[14] This connection is also recognized by F. SCHWEITZER, *Religious individualization: new challenges to education for tolerance*, in *BJRE* 29 (2007), 89-100; A. CASSON, *The right to "bricolage": Catholic pupils' perception of their religious identity and the implications for Catholic schools in England*, in *JBV* 32 (2011), 207-218; T. ELSHOF, *The Challenge of Religious Education to Deal with Past and Present Catholicism*, in *BJRE* (2016) (accepted).

[15] See T. ZONDERVAN & J.M. PRAAMSMA, *'Leren voor het leven'; een terugblik op de artikelen*, in *Narthex* 15 (2015), 85-89. These findings are supported by research that indicates the vulnerability of the role of Witness: B. ROEBBEN, *The Vulnerability of the Postmodern Educator as Locus Theologicus: A Study in Practical Theology*, in *Religious Education* 96 (2001), 175-192, and by the deficient way in which the Specialist-role is worked out: VERMEER, *Meta-concepts* (n. 3).

[16] The reason being that this does not do justice to the pupils' need for authenticity in religious/philosophical terms, ROEBBEN, *Inclusieve Godsdienstpedagogiek* (n. 9).

[17] VERMEER, *Meta-concepts* (n. 3).

The problems that both prospective and already employed teachers face with the implementation of the roles of Witness and Specialist indicate that the theme of this chapter is relevant to both groups.[18]

STORIES ABOUT JESUS AND THE PROFESSIONAL ROLES

The educational lectures about Jesus in the New Testament are based on Alfred Läpple's chapter on catechetical structures in the Holy Scriptures, in his *Kleine Geschichte der Katechese*.[19] His approach to biblical texts is remarkable and includes three characteristics.[20]

While catechetics is usually particularly interested in Biblical texts in which teaching is very specifically thematised, for example teaching within Jewish traditions or Jesus as a teacher,[21] Läpple believes that all Scripture is catechetical in nature: all stories are intended to give instruction.

Another distinguishing perspective is his view that the origin and development of biblical texts express catechetical processes. Therefore Bible stories (about the Jewish people and of Jesus' life) not only initiate catechetical processes, but Scripture itself is also a result of such catechetical processes.

The third point by which Läpple stands out, concerns his view that biblical texts express the development of religious tradition.[22] Within biblical texts, that express catechetical processes of a specific historical context (point 2), one can also distinguish processes of transformation when these texts are transmitted to another historical context. According

---

[18] Firstly, by providing insight into the interconnectedness these roles appear to have. In addition, it clarifies that, as well as how, the encounter with Jesus-stories in the Bible can contribute to fulfilling these roles in their correlation. Through this approach, this research, despite its modest scale, could be a valuable contribution to current RE teaching.

[19] A. LÄPPLE, *Kleine Geschichte der Katechese,* München, Kösel, 1981. This book is discussed because of the contextual approach to catechetics.

[20] The catechesis in the Bible is dealt with on pp. 19-40. It is striking – and also somewhat Catholic – that attention given to the teaching of the Old Testament remains relatively neglected when compared to Protestant catechetical textbooks. Within the Protestant catechesis little attention is given to faith in the Middle Ages.

[21] See for example: S. LEIMGRUBER, *Konzeptionelle Entwicklungslinien der Religionsdidaktik*, in G. HILGER – S. LEIMGRUBER – H.-G. ZIEBERTZ (eds.), *Religionsdidaktik: Ein Leitfaden für Studium und Beruf*, München, Kösel 2007, chapter I.3 1-5, pp. 42-48; R. LACHMANN, *History of religious education until the beginning of the 20th century – didactical highlights,* in: M. ROTHGANGEL – TH. SCHLAG – FR. SCHWEITZER (eds.), *Basics of Religious Education,* Bristol CT, Vandenhoeck & Ruprecht LLC, 2014, 45-62.

[22] In his contribution to this volume, Peter Tomson demonstrates a development of tradition in the Pauline Epistles, p. .

to Läpple, biblical authors were not oriented towards restoration and archiving traditions; their openness towards the transformation of traditional texts was interwoven with their search for texts that were comprehensible to a specific historical audience, and relevant to their contextual questions and needs. In view of the new context, the transmitted traditional stories were abridged, made longer or provided with new characteristics.[23]

The future teachers' papers express that these points made by Läpple make this approach to the Bible appropriate for the education of prospective RE teachers, despite the fact that in some aspects, Läpple is dated. His perspective is relevant to the three professional roles.

1. The religious teacher as a Specialist

The historical and the contextual perspective both prove to be new to several prospective teachers, and are of relevance. This approach contributes to a new awareness, namely that religion can be regarded as being a living tradition. The realization that each of the (biblical) stories deals with life's experiences and the questions of ordinary people from earlier times in a contextual way, makes it possible to involve them in the questions and experiences of the contemporary context. Moreover, it offers a perspective to identify diversity in a positive way: contributing to the development of tradition. Additionally, the Gospel narratives (and the Scriptures in a broader sense) are appealing, because as a part of the Jewish and Christian tradition, these stories had a huge influence on Western society: on its history, its values, its art and culture.

Even such a fairly rudimentary knowledge of the origins and contents of the Scriptures thus contributes to the role of a teacher as Specialist. The presented knowledge about the contextuality of the stories and the ethical challenges, religious practices or rituals that are discussed in them, could be introduced meaningfully into their classes. Therefore this knowledge is valuable: it promotes the religious and world view development of pupils, their thinking and their language skills.[24]

---

[23] LÄPPLE, *Kleine Geschichte* (n. 19), p. 29.
[24] V. BAUMFIELD, *Democratic RE: Preparing Young People for Citizenship*, in *BJRE* 25 (2003), 173-184; F. SCHWEITZER, *Religion and Education: A Public Issue and its Relationship to the Religions and Religious Traditions*, in *Religious Education: The Journal of the Religious Education Association* 108 (2013), 250-254; R. ENGLERT, *Religion gibt zu denken: Eine Religionsdidaktik in 19 Lehrstücken*, München, Kösel Verlag, 2013; C. GÄRTNER, *Religionsunterricht – ein Auslaufmodell?: Begründungen und Grundlagen*

2. The religious teacher as a Witness

The knowledge provided is not only important for the role as a Specialist; it also changes the teacher as a person and has bearing on the Witness role: the enthusiasm, inspiration and spirituality. The papers indicate three relevant aspects.

Firstly, becoming acquainted with biblical Jesus-stories contributes to the awareness of prospective teachers on how they relate to the Christian religion. It leads to an awakening.

This brings us to the second aspect: the impact this awakening has. Future teachers realize that stories that they consider to be appealing or challenging for themselves, become important for their profession as well. When texts or insights have become eye-openers for teachers or have become something they are excited about, they will also be able to imagine their students having this same experience. They expect that their own enthusiasm will have an impact on their students, because their personal enthusiasm is reflected in the preparation of better classes.

Thirdly, the papers illustrate a transition that is going on concerning the Witness-role. The previous meaning that being a witness implies the 'bringing' of religious tradition, is changing into an awareness that being a witness implies being a 'carrier' of this or these tradition(s).[25] The future teachers' papers express this transformation in their emphatic resistance against playing a Witness-role, which is a part and an extension of the church's proclamation,[26] while it is considered appealing when one's personal spirituality or religiosity can play a role in a dialogical way.[27] Being a 'carrier' of religious traditions does not only take the desire

---

religiöser Bildung in der Schule, Paderborn, Schöning, 2015. The prospective teachers believe that this development will benefit from the teacher's broad multi-religious experience. Eq. note 9.

[25] This is particularly noticeable in ROEBBEN, *Inclusieve godsdienstpedagogiek* (n. 9), pp. 10, 137-158. Other recent studies, for example, ADAMS, *Religious Education Teacher* (n. 8), relate the personal position only to the Christian tradition. Roebben has a more diverse view on the role of Witness.

[26] In the Netherlands, this approach emerged in the second half of the last century, especially in the kerygmatic doctrines. That was a few decades later than in Germany, where Leimgruber discusses this in his publication, see LEIMGRUBER, *Konzeptionelle Entwicklungslinien* (n. 21), pp. 45-47; J. VAN DER VEN, *Kritische Godsdienstdidactiek*, Kampen, Kok, 1982, pp. 383-384. Van der Ven distinguishes three types of proclamation: 1. The teacher confesses the faith of the Church in class (following Jungmann). 2. The teacher refers students to the proclamation within church life (following Stallmann). 3. The proclamation which is intrinsically possible but occasional in nature (following Nipkow).

[27] ROEBBEN *Seeking Sense* (n. 3).

for authenticity in education seriously, but it also takes the individual and fragmented ways of religious commitment into account, as well as the broader religious educational goals.

The fact that the 'carrier' approach of the Witness-role is considered relevant by prospective teachers, implies that religious teachers as a whole might benefit from the transition concerning this professional role.

3. The religious teacher as a Moderator

According to the students, the Gospel texts about Jesus as a teacher are the most intriguing. Läpple distinguishes the following features:[28] Jesus' teaching is tailored to his audience: he starts from specific needs and questions, and adapts his message to the life and setting of his audience. Moreover, he speaks in a concrete way which is easily understood and recognized. He uses the (Jewish) teaching methods of the time: narratives and dialogical learning. He tells parables and uses metaphors that are familiar, appealing and sometimes confronting.[29] In addition, a deeper dimension emerges, which clarifies difficult issues to people of different backgrounds, generations and continents. His way of talking is credible because he integrates doctrine and life and embodies what he professes. In these conversations he does not turn away from confrontation. His teaching is not optional, but can rather be seen as an invitation: Jesus' life and teaching focuses on repentance and imitation and challenges his audience to do the same. In addition, he calls on his audience to proclaim the Good News of the nearness of God's Kingdom.

Prospective teachers appreciate some aspects concerning this perspective of Jesus' teaching, while other aspects remain underexposed.

It appeals to them that Jesus takes people seriously, treats them with respect, treats them equally and responds to their questions and concerns. The way he treats people expresses authenticity, humanity, credibility and openness. According to the papers, these are all qualities that can serve as a model to prospective teachers in their pedagogical attitude to their own pupils. These qualities actually also serve as a model for the pedagogical attitude of the church: the appreciation of Jesus' attitude ventilates a lot of critique on church life. In addition, Jesus' teaching methods are held in high esteem because of their concreteness, their search for dialogue, and their open answers. Therefore Jesus' teaching also serves as an example

---

[28] LÄPPLE, *Kleine Geschichte* (n. 19), pp. 30-34.
[29] See L. Thurén's article on parables in this volume.

when looking at it from a didactical point of view: for their own professional teachings and for the teaching by the church.

Lastly, the reciprocity of Jesus' model of teaching appears to be appealing. It concurs with the prospective teachers' realization that not only students gain new insights, but that teachers also learn from their students and that it is important to be open to this. Occasionally, this dialogic learning is linked to the Jewish *lernen*.[30] The questions and topics that are raised in the parables and stories of Jesus as a Jewish rabbi are not only an invitation for reflection for students, but also for teachers. Another eye-opener is the realization that teaching religion is (also) about asking the right questions, and that good listening skills are not only expected from students but from teachers as well.[31]

The reason why prospective teachers find the stories that provide a model of teaching and apprenticeship so fascinating is the link with their profession. These stories strengthen them in their role of Moderator by expressing and expanding their pedagogical and didactic insights and intuitions. They thus provide a learning model from which education in general can benefit.

However, an one-sidedness can be identified. Biblical stories that reveal the refractory and challenging character of Jesus' teaching are often considered much less relevant by the aspiring teachers. This bias in their approach to stories about Jesus is accompanied by a similar bias in their perspective on the educational situation, which is rather rosy and harmonious. This raises the question whether such a selection can withstand the reality of RE teaching. Some papers do point out that actual teaching practice looks different and that the predominant harmonious ideal is too ambitious, even for RE teaching for pupils who are verbally strong, reasonably interested and have a good mutual rapport with the teacher. It is simply unrealistic for educational situations which are less ideal, in view of the relationships, the interest of students and group dynamics. Religious and cultural diversity are relevant here. The western feminine education culture (with goals such as individual expression and development) does not always match effortlessly with the (western or Islamic) masculine

---

[30] See the contribution of Van der Watt about the teaching of the Gospel of John in this volume.
[31] The contributions in this book by B.J. Koet, particularly the final section of 'Learning from children', p. . B.J. KOET, *Elijah as Reconciler of Father and Son: From 1Kings 16:34 and Mallachi 3:22-24 to Ben Sira 48:1-11 and Luke 1: 13-17*, in J. CORLEY – H. VAN GROL (eds.), *Rewriting Biblical History: Essays on Chronicles and Ben Sira in Honor of Pancratius Beentjes*, Berlin, De Gruyter, 2011, pp. 173-190.

street culture (where the role of the group and (family) honour are more important)[32]. The intractability of educational practices therefore requires a less one-sided perspective on the role of Moderator. RE teachers benefit from models of teaching and learning that take this into consideration. In addition to the above-mentioned stories, the actual practice benefits from stories about an uncomprehending, angry, dismissive or sarcastic Jesus. These stories could possibly promote a reflective attitude amongst teachers on the intractability and the confrontations that are also part of religious education.

Concluding Remarks

Against the background of the models of biblical teaching and learning discussed in this volume, I wish to end this case study of the students of my lectures for future RE teachers, by making some concluding remarks.

a. This contribution has clarified that the catechetical proposition that all biblical texts have an instructive intent appeals to prospective teachers of RE. This is evident from the way Bible stories about Jesus appear to have relevance for their professionalism, first of all in the role of Specialist. The familiarity of teachers with Bible stories about Jesus (and with Bible stories and the Christian tradition in general) stimulates their ability to guide students in recognizing religiosity in personal, family and social life. Being familiar with Bible stories also strengthens the role of Witness: it contributes to their awareness of and reflection on their own relationship to the Christian tradition. This is reflected in the authenticity with which they teach, and thus promotes the religious development of students. Knowledge of Bible stories about Jesus also provides an important contribution to the role of Moderator: these stories articulate a pedagogical and didactical attitude and are thus a model of teaching in which listening, equality and openness are central.

b. The empirical material subsequently shows that the roles are intertwined: the familiarity with Jesus-stories has an affective layer which influences one's own enthusiasm and personal inspiration and thus influences the role of Witness. Being familiar with Jesus-stories helps to

---

[32] I. EL HADIOUI, *Hoe de straat de school binnendringt: Denken vanuit de pedagogische driehoek van de thuiscultuur, de schoolcultuur en de straatcultuur*. Amsterdam, Van Gennep, 2011; L. JANELLE DANCE, *Tough Fronts: The Impact of Street Culture on Schooling*, Oxford, Routledge, 2002.

express pedagogical and didactical intuitions and attitudes, and thus also influences the role of Moderator. The realization that stories about Jesus as a catechist are considered so interesting by prospective teachers is consistent with the observation that the role of Moderator is deemed to be the least difficult of the three within the profession. This insight can be used in teacher education: stories that concur with the role of Moderator can be used as a starting point to discuss other stories. Becoming acquainted with Biblical narratives provides a greater range of starting points for lessons with an emphasis on content, with room for reflection and personal commitment.

c. However, the professional role of Moderator also benefits from biblical stories that provide learning models which are relevant to contradicting, challenging and less ideal teaching situations. This could not only include non-empathic or uncomprehending Jesus-stories, but also other stories from both the Old Testament and the New Testament, such as from Moses or Paul. Such lesser known and less comprehensible stories also contribute to the other roles of Witness and Specialist. They deepen the understanding of the role of the Christian religion in the past and the present, and they present a challenge for a renewed reflection on the personal bond with this religion.

d. The empirical material indicates a tendency of prospective teachers to discover aspects of Bible stories they (think they) already know. This calls for a more active supply of relatively unknown or contradicting and challenging texts, so that these will come alive and their relevance will be tested. This could be enhanced by providing prospective teachers with biblical texts that they can read themselves. The teachers can therefore experience for themselves what the text tells them. Teachers who are willing to accept the text as a teacher and are prepared to listen to the uniqueness, the distinctiveness and the newness of biblical texts, contribute to their own ability to hear the uniqueness, the distinctiveness and the novelty found within the stories of their students.

e. Stories about Jesus (and the Scriptures in a broader sense) seem to be relevant to the professionalism of RE teachers, even if they are non-believers or if there is an educational goal that is not aimed at religious initiation but is focused on ideological formation. The empirical material shows that (in the context of the processes of detraditionalization, individualization and pluralization), the teacher roles of Specialist and Witness benefit from a broader religious approach: being familiar with other traditions together with the Christian tradition contributes to their professionalism. It also benefits their professionalism if they are aware of their personal bond with the Christian and other traditions; in this respect, the material illustrates all current trends.

f. Nonetheless, as this contribution clarifies, the Bible offers various models for teachers and students, which can be implemented at different levels. Getting acquainted with more models of teaching, in particular with the more contradicting ones, contributes to a more dynamic instruction that increases the involvement of teachers and students in specific situations. Contemporary religious and cultural diversity requires familiarity with Biblical teaching models which discuss inequality, subordination, coarseness, ethnicity and disharmony, not only as substantive ethical themes to discuss within lessons, but also as themes that sometimes characterize educational situations and relationships. The newness of this empirical data is that religious and cultural pluralism is relevant to the role of Moderator, and that biblical stories create models to think about and to deal with this plurality. The levels of communication which can be distinguished within texts allow such texts to be read and discussed, especially in intractable learning circumstances and strained relations.

INDEX OF REFERENCES

Bible

Genesis
1,26-28	78
1,27	215
3,7	120
4,1-6	120
9,6-7	215
9,7	215
9,15-27	120
18,19	180
45,4-5	120
50,20	120

Exodus
15,20	160
17,9	24
17,20	22
20,12	180
20,24	210-212
23,6	94
23,20	156
25,31-40	104
31,10	100
32,1	22
32,1-6	19
32	4, 9-28
32,4	21-22
32,5	22
32,7	22
32,7-8	26
32,8	23
32,7-13	19
32,9	26
32,9-10	26
32,10	22, 26
32,11	22
32,11-12	26
32,12	26
32,13	22, 24, 26
32,14	19-20, 27
32,15-16	19-20, 24
32,17	24
32,17-18	19-20, 24
32,19	27
32,19-20	19-20, 25, 27
32,20	23, 25, 27
32,21-29	19-20
32,23	22
32,24	23
32,25	24
32,25-29	27
32,27	27-28
32,30	20-21, 25
32,32	21
32,30-34	19-20
32,34	21
32,35	19, 21, 23, 28
34,6-7	115
34,24	212-213
37,17-24	104
46,3	22

Leviticus
4-5	115
6	115
25	94
25,39	94

Numbers
8,26	66
11,15	66
19,20	100
25	25

Deuteronomy
1,1	3
6,6-25	179
15,4	94
18,15-18	2
22,13-29	95
25,5 10	120
25,24-25	199
29,3-6	123

29,23	66	9,5-12	77, 79
30,16	180	9,16-18	85
		9,24	79
Joshua		13,1-3	85
9,4-27	120	24	79
24,26	100	30,20	85
		31,35	85
1 Samuel		38,1-38	77
2,14	66	38-41	75
12,12	100	38,1-40,2	71
		38,1-42,6	76-77
2 Samuel		38,1-42,7	74
6,5	160	38,2	84-85
6,14	160	38,4-7	77
6,15	160	38,8-11	77
22,44	65	38,12-21	77
		38,37	77
1 Kings		38,18	77
1,50-53	103	38,22-30	77
7,50	104	38,31-33	77
8,6	100	38,34-38	77
12,28	21	38,39-39,30	77
17,1	3	39,19-25	80
17	152	40,3-5	77
		40,6-41,34	77
2 Kings		40,8	79
5	152	40,15	80
12,13	104	40,19	81
22,4	104	41,1-2	81
23,4	104	41,10-11	81
		41,33-34	81
1 Chronicles		42,1-6	77
4,14	179	42,2-5	83
9,19	104	42,2-6	82
9,22	104	42,3	85
15,29	160	42,5-6	86
16,31	100	42,6	82-84
22,19	100	42,7-8	86
		42,7-9	86
2 Chronicles			
3,7	104		
23,4	100	*Psalms*	
23,15	100	1,1	158
23,17	100	2,12	158
23,18	100	8,2	65
34,9	104	8,7-9	78
		12	43
Job		14	43
1,1-2,13	74	18	51
1,19	76	18,44	65

18,48	65	94:22-23	34
25,18	115	106,46	57
32,1-4	115	110,1	202
32,3	158	119,1	180
33,2-3	67	119,27	103
33,9	67	120	69
33,12	67	120-134	68
33,15	67	120-135	69
52	43	135-136	68-69
64,1-2	38	137,1	56
64,1-4	37	137,1-2	56
64	5, 29-47	137,1-3	52
64,2	29-30, 32, 44	137	5, 49-50, 52-57, 67-69
64,2-3	29, 37, 42, 45	137-145	69
64,2-4	37	137,3	56-57
64,2-7a	38	137,3-4	56
64,2-7	37-38	137,4	56
64,3	30, 32	137,4-5	52, 56
64,3-6	38	137,5	56
64,4	31	137,5-6	56
64,4-5a	30	137,6	56
64,4-5	37, 46	137,7	56
64,4-7	37-39, 42	137,7-8	56
64,5	42-43	137,7-9	52
64,5-7a	37	137,8	52
64,5-7	37, 46	137,8-9	56
64,5b	33	137,9	52
64,5b-7	30	137-145	49-71
64,6	40	138,1-3	60
64,6-7	37	138	59-60
64,7a	38	138-143	5, 49, 52-54, 59, 64
64,7	31, 38-39, 42	138-145	5, 50, 59, 68
64,7-9	42	138,4-6	60
64,7b-11	37	138,7	60
64,8	32, 34, 38, 40, 44	138,7-8	60
64,8-9	37-39, 41-42	139,1-18	61
64,8-10	30, 32, 37, 40-41, 46	139	59-62
64,8-11	37	139,19-24	61
64,9	31, 34, 41	139,20	61
64,10-11	37-39, 41-42	139,23-24	61
64,11	30, 32, 34, 37, 39, 43, 46	140	59, 61-62
		141	59, 61-62
68,19	217	141,3-4	62
72,20	70	141,5-7	62
73,17	100	141,8-10	62
74,13-14	80	142	59, 62
89,4	65	142,8	52, 62
89,10	80	143	59, 62-64, 67
89,51	65	143,2	62, 64

143,8	62	11,17	214, 216
143,10	63	23,20	147, 165
143,12	52, 63	23,22	179
144,1-2	50, 64	23,22-25	180
144,1-8	5, 49, 51, 53-54		
144	52, 59, 63-71	*Ecclesiastes*	
144,3-4	64, 67	3,1	160
144,5-6	64	3,4	160
144,7-8	51, 64	9,4	210
144,9	51		
144,9-10a	66	*Isaiah*	
144,9-11	50	5,12	160
144,9-15	50-53	6,1	100, 104
144,10	50-52	6	104
144,10c-11	66	6,4	104
144,11	51, 67	6,5	104
144,12	52, 54, 66	6,6	104
144,12-14	66	6,7	104
144,12-15	50, 66, 68	7,9	90
144,13	66	12,3	211
144,14-15	66	27,10	80
144,15	52	35,4-6	152
145,1-2	70	35,5-6	152
145,1-3	70	40,3-5	163
145,1-7	70	43,25	115
145	54, 59, 69-71	51,9	80
145,3	70	52,13	123
145,4-5	70	53,11	123
145,4-7	70	58,6	163
145,6-7	70	61,1-2	163
145,8-9	70		
145,10	50, 70	*Jeremiah*	
145,10-11	70	8,6	83
145,10-12	70	10,10	100
145,12-13	70	14,17	22
145,13	70	22,8	66
145,13-14	70	31,19	83
145,13-20	71	35,4	104
145,15-16	70	52,19	104
145,17-18	70	52,24	104
145,19-21	70		
145,21	60, 70-71	*Lamentations*	
146-150	68	2,20	100
Proverbs		*Ezekiel*	
1,8	179-180	1	201
2,6	180	2	4,13 66
4,1	180	13	96
6,20	179-180	16,1-63	120

20,33	100	7,11	99, 101
40,6	104	7,12	98, 102
40,7	104	7,13	98-100
41,16	104	7,15	98, 102
43,8	104	7,16-17	101
48,10	100	7,17	99, 101
		9,1	104
Daniel		9,1-4	89, 102-105
7,13	202	9,3	102, 105
7,13-14	135	9,4	105
		9,5-6	105
Hosea		9,11	106
1-6	119	9,11-15	89, 106
1,9	22	9,14-15	106
1,12	22		
2,9-10	120	*Jonah*	
2,22	22	3,9-10	84
Joel		*Zephaniah*	
2,12	160	2,14	104
		3,15	100
Amos			
1,1	91, 93	*Zechariah*	
1,1-2	89, 91-93, 103	12,2	104
1,2	91-93, 97-98	14,9	100
1,3-2,9	97		
1,3-2,16	89, 93-98, 105	*Malachi*	
2,4	94, 96	1,14	100
2,6-7	94	3,1	156
2,7	95	3,23	3
2,9	95		
2,10	96-98	*1 Maccabees*	
2,10-11	97	1,54-58	180
2,10-16	97-98	2,15-28	180
2,11	97	4,36-43	180
2,12	97		
2,12-16	97	*Ben Sira*	
2,13	97	48,10	3
3,1	97		
3,1-2	97	*Wisdom*	
7,1-9	99	6,4	158
7,2	99	9,13	158
7,3	99	10,21	123
7,5	99		
7,6	99	*Matthew*	
7,8	99	1,21	115, 122
7,9	99	3,4	165
7,10	93	4,2	120
7,10-17	89, 92, 98-102, 104-105	4,23-9,37	114

5	145	8,16	114, 122
5-6	143-144	8,17	114
5-7	114	8,18	109, 111, 116-117, 121
5,14-16	123	8,18-22	115-116
5,17-21	143	8,18-9,17	114-124
5,20	115, 141	8,19	107, 109, 115-116
5,21	144	8,19-20	109, 111
5,21-22	144	8,19-22	116
5,22	141, 144	8,20	109, 112, 115
5,27-30	144	8,21	109, 111, 116
5,28-29	143	8,21-22	109, 115
5,29	144	8,22	109, 146
5,31-32	144	8,23	116-117, 121, 124
5,33-37	144	8,23-9,1	116-117
5,43-48	143-144	8,25	109, 112
5,48	145	8,26	109-110, 115
6,1-4	143	8,27	112, 115, 117, 124
6,1-6	144	8,28	121
6,6	143	8,28-34	110, 112
6,12-14	144	8,28-9,1	117
6,12-15	146	8,29	115
6,16-17	144	8,31	110
6,16-18	120, 143	8,32	110, 112
7	114	9,1	121
7,28-29	114, 121, 124	9,1-8	115
7,29	116	9,1-17	120
8-9	6, 107-125	9,2	115-118, 123
8,1	111, 116, 124	9,2-8	117-118
8,1-4	108	9,3	110
8,1-15	114	9,3-5	110, 117
8,1-17	113-114	9,4	115
8,1-9,17	121	9,5	110, 115, 118
8,2	112, 121-122	9,6	110, 118
8,2-4	114	9,6-7	110
8,3	122	9,7	110, 118
8,4	123	9,9	110, 112, 118, 124
8,5	121	9,9-10	121
8,5-9	114	9,9-13	115
8,5-13	108-110, 114, 116, 151	9,9-17	118-121
8,7	122	9.10	159
8,8	122	9,11	115, 119
8,8-9	121	9,11-13	122
8,9	114, 116-118	9,12-13	119
8,9-10	117	9,14	115
8,10	117	9,14-17	107, 115, 122, 159
8,11	121	9,15	115, 120
8,13	122	9,16-17	122
8,14-15	114	9,17	120

9,18	121-122	25,32-33	134-136, 139
9,18-26	121-122	25,34	127, 136
9,18-34	121-124	25,34-45	131, 140, 143
9,20	121	25,34-46	135
9,20-21	122	25,41	141, 144
9,21	121	25,44-45	145
9,22	121-122	25,46	135, 144
9,27	121-122	26,1	142
9,27-31	122-123	26-28	145
9,28	122	26,20-35	120
9,30	110, 122	26,28	145
9,30-31	112	26,29	120
9,31	110	28,10	120
9,32	121	28,20	124
9,32-33	123		
9,32-34	123-124	*Mark*	
10,5	124	1,1	203
10,10	199	1,6	165
11,1-19	147	1,11	202
11,2	159	2,15	159
11,3	159	2,18-22	159
11,5	123	4,11	202
11,19	148	5,23	121
12,10	224	7,3	220
12,22	123	7,5	194
12,48	146	8,31-33	202
15,26	146	9,2-7	202
16,17	204	9,33-38	164
18,1-5	164	10,12	198
18,23-34	136	10,13-16	164
19,13-15	164	10,45	202
19,21-26	145	12,36	203
19,24	145	14,62	202
19,26	145	16	205
22,2-13	136	16,6	202
24-25	141-146		
24,3	138, 142	*Luke*	
24,45-51	142	1,1	154
24,48-51	144	1,1-4	149
25,1-12	142	1-2	159, 162
25,11-12	142, 145	1-4	163
25,13	145	1,4	154
25,14-30	142, 144	1,5-56	163
25,24-27	145	1,5-2,52	149
25,26	143	1,7	164
25,31	127	1,15	160, 165
25,31-32	135, 138, 140	1,16-17	164
25,31-46	125-146	1,17	3

1,45	158	7,11	150-151
1,57-2,52	163	7,11-12	157
1,59	164	7,11-17	151
1,66	164	7,12	150-151
1,76	164	7,12-17	151
1,80	164	7,13	153
2,17	164	7,16	153
2,27	164	7,17	157
2,40	164	7,18	154-155, 159
2,43	164	7,18-23	159
2,46-47	164	7,18-24	151
3,1-4,30	163	7,18-35	147-168
3-4	162	7,19	151, 153, 155, 159
3,2	150	7,20	151, 153, 159
3,4-6	163	7,21	153
3,21-4,44	150	7,21-22	156
4,14-9,50	150	7,22	151-152
4,16-20	151	7,23	156-158, 161, 163
4,18	152	7,24	148, 151, 156, 158-159
4,18-19	152, 163	7,24-28	158
4,22	153	7,25	156
4,25-27	152	7,26	153, 156
4,28-30	157	7,28	153, 163
4,36	153	7,29	18, 156-159, 161
5,1-6,11	150	7,29-30	148, 155, 157-158, 163
5,17-6,11	120	7,30	148, 152, 157-159, 161
5,21	153	7,30-34	153
5,27-32	159	7,31	156-157
5,29	159	7,31-32	160, 164
5,33-39	159	7,31-34	149, 158
6,12-49	150	7,31-35	6, 148, 159, 165
6,13	160	7,32	157, 160
6,20	158	7,33	148, 157, 159-160
6,20-49	150	7,33-34	152
6,25	160	7,34	149, 152, 160, 164-165
7,1	150-151	7,35	6, 157-158, 160-161, 163
7,1-10	151	7,36-50	152-153
7,1-11	151	7,37	152
7,1-17	151	7,39	152-153
7	150	7,42	153
7,1-8,3	150	7,43	153
7,2	151	7,49	153
7,3	151	7,50	153
7,4	151	8,1	152
7,6	151, 153	8,1-3	150-151
7,7	151	8,1-21	150
7,9	151, 153	8,22-56	150
7,10	151	8,25	153

8,42	121	3,32-33	181
9,1-17	150	4,8	175
9,1-50	153	4,31	172-173
9,9	153	4,31-38	182
9,18-22	153	4,43-54	151
9,18-27	150	5,1-17	182
9,20	153	5,1-18	178
9,24	153	5,2	181
9,28-36	150	5,17-23	176, 181
9,46-48	164	5,19	178
9,47	164	5,19-20	180
9,48	164	5,19-23	169, 178, 181
9,51-19,27	150	5,23	181
10,7	199	5,39-40	173
10,25-28	141	5,47	170, 173
10,30-35	143	6,5	175
10,30-37	130, 133	6,25	172
10,38-42	165	6,45	170
11,13	164	6,59	176
11,19	158	6,61	173
11,28	158	6,66	173, 176
14,1-6	165	7,14	181
14,7-11	165	7,15	170, 173, 175-176, 181
14,16-24	136	7,15-16	181
14,26	164	7,16	170
14,31-32	136	7,16-17	177
15,31	164	7,16-24	172
18,15-17	164	7,17	170
18,29	164	7,28	176-177, 181
19,44	164	7,35	176-177
20:1	152	8,4	170, 172
20,31	164	8,13	177
24	204-205	8,20	176-177, 181
		8,22	178
John		8,28	169, 176-178, 180
1,14-18	184	8,54	177
1,18	180	9	177
1,38	170, 172-173	9,2	172-173
1,39	175	9,2-4	175
1,43	175	9,28-34	178
1,49	172-173	9,34	176-177, 183
2,1-11	182	10,17-18	182
2,23-24	170	10,23	181
3,2	170, 172	10,28-30	181
3,3-36	182	11,5-16	175
3,10	170-171, 183	11,8	172-173
3,26	172-173, 183	11,16	175
3,31-36	176	11,20-27	182

11,21-22	171	13,36	158
11,23-27	171	20,27	158
11,24-26	182	22,3	220
11,28	170-171	22,17-22	204
11,32	171		
11,54	181	*Romans*	
12	170	1,16-17	191
12,20-21	175	2,10-11	191
13,1-17	182	4	128
13-16	175	6,17	193
13,6-10	175	7,1-2	198
13,13	171	9-11	191
13,13-14	169-170, 172	16,17	193
13,15	171		
13,29	175	*1 Corinthians*	
13,34-35	171, 175	7,1	196
13,36-38	175	7,1-7	196
14-16	182	7	193, 196, 198
14,6-10	175	7,5	196
14,6-25	183	7,8-9	196
14,9-10	181	7,10	195
14,15-17	183	7,10-11	195-197
14,26	170, 176-177, 182-184	7,12-16	196
15,1-8	175	7,17-24	197
15,9-17	175	7,25-38	197
15,14-17	175	7,32-35	196
15,26	184	7,39-40	197
15,26-27	183-184	8,1-11,1	198
16,13-15	182	9,1-10,22	198
17,6-8	175	9,14	195, 198
17,18	176, 183-184	10,23-11,1	198
18-20	182	11	193
18,10	175	11,23-25	189, 204
18,19	170, 176-177	11,23-26	195
18,20	176-177	14	193
18,20-21	181	15,1-7	195
18,28	170, 176	15	193, 203
20,16	170, 172-173	15,3-8	189, 204
20,19	172	15,5	205
20,21-22	176, 183	15,50	204
20,21-23	184		
20,30-31	90, 176	*2 Corinthians*	
		12,1-5	204
Acts		12,2-4	200
1,1	154		
1	205	*Galatians*	
2,23	158	1,7	189-190
9,36	194	1,11-16	204

1,12	7, 188, 204	**Early Christian Literature**	
1,13-2,21	190		
1,18-19	205	*Gospel of Thomas*	
2,1	204	logion 4	164
2,1-10	204	logion 21	164
2,7	189		
2,7-10	189	*Didache*	
2,11-14	190	1,3	193
2,12	190	13,2	199
3	128		
5,11	190	*Epistle of Barnabas*	
6,12	189-190	18,1	193
6,12-13	190		

Colossians
2,7   193

Philo and Josephus

Philo
Legum all. 2,90   179
Spec. Leg. 2.236 180

1 Thessalonians
4,1   186, 193

Josephus
Ant 1.2.3   180
Ant. 1.3.1   180

2 Thessalonians
2,15   194

Ant 13.297   220
Ad Ap. 2.204 180

1 Timothy
5,18   199

2 Timothy
2,24   7

Rabbinic Literature

Hebrews
6,4-6   145
6,13-7,10 128

Mišnah
Ber 2,6-7   175
Peah 2,6   185
Sukkah 5,1   211
Hag 1,1   202
Hag 2,1   201
Avot 1,3   224
Avot 1,4-12 185
Avot 1,4-15 163
Avot 1,12   221
Avot 2,5   209
Avot 2,6   211
Avot 2,12   217
Avot 5,7   175

James
2,21-24   128

Old Testament Apocrypha

Testament of Joseph
1,6   131

Psalms of Solomon
4,23   158

Tosephta
Peah 4,10   209
Šabb 19,1   214
Pes 4,13   208, 214

1 Enoch
62,2-5   135
69,27-29   135

Sukkah 4,3	210		Avot de-Rabbi Natan A	
Hag 2,1	202		12	210, 212, 230
Sota 13,3	209, 214		15	218
			26	221

Talmud Bavli

Ber 5b	174		*Avot de-Rabbi Natan B*	
Ber 23a	174		29	185, 218-219
Ber 23b	174		30	216
Ber 24a	174			
Ber 60a	174		*Midraš Rabbah*	
Šabb 3b	175		Berešit 1,21	224
Šabb 12b	174		Wayiqra 36,1	224
Šabb 31b	207		Qohelet 9,8	224
Šabb 108b	174		Cant 8,7	174
Šabb 112b	174			
Erub 30a	174		*Sifre Devarim*	
Yoma 28a	175		357	208
Yoma 35b	213			
Sukkah 53a	211		*Pesiqta Rabbati*	
Beiṣa 16a	217		23	217
Beiṣa 30v-31a	218			
Roš Haš 34b	174		*Derek Ereṣ Zuta*	
Hag 12a	224		1	175
Ket 67b	209			
Qid 82a-b	180			
Sanh 101a	174		**Ancient World**	

Talmud Yerušalmi

Šabb 19,1	208, 214
Pes 6,1	208
Hag 2,1	174, 202, 224
Ned 5,6	209
Sot 1,4	175
B. Meṣi 2,3	174

Plato
  Crit. 17,25   179

Plutarch
  Marc. Cat. 20,4-7 179

Contributions to Biblical Exegesis and Theology

1. J.A. Loader, *A Tale of Two Cities, Sodom and Gomorrah in the Old Testament, early Jewish and early Christian Traditions*, Kampen, 1990
2. P.W. Van der Horst, *Ancient Jewish Epitaphs. An Introductory Survey of a Millennium of Jewish Funerary Epigraphy (300 BCB-700 CE)*, Kampen, 1991
3. E. Talstra, *Solomon's Prayer. Synchrony and Diachrony in the Composition of 1 Kings 8, 14-61*, Kampen, 1993
4. R. Stahl, *Von Weltengagement zu Weltüberwindung: Theologische Positionen im Danielbuch*, Kampen, 1994
5. J.N. Bremmer, *Sacred History and Sacred Texts in early Judaism. A Symposium in Honour of A.S. van der Woude*, Kampen, 1992
6. K. Larkin, *The Eschatology of Second Zechariah: A Study of the Formation of a Mantological Wisdom Anthology*, Kampen, 1994
7. B. Aland, *New Testament Textual Criticism, Exegesis and Church History: A Discussion of Methods*, Kampen, 1994
8. P.W. Van der Horst, *Hellenism-Judaism-Christianity: Essays on their Interaction*, Kampen, Second Enlarged Edition, 1998
9. C. Houtman, *Der Pentateuch: die Geschichte seiner Erforschung neben einer Auswertung*, Kampen, 1994
10. J. Van Seters, *The Life of Moses. The Yahwist as Historian in Exodus-Numbers*, Kampen, 1994
11. Tj. Baarda, *Essays on the Diatessaron*, Kampen, 1994
12. Gert J. Steyn, *Septuagint Quotations in the Context of the Petrine and Pauline Speeches of the Acta Apostolorum*, Kampen, 1995
13. D.V. Edelman, *The Triumph of Elohim, From Yahwisms to Judaisms*, Kampen, 1995
14. J.E. Revell, *The Designation of the Individual. Expressive Usage in Biblical Narrative*, Kampen, 1996
15. M. Menken, *Old Testament Quotations in the Fourth Gospel*, Kampen, 1996
16. V. Koperski, *The Knowledge of Christ Jesus my Lord. The High Christology of Philippians 3:7-11*, Kampen, 1996
17. M.C. De Boer, *Johannine Perspectives on the Death of Jesus*, Kampen, 1996
18. R.D. Anderson, *Ancient Rhetorical Theory and Paul*, Revised edition, Leuven, 1998
19. L.C. Jonker, *Exclusivity and Variety, Perspectives on Multi-dimensional Exegesis*, Kampen, 1996
20. L.V. Rutgers, *The Hidden Heritage of Diaspora Judaism*, Leuven, 1998
21. K. van der Toorn (ed.), *The Image and the Book*, Leuven, 1998
22. L.V. Rutgers, P.W. van der Horst (eds.), *The Use of Sacred Books in the Ancient World*, Leuven, 1998
23. E.R. Ekblad Jr., *Isaiah's Servant Poems According to the Septuagint. An Exegetical and Theological Study*, Leuven, 1999
24. R.D. Anderson Jr., *Glossary of Greek Rhetorical Terms*, Leuven, 2000
25. T. Stordalen, *Echoes of Eden*, Leuven, 2000
26. H. Lalleman-de Winkel, *Jeremiah in Prophetic Tradition*, Leuven, 2000
27. J.F.M. Smit, *About the Idol Offerings. Rhetoric, Social Context and Theology of Paul's Discourse in First Corinthians 8:1-11:1*, Leuven, 2000
28. T.J. Horner, *Listening to Trypho. Justin Martyr's Dialogue Reconsidered*, Leuven, 2001
29. D.G. Powers, *Salvation through Participation. An Examination of the Notion of the Believers' Corporate Unity with Christ in Early Christian Soteriology*, Leuven, 2001
30. J.S. Kloppenborg, P. Hoffmann, J.M. Robinson, M.C. Moreland (eds.), *The Sayings Gospel Q in Greek and English with Parallels from the Gospels of Mark and Thomas*, Leuven, 2001
31. M.K. Birge, *The Language of Belonging. A Rhetorical Analysis of Kinship Language in First Corinthians*, Leuven, 2004

32. P.W. van der Horst, *Japheth in the Tents of Shem. Studies on Jewish Hellenism in Antiquity*, Leuven, 2002
33. P.W. van der Horst, M.J.J. Menken, J.F.M. Smit, G. van Oyen (eds.), *Persuasion and Dissuasion in Early Christianity, Ancient Judaism, and Hellenism*, Leuven, 2003
34. L.J. Lietaert Peerbolte, *Paul the Missionary*, Leuven, 2003
35. L.M. Teugels, *Bible and midrash. The Story of 'The Wooing of Rebekah'* (Gen. 24), Leuven, 2004
36. H.W. Shin, *Textual Criticism and the Synoptic Problem in Historical Jesus Research. The Search for Valid Criteria*, Leuven, 2004
37. A. Volgers, C. Zamagni (eds.), *Erotapokriseis. Early Christian Question-and-Answer Literature in Context*, Leuven, 2004
38. L.E. Galloway, *Freedom in the Gospel. Paul's Exemplum in 1 Cor 9 in Conversation with the Discourses of Epictetus and Philo*, Leuven, 2004
39. C. Houtman, K. Spronk, *Ein Held des Glaubens? Rezeptionsgeschichtliche Studien zu den Simson-Erzählungen*, Leuven, 2004
40. H. Kahana, Esther. *Juxtaposition of the Septuagint Translation with the Hebrew Text*, Leuven, 2005
41. V.A. Pizzuto, *A Cosmic Leap of Faith. An Authorial, Structural, and Theological Investigation of the Cosmic Christology in Col 1:15-20*, Leuven, 2005
42. B.J. Koet, *Dreams and Scripture in Luke-Acts. Collected Essays*, Leuven, 2006
43. P.C Beentjes. *"Happy the One Who Meditates on Wisdom" (SIR. 14,20). Collected Essays on the Book of Ben Sira*, Leuven, 2006
44. R. Roukema, L.J. Lietaert Peerbolte, K. Spronk, J.W. Wesselius (eds.), *The Interpretation of Exodus. Studies in Honour of Cornelis Houtman*, Leuven, 2006
45. G. van Oyen, T. Shepherd (eds.), *The Trial and Death of Jesus. Essays on the Passion Narrative in Mark*, Leuven, 2006
46. B. Thettayil, *In Spirit and Truth. An Exegetical Study of John 4:19-26 and a Theological Investigation of the Replacement Theme in the Fourth Gospel*, Leuven, 2007
47. T.A.W. van der Louw, *Transformations in the Septuagint. Towards an Interaction of Septuagint Studies and Translation Studies*, Leuven, 2007
48. W. Hilbrands, *Heilige oder Hure? Die Rezeptionsgeschichte von Juda und Tamar (Genesis 38) von der Antike bis zur Reformationszeit*, Leuven, 2007
49. J. Joosten, P.J. Tomson (eds.), *Voces Biblicae. Septuagint Greek and its Significance for the New Testament*, Leuven, 2007
50. A. Aejmelaeus, *On the Trail of the Septuagint Translators. Collected Essays*, Leuven, 2007
51. S. Janse, *"You are My Son". The Reception History of Psalm 2 in Early Judaism and the Early Church*, Leuven, 2009
52. K. De Troyer, A. Lange, L.L. Schulte (eds.), *Prophecy after the Prophets? The Contribution of the Dead Sea Scrolls to the Understanding of Biblical and Extra-Biblical Prophecy*, Leuven, 2009
53. C.M. Tuckett (ed.), *Feasts and Festivals*, Leuven, 2009
54. M. Labahn, O. Lehtipuu (eds.), *Anthropology in the New Testament and its Ancient Context*, Leuven, 2010
55. A. van der Kooij, M. van der Meer (eds.), *The Old Greek of Isaiah: Issues and Perspectives*, Leuven, 2010
56. J. Smith, *Translated Hallelujehs. A Linguistic and Exegetical Commentary on Select Septuagint Psalms*, Leuven, 2011
57. N. Dávid, A. Lange (eds.), *Qumran and the Bible. Studying the Jewish and Christian Scriptures in Light of the Dead Sea Scrolls*, Leuven, 2010
58. J. Chanikuzhy, *Jesus, the Eschatological Temple. An Exegetical Study of Jn 2,13-22 in the Light of the Pre 70 C.E. Eschatological Temple Hopes and the Synoptic Temple Action*, Leuven, 2011

59. H. Wenzel, *Reading Zechariah with Zechariah 1:1–6 as the Introduction to the Entire Book*, Leuven, 2011
60. M. Labahn, O. Lehtipuu (eds.), *Imagery in the Booky of Revelation*, Leuven, 2011
61. K. De Troyer, A. Lange, J.S. Adcock (eds.), *The Qumran Legal Texts between the Hebrew Bible and Its Interpretation*, Leuven, 2011
62. B. Lang, *Buch der Kriege – Buch des Himmels. Kleine Schriften zur Exegese und Theologie*, Leuven, 2011
63. H.-J. Inkelaar, *Conflict over Wisdom. The Theme of 1 Corinthians 1-4 Rooted in Scripture*, Leuven, 2011
64. K.-J. Lee, *The Authority and Authorization of Torah in the Persion Period*, Leuven, 2011
65. K.M. Rochester, *Prophetic Ministry in Jeremiah and Ezekiel*, Leuven, 2012
66. T. Law, A. Salvesen (eds.), *Greek Scripture and the Rabbis*, Leuven, 2012
67. K. Finsterbusch, A. Lange (eds.), *What is Bible?*, Leuven, 2012
68. J. Cook, A. van der Kooij, *Law, Prophets, and Wisdom. On the Provenance of Translators and their Books in the Septuagint Version*, Leuven, 2012
69. P.N. De Andrado, *The Akedah Servant Complex. The Soteriological Linkage of Genesis 22 and Isaiah 53 in Ancient Jewish and Early Christian Writings*, Leuven, 2013
70. F. Shaw, *The Earliest Non-Mystical Jewish Use of Iaω*, Leuven, 2014
71. E. Blachman, *The Transformation of Tamar (Genesis 38) in the History of Jewish Interpretation*, Leuven, 2013
72. K. De Troyer, T. Law, M. Liljeström (eds.), *In the Footsteps of Sherlock Holmes. Studies in the Biblical Text in Honour of Anneli Aejmelaeus*, Leuven, 2014
73. T. Do, *Re-thinking the Death of Jesus. An Exegetical and Theological Study of Hilasmos and Agape in 1 John 2:1-2 and 4:7-10*, Leuven, 2014
74. T. Miller, *Three Versions of Esther. Their Relationship to Anti-Semitic and Feminist Critique of the Story*, Leuven, 2014
75. E.B. Tracy, *See Me! Hear Me! Divine/Human Relational Dialogue in Genesis*, Leuven, 2014
76. J.D. Findlay, *From Prophet to Priest. The Characterization of Aaron in the Pentateuch*, Leuven, forthcoming
77. M.J.J. Menken, *Studies in John's Gospel and Epistles. Collected Essays*, Leuven, 2015
78. L.L. Schulte, *My Shepherd, though You Do not Know Me. The Persian Royal Propaganda Model in the Nehemiah Memoir*, Leuven, 2016
79. S.E. Humble, *A Divine Round Trip. The Literary and Christological Function of the Descent/Ascent Leitmotif in the Gospel of John*, Leuven, 2016
80. R.D. Miller, *Between Israelite Religion and Old Testament Theology. Essays on Archaeology, History, and Hermeneutics*, Leuven, 2016
81. L. Dequeker, *Studia Hierosolymitana*, Leuven, 2016
82. K. Finsterbusch, A. Lange (eds.), *Texts and Contexts of Jeremiah. The Exegesis of Jeremiah 1 and 10 in Light of Text and Reception History*, Leuven, 2016
83. J.S. Adcock, *"Oh God of Battles! Steal My Soldiers' Hearts!" A Study of the Hebrew and Greek Text Forms of Jeremiah 10:1-18*, Leuven, 2017
84. R. Müller, J. Pakkala (eds.), *Insights into Editing in the Hebrew Bible and the Ancient Near East. What Does Documented Evidence Tell Us about the Transmission of Authoritative Texts?*, Leuven, 2017
85. R. Burnet, D. Luciani, G. van Oyen (eds.), *The Epistle to the Hebrews. Writing at the Borders*, Leuven, 2016
86. M.K. Korada, *The Rationale for Aniconism in the Old Testament. A Study of Select Texts*, Leuven, 2017
87. P.C. Beentjes, *"With All Your Soul Fear the Lord" (Sir. 7:27). Collected Essays on the Book of Ben Sira II*, Leuven, 2017

PRINTED ON PERMANENT PAPER • IMPRIME SUR PAPIER PERMANENT • GEDRUKT OP DUURZAAM PAPIER - ISO 9706

N.V. PEETERS S.A., WAROTSTRAAT 50, B-3020 HERENT